Semantic Technologies for E-Government

Semantic Technologies for E-Government

Tomas Vitvar · Vassilios Peristeras ·
Konstantinos Tarabanis
Editors

Semantic Technologies for E-Government

 Springer

Editors

Tomas Vitvar
Universität Innsbruck
Institute of Computer Science
ICT - Technologiepark
Technikerstr. 21a
6020 Innsbruck
Austria
tomas@vitvar.com

Konstantinos Tarabanis
University of Macedonia
Information Systems Lab.
Egnatia Street 156
540 06 Thessaloniki
Greece
kat@uom.gr

Vassilios Peristeras
National University of Ireland, Galway
Digital Enterprise Research Institute (DERI)
IDA Business Park, Lower Dangan
University Road, Galway
Ireland
vassilios.peristeras@deri.org

ACM Computing Classification (1998): J.1, H.3.5, H.4, I.2

ISBN: 978-3-642-42433-5   ISBN: 978-3-642-03507-4 (eBook)
DOI 10.1007/978-3-642-03507-4
Springer Heidelberg Dordrecht London New York

© Springer-Verlag Berlin Heidelberg 2010
Softcover re-print of the Hardcover 1st edition 2010
This work is subject to copyright. All rights are reserved, whether the whole or part of the material is concerned, specifically the rights of translation, reprinting, reuse of illustrations, recitation, broadcasting, reproduction on microfilm or in any other way, and storage in data banks. Duplication of this publication or parts thereof is permitted only under the provisions of the German Copyright Law of September 9, 1965, in its current version, and permission for use must always be obtained from Springer. Violations are liable to prosecution under the German Copyright Law.
The use of general descriptive names, registered names, trademarks, etc. in this publication does not imply, even in the absence of a specific statement, that such names are exempt from the relevant protective laws and regulations and therefore free for general use.

Cover design: KuenkelLopka GmbH, Heidelberg

Printed on acid-free paper

Springer is part of Springer Science+Business Media (www.springer.com)

This book is dedicated to our children
Klára, Tomáš,
Vassiliki-Emmanouela,
Constantine & Athanasios

Foreword

The European Union is unique in its diversity. This encompasses different technical architectures, different sorts of organizations, different languages, different ways of seeing things, different ways of finding solutions, etc. This diversity can sometimes be difficult to work with when in government or administration, but it is also an incredible source of wealth. It allows us to see things that we normally would not see and to do things that we normally would not do. We must therefore learn to exploit our diversity to our mutual benefit.

Semantic technology is an important contribution to that achievement. In my own area, ICT for governments and public services, semantic technology holds the promise of a better governance system that works across national borders and institutional boundaries, to the benefit of all European citizens. Under the 6th IST Research Framework Programme, the Commission DG Information Society and Media has supported research into the development of semantic technologies for public administrations – and the supported projects are documented in this book.

This book is a significant testimony of progress in the area of semantic technologies for public administrations and also shows the European Commission's continued support to research that combines societal aspects and scientific excellence for the benefit of all European Citizens.

Mechthild Rohen
Head of Unit for ICT for Governments and Public Service

Acknowlegements

There were many contributors to the editing, writing, and reviewing of this book. First, we thank all the authors for their contributions as well as their attitude in providing the editors with timely updates and responses to editing requests. Special thanks go to all people who helped with the review process that significantly contributed to the quality of the book: Michele Missikof, Tania Di Mascio, Marco Luca Sbodio, Ralf Klischewski, Ljiljana Stojanovic, Maciej Zaremba, Tomas Sabol, Karol Furdik, Luis Álvarez Sabucedo, and Efthimios Tambouris. We thank to Jana Viskova for her contributions to chapter 1. We also thank Ralf Gerstner from Springer Germany for his great attitude and support for this book project during the editing and production process.

Last but not least, we gratefully acknowledge the support, encouragement, and patience of our wives.

Contents

Contributors

Jean-Paul Barthès CNRS Heudiasyc, UMR 6599, Université de Technologie de Compiègne, Centre de Recherches de Royallieu, BP 20529, 60205 COMPIEGNE cedex, France

Norbert Benamou Business Flow Consulting, 196 rue Houdan, F-92330 Sceaux, France

Irene Celino CEFRIEL – Politecnico of Milano, Via Fucini 2, 20133 Milano, Italy

Dario Cerizza CEFRIEL – Politecnico of Milano, Via Fucini 2, 20133 Milano, Italy

Mirko Cesarini Università di Milano-Bicocca, Via dell'Innovazione, 20100 Milano, Italy

Flavio De Paoli Università di Milano-Bicocca, Via dell'Innovazione, 20100 Milano, Italy

Emanuele Della Valle CEFRIEL – Politecnico of Milano, Via Fucini 2, 20133 Milano, Italy

Jacky Estublier Equipe Adele, LSR, Université Joseph Fourier, F-38041 Grenoble Cedex 9, France

Daniela Feldkamp School of Business, University of Applied Sciences Northwestern Switzerland FHNW, Riggenbachstrasse 16, 4600 Olten, Switzerland

MariaGrazia Fugini CEFRIEL – Politecnico of Milano, Via Fucini 2, 20133 Milano, Italy

Karol Furdík   Intersoft, a.s., Floriánska 19, 040 01 Košice, Slovakia

Lemonia Giantsiou   University of Macedonia, 156 Egnatia str., Thessaloniki 54006, Greece

Asuncion Gómez Pérez   Universidad Politecnica de Madrid, 28660 Boadilla del Monte, Madrid, Spain

Pascal Guarrera   Le Forem, Boulevard Tirou 104, 6000 Charleroi, Belgium

Knut Hinkelmann   School of Business, University of Applied Sciences Northwestern Switzerland FHNW, Riggenbachstrasse. 16, 4600 Olten, Switzerland

Mick Kerrigan   STI Innsbruck, University of Innsbruck, Technikerstraße 21a, 6020 Innsbruck, Austria

Ralf Klischewski   Faculty of Management Technology, German University in Cairo (GUC), Al Tagamoa Al Khames, New Cairo City 11835, Egypt

Nikolaos Loutas   Center for Research and Technology Hellas, 1st km Charilaou-Thermis Rd, Thessaloniki 57001, Greece

Marián Mach   Faculty of Electrical Engineering and Informatics, Technical University of Košice, Letna 9, 040 01 Košice, Slovak Republic

Mario Mezzanzanica   Università di Milano-Bicocca, Via dell'Innovazione, 20100 Milano, Italy

Michele Missikoff   Institute of Systems Analysis and Informatics "Antonio Ruberti", National Research Council, Viale Manzoni 30, 00185 Rome, Italy

Adrian Mocan   SAP Research, Chemnitzer Straße 48, 01187 Dresden, Germany

Claude Moulin   CNRS Heudiasyc, UMR 6599, Université de Technologie de Compiègne, Centre de Recherches de Royallieu, BP 20529, 60205 COMPIEGNE cedex, France

Sanaullah Nazir   Digital Enterprise Research Institute, National University of Ireland, Lower Dangan, Galway, Ireland

Matteo Palmonari   Department of Informatics, Systems and Communication (DISCo), University of Milan, Bicocca viale Sarca 336, U14 Building, Milan, Italy

Vassilios Peristeras Digital Enterprise Research Institute, National University of Ireland, Lower Dangan, Galway, Ireland

Jaime Ramìrez Universidad Politecnica de Madrid, 28660 Boadilla del Monte, Madrid, Spain

Tomáš Sabol Faculty of Economics, Technical University of Košice, Letna 9, 040 01 Košice, Slovak Republic

Konstantinos Samiotis Research & Innovation, PLANET S.A., 64, L. Riencourt Str., Apollon Tower, 115 23 Athens, Greece

Marco Luca Sbodio Hewlett-Packard, Italy Innovation Center, Corso Trapani 16, 10139 Torino, Italy

Kay-Uwe Schmidt SAP AG, Vincenz-Prießnitz-Straße 1, 76131 Karlsruhe, Germany

Ljiljana Stojanovic FZI Forschungszentrum Informatik, Haid-und-Neu-Straße 10-14, 76131 Karlsruhe, Germany

Nenad Stojanovic FZI Forschungszentrum Informatik, Haid-und-Neu-Straße 10-14, 76131 Karlsruhe, Germany

Francesco Taglino Institute of Systems Analysis and Informatics "Antonio Ruberti", National Research Council, Viale Manzoni 30, 00185 Rome, Italy

Konstantinos Tarabanis University of Macedonia, Thessaloniki, Greece

Susan Marie Thomas SAP AG, Vincenz-Prießnitz-Straße 1, 76131 Karlsruhe, Germany

Barbara Thönssen School of Business, University of Applied Sciences Northwestern Switzerland FHNW, Riggenbachstrasse. 16, 4600 Olten, Switzerland

Stefan Ukena Faculty of Management Technology, German University in Cairo (GUC), Al Tagamoa Al Khames, New Cairo City 11835, Egypt

Boris Villazon Universidad Politecnica de Madrid, 28660 Boadilla del Monte, Madrid, Spain

Gianluigi Viscusi Department of Informatics, Systems and Communication (DISCo), University of Milan, Bicoccaviale Sarca 336, U14 Building, Milan, Italy

Tomáš Vitvar   University of Innsbruck, Technikestrasse 21a, 6020 Innsbruck, Austria

Xia Wang   Digital Enterprise Research Institute, National University of Ireland, Lower Dangan, Galway, Ireland

Gang Zhao   Le Forem, Boulevard Tirou 104, 6000 Charleroi, Belgium

Semantic Technologies for E-Government: An Overview

Tomáš Vitvar, Vassilios Peristeras, and Konstantinos Tarabanis

Semantics, in the context of information systems, allows for a rich description of information or behavioural models that improve application processing, integration, and performance. Research and development into semantic technologies is today centred around Semantic Web, which covers various areas of computer science including knowledge engineering, software and service engineering, data interoperability, logical languages, user experience, social networks, and last but not least, business applications. While a vast number of different semantic technologies already exist, it is not fully clear how industry may profit from them and what they bring on top of other solutions already available in the market. For this reason, many research efforts focus on showcasing semantic technologies in various domains, such as e-business, e-health, e-learning, telecommunications, transport, and e-Government.

E-Government, like other mentioned areas, is facing several problems in systems and information integration, information extraction, and information representation across heterogeneous organizations. In particular, e-Government faces big challenges to achieve interoperability and integration, taking into account differences in laws, regulations, services, administrative processes, and different languages across regions and countries. Such differences are related to a great variety of computer-based solutions used at various levels and create the requirement for technical, content, and process integration. On the other hand, semantic technologies have been of interest to the research community for the last 7–8 years, and as any other research domain, they require a large, dynamic, heterogeneous, and shared information space to be effectively tested and evaluated. Therefore, the combination of these two areas is very much natural. E-Government provides an ideal test-bed for semantic technologies research and, on the other hand, semantic technologies provide an ideal platform for the vision of a knowledge-based, citizen-centric, and citizen-empowering, distributed and integrated e-Government. In addition,

T. Vitvar (✉)
University of Innsbruck, Technikestrasse 21a, 6020, Innsbruck, Austria

T. Vitvar et al. (eds.), *Semantic Technologies for E-Government*,
DOI 10.1007/978-3-642-03507-4_1, © Springer-Verlag Berlin Heidelberg 2010

e-Government has some specific features as opposed to traditional e-business scenarios, which are of interest to semantic technologies research and on which semantic technologies could be properly demonstrated. From these reasons, the interest in using semantic technologies applied and customized for e-Government was naturally triggered by the research and academic community. However, e-Government empowered by semantic technologies has also recently reached developers and various public administration agencies. In the last 2–3 years, we witnessed the first applications of semantic technologies in real, operational e-Government systems that address these challenges, such as in the UK[1] and in the USA.[2]

In this book, we present the latest results from the EU-funded e-Government projects supported by the 6th Framework Program. The major goal of these projects was to use semantic technologies in order to improve or even revolutionize the use of ICT in public administration systems. The projects have demonstrated the added value of semantic technologies in e-Government, provided a valuable environment with particular domain-specific difficulties and shortcomings that have to be handled in semantic technologies development, verified various approaches in semantic technologies development as the most suitable for e-Government, and revealed new challenges for further research. In this introductory chapter, we will summarize all these issues; we present their basic underlying concepts and technologies and we provide a summary of the book's chapters and their relations.

1 E-Government: A Suitable Application Domain for Semantic Technologies

This book gives an overview of how semantic technologies have been applied in different e-Government projects. The projects have used a wide spectrum of semantic technologies, including formal domain models expressed as content ontologies, formal service models expressed as service ontologies, semantic enhancements of business process models, semantic Service Oriented Architectures (SOAs) based on Semantic Web Services (SWS) frameworks, and ontology-based knowledge management.

Applying such technologies in the e-Government domain has proven to be challenging mainly for the following reasons:

1. Public administration (PA) is a huge, diverged, and distributed environment layered in clearly defined organizational levels (e.g., local, regional, state, and national). Additionally, currently, there are severe malfunctioning problems causing a lot of distress, embarrassment, and waste of valuable resources;

---

[1]http://webbackplane.com/mark-birbeck/blog/2009/04/23/more-rdfa-goodness-from-uk-government-web-sites.
[2]http://semanticcommunity.wik.is/Federal_Semantic_Interoperability_Community_of_Practice.

thus, a great potential for improvement exists. These characteristics make the PA domain suitable and a challenging candidate for testing and applying semantic technologies and solutions on a large scale.

2. Public administration is hierarchically organized, which means that there is a rather clear line of command, central coordination and rigidly defined corpus of rules (e.g., laws) that explicitly define systems' behaviour. These characteristics describe a domain which is relatively easy to be *standardized* when compared with the totally decentralized and competitive environment in the private sector.

3. Governments, not businesses, remain the major information processing entities in the world. The need to combine vast amount of real-time and archived data in critical domains gives a unique test-bed for testing semantic technologies. Moreover, public administration is currently considered the heaviest service industry, with a service production distributed in hundreds (even thousands) of partially independent agencies, which means that architectural paradigms like SOA and technologies adding semantics to the core "service" notion are particularly suitable and fit well with these structural characteristics of the domain.

4. In this distributed environment there is an increasing need for collaboration and interoperation among different agencies and actors. Currently, each agency acts as an isolated legacy system and thus effective communication with other legacy systems (agencies) becomes very difficult. Semantic interoperability is perceived as a key aspect to be adequately addressed in this environment, in order to make feasible direct interoperation and communication between public administration entities.

5. Through the implementation of EU policies, there is an increasing need for collaboration and interoperation among the Member States Administrations (MSA). Each separate national Public Administration system can be perceived as a separate legacy system with complexity and severe malfunctioning problems in its interior and less capable of effective communication with other legacy systems (other MSAs). Semantic interoperability is of great importance for communication between MSAs and could be considered as an infrastructure for further development of broader EU policies.

2 Difficulties in Applying Semantic Technologies in E-Government

Taking into account the challenges described above, we further point out some domain-specific shortcomings that make the application of semantic technologies in national and cross-border services difficult:

1. Public administration is politically driven, which means that decisions are not always taken rationally but based on political criteria. This means, for example, that the semantic standardization process should pass through several types of central "controls," of which technical excellence is just one.

2. Public administration is still not sufficiently modelled, partly due to its size and complexity, and consequently there are no widely accepted representations/models/definitions describing the domain. As an example, even heavily used and core terms in the field like e-Governance, e-Government, e-Democracy, e-Participation, and e-Services are ill-defined, used in different ways and result in a lot of ambiguity and different interpretations.
3. While the size and complexity make the domain a challenging field for applying semantic technologies, at the same time they cause confusion especially to technical people without anin-depth domain knowledge. The application of semantic technologies has not been coupled so far with a clear business view and development plan for the domain. Due to this situation, e-Government initiatives are still usually and mostly technology driven and thus lack a broader business perspective.
4. A conservative organizational culture is prominent in public administration. As a result, we may witness intense reluctance or even resistance of PA actors for technologies which potentially can introduce dramatic changes in the current modus operandi. PA is usually a late adopter and not a pioneering environment where innovations can easily flourish.
5. Finally, and with regard to the notion of the Pan-European e-Government Services (PEGS), it is important to mention that policies related to public administration are institutionally out of the EU mandate. Although the notion and the need to move toward a European Administrative Space has been discussed in theory for some years now (e.g., in European Public Administration Network), there is still no EU mandate for developing common policies for the European public administrations.

3 Concepts and Technologies

The work presented in this book builds on a number of various concepts and technologies that underpin the research and development into e-Government empowered by semantic technologies. Development of semantic technologies closely relates to development of other technologies that enhance their capabilities, among other things, with automation support, seamless integration, user-centric capabilities, personalization, etc. In this section, we present a short introduction to several underlying concepts and technologies that are exploited to provide solutions in this book. In particular, we present the state-of-the-art technical advances in the areas of semantic web, service-oriented computing, web 2.0, and SWS.

3.1 Semantic Web

The core idea of the Semantic Web is to make information available on the web understandable not only by humans but also by machines. Semantic Web builds an additional layer on top of the existing World Wide Web, in which the information has well-defined semantics enabling the Web to become the universal medium for data, information and knowledge exchange.[3] Although activities around the Semantic Web are today mainly driven by the W3C's Semantic Web activity,[4] there are also a number of activities happening outside of the W3C in various centres focused on the development of semantic web specifications and technologies. The goal of all these activities is to define a set of design principles and enabling technologies that include languages for the semantic web such as RDF, RDFS, OWL, SPARQL, and WSML (Roman et al. 2005), annotation mechanisms such as RDFa, GRDDL, and SAWSDL (Kopecký et al. 2007), vocabularies and ontologies such as SKOS, SIOC,[5] FOAF,[6] WSMO (Roman et al. 2005), and OWL-S (Martin et al. 2004), etc. In the following sections, we introduce some of these concepts in more detail.

3.2   Ontology and Ontology Languages

Ontologies and languages that can be used to describe them are in the core of the Semantic Web. The ontology as defined (in Gruber 1993) is a formal, explicit specification of a shared conceptualization of some domain knowledge.

- The "formal" and "explicit" means, that the ontology expresses the knowledge using some ontology language that is capable of certain semantic expressivity backed up by formal semantics.
- The "shared" means that the ontology is shared by all members of a community, meaning that every member of the community agrees to use and follow the ontology. The ontology thus becomes a social commitment for the community.
- The "conceptualization" means that the ontology defines concepts of the domain at a proper level of abstraction relevant to specific modelling requirements.

In practical terms, an ontology is a description of some domain knowledge (e.g., knowledge within an information or process model) usually expressed in some ontology language. The ontology is a valid description of a domain knowledge while at the same time domain members agree to follow the ontology for describing domain concepts. The ontology is one of the means to maintain interoperability within the domain by using common descriptions on which a communication and information interchange between domain members is based. From a software engineering viewpoint, engineers should first explore the domain and find or develop all appropriate reference ontologies they can use to describe a system's data and process models. Ideally, engineers use one or more ontologies as a base

---

[3]http://www.w3.org/2001/sw/Activity.html.
[4]http://www.w3.org/2001/sw/.
[5]http://sioc-project.org/.
[6]http://www.foaf-project.org/.

line that they further extend according to their particular domain-specific requirements. A number of research results presented in this book define a reference ontology describing various aspects of the e-Government domain that could be reused in the public administration's systems development.

The ontology is expressed in a language that is, depending on the language expressivity, capable of expressing declarative (i.e., concepts, attributes, relations) and procedural knowledge (also called axioms, implicit knowledge or rules). Today, ontology languages are the major output of the W3C Semantic Web activity, producing several language recommendations for representation and exchange of knowledge. Such languages include RDF, RDF Schema (RDFS), Web Ontology Language (OWL), Rule Interchange Format (RIF) or Web Service Modeling Language (WSML). We will introduce these languages in the following paragraphs.

RDF. The Resource Description Framework (RDF) represents information in graph-based models with so called triples, i.e., statements in the form <subject, predicate, object>. The subjects and objects link the triples into a graph. Thus, RDF can be used to represent the syntax of data using graph models while it does not define any semantics for any of the subjects, predicates and objects. RDF provides various serializations including RDF/XML and Notation 3 (N3).[7]

RDFS. On top of RDF, RDF Schema (RDFS) defines constructs that allow the expression of some semantics for the RDF model. RDFS allows the definition of classes describing the terminology of the domain of discourse, properties of those classes as well as class and property hierarchies (i.e., subClassOf and subPropertyOf). Thus, RDFS provides the minimal set of constructs that allow the specification of lightweight ontologies.

On top of RDFS: OWL, WSML, and RIF. Where the expressivity of the RDFS is not sufficient for modelling the required knowledge, various specializations of RDFS can be used. Such specializations are being developed both inside and outside of W3C along the lines of knowledge representation paradigms of Description Logic (DL) and Logic Programming (LP). The Web Ontology Language (OWL) provides further vocabulary along with a formalism based on DL. On the other hand, Web Service Modeling Language (WSML) defines several variants allowing for both paradigms of DL (WSML-DL) and Logic Programming (WSML-Flight, WSML-Rule). All WSML variants can be represented using RDF and they are layered on top of RDFS. While WSML-DL has a direct mapping to OWL, WSML-Rule is the basis of the Web Rule Language (WRL) specification which served as an input for the W3C Rule Interchange Format Working Group (RIF WG). RIF WG aims to produce a core rule language for the Semantic Web together with extensions that allow rules to be translated between different rule languages. The detailed description of WSML and its compliance with standards can be found in Bruijn et al. 2007.

---

[7]http://www.w3.org/DesignIssues/Notation3.html.

3.3   Ontology Mediation

Ontologies are major means to provide the interoperability in a domain. However, it is not realistic to assume that there will always be a single ontology describing a complete domain for various reasons; e.g., there are no strict borders between domains. For this reason, the other approach to maintain interoperability in a domain or across different domains is through ontology mediation (also called ontology mapping or ontology alignment). In general terms, ontology mediation resolves interoperability conflicts between two different ontologies.

The ontology mediation usually has two stages: the first stage involves creation of alignments between source and target ontologies during design-time while the second stage takes care of applying alignments to resolve interoperability conflicts on instance data. Since the interoperability problems can greatly vary in their nature and severity, fully automatic solutions for the creation of alignments is not feasible in real-world case scenarios due to lesser than 100% precision and recall of existing methods.[8] For this reason, the design-time stage usually relies on manual support from domain experts.

In general, an alignment consists of mapping rules expressing the semantic relationships that exist between two ontologies. In particular, a mapping can specify that classes from two ontologies are equivalent while corresponding rules use logical expressions to unambiguously define how the data encapsulated in an instance of one class can be encapsulated in instances of the second class. (More information on ontology alignment can be found in Euzenat and Shvaiko 2007).

3.4   Semantic and Non-Semantic Descriptions

Semantic descriptions must usually co-exist with other already existing descriptions. Semantics enrich existing descriptions with additional expressivity that systems can use for advanced content manipulation and provisioning. Semantic description usually refers to a description of a resource, e.g., service, message, data, and alike expressed in a semantic language, that is, in a language that allows formal definition of semantic information (e.g., classes of concepts, relations between classes, axioms, etc.), while at the same time some logical foundations for the language exist. For example, every description in RDFS, OWL, RIF, WSML is the semantic description. On the other hand, non-semantic description is a description of a resource, e.g., service, message, data, and alike which is captured in a language that does not allow expression of semantic information. In this respect, any description in XML, XML Schema, or any other proprietary format is the non-semantic description.

---

[8]The "Ontology Alignment Evaluation Initiative 2006" (Euzenat et al. 2006) shows that the best five systems' scores vary between 61% and 81% for precision and between 65% and 71% for recall.

Please note, that in the IT world, there might be different views on what semantics are about. People might call semantics a description of data in XML Schema with attributes' types, restriction on values, etc. However, XML Schema does not comply with our semantic description definition as it does not allow expression of classes, their properties, nor relationships between classes, while it does not have any logical foundation. In addition, the XML is often used as a serialization format of semantic descriptions, for example, a description captured in RDFS may be formatted in XML (such serialization is called RDF/XML). Thus, XML is usually understood as the language capturing the syntax. The semantic vs. non-semantic description definition we use is based on the Semantic Web point of view.

3.5 Semantic Annotations

Semantics add an additional layer on top of non-semantic descriptions enriching the content with more expressivity than the non-semantic descriptions provide. For this reason, semantic technologies define a number of - so called - annotation mechanisms that allow to extend non-semantic descriptions with semantics. In general, annotation mechanisms can be grouped in annotations of structured and unstructured data. Semantic annotation of unstructured data (i.e., natural text) defines methods and tools that allow to extract semantic information from unstructured text (usually by using natural language processing techniques) and annotate text structures with semantic information. On the other hand, semantic annotation of structured data allows to link descriptions available in XML or HTML with semantic information. Methods, tools, and specifications for semantic annotations of structured information have been recently actively developed in W3C. The major relevant specifications include Semantic Annotations for WSDL and XML Schema (SAWSDL), RDFa, and Gleaning Resource Descriptions from Dialects of Languages (GRDDL).

SAWSDL follows the bottom-up modelling approach to services by defining a set of extensions for WSDL and associated XML Schema in order to extend them with arbitrary semantic descriptions. SAWSDL has been created as a requirement for supporting incremental enhancements of service descriptions towards semantics. In SAWSDL semantic annotations are XML attributes added to WSDL and associated XML Schema documents. SAWSDL defines two types of extension attributes, namely *model references* that are explicit identifiers of concepts in some semantic model and *schema mappings* that are identifiers of mappings (transformations) from WSDL to concepts in some semantic model or vice versa.

RDFa belongs to the family of *microformats* whose general goal is to enhance HTML markup with metadata so that an agent can extract this metadata and further process it. RDFa as well as other microformats[9] address the fact that today's web is

---

[9]http://www.microformats.org.

built predominantly for human consumption. RDFa allows to embed RDF in XHTML by defining a set of XHTML extensions, that is, RDFa uses attributes from XHTML's meta and link elements and makes them general and usable on all elements. In order to provide an agent processing the RDFa annotation with the information of how the agent should extract the RDF data, W3C defines a markup format for GRDDL that enables users to obtain RDF triples from XML documents including XHTML. GRDDL primarily uses XSLT in order to extract the RDF data, however, it was intended to be more general so that other implementations are possible too.

3.6   Service Oriented Architecture

SOA is a software architectural paradigm where software functionalities are abstracted as services with well-defined and described interfaces independent of operating systems, programming languages or any other technologies which under-line the applications. In SOA, systems group functionalities into business processes and expose these as interoperable services accessible on the network through standardized messaging mechanisms.

The service in SOA is a software entity which conforms to the following principles: *reusability* (service can be reused in multiple business processes), *encapsulation* (many services can be consolidated to be used in a business process), *loose coupling* (services minimize dependability between each other but maintain awareness of each other), *contracting* (services adhere to a communication agreement by means of a standard service interface description), *abstraction* (services hide the implementation details between each other), *composability* (services can be composed to complex business processes), *autonomy* (services have control over a logic they encapsulate), *discoverability* (service interfaces are designed to be descriptive so that their functionality can be discovered).

One of the realizations of the SOA architecture is Web Services described using the Web Service Description Language (WSDL). WSDL is an XML-based lan-guage used to describe Web Services' abstract and concrete interfaces. The abstract part defines an information model usually in XML Schema for input, output and fault messages as well as interfaces with sets of operations. The concrete part defines binding for interfaces and their operations, defining on the wire message serializations as well as where the service can be physically accessed (endpoints).

3.7   Semantic Web Services

Web services and particularly technologies that enable them, such as WSDL are widely acknowledged for their potential to revolutionize computing and especially

Information Systems. The major driver behind adoption of web services in enterprises is to address requirements for flexibility, dynamism and integration.

However, with increasing number of services, existing technology proves difficult to scale without a proper degree of automation. Web Services' success depends on resolving fundamental challenges that existing technologies do not sufficiently address, namely search, integration and interoperability. In large-scale, open and service-centric environments, thousands of services will have to be discovered, adapted, and orchestrated based on user needs. In order to address these problems, SWS is an emerging approach for designing an architecture that would provide a flexible integration, more adaptive to changes which may occur over a software system's lifetime. SWS define the architecture as an extension of the current web service technology by adding a semantic layer.

Figure 1 depicts the SWS environment describing two types of users, namely a *service engineer* and an *end-user*. While end-users' aim is to consume the services' functionality that provide a solution for users' goals, service engineers perform activities of the so called *service life-cycle*. The service life-cycle includes the following stages: modelling of service descriptions and implementation of physical services, assembling complex services and deploying services' descriptions for the use of the intelligent agent. The intelligent agent is the core of the SWS environment. The agent hosts various services' *use tasks* such as discovery, selection, composition, mediation, and invocation. Depending on the level of automation, the agent, with help of the use tasks, may support the service engineer when *assembling* services and the end-user when *consuming* services' functionality.

The SWS environment adopts the so called *Problem Solving Principle* describing the integration in which an user formulates a goal he/she wants to achieve while the intelligent agent solves this goal by means of explicitly defined models on which the agent operates and the agent's processing logic. Ultimately, the user is

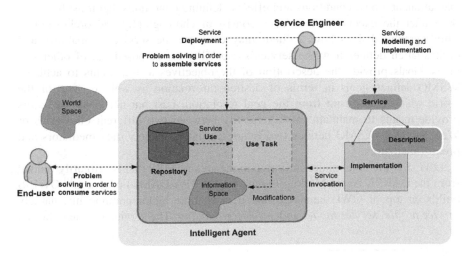

Fig. 1 SWS environment

not aware of the processing logic but only what he/she wants to achieve and a desired quality of the goal resolution. From this respect, the agent always tries to find an optimal solution for users' *goals*.

The agent uses services' descriptions (stored in the repository) on which the use tasks operate. The service descriptions usually have two layers, the semantic layer describing the service by using some service model and a semantic language and the non-semantic layer defining the underlying service technology used for service communication or invocation. In addition, the agent maintains the information space which reflects a state of the agent at some point in time during the agent's operation. The agent modifies the information space by adding, removing or updating information in the space. In addition, the SWS environment also defines a *world space* that is a space which is external to the agent. The agent assumes that such space exists but it does not have any access to it.

WSMO is one of the leading initiatives in the SWS, defining a conceptual model with all relevant aspects of Web Services so that the total or partial automation of service use tasks is possible. WSMO development has been primarily funded from EU FP6 and FP7 projects. WSMO uses the WSML set of languages for describing its elements. WSMO also specifies a reference architecture for WSMX, the Semantic Web Service execution environment. WSMO, WSML, and WSMX thus form a complete framework for modelling, describing, and executing SWS.

WSMO defines four major top-level components using which the Semantic Web Service environment can be described, namely *ontologies*, *web services*, *goals*, and *mediators*. Ontologies provide a formal definition of an information model for all WSMO components while they are the primary facilitators of interoperability. Web Services define functional capability they offer and one or more interfaces that enable a client to access the capability. WSMO models the capability using pre-conditions and assumptions defining conditions that must hold in a state of the information space and the world outside that space before the service's execution, and post-conditions and effects, defining conditions that must hold in a state after the execution. Interfaces consist of choreography and orchestration. Choreography defines how a client may consume the service's capability and orchestration defines how the service's capability is composed out of other services. Goals provide the description of the objectives a user wants to achieve. WSMO defines goals in terms of desired information as well as state of the world which must result from the goal resolution. Last but not least, mediators provide means to maintain interoperability between two different ontologies or Web Services. WSMO defines two major mediators namely data mediators and process mediators.

OWL-S is the other major initiative in the area of SWS that is primarily funded from the DARPA Agent Markup Language (DARPA DAML) program.[10] OWL-S builds on top of OWL language and defines three major components, namely *service profile*, *service model* and *service grounding*. The service profile defines a

---

[10]http://www.daml.org/about.html.

service capability that a client may use to search for services, service model defines a Web service's behaviour, that is, how a client may consume the service's functionality, and service grounding links a service model and the description of the concrete Web service in a form of the WSDL. In addition, some technologies are building on the OWL-S model. Among others, OWL-S virtual machine provides a general purpose client for the invocation of Web services based on OWL-S descriptions.

METEOR-S is a collection of tools and specifications that aim to enhance integration of services and processes in the SOA architecture while extending state of the art standards. One of the major specifications in this area is WSDL-S (Sivashanmugam et al. 2003) defining a simple extension for WSDL in the form of annotations for model references and schema mapping as well as service's capabilities (conditions and effects). WSDL-S has been created as a result of collaboration between University of Georgia in the USA and IBM. WSDL-S became the major input for the SAWSDL WG group and significantly influenced the SAWSDL specification.

3.8   Service Modeling Approaches

As we have already mentioned, the service descriptions follow some service model which the service engineer uses in order to model services in the SWS environment. There are two important modelling approaches that underpin the service models, namely *bottom-up* and *top-down* modelling of services.

In the top-down modelling approach, the service engineer first models semantics of the service and only after that he/she defines the service's communication technology. The top-down approach assumes that messages exchanged in services' interactions are semantic messages while leaving transformations between semantic models and non-semantic models to services' implementations. Typically, if a service already exists in the environment (e.g., enterprise environment, web environment, etc.), it is necessary that the service engineer, apart from modelling the service's semantics also creates a service *adapter* which implements transformations between service's semantic and non-semantic descriptions. A typical example of top-down modelling approach is the WSMO ontology.

In the bottom-up modelling approach, the service engineer models the semantics of the service according to the existing services already available in the running environment. In other words, the service engineer adds the semantic layer on the top of the non-semantic layer by providing semantic descriptions to already existing non-semantic service descriptions. This approach allows for the reuse of existing techniques and tools for service engineering and extends these techniques with additional steps of semantic service modelling. It is important to note that this approach is currently the least developed in the current SWS research, however, the first step towards this approach has already been made in W3C with SAWSDL recommendation.

3.9   Web 2.0

Web 2.0 builds on the Web principles and defines several revolutionary concepts that drive the current development of distributed web applications. The Web 2.0 concepts include: *read-write web*, *programmable web*, and *democratized web*.

Read-write web promotes the user as an active participant in producing the web content, thus shifting traditional content consumers to Web 2.0 *prosumers*, that is, the producer and the consumer of the Web content. Read-Write Web further allows for so called collective intelligence, empowering the sophistication of web applications by users' knowledge. Typical examples of the read-write web are Wikipedia, Flikr, and Digg.

Programmable web extends the current web with web APIs that advocate Web applications not only to provide contents for human users but also functionality for other Web applications. Programmable Web also defines a concept of a *mashup*, that is, applications that combine data and functionality from multiple applications on the web thus creating new value-added applications. Typical examples of mashups are arbitrary information displayed on a Google map such as property being offered for rental in particular areas.

Democratized web builds on the power of users on the Web whose main idea is that anyone can participate in production or selection of ideas. Typical examples are Wikipedia, the encyclopedia by amateurs, and blogs, news by amateurs. The principle of democratized web allows to realize the *long tail* (Anderson 2004) further, a concept utilized by Amazon or eBay in their recommendation engines. This allows consumers to reach out for the less popular goods with the help of the most popular goods. This concept is well known through messages such as "if you like Britney Spears, you will love . . .".

Web 2.0 is finally providing what the Web was meant to be in its original thoughts. This includes rich user experience implemented through AJAX, aggregation of content and its ranking, collective intelligence, human computation, etc.

3.10   Standardization

Many underlying semantic technologies discussed in this chapter are standardized in W3C as part of the Semantic Web activity.[11] W3C, however, does not only work on standards in the area of core technologies that underpin the development of novel systems and applications on the Web, but also recently looks at the vertical standardization activities. In this respect, W3C has established the e-Government Activity[12] and the E-Government Interest Group (eGov IG).[13] The main goal of the

---

[11]http://www.w3.org/2001/sw/.

[12]http://www.w3.org/2007/eGov/.

[13]http://www.w3.org/2008/02/eGov/ig-charter.

eGov IG is to "explore how to improve access to government through better use of the Web and achieve better government transparency using open Web standards at any government level (local, state, national and multi-national)." The eGov IG is a forum supporting researchers, developers, solution providers, and users of government services who use the Web as the delivery channel and enable broader collaboration across eGov practitioners.

The European Committe for Standardization (CEN) has been also active in the e-Government field. First, a focal group was created; it produced an "e-Government Standards Roadmap" in February 2008. Based on this roadmap a new group, "Discovery of and Access to e-Government Resources (CEN/ISSS WS/eGov-Share)" was formed and produced a report under the title "Sharing e-Government resources: a practical approach for designers and developers."

4 Organization of the Book

The work presented in this book targets various aspects of research and development in e-Government empowered by semantic technologies while at the same time this work describes research results of various projects funded from the EU FP6 program. We organize the book into three major parts describing

- *Architectures and process integration*
- *Ontologies and interoperability* and
- *Portals and user interactions*

Although the work presented in these three parts comes from different projects, it is closely related. While architectures describe an overall picture for e-Government systems and their seamless integration using service technologies, the work presented in ontologies and interoperability mainly deals with interoperability issues within such architectures that can be achieved by using commonly agreed upon vocabularies or various mediation techniques. Portals and interactions then look at how e-Government may be improved by means of sophisticated portals built on top of the cutting-edge Web and semantic technologies and how such approaches contribute to optimal interactions between public servants and various e-Government clients. We briefly present the structure and content of these three parts below.

4.1 Part I: Architectures and Process Integration

Every information system must have a properly designed architecture while at the same time the development of the system should follow appropriate engineering approaches for architecture design, implementation and deployment. Architectures designed for e-Government systems usually try to solve the important problem that many heterogeneous and diverse public administrations face today, which is integration of systems and services involving multiple sites in various regions.

The work presented in this part describes overall architectures of e-Government systems that mainly build on paradigms of SWS aiming at automation of service use tasks such as service discovery, composition, mediation, and invocation. In this respect, one of the main concerns lies in the integration of processes that the architecture facilitates, that is, processes spanning across multiple public administrations within and outside various e-Government regions involving multiple stakeholders such as public servants, citizens, and businesses. Designing such architectures, modelling of processes, and providing a proper technological foundation for their seamless execution were the major challenges targeted by a number of research projects. This part contains four chapters:

Chapter 2, *Pan-European E-government Service Architecture*, describes a novel approach to designing and implementing the architecture for e-Government systems that spans across multiple states within the EU. Such architectures will be the most important artifacts in future integration of EU e-Governments that will bring new challenges to integration of data and processes coming from diverse EU member states laws and procedures. This work describes the overall architecture for pan-European e-Government systems while at the same time incorporating the latest results from SWS research centred around development of Web Service Modeling Ontology (WSMO) and Semantic Execution Environment (SEE). This work uses the extension of WSMO, called WSMO-PA, for semantic description of public administration services, and describes the underlying technology so that the architecture can be realized in a distributed environment provided by pan-European e-Government services. This chapter presents research results from the EU project SemanticGov.

Chapter 3, *Employing Semantic Technologies for Orchestration of Government Services*, describes a functional architecture for a novel e-Government system that addresses an important trend of refocusing from provisioning of individual e-Government services, to more complex scenarios that require cross-organizational cooperation and information sharing. The authors emphasize major obstacles that service consumers usually encounter today, namely how e-Government services relevant to service consumers' situation could be identified and how the services could be combined so that the services can provide a solution to a particular life situation. The authors claim that increasing number of services on providers' side (both available in electronic as well as non-electronic form) calls for seamless service integration and interoperability which in turn will increase service consumers' comfort. The authors use the SWS technology for composition of electronic as well as non-electronic services within a scope of complex scenarios and discuss how such techniques can be customized according to users' contexts. They show how the scenarios can be executed in an automatic way in case of electronic services, and how the system can provide users with relevant contextual information in case of non-electronic services (e.g., required documents, contact points, fees, deadlines, etc.). The chapter presents research results from the EU project Access-eGov.

Chapter 4, *Modeling Knowledge-Intensive Processes Using Semantics*, describes a solution for a problem that lies in automation of e-government processes that are knowledge intensive and highly compliance relevant. The authors show how to semantically enrich processes' models with business rules in order to achieve flexibility through automation that better deal with exceptional, and unpredictable situations. In order to keep the process models slim, they apply four types of rules, each targeting a specific problem: resource allocation, consistency checking, decision support, and variable task selection and planning. Using these rules, the solution allows to explicitly model processes that can be automatically executed. The chapter describes research results from the EU project FIT.

Chapter 5, *E-Government Goes Semantic Web: How Administrations Can Transform Their Information Processes*, describes steps which guide public administrations in transforming information processes to the Semantic Web. In a field test in Schleswig-Holstein in Germany, the authors describe reconstruction of e-government information processing in terms of how semantic technologies must be employed to support information provision as well as information consumption; they compare required contribution to the transformation with capabilities and expectations of public administrations, and finally they review experience from transformation with focus on successful transformation of e-government into the Semantic Web. The process of adopting semantic web technologies for information processing helps public administrations when integrating heterogeneous e-government services in geographically and hierarchically distributed public administrations. The chapter describes research results from the EU project Access-eGov.

4.2   Part II: Ontologies and Interoperability

Public administration is a huge, diverged, and distributed environment layered in local, regional, state, national, and community organizational levels. Each such level may have different policies and rules which in turn form diverse organizational, information, and process communication patterns. A key challenge in public administration systems' integration lies in achieving interoperability at such levels starting at local, regional levels, and with increasing abstraction eventually targeting national and EU levels. Semantic technologies may provide a solution for such interoperability through its two key concepts, namely ontologies and mediation. Ontologies are commonly agreed domain models that describe information and process structures and which, by means of semantic languages, define information unambiguously and with higher semantic expressivity than traditional technologies provide. Ontologies created as a result of a common agreement on how to describe domain concepts thus provide an infrastructure for interoperability. As it is not usually possible to adopt ontologies that do not overlap in what they describe, semantic technologies also provide solutions that allow achieve interoperability through mapping of ontologies and their mediation. Designing ontologies with a goal to support interoperability and building supporting infrastructures was a key challenge in a number of research projects. This part presents four chapters:

Chapter 6, *A Semantic Cooperation and Interoperability Platform for the European Chambers of Commerce*, addresses the important issue of diversity of cultural and organizational models of different Chambers of Commerce (CoC) in Europe. The work describes a semantically enabled service-oriented platform that facilitates the CoC's collaboration and interoperability. The platform operates on semantic annotations of business processes that model the activities (i.e., the services available to the citizens) of the CoC at an organizational level, and concrete services which represent actual implementations (manual or automatic) of such activities. The platform also runs a semantic search and discovery mechanism that is able to select the proper concrete services with respect to the user request, in order to make the business process executable. The semantic annotation is based on a weighted reference ontology, where each concept is enriched with a weight that represents the selectivity power of a concept to characterize a given resource (a business process activity or a concrete service), and is represented as an ontology-based feature vector. The semantic search and discovery uses a similarity matchmaking algorithm that can compute a similarity degree between the semantic annotation associated to the business process activities and annotations associated with concrete services. The chapter describes research results of the EU IST LD-CAST project.

Chapter 7, *SEEMP: A Networked Marketplace for Employment Services*, describes a solution for employment services in the context of local governments. Employment services represent an important topic due to their social implications such as sustainability, workforce mobility, worker's re-qualification paths, and training for fresh graduates and students. Many administrations started their own e-government projects addressing these issues, however, with no wider perspectives such as country, cross-border, or European. The SEEMP system presented in this chapter overcomes this issue in different ways: starting bilateral communications with near-border similar offices, building a federation of the local employment services, and merging isolated trails. The SEEMP system relies on a distributed semantic SOA able to federate local projects, to create geographically aggregated services for employment by leveraging existing local ones. The chapter presents the social and technical aspects of the SEEMP system showing its integration with other systems at the country level. This chapter descries research results of the EU IST SEEMP project.

Chapter 8, *Semantic Repositories for E-Government Initiatives: Integrating Knowledge and Services*, describes the usage of semantic repositories for e-government together with techniques and experiences where conceptual models and ontologies are used at different levels in e-government initiatives. This work contributes to trends of semantic models and technologies adoption in traditional repository technologies, at the back-end and front-end architecture levels. Semantic repositories support interoperability among different administrations, that is, improving government to government interactions. Exploitation of semantic repositories is related to strategic planning where the improved access to information provides a clear and unified view of existing resources. This chapter describes research results from the EU IST SEEMP project.

Chapter 9, *Toward an E-Government Semantic Platform*, describes some major aspects of an e-Government platform where semantics underpins more traditional technologies to enable new capabilities, and to overcome technical and cultural challenges. Firstly, the authors recognize that shared knowledge representation is a key resource to enable the use of semantic technologies, and therefore they present the engineering and the structure of a core ontology for the e-Government domain. Such ontology serves as a common foundation to develop various capabilities of a semantic platform. Secondly, they realize that civil servants are increasingly required to face new situations, and that better access to information and services is a key to better public service. Hence the chapter presents how knowledge management tools enhanced with semantic indexing of resources can support a community of practice. Finally, the authors acknowledge the growing need for interoperability among heterogeneous systems; e-Government environments are moving to the paradigm of SOA, which facilitates the creation of business processes packaged as services. In this respect, they describe how SWS can improve the level of automation in the creation of such processes. The chapter also presents a real-world use case, where semantic technologies have brought added value to an application that re-engineers a typical e-Government process in the domain of social services and health-care. The chapter describes the research results from the EU IST Terregov project.

4.3   Part III: Portals and User Interaction

One critical e-Government goal is to allow its users, that is, citizens, businesses, and other public administrations, to interact efficiently with public administration offices and provide the best possible solutions for users' needs. The interactions between e-Government users and public administrations involve many aspects such as ability to specify users' request in a form suitable for public administrations to handle the request, ability to inform users about public administration policies, rules and operations, ability to provide all relevant information to users according to their current life situations, ability to pro-actively approach users with services suitable to their current life events, ability to provide users with central point of contact and one-stop-government, etc. Many e-Government systems today provide their services through e-Government portals through which users can interact with public administration offices. Development of e-Government portals empowered by semantic technologies that could provide a better experience for users through enhanced capabilities of personalized and focused e-Government were key research challenges in a number of EU research projects. This part presents three chapters:

Chapter 10, *Semantic-Based Knowledge Management in E-Government: Modeling Attention for Pro-active Information Delivery*, addresses challenges for a more productive and informative environment within Public Administration (PA) organizations. Authors' propositions are realized in a modern portal-like tool that enables public administrators to take proactive and grounded decisions that are in accordance with the related legislation as well as other sources of related knowledge (e.g., PA regulations, previous cases, local policies, including relevant web resources etc.). To achieve this, authors empower user interactions by managing users' attention which goes beyond informing a user about changes in relevant information towards proactively supporting the user to react on these changes, depending on her/his current working context and taking into account her/his preferences. The approach is based on an expressive attention model, which is realized by combining ECA (Event-Condition-Action) rules with ontologies. This chapter presents the system's architecture and describes its main components. The chapter also describes the research results from the EU IST SAKE project.

Chapter 11, *Personalization in E-Government: An Approach That Combines Semantic and Web 2.0*, presents a novel approach for achieving adaptivity of e-Government portals, that combines the power of Web 2.0 technologies (in particular Ajax) with semantic web technologies. The authors tackle the important problem today when a technology is the centre of the project and not the user, although the user, e.g., the citizen or business person, is the one who will in the end use all the new and exciting online e-Government services. To confront different citizens with a one-size-fits-all Web interface is not an optimal way to deliver public sector services, because every person is an individual with different knowledge, abilities, skills, and preferences. For this reason, many people tend to use conventional public administration offices rather than e-Government services. To transfer some of these people to e-Government portals, it is necessary to build adaptive portals for public services. Such user-adaptive portals will increase the usability, and thus, the acceptance of e-Government, enabling administrations to achieve the, as yet, elusive efficiency gains and user satisfaction that are the primary goals of e-Government projects. The solution proposed by the authors provides a semantic framework for capturing the meaning of a user's behaviour in a portal, recognizing the user's situation (i.e., problem in the usage of the portal), and applying certain rules, allowing the portal's behaviour to adapt to this situation. The authors also present two use cases showcasing the benefits of the portal. The chapter describes the research results from the EU IST FIT project.

Chapter 12, *A Semantically Enabled Portal for Facilitating the Public Service Provision*, describes a solution for complex public services focused on actual users' needs and/or profiles. In order to address problems like complex legislation and vague pre-conditions based on multiple details for citizens' profiles, the authors describe a solution that helps users to express their needs and discover PA services that address these specific and personalized needs. The solution comprises of a user-friendly, self-explanatory platform supporting users in searching for appropriate services while offering them the necessary guidance through the public service provision process. Also, the platform provides users with information about their eligibility for services, together with rich and well structured service descriptions. The chapter describes the research results from the EU IST SemanticGov project.

5   Further Research

There is already some criticism that semantic technologies do not deliver as fast as they should, even pessimistic voices saying that semantics may become what AI was in the 1970s, failing to address the raised expectations and promises. The software industry seems somehow addicted to short product lifecycles, and it is true that the Semantic Web rhetoric is already out there for a decade without having yet given mass implementation examples; not only in e-Government but also in other domains.

However, approaches like this fail to realize the particular characteristics of semantic technologies. Amongst others, semantic technologies, in order to take off, need commonly accepted ontologies or formal semantics in whatever format. Currently there is already a great stack of tools and applications that can effectively manage, process, and present semantic data. We already have enough capable languages and querying mechanisms that improve at a fast pace. What we miss, though, is large quantity of semantic data. This has to do, not only with the (not that advanced) tools we have for manual and automatic annotation of content, but also with something that needs more time and effort to be developed: standardized vocabularies, ontologies, and models that are shared and used by large communities and that could be used on a massive scale to provide the metadata to existing content. This fact clearly reflects on many book chapters where almost all projects had to develop their own domain representations, models, and ontologies to overcome the lack of global or at least widely adopted domain models. For example, and as already discussed, using RDFa, it has become easy to annotate common HTML web pages, and there are already real examples in the UK.[14] However, in e-Government we still miss the agreed upon terminology to use in order to generate real value from this technology. The previous example only brings limited value to a municipality that annotates descriptions of all social services available on the web using a terminology that is not used by anyone else.

These issues trigger a discussion about one critical aspect of ontologies, which is the cornerstone of semantic technologies: ontologies are social contracts or agreements where people agree on domain concepts describing a domain. When developing ontologies, public administrations have one important advantage and, on the other hand, one serious disadvantage when compared to other domains. The advantage is that the public agencies are not competing with each other and they belong to a broader system of collaborating entities which is governed by laws. This makes coordination and standards adoption easier. The disadvantage is that they are so large in size, so complex in their organization, and so diversified in power structures that coordination through standardization becomes eventually a great challenge.

---

[14]http://webbackplane.com/mark-birbeck/blog/2009/04/23/more-rdfa-goodness-from-uk-government-web-sites.

Are there means and policy vehicles that could accommodate the creation of common metadata in governments? We think yes. National interoperability frameworks are drafted and adopted in one country after another. While the first focus of such frameworks has been on technical issues, protocols etc., the current focus is shifted towards more content-related standards, for example, common xml schemas. In this setting, it is foreseeable that simple vocabularies could be proposed and adopted to guide developers of e-Government systems. To this end, governments should first review the currently available vocabularies and adopt (or adapt) some of them based on specific criteria. This exercise is all together new for governments so adequate processes should be put in place. Governments could go even further to develop domain-specific specializations of existing semantic web standards, for example, FOAF-Citizen, SIOC-Politics, Common Service Model as discussed in the W3C eGov IG Group,[15] etc.

The critical success factors here are related to wide adoption, reusability, extensibility, and real usage; in this direction simplicity and consensus are key factors. Certain central and strategic units could and should evangelize the adoption of such vocabularies: for example, in EU the Commission through its IDABC program, in US the CIO Council, the Semantic Interoperability Community of Practice (SICOP), OMB/GSA, and W3C through its eGov Interest Group and future groups and committees could play such roles. National Interoperability Strategies could also have a significant role to this direction by endorsing these types of vocabularies and empowering them with "official" or even legal support. With such activities at the background, annotating public data using such domain-specific vocabularies could start creating for governmental information, what Tim Burners Lee calls "a rapidly growing Linked Open Data cloud."[16]

References

B. Adida, M. Birbeck (eds.), RDFa Primer. W3C Recommendation, http://www.w3.org/TR/xhtml-rdfa-primer/

C. Anderson, The Long Tail. Wired, October 2004

D. Beckett (eds.), RDF/XML Syntax Specification, W3C Recommendation, http://www.w3.org/TR/rdf-syntax-grammar/

D. Brickley, R. Guha (eds.), RDF Vocabulary Description Language 1.0: RDF Schema. W3C Recommendation, http://www.w3.org/TR/rdf-schema/

J. Bruijn, D. Fensel, H. Lausen, D34v0.1: The Web Compliance of WSML. Technical report, DERI, 2007, http://www.wsmo.org/TR/d34/v0.1/

E. Christensen, F. Curbera, G. Meredith, S. Weerawarana, Web Service Description Language (WSDL) 1.1. W3C Recommendation, http://www.w3.org/TR/wsdl 22

D. Connoly (eds.), Gleaning Resource Descriptions from Dialects of Languages (GRDDL). W3C Recommendation, http://www.w3.org/TR/grddl/

---

[15]http://www.w3.org/2007/eGov/IG/wiki/Use_Case_9_Common_Service_Model.

[16]http://www.thenationaldialogue.org/ideas/linked-open-data.

J. Euzenat, P. Shvaiko, *Ontology Matching* (Springer, Heidelberg, 2007)

J. Euzenat, et al, Results of the ontology alignment evaluation initiative 2006. in *Proceedings of International Workshop on Ontology Matching (OM-2006)*, vol. 225. CEUR Workshop Proceedings, Athens, Georgia, USA, November 2006, pp. 73–95

T.R. Gruber, A translation approach to portable ontology specifications. Knowl. Acquis. **5**(2), 199–220 (1993)

J. Kopecký, T. Vitvar, C. Bournez, J. Farrell, SAWSDL: semantic annotations for WSDL and XML schema. IEEE Internet Comput. **11**(6), 60–67 (2007)

F. Manola, E. Miller (eds.), RDF Primer. W3C Recommendation, http://www.w3.org/TR/rdf-primer/

D. Martin et al., in Bringing semantics to web services: the OWL-S approach, *Proceedings of the 1st International Workshop Semantic Web Services and Web Process Composition (SWSWPC 04)* (Springer, Heidelberg, 2004) pp. 26–42

D. McGuinness, F. Harmelen (eds.), OWL Web Ontology Language Overview. W3C Recommendation, http://www.w3.org/TR/owl-features/

A. Miles, S. Bechhofer (eds.), SKOS Simple Knowledge Organization System Reference. W3C Candidate Recommendation, http://www.w3.org/TR/skos-reference/

E. Prud'hommeaux, A. Seaborne (eds.), SPARQL Query Language (GRDDL). W3C Reccomendation, http://www.w3.org/TR/skos-reference/

D. Roman, U. Keller, H. Lausen, J. Bruijn, R. Lara, M. Stollberg, A. Polleres, C. Feier, C. Bussler, D. Fensel, Web service modeling ontology. Appl. Ontol. **1**(1), 77–106 (2005)

K. Sivashanmugam, K. Verma, A. Sheth, J. Miller, Adding semantics to web services standards, in *2E Proceedings of the 1st International Conference on Web Services (ICWS'03)*, Las Vegas, Nevada (June 2003) pp. 395–401

Part I

Architectures and Process Integration

Pan-European E-Government Services Architecture

Tomáš Vitvar, Adrian Mocan, Sanaullah Nazir, and Xia Wang

1 Introduction

E-Government has been the center of interest for public administrations, citizens and businesses, as well as software vendors for several years. E-Government enables customers and members of the public and private sectors to take advantage of automated administration processes accessible on-line. These activities involve electronic exchange of information to acquire or provide products or services, to place or receive orders, or to complete financial transactions. All such communications must be performed securely, while at the same time maintaining the privacy of involved parties. E-Government allows citizens and businesses to process requests on-line, and with minimal physical interactions with public bodies. Since a complex information support often needs to be developed incrementally, e-Government services were first available as single services in specific sectors and for specific users. While these services are being further developed and expanded to be available in more sectors and for more users, their growing number leads to requirements of total or partial automation of certain tasks, for example, discovery, selection, composition and mediation of services. In addition, extensive numbers of such services are available in different sectors, and their provisioning in complex scenarios requires a good information strategy along with a good *architectural* and *technological* basis. The main goal is to identify and define methods, standards, technologies as well as legislation to be used within the whole development process and provisioning of complex e-Government systems. In the EU, the e-Government information strategy can be seen at two levels as (1) a European strategy driven by the European Commission to enable e-Government services across the EU member states and (2) national strategies to form a national e-Government available within a particular EU member state. The initiative which aims to develop the European

T. Vitvar (✉)
University of Innsbruck, Technikestrasse 21a, 6020 Innsbruck, Austria

T. Vitvar et al. (eds.), *Semantic Technologies for E-Government*,
DOI 10.1007/978-3-642-03507-4_2, © Springer-Verlag Berlin Heidelberg 2010

strategy at the EU level is called IDABC.[1] Based on the fundamental principles of the EU, the goal of IDABC is to promote development and integration of EU sector systems (e.g. transport, health), to develop on-line front-office services, and most importantly to develop a European E-Government Framework. The purpose of this framework is to define methods, standards and technologies to enable seamless integration of e-Government services on a Europe-wide scale. On the other hand, every national strategy aims to build national e-Government services. With the aim of being aligned with IDABC, different national initiatives exist, such as GovTalk[2] in the UK, or REACH in Ireland.[3]

With respect to ongoing activities in e-Government within the national and European initiatives, this work is the design of the architecture that enables seamless integration and provisioning of e-Government services on a Europe-wide scale. The work presented in this chapter provides the overview of the architecture developed in the EU FP6 Framework Program called SemanticGov.[4] SemanticGov architecture builds on the underlying concepts and technologies of semantic, and distributed systems, and provides a novel technology, allowing to achieve the vision of a knowledge-based, citizen-centric, and citizen-empowering, distributed and integrated e-Government.

2 Conceptual Architecture

In this section we define the conceptual SemanticGov architecture (depicted in Fig. 1), in several layers and building on several governing principles. We identify the architecture layers as: (1) Stakeholders Layer forming several groups of users of the architecture, (2) Problem Solving Layer for building the environment for stakeholders' access to the architecture, (3) Service Requesters Layer as client systems of the architecture, (4) Middleware Layer providing the intelligence for the integration and interoperation of business services, and (5) Service Providers Layer for exposing the functionality of back-end systems as Public Administration Services (PA Services).

2.1 Governing Principles

The architecture builds on a number of principles which define essential background knowledge governing architecture research, design and implementation.

---

[1]Interoperable Delivery of European e-Government Services to public Administrations, Businesses and Citizens (IDABC) was established through the Decision 2004/387/EC of the European Parliament.

[2]http://www.govtalk.gov.uk.

[3]http://www.reach.ie.

[4]http://www.semantic-gov.org.

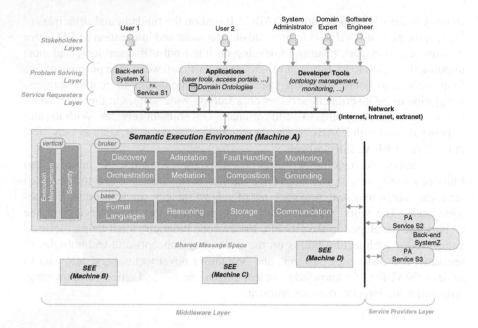

Fig. 1 Global SemanticGov architecture

These principles reflect fundamental aspects for service-oriented and distributed environments which promote intelligent and seamless integration and provisioning of business services, and in turn provide additional value to the e-Government domain. These principles include:

- *Service Oriented Principle* represents a distinct approach in analysis, design, and implementation which further introduces particular principles of service reusability, loose coupling, abstraction, composability, autonomy, and discoverability.

    With respect to the service orientation which enables a service level view on the PA domain, we further distinguish two types of services in this architecture: (1) *PA Services* and (2) *Middleware Services*. PA services are provided by various PAs at various PA levels – they are the subject of integration and interoperation providing certain value for citizens and businesses (e.g. issuance of a birth certificate). On the other hand, middleware services are the main facilitators for integration and interoperation of PA services at the member state and EU levels (e.g. discovery, interoperability, etc.).

- *Semantic Principle* allows a rich and formal description of information, and behavioral models enabling automation of certain tasks by means of logical reasoning. Combined with the service oriented principle, semantics allows to define scalable, semantically rich and formal service models and ontologies, allowing to promote total or partial automation of tasks such as service discovery, contracting, negotiation, mediation, composition, invocation, etc.

Semantic service oriented approach to modeling and implementation of the PA domain enables scalable and seamless interoperation, reusability, discovery, composition, etc. of e-Government services at the national as well as EU level.

- *Problem Solving Principle* reflects Problem Solving Methods as one of the fundamental concepts of artificial intelligence. It underpins the ultimate goal of the architecture which lies in so-called goal-based discovery and invocation of services. Users (service requester's) describe requests as goals semantically and independently from services, while the architecture solves those goals by means of logical reasoning over goal and service descriptions. Ultimately, users do not need to be aware of processing logic, but only care about the result and its desired quality.

  Problem solving is natural to the e-Government domain where a client has a need and wants to solve his need, although he/she ultimately does not care about how his/her need should be solved. The client rather cares about real world effects of his/her needs.

- *Distributed Principle* allows aggregating the power of several computing entities to collaboratively run a task in a transparent and coherent way, so that from a service requester's perspective they can appear as a single and centralized system. This principle allows executing a process across a number of components/services over the network which in turn can promote scalability and quality of the process.

  Distributed principle is natural for the PA domain. Depending on the particular law of a country/region, various PAs are distributed geographically together with responsibilities and performing activities. For the architecture design, it is important to take this aspect into account, with the possibility to distribute functionality of the architecture according to various geographical locations and functional PA levels.

2.2   Stakeholders Layer

Stakeholders form the group of various users who use the functionality of the architecture for various purposes. Two basic groups of stakeholders are identified: users, and engineers. Users form the group of those stakeholders to which the architecture provides end-user functionality through specialized applications. For example, users can perform electronic exchange of information to acquire or provide products or services, to place or receive orders, or to perform financial transactions. In general, the goal is to allow users to interact with back-end processes on-line, while at the same time reduce their physical interactions with back-office operations. On the other hand, the group of engineers form those stakeholders who perform development and administrative tasks in the architecture.

These tasks should support the whole SOA lifecycle including service modeling, creation (assembling), deployment (publishing), and management. Different types of engineers could be involved in this process, ranging from domain experts (modeling, creation), system administrators (deployment, management) and software engineers.

In the e-Government domain, the stakeholders are identified as (1) *citizens*, (2) *businesses*, and (3) *public servants*. Citizens and businesses are understood as e-Government users who consume e-Government services and processes according to their needs, through functionality provided by the *problem solving layer* (e.g. access portals). Public servants are domain experts and administrators who access the e-Government systems in order to manage, configure, create and maintain e-Government services. All groups perform certain activities (e.g. trigger processes) in the system.

2.3 Problem-Solving Layer

The problem-solving layer contains applications and tools which support stakeholders during formulation of problems/requests, and generates descriptions of such requests as formal goals (e.g. e-Government access portals). Through the problem solving layer, a user will be able to solve his/her problems; that means to formulate a problem, interact with the architecture during processing and get his/her desired results. This layer contains back-end systems which can directly interact with the middleware within business processes running in those back-end systems, specialized applications built for a specific purpose in a particular domain which also provide specific domain ontologies, and developer tools providing functionality for development and administrative tasks within the architecture.

Developer tools provide a specific functionality for engineers, i.e. domain experts, system administrators and software engineers. The functionality of developer tools covers the whole SOA lifecycle including service modeling, creation (assembling), deployment (publishing), and management. These tasks are supported by an Integrated Development Environment (IDE) for management of the architecture. The IDE aids developers through the development process including engineering of semantic descriptions (services, goals, and ontologies), creation of mediation mappings, and interfacing with architecture middleware and external systems. By combining this functionality, a developer will be allowed to create and manage ontologies, Web services, goals and mediators, create ontology to ontology mediation mappings and deploy these mappings to the middleware.

Applications provide a specialized functionality for architecture end-users. They provide specialized domain-specific ontologies, user interfaces and application functionality through which stakeholders interact with the architecture and its processes.

2.4   Service Requester's Layer

Service requesters act as client systems in client-server settings of the architecture. With respect to the problem solving principle, they are represented by goals created through problem/request formulation by which they describe requests as well as interfaces through which they wish to perform conversation with potential services.

2.5   Middleware Layer

Middleware is the core of the architecture providing the main intelligence for the integration and interoperation of e-Government Services. For the purposes of the architecture, we call this middleware Semantic Execution Environment (SEE) (Fig. 1 depicts the SEE conceptual architecture). The SEE defines the necessary conceptual functionality that is imposed on the architecture through the underlying principles. Each such functionality could be realized (totally or partially) by a number of so called middleware services. We further distinguish this functionality into the following layers: base layer, broker layer, and vertical layer. The SEE is the subject of work as part of the OASIS Semantic Execution Environment Technical Committee (OASIS SEE TC)[5], with reference implementation of WSMX.[6] WSMX is also the basis for the implementation of the middleware system for the SemanticGov architecture.

2.5.1   Vertical Layer

The vertical layer defines the middleware framework functionality that is used across the broker and base layers, but which remains invisible to them. In this respect, framework functionality always consumes functionality of broker and base layers, coordinating and managing overall execution processes in the middleware. For example, Discovery or Data Mediation is not aware of the overall coordination and distributed mechanism of Execution Management.

- *Execution Management* defines a control of various execution scenarios (called execution semantics) and handles distributed execution of middleware services.
- *Security* defines a secure communication, i.e. authentication, authorization, confidentiality, data encryption, traceability or non-repudiation support applied within execution scenarios in the architecture.

---

[5]http://www.oasis-open.org/committees/semantic-ex.
[6]http://www.wsmx.org.

2.5.2 Broker Layer

The broker layer defines the functionality which is directly required for a goal based invocation of Semantic Web Services. The broker layer includes:

- *Discovery* defines tasks for identifying and locating business services which can achieve a requester's goal.
- *Orchestration* defines the execution of a composite process (business process) together with a conversation between a service requester and a service provider within that process.
- *Monitoring* defines a monitoring of the execution of end point services; this monitoring may be used for gathering information on invoked services, e.g. QoS related or for identifying faults during execution.
- *Fault Handling* defines a handling of faults occurring within execution of end point Web services.
- *Adaptation* defines an adaptation within a particular execution scenario according to users preferences (e.g. service selection, negotiation, contracting).
- *Mediation* defines an interoperability at the functional, data and process levels.
- *Composition* defines a composition of services into an executable workflow (business process).
- *Grounding* defines a link between the semantic level (WSMO) and a non-semantic level (e.g. WSDL), used for service invocation.

2.5.3 Base Layer

The base layer defines functionality that is not directly required in a goal based invocation of business services; however, they are required by the broker layer for successful operation. Base layer includes:

- *Formal Languages* defines syntactical operations (e.g. parsing) with semantic languages used for semantic description of services, goals and ontologies.
- *Reasoning* defines reasoning functionality over semantic descriptions.
- *Storage* defines persistence mechanism for various elements (e.g. services, ontologies).
- *Communication* defines inbound and outbound communication of the middleware.

The SEE middleware can operate in a distributed manner when a number of middleware systems connected using a shared message space operate within a network of middleware systems, which empowers in this way a scalability of integration processes.

In the SemanticGov, the middleware layer is composed of two major building blocks: (1) *Member State Middleware*, and (2) *Communal Gateway*. Member State Middleware facilitates the integration of e-Government services provided by

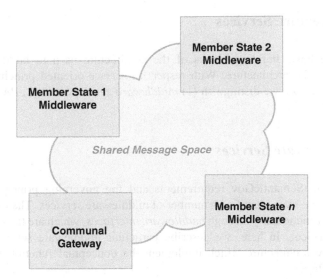

Fig. 2 Distributed middleware system for the SemanticGov

various PAs within the state as well as horizontal integration with the Communal Gateway. Communal Gateway facilitates the integration of member states at the EU level, i.e. integration and interoperation of cross-border PA services (Pan-European e-Government Services) that has been solving interoperability problems by means of data and process mediation. The integration process within both building blocks is maintained through a number of middleware services (Fig. 2).

2.6 Service Providers Layer

Service providers represent various back-end systems. Unlike back-end systems in service requesters layer which act as clients in client-server settings of the architecture, the back-end systems in service providers layer act as servers which provide certain functionality for certain purposes exposed as PA services to the architecture. The back-end systems could originate from one PA (one service provider) or multiple PAs (more service providers) interconnected over the network (internet, intranet or extranet). The PA services are the subject of integration and interoperation facilitated by the middleware layer. Since the middleware layer operates on the semantic description of services, additional semantic descriptions for PA services must exist. For this purpose, we define the WSMO-PA (Wang et al. 2007), an extension of the Web Service Modeling Ontology (WSMO (Roman et al. 2005)), with Public Administration concepts according to the GEA model. Such semantic description will be defined by a domain expert using the WSMO-PA framework as well as specific management tools.

3 Architecture Services

Services are basic building blocks of the architecture used to build processes facilitated by the architecture. With respect to service-oriented principles of the architecture design, we distinguish (1) *middleware services*, and (2) *PA services*.

3.1 Middleware Services

Following the SemanticGov requirements and the governing principles of the architecture, we have identified a number of middleware services. The middleware expose their functionality through *middleware interfaces*, which are then consumed by client services. In here, we describe particular middleware services for the SemanticGov architecture which implement the conceptual functionality of the middleware layer.

- *Operation* is in the core of the middleware intelligence which controls the integration process of e-Government services by means of *operational semantics* (also called *execution semantics*). It defines interactions of middleware services (e.g. discovery, composition, interoperability, etc.) along with integration of a member state middleware and the communal gateway. The exact form of the *execution semantics* depends on the functionality provided by the middleware to its users. For example, different execution semantics can exist and be available for (1) a client (a citizen) who wants to get all services from the repository which are related to registration of a birth certificate, or a (2) client (a system administrator) who wants to store an object (service, ontology) in the repository. Operational semantics is the description of behavior which is deployed to the middleware system, and according to which the middleware system behaves. The typical process is that the operational semantics is invoked through the event sent to the middleware generated at the problem-solving layer, followed by a set of invocations of middleware services and establishing the conversation between service requestor (client) and a set of back-office services. Operational semantics thus consumes various middleware services through their interfaces during processing. From the service provisioning point of view, the operational semantics supports both, design-time (e.g. service creation processes) as well as run-time (i.e. conversation between services, solving interoperability problems during run-time etc.) business processes.
- *Discovery* is the process of finding services which satisfy requests from citizens. The services are annotated with semantic description defined in the ontology. Services are described using the capability part of WSMO goal and web services, which contains preconditions, assumptions, effects and postconditions, thus enabling the description to define what the service does. Semantic web service discovery is a process of finding services which uses these annotations

for finding the service which meets the user goals, which is also described using semantic descriptions.

- *Registry and repository* services provide means to register and store PA services. SemanticGov defines a distributed discovery architecture, where each member state maintains its own registry/repository. Since PA service contains semantic descriptions as well as descriptions in WSDL (descriptions of XML schema, interfaces, operations, binding and endpoints), registry and repository allow storing and accessing both descriptions through distributed registry/repository mechanisms.
- *Composition* addresses the situation when a service needs to be aggregated by combining "parts of" available *component* Web Services. There are two possible approaches towards service composition: Design-time approach providing support tools for domain experts during service provisioning when system advices a domain expert how to compose business processes with respect to possible process configurations, and the run-time approach when the processes are composed on the fly for user (citizen) who interacts with the system. The SemanticGov architecture adopts the first approach.
- *Interoperability* provides functionality for maintaining interoperability among business services at data and process levels. Data level interoperability (Mocan and Cimpian 2005) needs to be solved when two services use incompatible information models thus data mediation between these models must be in place. Data mediation is performed in two phases: design-time and run-time phase. During the design-time phase, the mappings between information models are found and during run-time phase the mappings are executed. Process level interoperability (Cimpian and Mocan 2005) needs to be solved when two services use incompatible communication patterns.
- *Orchestration* drives a run-time conversation between service requestor and service provider according to defined composition of services (workflow). During the conversation, other middleware services could be used such as data and process mediation to allow solving interoperability problems between different information models and behavior of orchestrated services. More information about orchestration may be found in Vitvar et al. (2008).
- *Reasoner* provides reasoning functionality during the execution process, allowing reasoning on semantic descriptions of services.
- *Communication* manages all inbound and outbound communication from/to middleware. Communication service acts as the entry service to the middleware and triggers appropriate operational semantics on reception of an event, or ensures that all conversation is routed to appropriate running operation.

3.2   PA Services

PA services are subject to integration and provisioning facilitated by the middleware layer and by means of middleware services. PA services expose a certain functionality of a PA domain. In order to integrate PA services within the SemanticGov architecture, they must be available in WSMO-PA formalism.

4 Detail Architecture

Based on the conceptual architecture, in this section we describe several architecture components at the detail level. The detailed architecture design is based on several technologies that we chose for architecture development.

4.1 Technology

In this section we list all underlying and existing standards, models, techniques, software systems, etc. (commonly referred to as *technology*) which we use to build the architecture. This technology has been selected according to various pre-existing know-how of each partner with respect to overall project goals and technology direction of the project. This technology will be integrated within the scope of the SemanticGov architecture and is listed here for each building block according to the global view on the architecture (Table 1).

The SemanticGov architecture builds on the semantic technologies around WSMO, WSML, and WSMX.

4.1.1 WSMO, WSML, WSMX, WSMT

A general aim of the Semantic Web Services is to define a semantic mark-up for web services providing higher expressivity than traditional XML-based descriptions. One of the initiatives in this area is the Web Service Modelling Ontology (WSMO) (Roman et al. 2005). WSMO provides a conceptual model describing all

Table 1 Selected technology for the architecture

Architecture building block	Technology
Member state portal	Existing web standards and technologies (html, http, xml, xslt, servlets, etc.) and technology for semantic web services (WSMO4J, WSML2Reasoner, etc.)
Management tools	Web Service Modelling Toolkit (WSMT) – ontology editor, ontology mapping tool, management console
	WSMO Studio (ontology editor)
Middleware	Web Service Execution Environment (WSMX) – Framework
Operation	JavaSpaces/TupleSpaces, RMI, JMX
Discovery	Discovery techniques and components
Composition	Composition techniques and tools
Interoperability	Data and process mediation techniques and tools
Orchestration	WSMX orchestration engine
Repository and registry	ORDI for domain repositories (storing WSMO objects)
	CentraSite (storing WSDL and registering domain repositories)
PA services	Semantic descriptions: WSMO, WSML, WSMO-PA
	Non-semantic descriptions : WSDL

relevant aspects of general services which are accessible through a web service interface while at the same time adhering to the principles of loose coupling of services and strong mediation among them. WSMO defines an underlying model for the WSMX, a Semantic Web Services execution environment as well as WSML (Roman et al. 2005), an ontology language used for formal description of WSMO elements. Thus, WSMO, WSML and WSMX form a complete framework facilitating all relevant aspects of the Semantic Web Services.

WSMO top-level conceptual model consists of *Ontologies, Web Services, Goals*, and *Mediators. Ontologies* provide formal explicit specification of shared conceptualization that is formal semantics of information model used by other components (goals, web services, and mediators). WSMO ontologies also provide one of the solutions for handling interoperability among some components (goals, web services), achieved through common (domain) ontology. *Web Services* provide functionality for a certain purpose, which is semantically described. Such description includes non-functional properties, capability and interfaces. Capability of a web service is modeled by preconditions and assumptions defining conditions under which the execution of the web service can be performed, as well as postconditions and effects defining conditions which must hold after a successful execution of the web service. The interface for every web service is modeled as choreography describing communication pattern (interactions) with this web service and orchestration describing partial functionality required from other web services. *Goals* provide description of objectives of a service requester (user) that he or she wants to achieve. WSMO goals are described in terms of conditions which must hold before and after the execution of given services. The WSMO goal is characterized by a requested capability and requested interfaces. *Mediators* describe elements that aim to overcome semantic or behavioral mismatches that appear between different components that build up a WSMO description.

WSMX is the middleware system built specifically to enact Semantic Service Oriented Architectures and facilitates the integration process between different systems. The integration process is defined by the operational semantics (also called execution semantics) of WSMX, which defines the interactions of middleware services including discovery, mediation, invocation, choreography, repository services, etc.

The Web Service Modeling Toolkit (WSMT) is an integrated development environment for WSMO. The WSMT is implemented as a collection of plug-ins for the Eclipse framework such that it can be integrated with other toolkits like the Java Development Toolkit (JDT), or the Web Tools Platform (WTP), so that a developer can develop his java code, Web services and Semantic Web Services side by side in the one application. The main aim of the WSMT is to support the developer through the full Software Development Cycle of his Semantic Web Service from requirements, through design, implementation, testing, and deployment, such that the process of developing Semantic Web Services can become cheaper to perform and remove many of the tedious activities that the developer must currently perform.

4.1.2 Governance Enterprise Architecture

Governanace Enterprise Architecture (GEA) (Peristeras and Tarabanis 2004) is one of the major underlying concepts for the SemanticGov architecture, for modeling of PA services in particular.

The GEA object model for service provisioning has been created with a requirement to be generic enough so that it can cover all different application areas of public administration. This makes it highly reusable in different cases for the public service domain. The GEA model defines *Governance Entities* as two categories: *Political Entities* and *Public Administration Entities (PA)*. During execution time, PA entities have three kinds of roles: *Service Provider*, *Evidence Provider*, and *Consequence Receiver* (this means that PA services may have three kinds of capabilities: providing service, providing evidence, and receiving consequence).

Political Entities define *PA Services*. *PA Entities* through their role as *Service Provider* offer real services. *PA Services* are governed by *Preconditions* usually specified by legal acts, i.e. *Laws*. *PA service* defines three outcomes, which are *Output* (a kind of document decision yielded by service provider and returned to the client), *Effect* (the result of executing a service changing the state of the world, e.g. transferring money to an account), and *Consequence* (the information about an executed PA service that needs to be forwarded to interested parties, i.e. to an appointed consequence receiver).

Societal Entities (e.g. citizen, business) have *Needs* related to specific *Goals*. A *Need* is an informal description of the *Goal*, as experienced from a client's perspective. Also a *Societal Entity* requests a *Public Administration* service to serve its *Goals*.

Evidence is primarily pure information; it is stored in *Evidence Placeholders*, which, in turn, contain *Pieces of Evidences*. *Preconditions* are validated by *Pieces of Evidence* and *Purposes of Evidence*. The direct relationship between *PA Service* and *Evidence Placeholder* depicts cases where *PA Services* preferably use specific types of *Evidence Placeholders*, e.g. when the law explicitly states that a birth certificate is needed for the execution of a particular service.

4.1.3 Technological Components

Following are brief descriptions of other relevant technologies used to build the SemanticGov architecture.

- *WSMO4J* is the API for WSMO services, ontologies, mediators and goals.
- *WSML2Reasoner* is a modular architecture which combines various validation, normalization, and transformation functionalities essential to the translation of ontology descriptions in WSML with the appropriate syntax of several underlying reasoning engines.

- *JavaSpaces* provides a distributed persistence and object exchange mechanism for Java objects. It can be used to store the system state and implement distributed algorithms. It is an implementation of the TupleSpaces idea.
- *TupleSpaces* is an implementation of the associative memory paradigm for parallel/distributed computing. It provides a repository of tuples that can be accessed concurrently.
- *RMI (Remote Method Invocation)* provides a means for invoking the methods of remote Java objects.
- *JMX (Java Management Extensions)* is a Java technology that supplies tools for managing and monitoring applications, system objects, devices (e.g. printers) and service-oriented networks. An interesting detail of the API is that classes can be dynamically constructed and changed.
- *ORDI (Ontology Representation and Data Integration)* allows the representation and basic management (storage, retrieval, exchange) of ontologies.
- *CentraSite* is the registry and repository developed by SoftwareAG supporting the whole SOA governance for managing the service oriented environment.
- *WSDL* (Christensen 2001) is an XML format for describing network services as a set of endpoints operating on messages containing either document-oriented or procedure-oriented information. The operations and messages are described abstractly, and then bound to a concrete network protocol and message format to define an endpoint.

4.2 Member State Portal

Member state portal implements some functionality of the problem solving layer of the SemanticGov architecture. Chapter 11 describes the member state portal of the SemanticGov architecture in detail.

4.3 Management Suite

All management activities in the SemanticGov architecture are performed by domain experts and engineers by using the SemanticGov management suite. Figure 3 shows the architecture of the management suite.

SemanticGov management suite consists of following components:

- *WSML Text Editor* provides capabilities for editing WSML descriptions (ontologies, goals, services, etc.) in text (e.g. syntax highlighting, code suggestions, etc.).
- *WSMO Visualizer* provides capabilities for visualizing and editing of WSMO services, WSMO ontologies and WSMO goals in a graphical way. More information about ontology visualization in the context of the SemantiGov architecture may be found in Kerrigan (2006).

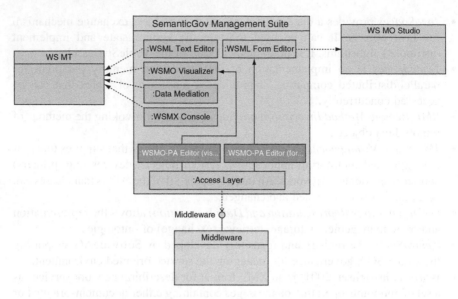

Fig. 3 SemanticGov management suite

- *Data Mediation* provides capabilities for design-time mediation of WSMO ontologies. More information about ontology mediation may be found in Euzenat and Shvaiko (2007), Mocan and Cimpian (2005), Scharffe and de Bruijn (2005).
- WSMO Form Editor provides capabilities for form-based editing of WSMO elements.
- *WSMO-PA Editor* is a tool for form-based editing of WSMO-PA services. WSMO-PA Editor has been built specifically to support domain experts and engineers during the service creation process. The functionality of the editor is based on the WSMO-PA specification, the formal service ontology for the PA domain.
- *Access Layer* provides access for various management components to the middleware through standard API (WSMO Registry API for retrieving and storing WSMO, Entry point API for accessing various operational semantics at the middleware layer). This API is based on the WSMX API developed in the DIP project and extended according to the functionality of the SemanticGov architecture.

4.4 WSMO-PA

WSMO-PA is a specification on how the WSMO service model can be used to model PA services. Thus, the WSMO-PA can be seen as an additional layer on top of the semantic service stack built on WSMO and GEA which contains both semantic as well as non-semantic descriptions.

Table 2 GEA-PA and
WSMO mapping

GEA-PA	WSMO
Societal entity, service provider, evidence provider, evidence, evidence placeholders, political entities, etc.	Ontology
PA Service	Service
– preconditions	– preconditions
– preconditions	– assumptions
– outputs	– postconditions
– effects	– effects
– consequences	– Orchestration, Choreography
Goal (Needs)	Goal
	Mediator
	NonFunctionalProperties

The mappings between GEA-PA and WSMO are illustrated in Table 2. We
discuss this mapping below in more detail.

- We build a GEA domain-specific ontology on top of the other established
  domain-neutral specifications of WSMO. Such a generic GEA ontology can be
  shared by all elements of the WSMO-PA service model. Every object entity of
  the PA service model is provided by a corresponding ontology class, their
  concepts, relations, functions, instances and axioms. In the GEA-PA service
  model, *Societal Entity*, *Service Provider*, *Evidence Provider*, *Evidence*, *Evidence Placeholder*, *Political Entity* and so on will be defined as subclasses of
  the general GEA Ontology.
- *PA service* is modeled as a WSMO web service. It is described by capabilities and interfaces. For the capabilities, we map the PA preconditions
  into WSMO preconditions; PA preconditions (or *Rules* of a specific PA service) can be also mapped to WSMO assumptions. The separation between
  precondition and assumption is based on whether required information is
  available in the information space (information used in assumptions are
  usually not included in the information space of service requester/provider).
  Finally, the PA outputs are mapped into WSMO post conditions, and the
  PA effects are mapped into WSMO effects. For the interfaces, the choreography and orchestration are two special concepts only appearing in WSMO
  model.
- *Societal Entities* act as clients (e.g. citizen, business), that present their
  goals by providing service *Needs*. Therefore, we map PA goal into WSMO
  goal.
- WSMO-PA includes the WSMO *nonFunctionalProperties* and WSMO mediators, as they play an important role in supporting dynamic operations such as
  discovery, composition, selection, and invocation of PA services.

4.5   Member State Middleware

Member State Middleware is the platform for integration of services provided by the PA domain. Member State Middleware provides a specific functionality which allows running tasks related to service usage processes including discovery, composition, mediation, and invocation of services. The middleware performs these tasks during *design-time* as well as *run-time* phases of the service provisioning. In this section we do not describe detailed functionalities of the middleware components, but a technology for the execution management of the middleware core. The execution management service is responsible for the management of a platform, and for orchestrating the individual functionality of middleware services according to defined execution semantics through which it facilitates the overall operation of the middleware. In here, middleware services are implemented as *functional components* (also called application components) of the middleware system. The execution management service takes the role of component management and coordination, inter-component messaging, and configuration of execution semantics. In particular, it manages interactions between other components through the exchange of messages containing instances of WSMO-PA concepts expressed in WSML, and provides the microkernel and messaging infrastructure for the middleware. The execution management service implements the middleware kernel utilizing Java Management Extensions (JMX). It is responsible for handling following three main functional requirements: (1) Management, (2) Communication and Coordination, and (3) Execution Semantics.

4.5.1   Management

We have made a clear separation between operational logic and management logic, treating them as orthogonal concepts. By not separating these two elements, it would become increasingly difficult to maintain the system and keep it flexible. Figure 4 shows an overview of the infrastructure provided by the management execution service to its components. This infrastructure primarily allows to manage and to monitor the system.

In the core of the management lies a management agent which offers several dedicated services. The most important one is the *bootstrap service* responsible for loading and configuring the functional component. Here, the management agent plays the role of a driver which is directly built into the application. The execution management service, in addition, employs self-management techniques through scheduled operations, and allows administration through a representation-independent management and monitoring interface. Through this interface, a number of management consoles can be interconnected, each serving different management purposes. In particular, terminal, web browser and eclipse management consoles already exist. The execution management service hosts a number of subsystems that provide services to components and enable inter-component communication. In addition, the service provides a number of other services including pool

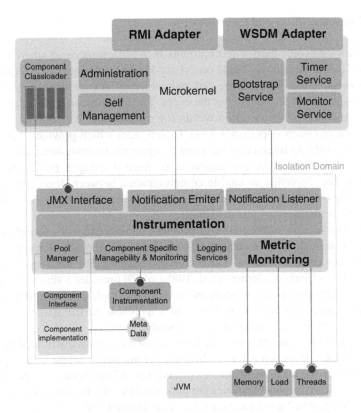

Fig. 4 Component management in the middleware execution management service

management which takes care of handling component instances, logging, transport and lifecycle services. The execution management service also exploits the underlying (virtual) machine's instrumentation to monitor performance and system health metrics. Although some general metrics can be captured for all components, the component metric monitoring allows capturing metrics specific to some components which require custom instrumentation. Such customization can be achieved by extending the configuration for the instrumentation of a specific component which is done independently from the implementation of the component itself.

With respect to the distributed principle of the architecture, the execution management service may act as a facade to distributed components. However, the preferred way for distribution is to organize the system as federations of agents. Each agent has its own execution management service and a particular subset of functional components. In order to hide the complexity of the federation for the management application, a single agent view is provided, i.e. single point of access to the management and administration interfaces. This is achieved by propagating requests within the federation via proxies, broadcasts or directories. A federation thus consists of a number of execution management services, each of them operating a kernel per one machine and hosting a number of functional components.

4.5.2   Communication and Coordination

The middleware avoids hard-wired bindings between components when the inter-component communication is based on events. If some functionality is required, an event representing the request is created and published. A component subscribed to this event type can fetch and process the event. The event-based approach naturally allows event-based communication within the middleware. As depicted in Fig. 5, the exchange of events is performed via TupleSpaces which provides a persistent shared space enabling interaction between components without direct exchange of events between them. This interaction is performed using a publish-subscribe mechanism. The TupleSpaces enable communication between distributed components running on both local as well as remote machines, while at the same time components are unaware of this distribution.

For this purpose, an additional layer provides components with a mechanism of communication with other components, which shields the actual mechanism of local or remote communication. The TupleSpace technology used in the middleware is based on Linda (Gelernter et al. 1985) which provides a shared distributed space where components can publish and subscribe to tuples. Subscription is based on templates and their matching with tuples available in the space. The space handles data transfer, synchronization and persistence.

The Tuple Space can, in addition, be composed of many distributed and synchronized TupleSpaces repositories. In order to maximize usage of components available within one machine, instances of distributed TupleSpaces are run on each machine, and newly produced entries are published locally. Before synchronization with other distributed TupleSpaces, a set of local template rules is executed in order

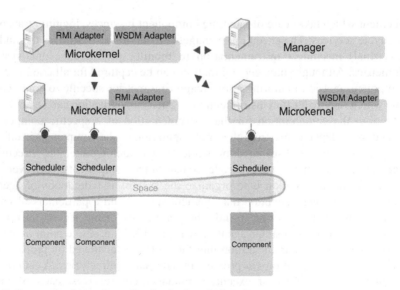

Fig. 5 Communication and coordination in the middleware

to check if there are any local components subscribed to the newly published event type. It means that by default (if not configured otherwise), local components have priority in receiving locally published entries. Through the infrastructure provided by the execution management, components implementations are separated from communications. This infrastructure is made available to each component implementation during instantiation of the component carried out by the execution management service during the bootstrap process. Through the use of JMX, this can occur both at start-up as well as after the system is up and running. The communication infrastructure has the responsibility to interact with the transport layer (a TupleSpaces instance). Through the transport layer, components subscribe to an event-type template. Similar mechanism applies when events are published in the TupleSpaces. In order to enable a component to request functionality from another component a proxy mechanism is used. When a component needs to invoke another component's functionality, the proxy creates the event for this purpose and publishes it on the TupleSpaces. At the same time, the proxy subscribes to the response event and takes care of the correlation. From the perspective of the invoking component, the proxy appears as the component being invoked. This principle is the same as one used by Remote Method Invocations (RMI) in object-oriented distributed systems.

4.5.3 Execution Semantics

Execution Semantics enable a combined execution of functional components as Fig. 6 depicts. Execution semantics define the logic of the middleware which realizes the middleware's behavior. The execution management service enables a general computation strategy by enforcing execution semantics, and operating on

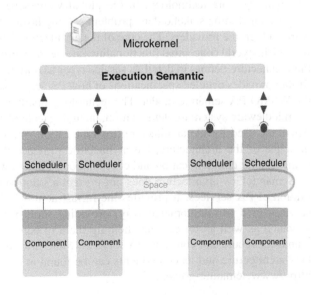

Fig. 6 Execution semantics

transport as well as component interfaces. It takes events from the TupleSpaces and invokes the appropriate components while keeping track of the current state of execution. Additional data obtained during execution can be preserved in the particular instance of execution semantics. The execution management service provides the framework that allows execution semantics to operate on a set of components without tying itself to a particular set of implementations. In particular, execution management service takes care of the execution semantics lifecycle, management and monitoring.

5 Conclusion

The SemanticGov architecture follows a new approach to integration and inter-operation of PA services by means of semantic languages and semantic service models. Building on the Web Service Modeling Ontology and Governance Enterprise Architecture, and taking into account governing principles of service orientation, semantic modeling and problem solving methods, the architecture provides a means for total or partial automation of tasks which are essential for better provisioning of e-Government services to its clients. An important aspect which underpins this integration lies in so called goal-based discovery and invocation of semantic services when users describe requests as goals semantically and independently from services, while architecture solves those goals by means of logical reasoning over semantic descriptions. Ultimately, users do not need to be aware of processing logic, but only care about the result and its desired quality.

With respect to underlying principles, the architecture is defined from several perspectives, such as global architecture, service architecture, and a detailed architecture with the core technology. In the global view, several architecture layers are identified including stakeholders, problem solving layer, service requesters, middleware and service providers. The core of the architecture lies in the middleware layer, for which several conceptual functionalities are defined. From the service perspective, the architecture defines in detail its service types as middleware and PA services, and further provides detailed specifications of how PA services can be modeled, based on the WSMO-PA semantic model. The technology finally presents the technology for the middleware system implementation, including technology of various components which are used for the architecture implementation. With respect to the distributed principle of the architecture, the architecture provides the support for distributed management, communication and coordination of middleware processes.

SemanticGov architecture does not present a solution for fully automated integration of PA services. It provides the infrastructure which will help to integrate services in a semi-automated way, providing tools for domain experts (public servants) as well as for citizens, helping them to better create, deploy, assemble, manage, execute and consume PA services. More information about the Semantic-Gov architecture and its components can be found at the SemanticGov web site at http://www.semantic-gov.org.

References

E. Christensen, F. Curbera, G. Meredith, S. Weerawarana, Web Service Description Language (WSDL) 1.1. W3C Recommendation (2001), http://www.w3.org/TR/wsdl

E. Cimpian, A. Mocan, WSMX process mediation based on choreographies, in *Proceedings of the 1st International Workshop on Web Service Choreography and Orchestration for Business Process Management at the BPM 2005*, Nancy, France, 2005

J. Euzenat, P. Shvaiko, *Ontology Matching* (Springer, Heidelberg, 2007)

D. Gelernter, N. Carriero, S. Chang, Parallel programming in Linda, in *Proceedings of the International Conference on Parallel Processing*, 1985, pp. 255–263

M. Kerrigan, *WSMOViz*: an ontology visualization approach for WSMO, in *Proceedings of the 10th International Conference on Information Visualization (IV06)*, July, 2006, London, England

A. Mocan and E. Cimpian, Mapping creation using a view based approach, in *Proceedings of the 1st International Workshop on Mediation in Semantic Web Services (Mediate 2005)*, Amsterdam, The Netherlands, December 2005

V. Peristeras, K.A. Tarabanis, Advancing the government enterprise architecture – GEA: The service execution object model. EGOV 2004, pp. 476–483

D. Roman, H. Lausen, U. Keller, Web service modeling ontology (WSMO), Technical report, WSMO Final Draft, April 2005, http://www.wsmo.org/TR/d2/v1.2/

F. Scharffe, J. de Bruijn, A language to specify mappings between ontologies, in IEEE Conference on Internet-Based Systems SITIS6, Yaounde, Cameroon, December 2005

T. Vitvar, M. Zaremba, A. Mocan, Formal model for semantic-driven service execution, in *The 7th International Semantic Web Conference (ISWC 2008)* (Springer, Heidelberg, 2008)

X. Wang, S. Goudos, V. Peristeras, T. Vitvar, A. Mocan, K. Tarabanis, WSMO-PA: formal specification of public administration service model on semantic web service ontology, in *Proceedings of the 40th Hawaii International Conference on System Sciences* (IEEE CS Press, Hawaii, USA, 2007)

Employing Semantic Technologies for the Orchestration of Government Services

Tomáš Sabol, Karol Furdík, and Marián Mach

1 Introduction

The main aim of the eGovernment is to provide efficient, secure, inclusive services for its citizens and businesses. The necessity to integrate services and information resources, to increase accessibility, to reduce the administrative burden on citizens and enterprises – these are only a few reasons why the paradigm of the eGovernment has been shifted from the supply-driven approach toward the connected governance, emphasizing the concept of *interoperability* (Archmann and Nielsen 2008).

On the EU level, the interoperability is explicitly addressed as one of the four main challenges, including in the i2010 strategy (i2010 2005). The Commission's Communication (Interoperability for Pan-European eGovernment Services 2006) strongly emphasizes the necessity of interoperable eGovernment services, based on standards, open specifications, and open interfaces. The Pan-European interoperability initiatives, such as the European Interoperability Framework (2004) and IDABC, as well as many projects supported by the European Commission within the IST Program and the Competitiveness and Innovation Program (CIP), illustrate the importance of interoperability on the EU level.

Interoperability was defined in Tambouris et al. (2007) as "*the ability of ICT systems and business processes they support to exchange data and to enable sharing of information and knowledge.*" Other definitions can be found, for example, in the Interoperability for Pan-European eGovernment Services (2006; Lueders 2005). Three types of interoperability on: (a) organizational; (b) semantic; and (c) technical levels were identified in the European Interoperability Framework (2004) and were also emphasized in the Commission's Communication (2006), and were further elaborated, for example, in Tambouris et al. (2007) and Laskaridis et al. (2007).

T. Sabol (✉)
Faculty of Economics, Technical University of Košice, Letna 9, 040 01 Košice, Slovak Republic

T. Vitvar et al. (eds.), *Semantic Technologies for E-Government*,
DOI 10.1007/978-3-642-03507-4_3, © Springer-Verlag Berlin Heidelberg 2010

The interoperability in the eGovernment is not only a technical issue concerned with the linking up of computer networks or of simple information exchange (Archmann and Nielsen 2008), but includes the reorganization of administrative processes (on all levels) to integrate services according to the user's requirements. From this point of view, an eGovernment solution also needs to address the *user-centric principle*, which means to design and provide government services from the perspective of service consumers – citizens or business users. This principle keeps the users in a central position when designing services and processes. It implies the need to integrate and orchestrate government services from various heterogeneous resources, usually provided by different institutions, into complex and customizable scenarios corresponding to life-events or business episodes which are then presented to the user in an easy-to-understand way. Access to particular services of the scenario is thus transparent and enabled, regardless of the existing institutional or role boundaries.

The user-centric interoperability, especially the semantic and organizational interoperability, can be achieved by employing *semantic technologies*, often accompanied by the use of technologies for workflow processing and business process modelling. The availability of formal and machine-readable descriptions of the meaning and context of the services, without the necessity to modify the services themselves, is one of the main advantages of this approach.

Service Oriented Architecture (SOA) implemented by the technology of web services is advantageous for the integration of government services, since it fits well with the requirements of the technical interoperability, namely by means of open interfaces, service interconnection, accessibility, and security. *Semantic Web Services*, or web services enhanced by a semantic description (McIlraith et al. 2001), are probably the most promising approach providing capabilities for discovery, composition, and interoperation of the involved services. Assuming the heterogeneity of services on data or process levels, the semantic grounding on a common and shareable knowledge base enables to make the services interoperable. Explicit semantic information accompanying the web services can be used for complex choreography and orchestration procedures and enables the exchange of information between two systems while taking into considering its precise meaning.

The demand for interoperable eGovernment solutions on one hand and availability of technologies and standards on the other hand, together with the existing R&D funds on the EU and national levels, have triggered quite a large number of projects in this area. However, despite the extensive ongoing research, the overall impact is still behind expectations (Archmann and Nielsen 2008; Abecker et al. 2006). One reason could be that application and testing of semantic technologies and solutions on a large scale in a vast, diverged, and distributed environment of public administration (PA) are a big challenge (cf. Wang et al. 2007). Another reason for this underachievement may be the lack of proper methodology, tools, and guidelines describing the procedures to design, develop, implement, and employ semantically enhanced eGovernment services in practice (Klischewski and Ukena 2007). The complexity of the knowledge modelling and semantic annotation processes needs to be dealt with using a user-oriented framework and a toolkit that is easy to use and understandable for public servants who will be the users of this toolkit.

To foster an easy implementation of integrated interoperable services in practice, the proposed solution has to be anchored in real conditions of PA. Although in general the number of electronically enabled services is growing, there are still many services available only in a "traditional" (i.e., non-electronic, face-to-face) form. The advantage of semantic technologies is that they enable the integration of traditional services (by means of their semantic descriptions and annotations) with electronic and web services, and distributed information resources (provided by different PAs or various external suppliers). Semantically described services of all forms, electronic and non-electronic, can be composed into complex scenarios corresponding to the life events of citizens (or business episodes of companies). These scenarios are presented to users (service consumers) through a proper interface, enabling the navigation and customization of the scenarios according to the situation of individual users. The customized scenario, tailored to the situational context of a concrete user, has usually a "hybrid" character: it consists of a combination of electronic and non-electronic (traditional) services. The electronic services in the scenario can be automatically executed by invoking corresponding web services, while in the case of traditional services the system provides the user with at least relevant supporting information.

This approach was adopted and elaborated within the R&D project Access-eGov (http://www.accessegov.org) supported by the European Commission within the 6th Framework Program (Furdik et al. 2007). The system designed, implemented, and deployed within the Access-eGov project targets and supports all the interoperability aspects, especially semantic and organizational interoperability. The following sections contain the description of the approach employed for the design and implementation of the Access-eGov system, especially focusing on the system components for orchestration of semantically annotated government services.

2   Problem Definition

The first problem users (citizens or businesses) in a given life event face is quite trivial – they need to identify which particular institution(s) provide(s) service(s) relevant to their life event. Subsequently, it is also important for users to know whether these services are available online, electronically, e.g., via web forms or through a web-service interface, or whether they are available only in a "traditional" (face-to-face) way, which means that the user has to personally visit a PA office. Sometimes, it is also confusing for the user to determine what the necessary inputs (documents, information) required for a service are, how the service fits into the life event, or how (if needed) to adapt (customize) the service to the user's situational context.

This situation is even more complex in real life. Citizens and businesses are rarely seeking one (atomic) government service. More often a set of services composed into a *scenario* (containing a non-linear sequence of services, including *if-then-else* branches) corresponding to their life event is needed. Assuming that only a limited number of government services are available online, the users usually have to deal with a combination of traditional (non-electronic) and electronic services – which means that they have to deal with *hybrid scenarios*. Carrying out a scenario consisting of a non-linear sequence of services as a workflow of interoperable e-services is also a challenging goal.

3 Conceptual Modelling of Integrated Government Services

The presented approach for enabling service interoperability follows the pattern of *front-office integration* (Mach et al. 2006). It does not require reorganization of the internal processes on the side of the PA (Fig. 1). Instead, an external integrator enables to leveraging currently offered services and providing them as one integrated service to users.

Integration of government services on the semantic level requires a specification of the common semantic basis, i.e., a conceptual model. Such a model contains a set of relevant entities – concepts, relations, properties, constraints, etc., that can serve as building blocks for annotation, i.e., a formal representation of potentially complex governmental services and their relationships. The conceptual model is strongly influenced by a technology applied to the semantic annotation.

Within the Access-eGov project it has been decided to apply the WSMO as a basic conceptual framework and implementation platform. This decision was made after a detailed survey and analysis of the existing approaches, investigating RDF/S, WSDL-S, and OWL-S ontologies for semantic description of web services, as

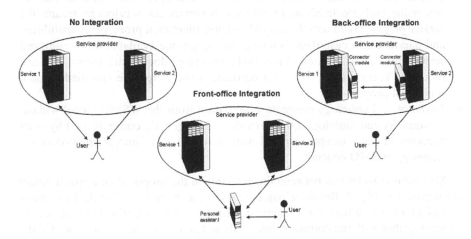

Fig. 1 Models of non-integrated government services, back-office and front-office integration of government services

well as BPEL4WS for modelling web services in a business process interaction (Bednar et al. 2006). The main reason for this decision was that WSMO, as a technically more advanced alternative, provides a consistent conceptual model for the semantic description of web services, with the inclusion of mediators and the distinction between goals and capabilities. The WSMO framework also includes the WSML language specification for ontology formalization (de Bruijn 2005) and the WSMX execution environment for discovery, selection, mediation, and invocation of Semantic Web Services. In addition to that, the WSMO conceptual model fits best to the architecture and functionality proposed for the Access-eGov system (Skokan and Bednar 2007); (Bednar et al. 2006).

3.1 Conceptual Model

The WSMO conceptual model (Roman et al. 2005) provides *Ontologies, Web services, Goals,* and *Mediators* as top-level elements for semantic description of general web services. However, for the modelling government services based on the life-event approach, the need to extend the WSMO conceptual model has arisen. The top-level elements were modified as follows:

- *Life Events* were added as formal models of users' needs consisting of multiple sub-goals organized into a *generic scenario* and expressed by an orchestrated construction of work-, control-, and data-flow sequences.
- *Goals* were reused from the WSMO model (Roman et al. 2005). They specify the objectives a user can have when consulting a single service, including functionality that the service should provide from the user's perspective.
- *Services* representing atomic activities provided by a PA were added as a generalization of the WSMO *Web service* concepts. This solution enables describing both electronic and traditional governmental services by means of a *service profile*, containing functional and non-functional properties, capabilities, and interfaces. In case there is no executable service available for a traditional service, textual description of required inputs (e.g., documents, forms, etc.) and requested actions (e.g., to visit a particular office, etc.) are specified as non-functional properties.
- *Mediator* and *Ontology* elements were reused from the WSMO model without changes. System ontologies that provide a set of generic concepts used by other elements of the conceptual model were designed as an implementation of the Ontology WSMO concept.

Structural correlations between the elements in the proposed conceptual model are depicted in Fig. 2. Resource ontologies serve as a repository of data structures and as a knowledge base for semantic descriptions of the identified concepts: Life events together with the corresponding goals and generic scenarios are stored in the *Life Events Ontology*; Services and their properties are described in the *Service Profiles Ontology*; and the *Domain Ontology* contains formal representations of

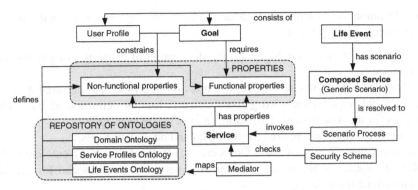

Fig. 2 Conceptual model adapted for eGovernment application

all relevant information related to the domain of the government, including eGovernment concepts. It covers non-functional properties such as organizational structures of PA (offices, access points, locations, and addresses), concepts describing quality of service (required documents, related laws, fees, and deadlines), security, trust, as well as concepts related to the user management and profiling.

The provided government services are conceptually described by functional and non-functional properties. *Functional properties* specify inputs, outputs, preconditions, and effects of a service. These properties are formally specified as logical expressions, consisting of terms that constrain type and property values of various resources required for, or provided by, the service. The types that are used to specify functional properties are defined in the *Service Profiles Ontology*.

Non-functional properties describe semi-structured information intended for service consumers during the service discovery procedure. Non-functional properties can be, for example, service name, description, information about the service provider, and properties that incorporate further requirements for the service capability (e.g., opening hours of the office, address and contact information, availability constraints, etc.).

3.2 Ontology Design

The conceptual model can be considered as a general background framework for semantic modelling and front-office integration of government services. To apply this general framework to a concrete set of services provided by a given PA, it is necessary to specify the conceptual elements of resource ontologies as semantic descriptions (models) of "real" public services – traditional (i.e., non-electronic) or electronic ones. In addition, to ensure the semantic interoperability of the described services as well as the user-centric principle, the descriptions should match the widely accepted standards available for the eGovernment domain. Having analyzed about 25 ontology resources and standards, the following ones were finally reused in the Access-eGov project:

- WSMO and Protege ontologies for the description of properties of government services;
- vCard ontology (www.w3.org/2006/vcard/) for addresses and personal data;
- SKOS ontology (www.w3.org/2004/02/skos/) for the definition of basic elements for the description of structure (hierarchy) of concepts;
- DublinCore (dublincore.org) for metadata and document types;
- SemanticGov, TerreGov, and OntoGov (cf. Related research) ontologies for the description of the process model of government services and for specific eGovernment concepts.

The available ontology resources were used to produce some fragments of the whole ontology structure, mostly comprising definitions of non-functional properties of services. The example below presents an implementation of the vCard ontology for the WSML representation of the ontology concept "Organization":

```
namespace{ _"http://www.accessegov.org/ontologies/core/",
dc _"http://purl.org/dc/elements/1.1/",
v _"http://www.w3.org/2006/vcard/ns#" }
concept Organization
v#relation ofType Link
v#organizationName ofType _string
v#organizationUnit ofType _string
v#addr ofType (1 1) v#Address
```

To obtain, encapsulate, and formally express the information needs and requirements of the service consumers and primary ontology users, the *requirement-driven approach* (Klischewski and Ukena 2007) was originally designed and developed within the Access-eGov project by one of the project partners (German University of Cairo). This approach proposes a systematic methodology for collecting, relating, and formalizing information needs in order to design specific semantic structures and descriptions of provided governmental services. The method consists of seven steps that include the identification of users' information needs and the required information quality, based on an analysis of the textual descriptions of use cases provided by the PAs. Further analysis of the use cases enables the creation of a glossary of the most important terms and a controlled vocabulary of these terms organized into a hierarchical structure. The procedure continues with an identification of relations between the terms and a distinction between the classes, instances, and attributes, which results in the production of an ontology-like networked structure. The fragment of this structure, designed for the pilot applications of the Access-eGov project, is depicted in Fig. 3.

The ontology-like structure is then transformed into the selected ontology formalization and the ontology concepts are semantically enhanced by proper process model elements. The procedure finishes with a verification of the produced formal ontologies on the sample real-world data provided by the PAs.

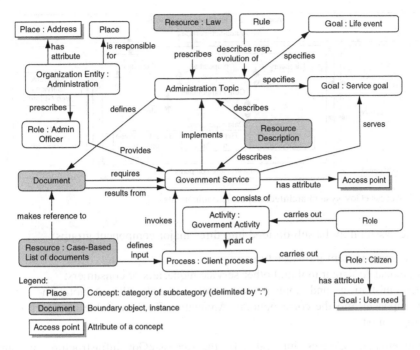

Fig. 3 Fragment of the Access-eGov ontology-like structure

Within the Access-eGov project, the steps of the requirement-driven procedure were performed by the project partner PAs in cooperation with knowledge engineers and system developers for the pilot applications carried out within the project. The process of creation of the Access-eGov resource ontologies is described in more detail in (Furdik et al. 2008). The resulting WSML formalization of the resource ontologies serves as a platform for further semantic front-office integration. The ontologies are used by specialized tools for the creation and maintenance of service instances (i.e., *Annotation Tool*) and by the tools for the presentation of annotated services to service consumers (i.e., *Personal Assistant Tool*).

4   Access-eGov System

The Access-eGov system was designed as a component-based enhancement to the existing eGovernment infrastructure. To address the interoperability between different types of legacy back-end systems, the implementation of web services in conjunction with service-oriented architecture was chosen as the most promising approach. The system's architecture, as presented in Fig. 4, is designed in a highly modularized way and is logically composed from a number of components interacting with each other as independent services.

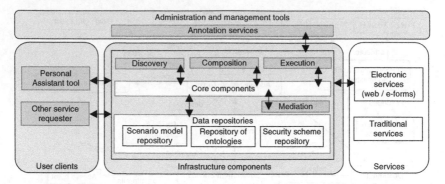

Fig. 4 Access-eGov system architecture, basic components

The system may be sub-divided into three major component groups:

1. The inner-system infrastructure;
2. Personal Assistant tool and other service requesters or consumers;
3. Administration and management tools, namely the Annotation service component and the corresponding Annotation Tool available as a web-based application.

Government services, integrated by the Access-eGov infrastructure, are supposed to be located on the premises of the provider and thus they are not an integral part of the Access-eGov system itself. The services are either electronic (available directly through web service interfaces or web forms) or traditional (non-electronic) that are semantically described and registered in the Access-eGov system. Of course, only the executable electronic services will expose an XML-based interface to the system infrastructure. It is supposed that public servantsannotate the services through an easy-to-use interface of a specialized annotation tool.

4.1   Basic System Modules and Components: Discovery of Services

The Access-eGov system infrastructure consists of the following functional modules:

- *Discovery* and *Composition* modules for building generic workflow structures out of external government services;
- *Execution* module for specification of a goal and execution of the retrieved (discovered and composed) services;
- *Core* module for basic system functionality and management.

The infrastructure also includes data repositories of persistently stored data on life events, goals, services, and generic scenarios, all the resource ontologies, as well as user management and security data.

The functional modules are further sub-divided into particular components. The *Core* module is composed of a built-in memory object model of resource ontologies, security and notification services, and a web-service entry point that makes infrastructure components available to the external services and tools – the Personal Assistant tool and the Annotation service component. The in-memory ontology objects enable to solve the heterogeneity problems at both process and data levels. The mediation on the data level is based on the mapping of semantic descriptions that characterize the services with the ontological concepts. The services registered in the Access-eGov system, originating from various independent resources, are integrated on a common semantic platform. The rules for ontological merging are employed to mediate the semantic extensions of the external web services, which are based on outer ontologies. In addition, these services are loosely coupled with the life events and goals; the data mediation together with semantic matching of capability interfaces is used for the retrieval of proper services for a given sub-goal or life event. The process mediation is handled by a dynamic workflow composition, based on the run-time data provided by system users – e.g., as answers to the customization questions or as values obtained from executed web services.

The *Discovery*, *Composition*, and *Execution* modules are responsible for managing the composed services, particularly for searching capabilities, orchestration, merging, chaining, or decomposition of elementary services according to the given scenario and for the execution of the services in a workflow sequence. During the process of service discovery, functional properties of goals and services are semantically compared and matched by the *Discovery* module to select the services capable to achieve these goals. Non-functional properties specified by the requester are then used to additionally filter or reorder the discovered services according to the user's preferences. In addition to the semantic discovery, full-text searching capabilities are also supported.

If the *Discovery* module is not able to find proper services to achieve a requested goal, semantic description of the goal is delegated to the *Composition* module that tries to orchestrate existing services to a new scenario to solve the goal. This process includes the decomposition of the complex goal to the atomic sub-goals and its consequent resolving by a semi-automatic approach based on generic scenarios defined for the life events. Finally, the *Execution* module for successfully identified and composed services creates and executes a process instance for the user scenario according to the specified process model.

4.2 Orchestration and Choreography Process Model

The Access-eGov process model is based on the WSMO specification of choreography and orchestration of web services (Scicluna et al. 2006). In this approach, the choreography interface describes the behavior of the service from the client's point of view; the orchestration interface defines how the functionality of the service is achieved in terms of the cooperation with other services, i.e., how the service operates from the provider's perspective. The WSMO choreography and orchestration description is based on the Abstract State Machines (ASM) (Gurevich 1995) methodology. It consists of the *if-then* rules that specify guarded transitions between the implicit states. The conditions (antecedents) of the rules define an expression, which must be held in a state in order to execute the rule's action (consequent). The states in the ontology are defined implicitly, as a set of instances, where the signature determines the available types. The ontology provides a vocabulary of transition rules and includes also the set of implicit state instances that change their values from one state to another while processing. Concepts of the ontology used for representing the states may have a specified grounding mechanism, which binds the service description to a concrete message specification, as to WSDL.

During the experiments carried out within the Access-eGov project, it has been found out that the current proposal of the WSMO specification is not adequate to these objectives, since models based on the state machines are not structured in a way suitable for interaction with human actors. Especially the WSMO specification is missing (or is not yet completed) for process mediators that are responsible for copying and transforming ASMs from one service to another. Based on the input or output instance, there is a necessity to derive a new ontology with an added grounding to each of the concepts that defines the status of the instance (i.e., input / static / output). For such reasons, it was decided to design and implement a workflow-based extension to the WSMO specification (Skokan and Bednar 2008). Besides the mentioned objectives, compatibility with the existing standards BPMN and BPEL4WS was also considered as an important requirement.

The Access-eGov process model is based on the workflow CASheW-s model (Norton et al. 2005), originally proposed for the OWL-S specification, with dataflow and WSMO mediation extensions. The proposed process model covers the service provider's and the consumer's perspectives used in dealing with interfaces, and therefore the same model can be used to specify both orchestration and choreography interfaces. A general structure of the model is depicted in Fig. 5. The elements used to construct service interfaces and relationships among them are state signatures, shared variables, and activities as workflow elements.

The state of a process is defined as a set of grounded facts. The elements that can be changed and that are used to express different states of the process execution are

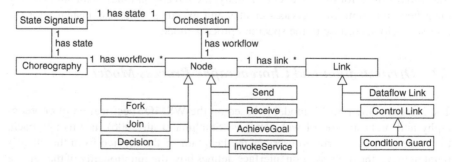

Fig. 5 Access-eGov process model for orchestration and choreography interfaces

instances of ontology concepts. The changes are expressed in terms of the creation of new instances or changes of the attribute values. The instances are assigned to *variables*, which are shared by workflow activities.

The workflow model consists of *activity nodes*. Atomic nodes (*Send*, *Receive*, *AchieveGoal*, and *InvokeService*) and control nodes (*Decision*, *Fork*, and *Join*) are used. Nodes are connected with *control links* representing a control flow. Each node has at least one input control link, except the root node representing the start activity of the workflow, which has no input links. The number of output links depends on the type of node. The *Fork* and *Decision* nodes have many output links; other nodes can have only one output link that determines the subsequent activity in the workflow. *End* nodes do not have any output links. The interface may have several *End* nodes defined, depending on the branches in the workflow.

Branching is defined by the *Decision* nodes. *While* or *Do-while* cycles are modelled by the *Decision* node and by backward control links pointing to an activity within the cycle. The *Decision* node represents an internal *if-then-else* decision, which is evaluated by the execution environment (cf. section 4.3). Service requesters cannot directly select a particular branch, i.e., defer a decision pattern, but the decision depends on the data received from the user.

The workflow can contain parallel threads created by the *Fork* and *Join* nodes. The *Fork* node has at least two output control links and each subsequent activity is executed in the parallel thread. The *Join* synchronizes parallel threads arriving to the node and waits until all the activities from the input links are finished.

The atomic activity nodes enable to specify the transition rules by means of pre- and post-conditions. The pre-conditions are activities that need to be performed before executing the service itself. The post-conditions define when and under what conditions the service provides an output. The following transition rules can be defined in the interface:

- *perform receive* $<$ *logical expression* $>$: service, before its execution, expects on its input a concept specified by a logical expression. The input concept can be a customization question or information that can be provided by the user directly, without the necessity to invoke an additional service (e.g., to fill in a form, to provide a payment, etc.);
- *perform send* $<$ *logical expression* $>$: service provides a concept as its output;
- *perform achieveGoal* $<$ *goal1* $>$: before executing the service, the *goal* needs to be solved;
- *perform invokeService* $<$ *service1* $>$: before executing the service, the user needs to obtain an output from *service1*;
- *if* $<$ *logical expression* $>$ *then* $<$ *list of transition rules* $>$ *endIf*: *if-then* rule is used for branching-in the process. If the logical expression is fulfilled, then all the transition rules in the list will be active, i.e., the user has to perform all of them. The transition rules usually refer to the customization questions, to which the user should provide the answers to better specify his/her life situation.

Reference syntax for orchestration and choreography process model was designed as an extension of the WSML (de Bruijn 2005).

4.3   Composition and Execution Environment

At the run-time, the *Composition* module is responsible for the orchestration of sub-goals specified in the process model interface of a life event or goal into a scenario, customized according to the inputs provided by the user. The generic scenario, formalized as a complex goal with the internal process model consisting of abstract activities, is resolved into a new composed service. In case all the inputs or preconditions of the resolved services are not available from the output of the previous activities, the workflow is actively modified in a so-called "chaining" procedure. It may also happen that the selection of a concrete service for the abstract activity depends on the outputs of previous activities and that it may not be possible to resolve the abstract activity at the time of its composition. In this case, the selection of a proper service needs to be postponed to the execution phase. To support the described functionality, the *Composition* module contains *Resolving* and *Composition* components.

The *Resolving component* is responsible for resolving goals into particular invocable and/or executable services. The goals, as formal expressions of the user's objectives by means of outputs, effects, and capability statements, cannot be executed directly. The only way to achieve the goal is to execute proper services retrieved from the ontology by the *Discovery* module, according to the semantic matching of the capability of the goal with the capability of services. If the goal is complex, i.e., orchestrated from other elements, then it is transformed into a composite service, sharing its orchestration model with the goal. In case of a simple atomic goal without an orchestration model, a service (or more services) able to resolve the goal(s) is/are selected and returned by the *Resolving* component. The selected service is expected to provide the same (or at least some) post-conditions defined by the goal.

The *Chaining component* attempts to actively modify the workflow of a specific process. This may happen in two possible situations: The first is when the execution of a process occurs in a state when a specific goal in the process can be fully or partially replaced by a specific service. The second occurs if a goal has to be inserted into a workflow after which it reaches the state when some of the required inputs (e.g., those to be obtained as a result of the receive activity) cannot be resolved. The chaining component then tries to compose the services by considering the effects and outputs of one service as preconditions and inputs of the following one in a recursive way, until a desired effect is reached.

The *Execution* module, as the core of the entire composition and execution environment (Fig. 6), is responsible for the processing and invocation of the discovered services. It interprets and executes the service's process model, and then subsequently invokes the service itself. The module supports the processing of simple atomic services (available as web, electronic, or traditional services), as well as of composed services with a process model defined in the orchestration interface. If the service is available as a web service, communication is performed directly by invoking this external service. In the case of traditional (non-electronic)

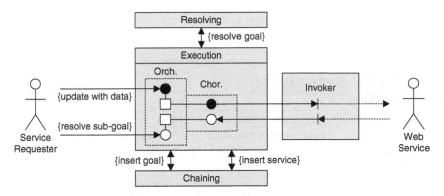

Fig. 6 Schema of the composition and execution environment

service, it is represented by a proxy – a person who will execute the service (e.g., by a personal visit to a governmental institution) on behalf of the execution environment – and will then provide information about the obtained results back into the system.

To invoke a service, the module creates a new process instance labeled by an execution context. It includes a reference to the service itself, the values of process variables (represented as ontology instances), and the current state of the process activity (i.e., one which is not active, has started, or is already finished). The process variables consist of inputs from the service requester, shared variables used for the control and data flow, and outputs of the already finished activities. The context container is persistent and is used to store the process state when the process is suspended to wait for the asynchronous invocation of a web service, or for manual updates that will be provided by the user.

4.4 Interface Components and User-Side Tools

The Access-eGov system includes components and reference implementations of client-side tools that expose the functionality of infrastructure modules for users. On the side of service providers, it is the *Annotation service component* and a set of components for system administration and maintenance that are functionally integrated into the *Annotation Tool*. This client-side tool enables the customization and enhancement of semantic descriptions of government services by means of *semantic annotation* (Furdik et al. 2008). In particular, it provides a set of forms for PA officers to specify preconditions and non-functional properties as parameters of the services. The Annotation Tool, implemented as a standard Web application using the extended WSMO object model and JSF technology, provides a template mechanism of service types to ease the maintenance of predefined workflow sequences for the annotated services. It also supports a role-based user access control, multilingualism on both interface and data levels, as well as a simple

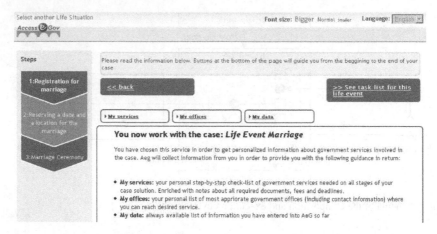

Fig. 7 Web interface of the Personal Assistant tool

"content grabber" functionality that enables to annotate external web pages and semantically integrate their content into a unified eGovernment application.

On the side of service consumers (citizens or businesses), the Access-eGov provides interface components for service requesters and the *Personal Assistant tool* as a reference client-side application (Fig. 7). It enables interactive browsing, discovery, and execution of proper services according to the specified life event or goal, customized by user's inputs to meet the specific life situation or business episode.

The Personal Assistant tool is implemented as a Web application using JSF technology and the extended WSMO object model. The layout, structure, and ordering of tabs in the interface are dynamically created from the annotated services, customized by the data entered by users. After selecting a life event, the corresponding navigation structure of sub-goals and services is displayed to users in the form of textual information, a hyperlink, a field for inserting a specified input value, or an interface for the invocation of a web service. Users can browse sub-goals and provide inputs when a customization input is requested. The system then automatically resolves the sub-goals and navigates the user to a new set of sub-goals and services inferred from the conceptual model. Electronic services can be invoked directly; traditional services are provided in a form of textual description of required actions. Finally, the user obtains all available information on the life event customized to his/her case and also has the possibility to execute actions required for particular services needed to accomplish the given life event.

5 Application Examples

Examples presented in this section describe the front-office integration of semantically enriched services as it was accomplished by employing the Access-eGov system in the PA environment. The first example explains the behavior of the inner system components during the service composition and execution; the other examples present pilot applications using which the Access-eGov system was tested and evaluated.

5.1 Example on the Composition and Execution of Services

This example is based on the Slovak pilot application of the Access-eGov system (cf. Sect. 5.2) and describes a real use case of the *"Building a house"* life event. Although this example is a bit simplified and adapted for explanation purposes (to reduce complexity and avoid unnecessary details), it offers a clear picture on how this approach can be used in the government domain to integrate electronic and traditional services.

Let us suppose that a citizen is faced with a specific life event – he/she wants to build a new house. The process model of this life event, as a top-level goal, can be formalized by means of an orchestration interface as follows:

```
goal _"buildHouseLifeEventGoal"
 capability
precondition
 definedBy ? request memberOf bp#buildingPermissionRequest
   and
  ? ZonePlanningAvailable menberOf _boolean
postcondition
 definedBy ? permission memberOf bp#buildingPermission
orchestration
workflow
  receive (? request memberOf bp#buildingPermissionRequest
   and
  ? zonePlanningAvailable memberOf _boolean)
  from _"buildHouseLifeEvent? requester"
  switch
  if ? ZonePlanningAvailable = true then
  receive (? plan memberOf bp#zonePlan) from
   _"buildHouseLifeEvent? requester"
   send (? request and ? plan) to _"zoneLocationPlanGoal"
   receive (? locationStatement memberOf
     bp#buildingLocationStatement)   from  _"zoneLocation-
PlanGoal"
  endIf
  otherwise
  send (? request) to _"landUsePlanGoal"
   receive (? locationStatement memberOf
     bp#buildingLocationStatement) from _"landUsePlanGoal"
  endSwitch
```

```
send (? request and ? locationStatement) to
 _"buildingPermissionGoal"
receive (? permission memberOf bp#buildingPermission)
 from _"buildingPermissionGoal"
send (? permission) to _"buildHouseLifeEvent? requester"
```

The life event defines a process that starts with a request to obtain the required information, i.e., a request for building permission and information on the availability of a zone plan, from a requester – citizen. The process, depicted in Fig. 8, continues by a workflow sequence of a few sub-goals; finally, a new building permission is provided to the citizen as an output.

The *Execution* module (*EXE*) starts to interpret the top-level goal (Fig. 6). Since the interpretation is enabled for services only, the goal is decomposed and processed by the *Resolving* component (*RES*), which calls for the *Discovery* component (*DIS*) to retrieve the corresponding services from the ontology (using the semantic matching of capabilities). As a result, the top-level goal is transformed into a composite service with the same capability and orchestration interface. A new process instance (referenced as *PI1*) is created and the EXE starts to interpret activities defined in the orchestration process model. The *Goal/Scenario execution* component (*GSE*) creates one token referring to the first activity in the sequence and associates the service requester with the citizen.

Since the next activity expects an input from the citizen, the process is suspended and the *EXE* waits for inputs. The process context is saved persistently. The citizen, using an appropriate client, asynchronously inspects the state of the process and updates the execution by providing new input data. The *EXE* then adds the received data (in this case, a negative answer regarding availability of a zone plan and an instance of the *bp#buildingPermissionRequest* concept) to the process state ontology and binds the instances to the *?request* and *?zonePlanningAvailable* shared variables.

The token is then moved to the subsequent activity – to fulfil the sub-goal *landUsePlanGoal*. Since no such goal is defined in the ontology, the sub-goal is considered to be atomic. The *EXE* calls *RES* to resolve this goal. This attempt results in providing the following service:

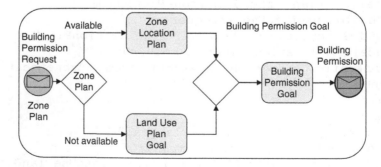

Fig. 8 Example "Obtaining a building permission"

Service _"landUsePlanService"
capability
```
precondition
definedBy ? info memberOf bp#landUsePlanInfo and
 ? request memberOf bp#buildingPermissionRequest
postcondition
definedBy ? locationStatement memberOf bp#buildingLoca-
   tionStatement
 and ? info memberOf bp#landUsePlanInfo
```
choreography
```
workflow
  receive (? info memberOf bp#landUsePlanInfo)
  from _"landUsePlanService? requester"
  receive (? request memberOf bp#buildingPermissionRequest)
  from _"landUsePlanService? requester"
  send (? info memberOf bp#landUsePlanInfo)
  to _"landUsePlanService? requester"
  send    (? locationStatement    memberOf    bp#buildingLoca-
   tionStatement)
  to _"landUsePlanService? requester"
```

The *Chaining* component (*CHAN*) modifies the parent workflow by replacing the pair of *send* and *receive* activities accessing the *landUsePlanGoal*, with similar activities of the selected service. Since the service requires more inputs as a precondition of the parent goal, an additional *receive* activity is inserted before the activities are replaced in order to obtain the missing inputs to enable correct service invocation. As a result, the fragment of the workflow of the *PI1* process instance:

```
send (? request) to _"landUsePlanGoal"
receive (? locationStatement memberOf
bp#buildingLocationStatement) from _"landUsePlanGoal"
```

is modified into a fragment of the following form:

```
receive (? info memberOf bp#landUsePlanInfo)
send (? info and ? request) to _"landUsePlanService"
  receive   (? locationStatement   memberOf   bp#buildingLoca-
   tionStatement
  and ? info memberOf bp#landUsePlanInfo) from _"landUse-
  PlanService"
```

The token is moved to the first *receive* activity (Fig. 9). Since the activity has no source specified, the *EXE* first tries to obtain an instance of *bp#landUsePlanInfo* from the citizen. Execution of the *PI1* process instance is suspended, the process context is persistently saved, and the *EXE* waits for inputs from the citizen. Let us suppose that the citizen (using a client) asynchronously updates the execution without entering new data (e.g., because the required information is not available for the citizen).

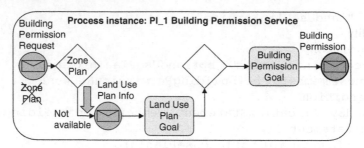

Fig. 9 Resolving and chaining the *"Land Use Plan Goal"*

As nothing can be bound to the *?info* variable, the *EXE* considers it as a new goal, which needs to be fulfilled. The *EXE* calls *CHAN* to insert this new goal into the workflow just at the place the token points to. Subsequently, the *RES* tries to resolve this new goal and provides the following service:

Service _"landUsePlanInfoService"
capability
precondition
  definedBy ? request memberOf bp#buildingPermissionRequest
postcondition
  definedBy ? info memberOf bp#landUsePlanInfo
choreography
workflow
  receive (? request memberOf bp#buildingPermissionRequest)
  from _"landUsePlanInfoService? requester"
  send (? info memberOf bp#landUsePlanInfo)
  to _"landUsePlanInfoService? requester"

The *CHAN* modifies the parent workflow by replacing the recently inserted goal with the access to this new service. Since the service requires only available instances as its pre-condition, no additional modifications of the workflow are required. As a result, the fragment of the workflow of the *PI1* process instance has the following form (the token is on the first activity of the fragment):

send (? request) to _"landUsePlanInfoService"
receive (? info memberOf bp#landUsePlanInfo)
 from _"landUsePlanInfoService"
send (? info and ? request) to _"landUsePlanService"
receive (? locationStatement memberOf bp#buildingLoca-
  tionStatement
and ? info memberOf bp#landUsePlanInfo) from _"landUsePlan-
  Service"

The *EXE* is ready to execute the first service. It creates a new process instance *PI2*, which will recursively interpret the activities specified in the choreography interface of the *landUsePlanInfoService*. *PI2* shares the process state ontology with the parent process instance *PI1*. The *EXE* creates two process links that will connect the parent and child process instances and passes the value of the *?request* variable to the link from *PI1* to *PI2*.

While the *PI1* process instance is suspended, the *EXE* interprets the choreography of the *landUsePlanInfoService* within the *PI2* process instance. Let us suppose that this service is available as a web service. It is invoked by the *Invocation* component (*INV*) and the web service output is returned to the process and the *PI2* instance is terminated. A new instance of the *bp#landUsePlanInfo* concept is added to the parent process and is associated with the *?info* variable.

The *EXE* continues to interpret the workflow within the *PI1* – the token is moved to the first activity relevant to the *landUsePlanService*. A new process instance *PI3* is created to interpret the choreography of this service in the same way as done previously (creating process links, creating and initiating a token), and *PI1* is suspended. The only difference is the fact that the service is a traditional one – in this case the citizen plays the role of a proxy for this service.

The instances *bp#landUsePlanInfo* and *bp#buildingPermissionRequest* are sent to the citizen, the token is moved, the process is suspended with persistent saving of context, and the *EXE* waits for inputs from the citizen. The citizen asynchronously inspects the state of the process, obtains the relevant information, and accesses the service – e.g., by visiting a public institution. After the citizen receives an output of the service, he/she asynchronously updates the execution with a new input data. The *EXE* then adds the received data, i.e., the instances *bp#buildingLocationStatement* and *bp#landUsePlanInfo*, into the process state ontology and binds these instances to the *?locationStatement* and *?info* shared variables. The output of the service is put into the process link from *PI3* to *PI1* and the *PI3* instance is terminated.

The *PI1* is resumed and the token is moved to the subsequent activity and interpretation of the top-level workflow continues. In order to resolve the next goal, the *RES* provides the service requiring an additional input. This situation is depicted in Fig. 10. The rest of the process can be executed in a similar way as described above in this section.

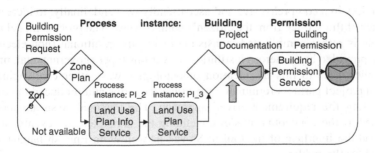

Fig. 10 The "Building Permission Service" resolved

5.2   Pilot Applications

The Access-eGov system was implemented, tested, and evaluated within three pilot applications and one lab test. The *lab test* took place in Egypt, German University in Cairo, and it focused on testing the functionality and technical capabilities of the whole system, especially from the service consumer's perspective through the use of the Personal Assistant tool. Consequently, after the tools were ready for installation and usage by the project user partners (PAs), three pilot applications in Germany, Slovakia, and Poland were carried out to test the applied approach within the real settings of PAs in three different EU countries.

The *German pilot application* was focused on the life event "Getting married" and related procedures, carried out by the Ministry of Finance of Schleswig-Holstein. The main objective of this pilot was to test the integration of different heterogeneous web resources containing the service information and making them accessible via a single platform but still leaving the data and its maintenance in the municipalities' legacy systems.

The registry offices of eleven municipalities from Schleswig-Holstein have been involved in the first trial, held from September 2007 till February 2008. In the first phase of the trial, the registry offices described the services provided by them following the steps of the requirement-driven approach (Klischewski and Ukena 2007) to produce the resource ontologies containing a semantic model of the life event. The administration officers then used the Annotation Tool to create semantic descriptions of the provided services. In the second phase of the trial, the Personal Assistant tool providing the support for the "Getting married" life event was tested and evaluated by the involved municipalities and general public. A more detailed description of the German field test, including the process of the conceptual model development and evaluation of both methodology and tools is presented in Bednar et al. (2008).

The *Slovak pilot*, dealing with the life event "Obtaining a building permit," has been carried out by the Kosice self-governing region and the municipality of Michalovce. It focused on supporting citizens during the process of obtaining a building permit, including complex services related to land-use planning and approval proceedings. The objective of this pilot was to make the whole process easier and transparent for citizens, to provide all relevant information about necessary services in a comprehensive and user-friendly way and, finally, to increase the efficiency of the service from the citizen's point of view. The process model of this life event is rather complicated, consisting of mostly traditional (non-electronic) services provided by numerous institutions of various types (governmental, private, and public). Due to this the creation of ontologies was rather challenging; the involved project partners formulated the usage scenarios and produced the ontologies – using the requirement-driven approach. The Personal Assistant tool was connected to the conceptual model containing the annotated life events and services, and the interface of the tool in Slovak as well as in English language was provided for the public.

The Polish pilot, focused on the life event "Establishing an enterprise," took place in the Silesian region and was performed by the Gliwice City Hall. The objective of this pilot application was to provide a single-entry point where users, citizens, and entrepreneurs could obtain all the relevant information and could be properly navigated by the system during the entire complex process. The municipality prepared scenarios containing a detailed description of all the steps in the process, e.g., registration in various institutions, possible paths of registration dependent on the individual user's case, and all the required documents and forms. According to the scenarios, relevant services, both electronic and traditional ones, were identified and information on service providers in the Gliwice area was collected. Using the requirement-driven approach, the data were formalized into an underlying conceptual model. From the user's perspective, the life event was modelled as a "dialogue," containing most frequent requests of citizens toward the municipality, office of statistics, tax office, etc. (i.e., information providers). The installations of the Annotation Tool and Personal Assistant tool were set up and connected with the produced conceptual model. The interface was then translated into Polish language and exposed for public testing.

The first trials of the pilot applications were evaluated using online questionnaires and "think aloud" sessions. The feedback from the tests shows that the Annotation Tool was relatively easy-to-use even by untrained annotation authors (public servants). Despite the fact that a few users found the process of semantic annotation "not so easy," the annotators managed to annotate all services and found the tool useful and efficient. As far as the Personal Assistant tool is concerned, the applied approach to the user-centric service integration has been proved as successful and efficient. However, users would welcome improvement of the user interface, especially regarding its structure, design, and navigation of services. The evaluation of the inner system infrastructure did not indicate any drawback in ontology and the underlying conceptual model. Minor comments were related to the translation of specialized terms (i.e., linguistic issues). However, the correctness of the ontology structure indicates that the methodology used for ontology development is correct and provides good results.

6   Related Research

Interoperability, semantic integration of services, user-centric design of portals enabling unified access to government services organized around life-events and business episodes, are high on the current research agenda. Intensive research is mostly focused on the development of platforms and solutions for the back-office integration of services, employing SOA and web services enriched by a semantic description (Abecker et al. 2006; Codagnone and Wimmer 2007). In the European context, this research can be documented, for example, by eGovernment projects supported by the European Commission within the Information Society Technologies program. Most of the solutions apply semantic technologies to ease the system design by modelling the citizen's behavior, enable or enhance the interoperability of services, provide a platform for the creation of semantically described web services, etc. Some EU R&D projects relevant to the Access-eGov solution are briefly described below.

OntoGov project (http://www.ontogov.com, 2003–2006) provides a solution for consistent composition, reconfiguration, and evolution of eGovernment services, based on the Semantic Web services, business modelling, and SOA principles (Apostolou et al. 2005). The solution includes a set of ontologies supporting the lifecycle of semantically described eGovernment services. The OntoGov approach focuses mainly on the software engineering side rather than on the detection and orchestration of government services. As a consequence of this, the interpretation of how the ontologies can be used in practical scenarios can be rather vague. In addition, maintenance and usage of the OntoGov solution requires expert knowledge and lacks a certain degree of transparency for public servants when using the system. However, the architecture and technical solution of the OntoGov can be seen as a holistic and complex platform for the integration of government services, provided as web services, on a semantic basis.

The *Terregov* project (http://www.terregov.eupm.net, 2003–2005) focused on the requirements of governments at local and regional levels for building a flexible and interoperable environment (interoperability centre) and tools to support the change toward semantically enriched eGovernment web services (Pérez and Labajo 2007). Terregov provides a specialized ontology as well as a SOA-based platform for enhancing existing government web services with a semantic description. Such Semantic Web services can then be detected, accessed, and orchestrated in an interoperable way.

The *DIP* project (http://dip.semanticweb.org, 2004–2006) represents probably the most complex approach toward the semantic interoperability in general, providing a platform and a wide range of tools for the semantic modelling of web services and processes. It includes the WSMO framework, accompanied with an integrated set of tools for efficient management of ontologies that serve as an underlying data model for Semantic Web services. For the eGovernment domain, DIP project provides ontology framework developed for the prototype of eGovernment Case Study in the Essex County Council, UK (Domingue et al. 2004).

The *SemanticGov* project (http://www.semantic-gov.org, 2006–2008) is aimed to support the provision of Pan-European services to resolve semantic incompatibilities between PAs (Vitvar et al. 2006). The focus is put on discovery, composition, mediation, and execution of semantically described government services within complex user-oriented scenarios. The solution provides a global ontology of semantic components needed for web service descriptions.

In addition to the projects mentioned above, there are many other initiatives, research groups and projects on local, national, and global levels, dealing with the interoperability and semantic integration of services. An intention to co-ordinate the research efforts in this area led to the establishment of such initiatives as the EIF IDABC program, Semantic Interoperability Centre Europe, and the eGovernment Interoperability Observatory of the Terregov project. Finally, the interoperability research in the eGovernment domain is supported by several initiatives and programs provided by the governments on the national level, for example in EU member countries, USA, Australia, etc. (Codagnone and Wimmer 2007).

Integration of government services in most of the projects described above is achieved by employing the web services technology and SOA, which enables the exchange of data and information in a flexible way. Interoperability, i.e., the meaningful co-operation and co-ordination of the services provided by different organizations, is then supported by enriching the web services with additional semantic information. The resulting Semantic Web services extend flexibility, reusability, and universal access of web services with the capabilities of semantics in areas of expressivity of mark-up, standardization of meaning, and reasoning. It enables invocation, composition, mediation, and automatic execution of services orchestrated into complex workflow scenarios (Gugliotta et al. 2008). The most frequently used frameworks and technologies for the semantic description of web services are based on semantic modelling formalisms such as RDF/S (RDF Vocabulary Description Language 1.0: RDF Schema 2004), OWL-S (OWL-S: semantic markup for web services 2004) and WSMO, or based on descriptive semantic extensions of web services – WSDL-S (Web Service Semantics – WSDL-S 2005) and SAWSDL (Semantic annotations for WSDL, XML schema 2007). For the WSMO framework, that is probably the most progressive in the Semantic Web service modelling, the WSMO-Lite (Vitvar et al. 2008) and MicroWSMO (Kopecky et al. 2008) need to be mentioned as the latest developmental works in the direction of the wider usability and easier development of the service-based solutions, together with the enhancements on the service grounding mechanism in SAWSDL (Kopecky et al. 2007).

Another important aspect of interoperability is the presentation of semantically integrated government services to the service consumers. Abiding with the user-centric principle means respecting the needs of service consumers during their communication and negotiation with a PA. In other words, the government services should be modelled and provided in a form that is transparent and easy to understand for the users, and which correspond to their life events or business episodes. The *life event approach* (Todorovski et al. 2006) is today probably the most popular, effective, and widely accepted way of modelling, integrating, and presenting government services from the perspective of users.

The *life event*, a basic concept of this approach, denotes a specific situation in the life of a citizen (and similarly a business episode in the life-cycle of an organization). A life event corresponds to a complex goal, which can be achieved by a sequence of sub-goals and services provided by the PA or another institution. The life event approach, in combination with semantic technologies and business process modelling principles, enables to integrate government services into a workflow structure, where sub-goals and services are orchestrated and moderated (i.e., adapted and customized) by specific conditions and inputs provided by the user – service consumer. The design and development of a framework for life-event-oriented eGovernment solutions is the main objective of the *OneStopGov* project (http://www.onestopgov-project.org, 2006–2008). The project provides life-event ontology and reference models containing a semantic description and generic workflow specification for representing customizable life-event concepts.

The approaches, projects, and technologies listed in this brief survey represent a mature platform for the application of semantic integration and interoperability in the eGovernment area. However, most of the proposed solutions still exist only as prototypes and are difficult to be adopted on a larger scale. One of the reasons can be the fact that these solutions are mostly oriented on back-office integration of services and require a significant reorganization of internal processes within a PA. In addition, the solutions rarely contain a proper methodology describing how semantic technologies can be adapted in practical applications. As already mentioned above, if a corresponding methodology is not available, transformation from a "traditional" to interoperable and semantically enhanced way of providing services is a difficult process within the PAs.

The Access-eGov project is addressing exactly this problem by supporting the transformation and semantic integration of the existing government services of all types – traditional (face-to-face) services, electronic services provided through web forms or emails, as well as web services. The Access-eGov solution is focused on the front-office and user-centric integration, providing a component-based enhancement of the existing eGovernment infrastructure based on Semantic Web technologies and distributed architectures (Service-oriented and peer-to-peer). The Access-eGov project also provides a methodology for semantic modelling of life events and services, based on the existing infrastructure and requirements of PA (i.e., the service provider).

7   Conclusion

This chapter presents main achievements of the Access-eGov R&D project targeting the front-office integration of government services based on utilization of semantic models and annotations. The technical information is complemented by illustrations of real use cases and the descriptions of pilot applications.

Feedback from the experience gained and the evaluation results of the first trial when testing the proposed architectural and software solution within three pilot applications in three EU countries in different, real operational environments have proven the feasibility of the applied approach. The user acceptance of the system indicates that the Access-eGov system can represent a very attractive alternative for service integration, especially in a heterogeneous environment with various ways of service delivery – from traditional, non-electronic services up to modern web services. The Access-eGov approach also supports an easy traditional upgrade of an individual to a web service (as new eGovernment services are one by one implemented in the given environment – municipality, region, or country) by simply adding a semantic description of the new web service to the system.

Based on the results of the evaluation of the first trial, the second version of the Access-eGov prototype was implemented, including improved user interface of the Personal Assistant, which will be tested in the second trials of the pilot applications. The Access-eGov project (as an R&D project co-funded by the European Commission within FP6) is planned to be finished in February 2009. Till then the software solution (implemented under the open-source licence), supporting ontologies and methodological guidelines will be available. More information on the Access-eGov project can be found at http://www.accessegov.org.

Acknowledgements The Access-eGov IST project No. FP6-2004-27020 is co-funded by The European Commission. The presented work was also based on research supported by the Slovak Grant Agency of the Ministry of Education and Academy of Science of the Slovak Republic within the 1/4074/07 Project "Methods for annotation, search, creation, and accessing knowledge employing metadata for semantic description of knowledge."

References

A. Abecker, A. Sheth, G. Mentzas, L. Stojanovich (eds.), *Proceedings AAAI Spring Symposium "Semantic Web Meets eGovernment"*, Stanford University, March 27–29, 2006. Technical report SS-06-06, AAAI Press, Menlo Park, CA, 2006

D. Apostolou, L. Stojanovic, T. Pariente Lobo, B. Thoenssen, Towards a semantically-driven software engineering environment for eGovernment. Lect. Notes Comput. Sci. **3416**, 157–168 (2005)

S. Archmann, M.M. Nielsen, in Interoperability and Its Importance to eGovernment – Success Factors and Barriers. ed. by F. Corradini, A. Polzonetti *MeTTeG08, Proceedings of the 2nd International Conference on Methodologies, Technologies and Tools Enabling e-Government, Corfu, Greece, 25–26 September 2008*, (Halley Editrice SRL, Greece, 2008), pp. 1–12

P. Bednar, S. Duerbeck, J. Hreno, M. Mach, L. Ryfa, R. Schillinger, Access-eGov Platform Architecture. Deliverable D3.1, Access-eGov Project, FP6-2004-27020, 2006

P. Bednar, K. Furdik, M. Kleimann, R. Klischewski, M. Skokan, S. Ukena, Semantic integration of e-Government services in Schleswig-Holstein. Lect. Notes Comput. Sci. **5184**, 315–327 (2008)

Business Process Execution Language for Web Services, version 1.1, http://www.ibm.com/developerworks/library/specification/ws-bpel/. Accessed 27 May 2009

C. Codagnone, M.A. Wimmer (eds.), *Roadmapping eGovernment Research Visions and Measures Towards Innovative Governments in 2020*. Results from the EC-funded Project eGovRTD2020, IST-2004-027139, eGovRTD2020 Project Consortium (2007)

Competitiveness and Innovation Programme ICT Policy Support Programme, http://ec.europa.eu/cip/. Accessed 27 May 2009

J. de Bruijn (ed.), D16.1v0.2 The Web Service Modeling Language WSML. WSML Final Draft, 20 March 2005, http://www.wsmo.org/TR/d16/d16.1/v0.2/

J. Domingue, L. Gutierrez, L. Cabral, M. Rowlatt, R. Davies, S. Galizia, Deliverable D9.3: e-Government Ontology. DIP project, WP 9: Case Study eGovernment, 2004

EC Projects and Activities, IST eGovernment projects, Sixth Framework Programme Call 4, http://ec.europa.eu/information_society/activities/egovernment/projects/index_en.htm. Accessed 27 May 2009

European Interoperability Framework for pan-European eGovernment Services, version 1.0. European Communities (2004), http://europa.eu.int/idabc/en/document/3761

K. Furdik, T. Sabol, P. Bednar, in *Framework for Integration of e-Government Services on a Semantic Basis*. Electronic Government, ed. by A. Grönlund, H.J. Scholl, M.A. Wimmer 6th International EGOV Conference. Proceedings of ongoing research, project contributions and workshops, (Trauner, Linz, 2007), pp. 71–78

K. Furdik, J. Hreno, T. Sabol, in *Conceptualisation and Semantic Annotation of eGovernment Services in WSMO*. ed. by V. Snasel Proceedings of Znalosti (Knowledge) 2008 (STU, Bratislava, 2008), pp. 66–77

A. Gugliotta et al., Deploying semantic web services-based applications in the e-Government domain. Lect. Notes Comput. Sci. **4900**, 96–132 (2008)

Y. Gurevich, in *Evolving Algebras 1993: Lipari Guide*, ed. by E. Börger in Specification and Validation Methods, (Oxford University Press, Oxford, 1995), pp. 9–36

i2010 – A European Information Society for Growth and Employment, COM (2005) 229 final of 1 June 2005, http://ec.europa.eu/i2010

IDABC – Interoperable Delivery of European eGovernment Services to Public Administrations, Businesses and Citizens, http://ec.europa.eu/idabc/. Accessed 27 May 2009

Interoperability for Pan-European eGovernment Services. Communication from the Commision to the Council and the Europena Parliament. COM(2006) 45 final, Brussels, 13.2.2006, http://europa.eu.int/idabc/servlets/ Doc?id = 24117

R. Klischewski, S. Ukena, in Designing Semantic e-Government Services Driven by User Requirements, ed. by A. Grönlund, H.J. Scholl, M.A. Wimmer Electronic Government, 6th International EGOV Conference. Proceedings of ongoing research, project contributions and workshops, (Trauner, Linz, 2007), pp. 133–140

J. Kopecky, T. Vitvar, C. Bournez, J. Farrell, SAWSDL: semantic annotations for WSDL and XML schema. IEEE Internet Comput. **11**(6), 60–67 (2007)

J. Kopecky, K. Gomadam, T. Vitvar, in hRESTS: An HTML Microformat for Describing RESTful Web Services. The 2008 IEEE/WIC/ACM International Conference on Web Intelligence (WI2008), November, 2008, Sydney, Australia (IEEE CS Press, Washington, DC, 2008)

G. Laskaridis et al., E-government and interoperability issues. Int. J. Comput. Sci. Netw. Secur. **7**(9), 28–38 (2007)

H. Lueders, Interoperability and Open Standards for eGovernment Services, in *Proceedings of 1st International Conference on Interoperability of Enterprise Software-Applications*, Switzerland, January 17, 2005

M. Mach, T. Sabol, J. Paralic, Integration of eGov services: back-office versus front-office integration. in *Proceedings of the Workshop Semantic Web for eGovernment, a Workshop at the 3rd European Semantic Web Conference, ESCW 2006*, Budva, Serbia – Monte Negro, 11–14 June 2006, pp. 48–52

S.A. McIlraith, T.C. Son, H. Zeng, Semantic web services. IEEE Intell. Syst. **16**, 46–53 (2001)

New Zealand eGovernment Programme. The user-centric principle, http://www.e.govt.nz/standards/fea/user-centric.html. Accessed 27 May 2009

B. Norton, S. Foster, A. Hughes, A compositional operational semantics for OWL-S. in Proceedings of 2nd International Workshop on Web Services and Formal Methods (WS-FM 2005), Versaillis, France, 1–3 September 2005

Owl-S: Semantic Markup for web services.owl-s Coalition 2004, http://www.daml.org/services/owl-s/1.1/

M. Pérez, S. Labajo, in An Innovative Semantic Based Solution for eGovernment Interoperability. IST Africa, Maputo, Mozambique, 9–11 May, 2007

RDF Vocabulary Description Language 1.0: RDF Schema. W3C Recommendation, 10 February 2004, http://www.w3.org/TR/rdf-schema/

D. Roman, H. Lausen, U. Keller (eds.), D2v1.2. *Web Service Modelling Ontology (WSMO)*. Technical report, WSMO Final Draft, 13 April 2005, http://www.wsmo.org/TR/d2/v1.2/

J. Scicluna, A. Polleres, D. Roman (eds.), *D14v.0.2. Ontology-based Choreography and Orchestration of WSMO Services*. WSMO Final Draft, 3rd February 2006, http://www.wsmo.org/TR/d14/v0.2/

Semantic annotations for WSDL and XML schema. W3C Recommendation, 28 August 2007, http://www.w3.org/2002/ws/sawsdl/

M. Skokan, P. Bednar, in *Access-eGov Architecture*. ed. by P. Mikulecky, J. Dvorsky, M. Kratky Proceedings of Znalosti (Knowledge) 2007 (VSB – Technical University of Ostrava, Ostrava, 2007), pp. 384–390

M. Skokan, P. Bednar, in *Semantic Orchestration of Services in eGovernment*. ed. by V. Snasel Proceedings of Znalosti (Knowledge) 2008, (STU, Bratislava, 2008), pp. 215–223

E. Tambouris, K. Tarabanis, V. Peristeras, N. Liotas, *Modinis Study on Interoperability at Local and Regional Level*. Final version: version 2.0, 20 April 2007, http://www.epractice.eu/document/3652

The eGovernment Interoperability Observatory, http://www.egovinterop.net. Accessed 27 May 2009

The Semantic Interoperability Centre Europe, http://www.semic.eu. Accessed 27 May 2009

The User-centric Principle. NewZealand eGovernment programme, http://www.e.govt.nz/standards/fea/user-centric.html.

L. Todorovski, A. Leben, M. Kunstelj, D. Cukjati, M. Vintar, Methodology for building models of life events for active portals, in Communication Proceedings of EGOV 2006 (Trauner, Linz, 2006), pp. 111–119

T. Vitvar, M. Kerrigan, A. van Overeem, V. Peristeras, K. Tarabanis, Infrastructure for the semantic pan-european e-government services. in *Proceedings of the 2006 AAAI Spring Symposium on The Semantic Web meets eGovernment (SWEG)* (Stanford University, California, USA, 2006)

T. Vitvar, J. Kopecky, J. Viskova, D. Fensel, WSMO-Lite Annotations for Web Services. in *The 5th European Semantic Web Conference 2008 (ESWC), Tenerife, Spain*, June 2008 (Springer, New York, 2008)

X. Wang, S. Goudos, V. Peristeras, T. Vitvar, A. Mocan, K. Tarabanis, WSMO-PA – Formal specification of public administration service model on semantic web service ontology. in *Proceedings of the the 40th Hawaii International Conference on System Sciences* (IEEE Computer Society, Hawaii, USA, 2007), p. 96a

Web Service Modelling Ontology, http://www.wsmo.org. Accessed 27 May 2009

Web Service Semantics – WSDL-S. W3C Member Submission, 7 November 2005, http://www.w3.org/Submission/WSDL-S/

The Modelling of Knowledge-Intensive Processes Using Semantics

Daniela Feldkamp, Knut Hinkelmann, and Barbara Thönssen

1 Motivation

In the "i2010 eGovernment Action Plan" it is stated that: "Member States have committed themselves to inclusive eGovernment objectives to ensure that by 2010 all citizens [...] become major beneficiaries of eGovernment, and European public administrations deliver public information and services that are more easily accessible and increasingly trusted by the public, through innovative use of ICT, increasing awareness of the benefits of eGovernment and improved skills and support for all users" (Commission of the European Communities 2006). For example, in the latest study on e-Government in Switzerland conducted by the University of St. Gallen, it was stated for the first time that measures for e-Government quality improvement are *change* (42% of the Swiss cantons, 19% of the Swiss municipalities) and *benchmarking (business) activities/processes* (41% of the Swiss cantons, 50% of the Swiss municipalities). But in the same study, design and IT-supported processes are considered a huge challenge (Schedler et al. 2007a, b). Thus, what Becker et al. already described still holds true: Although the benefit of having formal models of business processes is well known in public administrations, too few processes have been modelled and lesser still have been automated (Becker et al. 2003).

Dörfler sees the problem in the difference between e-Government services and traditional services. "E-government services differ from the traditional services offered by administrations in many ways. Therefore these new processes have to be modelled, preferably using special software. Business Process Modelling is a part of Knowledge Management because understanding the processes is the basis of an organisation's knowledge" (Dörfler 2003).

D. Feldkamp (✉)
School of BusinessUniversity of Applied Sciences Northwestern Switzerland FHNW, Riggenbachstrasse. 16, 4600, Olten, Switzerland

T. Vitvar et al. (eds.), *Semantic Technologies for E-Government*,
DOI 10.1007/978-3-642-03507-4_4, © Springer-Verlag Berlin Heidelberg 2010

As business processes in public administrations are highly knowledge-intensive (Feldkamp et al. 2007), the challenge is not only to *model* the new services but to model them *adequately*. As Karagiannis and Palkovits state: "It is not enough to use traditional modelling tools for the Business Process Management in e-government, it is moreover necessary to be aware of the flows, the necessary resources, the responsible roles and the competencies of the authorities" (Karagiannis et al. 2002).

To address these challenges we chose the following approach.

- Process models consist of two different types of tasks (activities): activities that are performed whenever the process is executed (static activities) and tasks performed under certain conditions (variable activities).
- Static and variable tasks are represented in the process model in different ways.
- The execution order[1] of static activities is defined during build time, whereas the decision as to which variable activities should be executed and in which order is taken during run time. This decision is based on conditions that can be represented as business rules.

  - *Variable task selection and planning rules* are used for selecting the appropriate activities and determining the order of their execution.

- There are three further rule types that enable knowledge support at execution time:

  - *Resource allocation rules* are used to select the appropriate resource for the respective activity. Resources can be either human resources – having implicit knowledge – or information, material and tools.
  - *Consistency checking rules* are used to check on conditions that have to hold on results of an activity or of the whole process.
  - *Decision supporting rules* not only check the consistency of the results, but also compute or suggest appropriate values. These rules can be applied either during the execution of an activity or for intelligent branching by the workflow enactment system to decide on the process flow.

With this approach process models can be simplified as only the "normal" flow or "process skeleton" is to be represented. Using the rules for modelling the handling of exceptional situations, unforeseeable events, unpredictable situations, and great variability and knowledge-intensive tasks makes the design and maintenance much easier for business people.

In this chapter we describe details of the representation of business rules for modelling knowledge-intensive processes and show how to apply and adapt this approach for e-Government.

Although the introduced approach is not limited to public administrations, we agree with Metaxiotis and Psarras, who state that "e-government and KM-based public administration are still in an early state of evolution" (Metaxiotis and Psarras

---

[1]This comprises sequence, branching, and parallelism.

2005) and, therefore, especially need easy-to-use tools to gain momentum. In the FIT project we developed a modelling tool (ATHENE) that provides a user interface for a semi-formal representation of the knowledge-intensive processes (Hinkelmann et al. 2007). These models are exported into an ontological representation that serves as an interchange model for a process execution environment. To validate this approach we implemented a transformation of this interchange model into the Business Process Execution Language (BPEL), which could be executed using ActiveBPEL as an example.[2]

2 The Three Phases of the Knowledge-Intensive Business Process Modelling Approach

In this section, we introduce an approach to address the challenge of modelling knowledge-intensive business processes not only by "analysing each activity [of a business process] and identifying the so-called 'Knowledge Intensive Tasks'" (Woitsch and Karagiannis 2005) but also by providing appropriate representations of the results.

Figure 1 depicts the 3-phase procedure for process modelling: phase 1 is about knowledge capturing and semi-formal descriptions, phase 2 is about the transformation

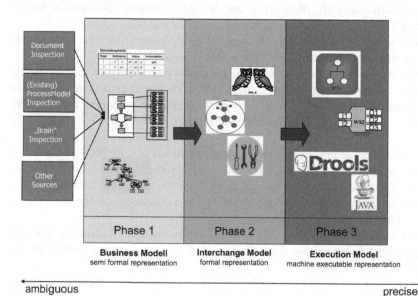

Fig. 1 3-Phase modelling approach

---

[2]ActiveBPEL http://www.activevos.com/community-open-source.php

into standardized formal representations (we use OWL and SWRL to express domain information and business rules, while the process models are represented in OWL-S (Martin 2008) during the FIT project; however, our approach is not restricted to the mentioned formats, and ontologies used in WSMO, for example, are also capable of presenting process models). In phase 3, the interchange models can automatically be migrated into machine-executable forms, e.g., OWL-S into BPEL (IBM and Microsoft 2007) for process execution, or rules for If-Then-Else Statements expressed in Java or JavaScript.

2.1 Phase 1: The Business Model

Even though, all information is kept in an ontology, it is important to hide the modelling complexity for the business user. Business people need an easy-to-understand and easy-to-use way for capturing their knowledge.

In Switzerland the eCH association[3] is currently working on a standard on business process modelling (Standard eCH-0075 2008). Defining content and metadata of process descriptions provides a good pattern for unified documentations. The sample solution eCH-0041 *Einreise mit Arbeitsbewilligung* (entry of a country having a working permission) provides an example (Hilfsmittel eCH-0041 2006). The eCH association suggests the use of a subset of the Business Process Management Notation (BPMN) (OMG 2006) for modelling e-Government processes (Hilfsmittel eCH-0074 2008). Even though the process descriptions aim to be comprehensive, they have some significant drawbacks:

* Knowledge is hidden in the paraphrases (e.g., business rules)
* Context and domain information (metadata) are related to the process but are modelled independently[4]
* Relations between the information (in-between metadata or between metadata and the process model) cannot be used for retrieval
* Reusing is limited as only the copies can be reused but not the actual models
* Exchanging is limited as no standardized exchange format is available

However, the drafted standard for business process modelling is a good starting point: the requested metadata can be used for term definition; the BPMN subset for e-Government can be used for process representation. Although Chappel claims that "everything starts with terms" (Chappel et al. 2005), process modelling and rule definition are highly interlinked and iterative procedures.

---

[3]eCH is an association that supports, works on, and approves standards, best practises and auxiliary material for the e-Government in Switzerland.

[4]Even though there is a separate catalogue listing e-Government services and their descriptions (Best Practice eCH-0015 2007) or a theme catalogue (e.g., lifecycle aspects, business situations (Standard Recommendation eCH-0049 2008), they are not modelled in a machine-processable way.

Most often, business people feel more familiar beginning with process modelling. Usually, in the first step only a "process skeleton" can be sketched, which means that only the main activities of a process are modelled. Especially important in knowledge-intensive processes is that the execution of some activities (in particular knowledge-intensive tasks – KIT) depends on particular circumstances. Taking the "Entry of country having a working permission process" as an example, the decision whether a person is allowed to enter Switzerland depends on many factors like country of origin, age, criminal record, earlier residence in Switzerland, kind of working permission, etc.

Figure 2 depicts such a skeleton for the "Entry of country having a working permission process" modelled with ATHENE using BPMN. Activities labelled with "KIT" indicate the knowledge-intensive parts of a process.

Introducing the "KIT" modelling object not only simplifies the process model, but also allows the modelling of those activities whose conditions are not given at the process start but should be executed depending on the case and circumstances during run time. Thus, we have an unforeseeable sequence of data collections, clarifications, and decision support which cannot be modelled exactly but must be determined at run time.

While modelling the process, especially the knowledge-intensive parts, the rules do appear naturally, e.g., reflecting law, regulations, or conditions for decisions.

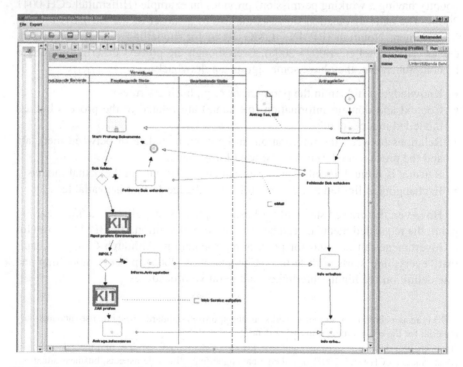

Fig. 2 Entry of country having a working permission process skeleton with knowledge-intensive parts

Therefore, in parallel to the process flow, business rules need to be modelled. As mentioned above, rules are used not only for the selection and planning of variable activities, but also for resource allocation, consistency checking, and decision support.

The Business Rules Group defines a "Business Rule" as "a statement that defines or constrains some aspect of the business. It is intended to assert business structure, or to control or influence the behaviour of the business" (Business Rule Group 2006). Keeping the rule modelling procedure as simple as possible and allowing business people to do the modelling without IT specialists, the well-understood and comprehensive classification scheme given by von Halle (2002, p. 27ff) was used during the FIT project.

In order to use the rules actively, they must not be captured in flat files and should be modelled in a semi-formal way. Figure 3 depicts a user interface for rule modelling.

The terms used for phrasing the rules have to be unified and "standardized." Again, instead of having a textual representation, terms could be represented using specific models (a domain model for e-Government specific expressions, a model for legal information, a document model, an organizational model, etc.). With the meta modelling approach of ATHENE, knowledge engineers can set up user-defined models for any type of information according to business needs, e.g., process elements compliant to the BPMN or rule types according to the von Halle classification (Hinkelmann et al. 2007).

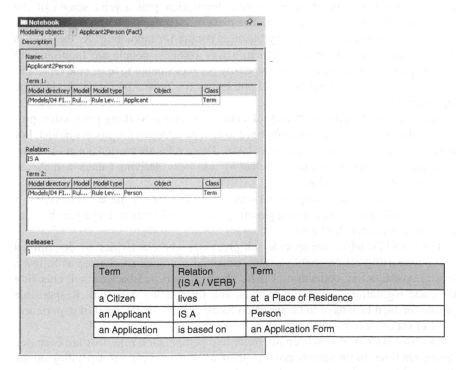

Fig. 3 Relating terms to build facts

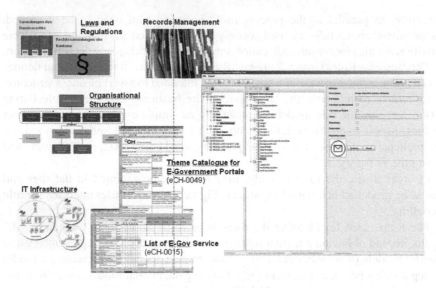

Fig. 4 Creating information models with ATHENE

Figure 4 depicts examples of various information types that need to be modelled in order to get a comprehensive service description plus a print screen of the ATHENE meta modelling function. The meta models can be set up by the knowledge engineer and can be used by business people for modelling. As the entities of the meta models are represented in a way business people are familiar with (e.g., organization's diagrams), or can easily get accustomed to (e.g., rule representation), modelling is simplified without losing the power of formal knowledge representation.

Again using the process "Entry of country having a working permission process," rules and context information have to now be added to the process model. For this, a set of rules are associated to the tasks. These rules are carried out at run time, affecting the process execution by selecting resources, deriving values, and checking constraints and guidelines.

Figure 5 depicts the mapping between process elements and the four types of rules (variable tasks selection and planning, resource allocation, intelligent branching, and constraints checking).

For the KITs, which are specific sub-processes whose activities are determined at run time using action-enabling rules, potential activities are defined as follows: formal investigation, collection of data, checking personal background, checking laws and regulations, involving experts, and formulating decisions. Responsible people for each task have to be allocated based on their skills, level of experience, level of expertise, etc.

Decision support depends on inference and computation rules that are executed during run time. In the sample process, there are two possibilities depending on the decision taken in the previous phases: One branch starts a sub-process to handle

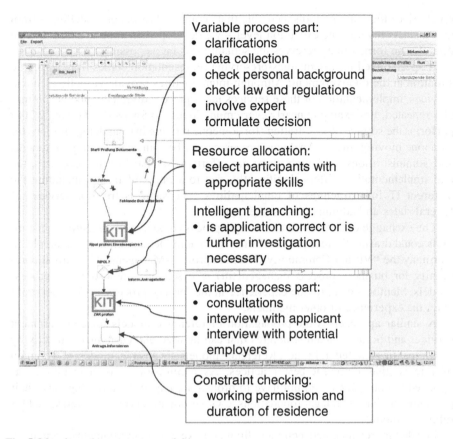

Fig. 5 Mapping rules to process models

further investigation on the application, and the other branch leads to another KIT dealing with details of the application.

In the same way that rules are mapped to processes, context information as described above can be added.

With this modelling approach, knowledge, often hidden in the paraphrases (e.g., in simple process documentations), can be made explicit and formalized without bothering business people with ontology modelling. Context and domain information can be independently modelled; therefore, relations between entities of models can be exploited, for example, for retrieval. The exchange of models is well supported as they are stored in standardized formats.

2.2 Phase 2: The Interchange Model

To implement the processes, a representation formalism is necessary that preserves the semantics of the models from the more informal models until the execution level. Since there are no tools available that support all levels of modelling – from the business level to the execution level – we developed an approach that uses an interchange format that preserves the semantics as far as possible.

A special need for a semantics-preserving representation comes from a specific situation in the e-Government: Although municipalities provide virtually identical services, implementation of these services takes place individually and is continually repeated. For example: nearly every municipality in Switzerland (about 2,700) performs the service of registration (for someone moving in) and deregistration (for someone moving away). Analogue processes can be found for local governments and administrations. Although, there are efforts to standardize the processes, the real implementation differs significantly, due to a range of factors including the different IT infrastructures of municipalities. The same is true for services of federal states and administrations like courts.

The exchange of experience and sample process models between similar institutions could drastically reduce the effort of service implementation. For example, in Germany the "Virtual Community Geschäftsprozess-Management[5]" (virtual community for business process management) is based on a repository of process models. Members can provide experience in the form of process models and profit from the experience of other members.

A similar approach is the propagation of reference models for e-Government services and organizational structures that can be used and customized directly by municipalities and federal states. Reference models are abstract models of a domain of interest that represent best practices. As administrative organizations – as opposed to companies – do not have to protect a competitive advantage and their processes are based on legal foundations, e-Government services are well suited for reference models.

For the interchange between modelling and execution environments, formalism with a precise semantics is necessary that integrates both process knowledge and business rules.

2.2.1 Semantics of Process Modelling

A first implementation and application of our approach was based on the von Halle classification for business rules (see above), for which we defined patterns for simple rule formulation. The von Halle scheme and the corresponding patterns, however, lack a clear semantics.

With the Semantics of Business Vocabulary and Business Rules (SBVR) specification, the OMG developed an approach to model the semantics of a business vocabulary and rules (OMG 2008). SBVR is not a modelling language but defines a vocabulary and rules for documenting the semantics of business vocabularies, facts,

---

[5]http://www.fhvr-berlin.de/vc-gpm/ (information available only in German).

and rules. Although the SBVR specification mainly uses structured English to represent the vocabulary, it can also be represented in other formalisms.

SBVR is designed to be used for business purposes, independent of information systems designs, but is applicable as input to transformations by IT staff into information system designs. It allows defining a precise semantics of a business vocabulary and business rules. SBVR deals with declarative rules expressed from a business perspective, while the mechanization of those rules in an automated system are outside the scope of SBVR (OMG 2008, p. 85).

We propose a representation formalism that uses ontologies to represent terms and facts. Ontologies have a precise semantics and at the same time there exist inference rules that can be automated.

The correspondence of SBVR to the web ontology language OWL is already described in the SBVR specification (OMG 2008, p. 118ff). In short, generic and individual noun concepts are mapped to classes and instances, respectively. Facts correspond to the OWL statement. Many of the predefined fact types have particular correpondences in OWL. For examples, the fact type "concept$_1$ specializes concept$_2$" corresponds to rdfs:subClassOf, if the concepts are noun concepts, and to rdfs:subPropertyOf if the concepts are binary-fact types. For many of the semantic formulations, too, a correspondence is specified e.g., cardinality restrictions, existential and universal quantifications, and complements. For details see (OMG 2008, p. 118ff).

This correspondence can be extended to business rules. Since facts types and noun concepts correspond to the OWL expression it is straightforward to use SWRL to represent business rules. However, there are some semantics subtleties in SBVR that need further consideration:

- Fact types can be defined according to the open and closed world semantics which has impact on how negation is interpreted. OWL is based on description logic and thus supports the open-world semantics with classical negation. Negating fact types defined according to the closed world assumption would need negation as failure which is not supported by SWRL.
- Rules can be formulated using alethic (necessity, possibility) and deontic (obligation, permission) modal operators. Modality is not supported in OWL or SWRL.
- For business rules different enforcement levels can be defined. While the von Halle classification distinguishes only between mandatory and guidelines, SBVR allows specifying any enforcement levels. In SBVR, however, the enforcement level is separated from the rules themselves. If, for instance, the rules detect an inconsistency, it is up to the user how he/she would react to it.

2.2.2 Ontological Modelling

Since it is not feasible for business people to model business knowledge and business processes using an ontology formalism, we promote a graphical modelling approach that allows the business users to draw their knowledge using symbols they are familiar with.

As mentioned in the previous sections the modelling tool ATHENE supports this approach. On a meta-level, the modelling objects are defined that can be used by the business users to draw their models. As a unique feature of ATHENE, each meta-model is represented as an ontology combining the domain model of the business vocabulary with a graphical representation.

A main advantage of this approach is that each model which is designed using these meta-models automatically has an ontological representation.

In order to model the knowledge-intensive processes as described above, meta-models are required for business processes, business rules, and for defining the business vocabulary. To conform with SBVR, the meta-models must conform to the compliance points for the business vocabulary and the business rules vocabulary by supporting the concepts of the corresponding clauses of the SBVR specification.

For some aspects of the business vocabulary, specific meta-models can be developed e.g., a document meta-model reflecting documents and their lifecycle, meta-models for organizational structure and IT infrastructure, and also domain-specific meta-models representing product models, for example.

Figure 6 sketches the modelling levels of ATHENE. On the meta-level different meta-models are defined. These meta-models define the object types that can be used for modelling. In the case of business processes the object types include activities, sub-process, branch, etc. For the business rules meta-model the object types are business rule, fact type, condition, quantifier, etc.

Figure 7 shows examples of ATHENE models and there relations to define knowledge-intensive processes. In the process model a rule set is linked to an activity. The rule set itself is a model containing various rules, each of which again has a graphical representation.

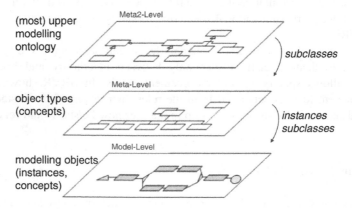

Fig. 6 Modelling levels in ATHENE

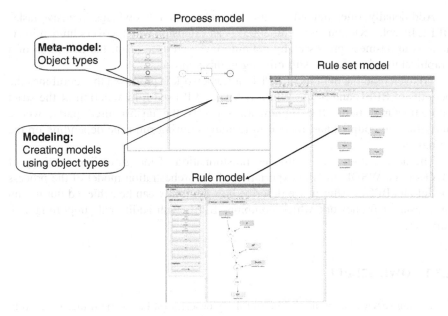

Fig. 7 Modeling knowledge-intensive processes in ATHENE

2.3 Phase 3: The Execution Model

The third phase of the modelling procedure is to transfer the high expressive interchange model to an executable format.

Contemporary Workflow Management Systems uses predefined process models, which are efficient for production and structured processes. But, as mentioned in the previous sections, they lack in supporting unstructured processes. Service oriented architecture (SOA) has evolved as key technology which provides the needed flexibility for agile enterprises by offering loosely coupled web services, which can be invoked during run time.

The Business Process Execution Language for Web Services (BPEL) combines the benefits of BPM and SOA by providing a language to specify the coordination and composition of web services. However, BPEL has two important deficits:

1. BPEL lacks the flexibility to deal with knowledge-intensive, weakly structured processes and
2. BPEL does not support the services that are performed by humans.

BPEL provides predefined control constructs, like sequence, to combine web services to a process. Modelling knowledge-intensive and unstructured process parts leads to complex and unmaintainable process models containing multiple decision points for several possible situations and events. A suitable approach would be, to couple the activities of the unstructured process part during run time depending on the actual case and situation.

Additionally, often human resources are involved in knowledge-intensive tasks. BPEL4People (Kloppmann et al. 2005) is an extension which covers human interactions in business processes by defining involved users. But, the definition of a graphical user interface is still missing in this approach.

To overcome the deficits of BPEL, a framework is proposed that combines the benefits of BPEL and SOA. While BPEL is still used for execution of the strict and structured parts, the framework supports the unstructured parts, whose activities are coupled and related to resources during run time depending on the actual case.

The next sections deal with the transformation of the grounding ontology of OWL-S into WSDL and the exportation of the orchestration model of the process model into BPEL. After it, we describe how flexibility can be achieved during run time using a framework which combines BPEL with additional supporting web services.

2.3.1 OWL-S2BPEL

In making services executable the ontology description has to be transformed into Web Service Description Language (WSDL) and BPEL. In the FIT project we used OWL-S as the interchange model for process models, as it is a service ontology. But, this is not a restriction of our approach, as any other process ontology could also be used.

OWL-S contains three main parts: the service profile, which describes the advertising and discovering of services; the process model, which describes the service's operation; and the grounding, which provides details on how to interoperate with a service (Martin et al. 2004). The information provided by the OWL-S grounding is used for the transformation into WSDL. It provides details of how to access the service, for instance, which port, which protocol, and which message formats are used. The OWL-S process model describes how services interact by using the concept atomic process, which contains details of a single process. Every OWL-S atomic process corresponds to a WSDL operation. Thus, the first step of transforming OWL-S into BPEL is to export the grounding description of the atomic processes into WSDL. These atomic processes can be combined to processes using control constructs similar to BPEL. For the export, these composite processes have to be retrieved and transferred to the equivalent BPEL control constructs (Singh and Feldkamp 2008; Tripathi et al. 2008).

As we have mentioned in the previous sections, flexibility cannot be achieved using standard control constructs. Therefore, we use the OWL-S control construct AnyOrder to express that the related atomic processes can be invoked depending on the actual case. During run time, rules select the atomic processes which have to be executed depending on the actual case. Therefore, an additional web service is needed which is able to invoke the rule engine and to interpret its results.

During the FIT project we implemented a framework that can be invoked as a web service by a BPEL engine and is able to invoke a rules engine, interpret its results and can invoke, control, and terminate additional web services which have to be executed depending on the fired rules.

2.3.2   Execution

After the transformation, the process can be executed. For the execution of the unstructured process part, two main components are necessary:

- *Rules Engine.* The rules engine is used to execute rules at run time.
- *Framework.* The framework is necessary to invoke the rules engine and to interpret the results.

Both components were implemented during the FIT project. In the next sections we briefly describe the components and a resulting layer architecture.

2.3.3   Layer Architecture

As mentioned in the previous section a framework and a rules engine were implemented supporting the unstructured parts of knowledge-intensive processes. Because of its flexibility the architecture is based on the layer architecture proposed by Geminiuc (2007). Instead of the restricted rules layer we use a more general "Application Layer" containing the rules engine, and also additional applications.

- *Business Process Layer.* The overall process is described and executed by a BPEL engine.
- *Web Service Layer BPEL* (and service-oriented architectures in general) exposes the existing application logic as web services. It is the aim of this layer to provide a standardized interface to business applications. Moreover functionality is modularized in order to be reused in various business contexts.
- *Application Layer.* The application layer contains every application which implements the web services.

The three layers are extended by a "Framework" Layer, which contains the framework connecting the abstract view of unstructured part with the technical view (like WSDL descriptions and input data of the activities belonging to the unstructured process part).

The framework provides the facilities to handle the rule set given by the BPEL engine, controlling the process instances of the unstructured part, like creation and termination as well as interfaces for user interface (Fig. 8).

Therefore, similar to the Workflow Reference Model, the framework provides several interfaces for e.g., a rules engine and a graphical user interface.

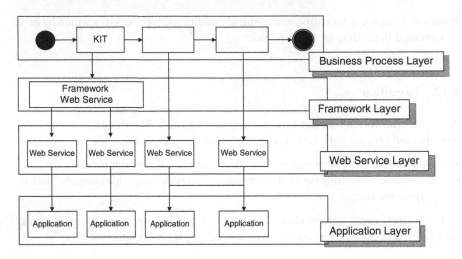

Fig. 8 Layer architecture

Fig. 9 RHEA architecture

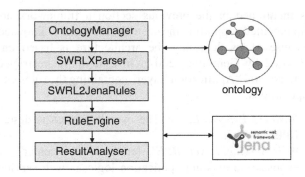

In the next section we describe the implemented rules engine RHEA and the framework itself.

2.3.4 RHEA

For the web-service orchestration during run time depending on the actual case and situation we use rules. To execute the rule, we have implemented during the FIT project a rules engine named RHEA which is able to execute SWRL rules (Fig. 9).

RHEA contains the following six components:

- *OntologyManager.* The OntologyManager loads the ontology and add the workflow relevant data to the ontology. This knowledge is used as knowledge base for the rule engine.

- *SWRLXParser*. The SWRLXParser parses the rule set and transfers the rule into an internal format.
- *SWRL2JenaRules*. This internal format is transformed into a Jena2[6] readable format. The advantage of using an internal format is that this part can be easily replaced by another rules engine format.
- *RuleEngine*. After loading the ontology and adding the workflow relevant data to the ontology, the parsed and transformed rules can be added to the knowledge base of the rule engine. After this step, the rules engine is able to execute the rules.
- *ResultAnalyser*. The fired rules and their consequences are analyzed by the ResultAnalyser. Various conflict resolution strategies exist. RHEA currently uses the first-in first-out strategy, for which results are dictated by the order of activation.

2.3.5 Architecture of the Framework

The previous section has described the rules engine. The interpretation of the fired results is done by an additional framework. The framework is responsible for the invocation of the rule engine, handling the rules engine's results, invocation, and termination of additional web services of the unstructured process part.

To provide the functionalities the framework contains the following four main components:

- *Controller*. The main component of the framework is the controller. The controller gets the rule set and invokes the rules engine. The controller is capable to invoke the rule engine and to deal with the returned results.
- *Rule Engine Adapter*. The rules engine adapter invokes a rule engine and returns its results to the controller.
- *GUI-Adapter*. The Graphical user interface is used as a work-list handler and provides the user interaction with the BPEL engine. Additionally, it is able to adapt the GUI depending on the selected resource and actual case and situation.
- *WSInvoker*. The WSInvoker is used to invoke the web services of the unstructured process parts. For instance, if the rules engine returns web service description, the WSInvoker invokes these web services.

3 Evaluation

To evaluate the introduced modelling approach, we create a questionnaire, which tries to figure out if the approach meets the end users' needs. During the FIT project we have two governmental end users, the municipality of

---

[6]JENA2, Jena – A Semantic Web Framework for Java, http://jena.sourceforge.net/

Vöcklabruck[7] (STADTVB) and the General Secretariat of Public Administration and e-Government[8] (YPESDDA).

The process used for the evaluation is as follows: First a practical exercise has been assigned to both end users, i.e., they were given a process model and asked to model rules and add them to the provided process model. The phrasing of rules was done by filling the Barbara von Halle's templates. After performing the tasks, a questionnaire has been used in both cases, which tries to figure out whether the use of the FIT approach for Adaptive Back Office meets users' needs.

The first part of the questionnaire contains two tasks, which should figure out, if rules can be easily created and added to the process model. Making the tasks easier for the people who answered the questionnaire, we have implemented two individual questionnaires containing the end users process models, which are implemented during the FIT project. Firstly, the evaluators have to create the rules using a provided Barbara von Halle template. After it, they should add the created rules to the process model using graphical representations.

All evaluators have to fill out the templates correctly. Half of the evaluators have filled out sheets which collect the terms and facts. All evaluators have to fill out the tables, which collects the rules itself. Conspicuously, the rules can be interpreted in other ways. The difficulty seems to be in distinguishing between action enabling rules and inference rules. All evaluators correctly relate the rules to the activities.

With the first two questions we wanted to know how the evaluators rated their own skills in the rule modelling and process modelling.

Of the evaluators 55.5% are not experienced and 22% of them are experienced rule modellers. Among them 44% said that they are experienced, and 44% said that they are inexperienced.

After these two questions we want to know the benefits and disadvantages of the FIT approach. The first four questions are directly referring to their tasks which they have performed first. We ask them to evaluate the following four situations:

- Having a process skeleton is a good starting point for agile process modelling.
- Phrasing rules in a semi-formal way (e.g., based on the notation of Barbara von Halle) is easy to understand.
- Having templates for rule phrasing makes rule phrasing easy.
- Adding rules to a task is easy.

The first question measures if having a process skeleton is a good starting point. The evaluators can use their experience as well as their knowledge that they gained during the execution of the tasks. Figure 10 shows that 66% of the evaluators

---

[7]The Municipality of Vöcklabruck (STADT VB) operates in the town hall of Vöcklabruck, a regional centre town in Upper Austria with 13,000 inhabitants and a "metropolitan area" of more than 100,000 people, living in a partly industrial, partly rural region.

[8]The General Secretariat of Public Administration and E-Government (YPESDDA) operates within the Ministry of Interior, Public Administration and Decentralization.

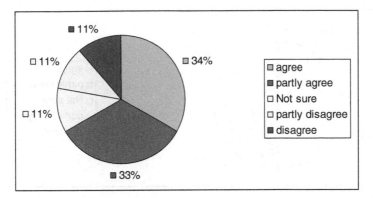

Fig. 10 Having a process skeleton is a good starting point for agile process modelling

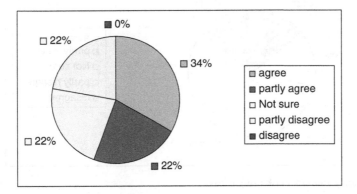

Fig. 11 Phrasing rules in a semi-formal way is easy to understand

indicate that having a process skeleton is a good starting point for agile process modelling.

The second question measures if phrasing rules in a semi-formal way is easy to understand. The task performed by the evaluators provided evidence that the task seems to be easy because the sheets were filled out by every evaluator. Additionally, Fig. 11 shows that 55% of the evaluators indicate that phrasing rules in a semi-formal way are easy to understand.

Figure 12 shows that 50% of the evaluators think that having templates makes rule phrasing easy. Only, 12.5% do not think that it makes it easier.

Adding rules to a task seems to be neutral for 57% and 28% of the evaluators think that it is difficult to add rules to a task. We have added in the question an example tool, which was used during the FIT project, the FIT extension of

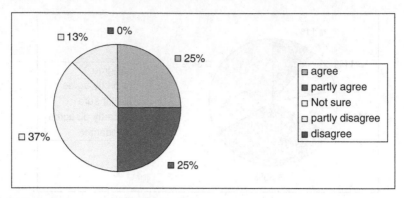

Fig. 12 Having templates for rule phrasing makes rule phrasing easy

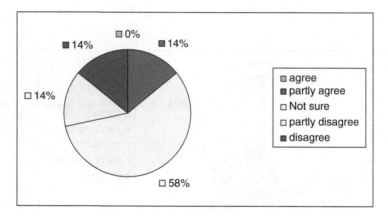

Fig. 13 Adding rules to a task using is easy

ADOeGov[9] provided by BOC.[10] Some of the evaluators indicate that they are not familiar with ADOeGov, so it is hard to answer this question. However, the task "Adding rules to task" is well executed by all evaluators (Fig. 13).

After these six questions, the next questions try to help understand the entire FIT-3 Phase modelling approach.

The first question measures if having flexible process execution meets users' needs. Figure 14 illustrates that most of the evaluators (78%) think that having flexible process execution meets users' needs.

The next question measures how the overall FIT 3-phase procedure is rated. Figure 15 shows that 78% of the evaluators rate the overall FIT approach for modelling processes high or very high.

---

[9]ADOeGov is a comprehensive modeling method for public administration, which has been developed within the FIT project

[10]BOC, http://www.boc-group.com [17.10.2008]

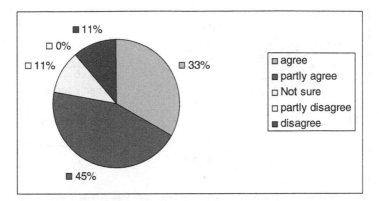

Fig. 14 Having flexible process execution meets users' needs

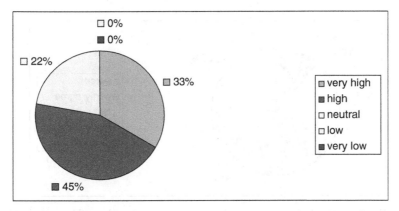

Fig. 15 How do you rate the overall FIT approach for modelling flexible processes?

The next question asks whether having a process skeleton and business rules is sufficient for modelling knowledge-intensive business processes. In this case, 56 % of the evaluators are neutral, 33% think that it is sufficient, and only 11% indicate that having a process skeleton plus business rules is not sufficient. The large number of people who have selected neutral could be due to the high number of inexperienced process and rule modellers (Fig. 16).

Figure 17 shows that a high number of evaluators (66%) think that the management of business rules becomes complex and unmaintainable very soon. Only 22% do not think so. One explanation for this could be due to the tasks the evaluators had to perform. Usually, the rules have to be combined into rule sets. This procedure was not carried out because of the small number of rules and to avoid making the evaluation unnecessarily complex. Because of this, the evaluators had to deal with a set of single rules instead of a single rules set.

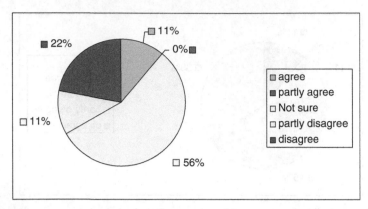

Fig. 16 Having a process skeleton plus business rules is not sufficient for modelling knowledge-intensive business processes

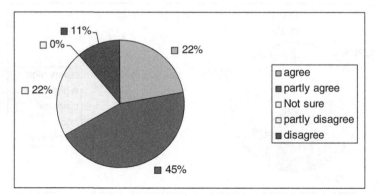

Fig. 17 The management of business rules becomes very soon complex and unmaintainable

The next question tries to measure whether the evaluators think that having rules or rule set repositories would decrease the effort for modelling significantly. Figure 18 illustrates that most of the evaluators (77%) agree that having rules and rule set repositories decreases the effort for modelling significantly.

Most of the evaluators indicate that having flexible process execution meets users' needs. The questionnaires show that the overall FIT modelling approach is highly rated and fulfills the users' requirements of having flexible processes.

The filled-out templates for rule phrasing and the answers show that phrasing rules in a semi-formal way is easy for the evaluators.

As many as 55% of the evaluators think that having process models that can be easily interchanged increases business efficiency and 43% think that having process models that can be easily exported/transformed into BPEL smoothes the path to automation significantly.

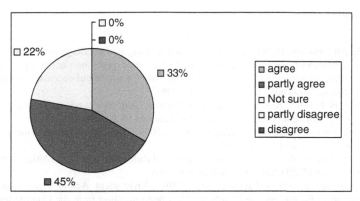

Fig. 18 Having a rules/rule set repository would decrease the effort for modelling significantly

4   Conclusion

This paper was motivated by the limitation of modelling and automating knowledge-intensive processes. To cope with knowledge-intensive processes we suggest allowing for flexibility of process execution as far as possible. This results in a separation of the fixed process part, for which the process flow is modelled at design time, and a flexible part, which is concretized at run time. The run-time decisions are supported in our modelling approach by adding four types of rules to process models. These rule types focus on one specific problem each: selection and planning of variable process parts, resource allocation, consistency checking, and decision support.

This modelling approach is complemented by a 3-phase procedure for process modelling. In the first phase, the knowledge is captured and described on the business level using semi-formal representations; phase 2 is about the transformation into standardized formal interchanged models, which can be transferred into machine executable forms. In phase 3, the interchange models are based on an ontological representation which is automatically generated by the ATHENE modelling environment. Additionally, we developed a framework which can execute the machine-executable processes.

An evaluation which was done during the FIT project shows that the 3-phase procedure fulfills the users' requirements for adaptive and flexible process models. It also shows that inexperienced process and rule modellers are able to model rules and processes. It also became clear, however, that the semantics of the business rules and the distinction between rule types are not always obvious. According to the results of the evaluation we switched from our first rule modelling approach to the SBVR specification. While SBVR allows defining a clear semantics of business vocabulary and rules, to exploit its full expressiveness additional research is required. For example, SBVR allows combining open and closed world semantics by defining fact types as either open or closed. Another point of research is the introduction of modal operators into ontological reasoning.

References

J. Becker, L. Algermissen, B. Niehaves, Prozessmodellierung als Grundlage des E-Government – Ein Vorgehensmodell zur prozessorientierten Organisationsgestaltung am Beispiel des kommunalen Baugenehmigungsverfahrens (2003), http://www.wi.uni-muenster.de/improot/is/pub_imperia/doc/1662.pdf. Accessed 04 Sep 2008

Best Practice eCH-0015 Struktur Prozessinventarliste, http://www.ech.ch/index.php?option=com_docman&task=doc_download&gid=326. Accessed 05 Jan 2007

Business Rule Group. What is a Business Rule? (2006), http://www.businessrulesgroup.org/defnbrg.shtml. Accessed 05 Dec 2006

O. Chappel, Term–Fact Modeling, the Key to Successful Rule-Based Systems (2005), http://www.brcommunity.com/b250.php. Accessed 28 Nov 2008

Commission of the European Communities: i2010 eGovernment Action Plan: Accelerating eGovernment in Europe for the Benefit of All. Communication from the Commission to the Council, The European Parliament, the European Economic and Social Committee and the Committee of the Regions. Brussels, SEC(2006) 511, http://ec.europa.eu/information_society/activities/egovernment/docs/highlights/comm_pdf_com_2006_0173_f_en_acte.pdf. Accessed 05 Sep 2008

A. Dörfler, Business Process Modelling and Help Systems as Part of KM in e-Government. Lect. Notes Comput. Sci. **2645**(N4), 297–303 (2003)

D. Feldkamp, K. Hinkelmann, B. Thönssen, KISS – Knowledge-Intensive Service Support: An Approach for Agile Process Management, in *Advances in Rule Interchange and Applications, International Symposium RuleML 2007*, ed. by A. Paschke, Y. Biletskiy (Springer, Heidelberg, 2007), pp. 25–38

K. Geminiuc, A services-oriented approach to business rules development (2007), http://www.oracle.com/technology/pub/articles/bpel_cookbook/geminiuc.html. Accessed 11 Oct 2008

Hilfsmittel (sample solution) eCH-0041Einreise mit Arbeitserlaubnis (2006), http://ech.ch/index.php?option=com_docman&task=doc_download&gid=392&Itemid=138&lang=en. Accessed 29 Nov 2008

Hilfsmittel (draft) eCH-0074 Geschäftsprozesse BPMN (2008), http://ech.ch/index.php?option=com_docman&task=doc_download&gid=2346&Itemid=138&lang=en. Accessed 29 Nov 2008

K. Hinkelmann, S. Nikles, B. Thönssen, L. von Arx, in *An Ontology-based Modelling Tool for Knowledge Intensive E-Government Services*. ed. by F. Corradini, A. Polzonetti, MeTTeG07, Proceedings of the 1st International Conference on Methodologies, Technologies and Tools Enabling E-Government, Halley Editrice SRL, Camrina, Italy, 27–28 September 2007, pp. 43–56

IBM and Microsoft and others (2007) Web services business process execution language (WS-BPEL) Version 2.0, http://docs.oasis-open.org/wsbpel/2.0/OS/wsbpel-v2.0-OS.html. Accessed 11 Oct 2008

D. Karagiannis, S. Palkovits, Prozessmodellierung in der öffentlichen Verwaltung – Ein ganzheitliches Rahmenwerk für E-Government, October 2002, for eGOV day 2003 (2002)

M. Kloppmann, D. König, et al., WS-BPEL, extension for people – BPEL4People (2005), http://download.boulder.ibm.com/ibmdl/pub/software/dw/specs/ws-bpel4people/BPEL4People_white_paper.pdf. Accessed 18 Oct 2008

D. Martin, M. Burstein, et al., OWL-S: semantic markup for web services, http://www.daml.org/services/owl-s/1.2/. Accessed 17 Oct 2008

K. Metaxiotis, J. Psarras, A conceptual analysis of knowledge management in e-government. Electron. Gov. **2**(1), 77–86 (2005)

OMG: BPMN, business process modelling notation, http://www.bpmn.org/. Accessed 27 Oct 2008

OMG, Semantics of business vocabulary and business rules (SBVR), v1.0, http://www.omg.org/docs/formal/08-01-02.pdf. Accessed 28 Oct 2008

K. Schedler, A. Collm, R. Hristova IV, Bericht zum Stand von E-Government in der Schweiz –
    Teil Kantone, Universität St. Gallen, 2007a, http://www.idt.unisg.ch/org/idt/ceegov.nsf/0/
    920543920addd0f0c12572c90055e199/$FILE/EGov%20Barometer06%20Teilbericht%
    20Kantone.pdf. Accessed 04 Sep 2008
K. Schedler, A. Collm, R. Hristova IV, Bericht zum Stand von E-Government in der Schweiz –
    Teil Gemeinden, Universität St. Gallen, 2007b, http://www.idt.unisg.ch/org/idt/ceegov.
    nsf/0/920543920addd0f0c12572c90055e199/$FILE/EGov_Barometer06_Teilbericht_Gemeinden.pdf.
    Accessed 04 Sep 2008
N. Singh, D. Feldkamp, *Making BPEL flexible.* in AI Meets Business Rules and Process Manage-
    ment, Papers from the AAAI Spring Symposium, Stanford University, 26–28 March 2008
    (AAAI Press, Menlo Park, CA)
Standard eCH-0075 Dokumentationsmodell Geschäftsarchitektur (2008), http://ech.ch/index.php?
    option=com_docman&task=doc_download&gid=2352&Itemid=181&lang=de. Accessed 29
    Nov 2008
Standard Recommendation eCH-0049 Themenkatalog für E-Government-Portale, http://ech.ch/
    index.php?option=com_docman&task=cat_view&gid=118&Itemid=181&lang=en. Accessed
    29 Nov 2008
U.K. Tripathi, K. Hinkelmann, D. Feldkamp, Life cycle for change management in business
    processes using semantic technologies. J. Comput. **3**, 24–31 (2008)
B. Von Halle, *Business Rules Applied, Building Better Systems Using the Business Rules Approach*
    (Wiley, New York, 2002)
R. Woitsch, D. Karagiannis, Process oriented knowledge management: a service based approach.
    J. Universal Comput. Sci. **11**(4), (2005), http://www.jucs.org/jucs_11_4/process_oriented_
    knowledge_management/Woitsch_R.pdf. Accessed 05 Sep 2008
Workflow Management Coalition, The workflow reference model, http://www.wfmc.org/standards/
    docs/tc003v11.pdf. Accessed 29 Nov 2008

E-Government Goes Semantic Web: How Administrations Can Transform Their Information Processes

Ralf Klischewski and Stefan Ukena

1 Introduction

E-government applications and services are built mainly on access to, retrieval of, integration of, and delivery of relevant information to citizens, businesses, and administrative users. In order to perform such information processing automatically through the Semantic Web,[1] machine-readable[2] enhancements of web resources are needed, based on the understanding of the content and context of the information in focus. While these enhancements are far from trivial to produce, administrations in their role of information and service providers so far find little guidance on how to migrate their web resources and enable a new quality of information processing; even research is still seeking best practices. Therefore, the underlying research question of this chapter is: what are the appropriate approaches which guide administrations in transforming their information processes toward the Semantic Web?

In search for answers, this chapter analyzes the challenges and possible solutions from the perspective of administrations: (a) the reconstruction of the information processing in the e-government in terms of how semantic technologies must be employed to support information provision and consumption through the Semantic Web; (b) the required contribution to the transformation is compared to the capabilities and expectations of administrations; and (c) available experience with the steps of transformation are reviewed and discussed as to what extent they can be expected to successfully drive the e-government to the Semantic Web.

R. Klischewski (✉)
Faculty of Management Technology, German University in Cairo (GUC), Al Tagamoa Al Khames, New Cairo City 11835, Egypt

[1]Semantic Web refers to both the vision of the Semantic Web as outlined by Berners Lee et al. (2001) and the Semantic Web technology stack suggested by the W3C (see http://www.w3.org/2001/sw/).

[2]By machine-readable data, we mean data that can easily be read and processed by computers in a way that is useful for human users of the system.

T. Vitvar et al. (eds.), *Semantic Technologies for E-Government*,
DOI 10.1007/978-3-642-03507-4_5, © Springer-Verlag Berlin Heidelberg 2010

This research builds on studying the case of Schleswig-Holstein, Germany, where semantic technologies have been used within the frame of the Access-eGov[3] project in order to semantically enhance electronic service interfaces with the aim of providing a new way of accessing and combining e-government services.

The structure of this chapter follows the above-mentioned approach. In the following section we revisit the visions and strategic goals related to the Semantic Web, identify the essential concepts of semantic information processing and interoperability, and introduce the case of the state of Schleswig-Holstein where transformation to the Semantic Web is under way. In the second section thereafter, we summarize the main challenges for administrations as well as the main motivators, and follow up how the Schleswig-Holstein state government positions itself in this uncertain situation. In the third section, we summarize the lessons learnt in Schleswig-Holstein with the aim of sharing this experience for the benefit of future adopters of semantic technologies in the e-government domain. In the conclusion, we finally zoom out of the case and point at possible generalizations as well as on future research.

2   Semantic-Based Information Processing in E-Government

Information processing is crucial for all e-government operations. Therefore, we look at how semantic technologies can or must be employed for the information provision and consumption in the e-government and how this can be linked to the Semantic Web.

The Semantic Web is both a vision of an enhanced World Wide Web and a technology stack (see below) to implement this vision. The vision roughly calls for changing the way that information resources and services are published on the Web so that machines can find and combine these resources and services. Opposed to this, the current web is by and large only comprehensible by humans. The Semantic Web has an informational as well as a functional aspect. The informational aspect unfolds its potential when machine agents are able to find relevant information based on a "machine understanding" while searching for and processing the information on behalf of their users. The functional aspect is related to Semantic Web services which allow for completely automated identification, activation, and combination of functional resources wrapped as services. In general, Semantic Web users (the demand side) are expected to gain an added value while searching for precise information in cases of (cf. Java et al. 2007):

- Conceptually searching for content (e.g., a business founder looking for all regulations governing the opening of a new business in a given region)

---

[3]Parties interested in implementing a solution based on the Access-eGov can find relevant information in the project deliverables D9.2 "Methodological Guidelines" and D6.2 "System and use documentation" available from www.access-egov.org.

- Context based querying (e.g., a citizen looking for marriage services in a given region that offers conducting legal marriages in a lighthouse)
- Reporting facts (e.g., any client looking for opening hours of a given administration)
- Knowledge sharing on the semantic web: structured knowledge of and about administration (e.g., business founding regulations in one country) can be also used to analyze yet unstructured information (e.g., business founding regulations in another country), thus enriching the results of the information search

For e-government the above potentials are relevant as far as they can be exploited for the integration of administrative information and processes.

2.1 *From Strategy to Implementation:* Semantic *Interoperability*

Citizens and business users all around the world – according to their needs and capabilities – increasingly use the Internet seeking for more support when interacting with the administration: the vision of the Semantic Web raises expectations toward the next generation of a one-stop government, including the delivery of complete and relevant information, integrated access to multiple services, and service provision on the basis of awareness of the user's context.

To this end, electronic information sharing and processing across the front-and back-end systems of public administrations (PAs) require a shared automatic interpretation of the electronic resources involved in order to enable a smooth operation and successful interaction across technical and organizational borders. The requirements of enabling integrated service delivery are known in principle (Wimmer and Tambouris 2002), but even more critical than the technical challenges is the strategic alignment of the PAs (cf. Kubicek et al. 2003) as the starting point for linking automated information processing and setting up a common infrastructure.

The vision of the Semantic Web entails a specific strategy on how to achieve the integration: the aim is to enable *semantic* interoperability through describing information and services in such a way that machines can "make sense" of these descriptions and thus automatically find and combine required information and services. This is done through formal semantics, in particular, by using the technology stack of knowledge representation standards that have been and are being developed for this purpose. The de-facto standard to describe information resources is the RDF-family of W3C standards (i.e., RDF, RDF-S, OWL).[4] For the formal semantic description of services there are several options, including OWL-S (Martin et al. 2004), WSML (Lausen et al. 2005), and more recently SAWSDL (Farrell and Lausen 2007).

---

[4]See the W3C Semantic Web portal at http://www.w3.org/2001/sw/ for more information.

The formal description of what certain data means is essential to facilitate automatic processing: For example, to plot the locations of addresses on a map, a system needs to "know" what the data elements of a given set of data refer to. If the system "knows" that a certain data element is the street address and another one contains the ZIP code, then this information can be used by the system to calculate and plot the corresponding position on the map (assuming that the address is valid and can be transformed to the appropriate coordinates, etc.). It is possible to do this using XML, as can be seen by efforts such as microformats.[5] However, because RDF was designed for this purpose from the beginning, it does not only make the task simpler, but it also provides a much better support for this than is possible with XML. Basically, today's semantic technologies and the idea of the Semantic Web are combining advancements in the area of artificial intelligence (knowledge representation and agent technology) with latest Internet technologies and infrastructure capabilities. Most of the envisioned applications are based on knowledge representation, intelligent retrieval, and facilitation of communication (or a combination of those).

Technically, the integration and combination of data from diverse sources is enabled through adding data to available resources in order to facilitate the semantic processing. In the context of the Semantic Web, the term "annotation" usually refers to semantic annotation, i.e., enriching digital content with information about its meaning and context in such a way that this semantic annotation is processible by machines (Berners-Lee et al. 2001). Semantic annotation enables software agents to process the content of Web-pages and other digital resources in a way that is meaningful to human users. The goal is to ensure that humans and machines "understand" the same information in the same or at least similar way. Semantic annotation can be applied to web resources in the form of semantic mark-up (semantic enhancements of a regular HTML mark-up) or, more generally, metadata. In its true sense, metadata is "data about data," but it may also be understood as information about information. Metadata is usually applied to a resource by annotating these resources with information that describes the content, structure, and context of a resource (Gill et al. 2008).

The production of metadata should be governed by one or more ontologies, a term which has received much attention, since ontologies are expected to serve as the knowledge bases for empowering Semantic Web applications and as the key enabler and mediator for semantic interoperability. Technically, ontology defines the "basic terms and relations comprising the vocabulary of a topic area as well as the rules for combining terms and relations to define extensions to the vocabulary" (Neches et al. 1991). In the context of semantic interoperability, ontologies are useful to control the vocabulary of metadata and values related to key terms, and to define formalized relationships between terms and concepts – all of which are prerequisites for software agents to make use of the metadata and annotated resources.

---

[5]http://microformats.org/.

The vision of the next-generation Internet (as originally promoted by Tim Berners-Lee and others) has inspired many to work on semantic technologies and standards such as RDF, OWL, WSMO, etc., of which the main aim is to facilitate integration and combination of data drawn from diverse sources. However, the availability of these technologies is not sufficient. Other prerequisites are standardized controlled vocabularies or even higher developed ontologies which describe the domain knowledge in a certain area of interest, i.e., domain-specific standards.

This also applies to e-government: Only when controlled vocabularies and/or ontologies covering the administrative domain are published and widely used can the vision of the Semantic Web for the government be realized. Throughout the last years, a number of countries have started initiatives in this direction. One of the first and most developed is the Integrated Public Sector Vocabulary IPSV/GLC[6] as an "encoding scheme" for populating the UK e-Government Metadata Standard (e-GMS) which lays down the elements, refinements, and encoding schemes to be used by government officers when creating metadata for their information resources, or when designing search engines for information systems. Similar lists of terms organized in a thesaurus-like structure have also been developed and standardized by other governments (e.g., AGIFT[7]). On a more advanced level, a Governance Enterprise Architecture reference model has been suggested, including detailed models and implementations in specific ontology languages like OWL-S and WSMO to cater to various aspects of interoperability (Goudos et al. 2006, Peristeras et al. 2006, Wang et al. 2007).

Semantic interoperability has been defined, for example, by Pollock and Hodgson (2004, p. 6) as a capability that enables enhanced automated discovery and usage of data (due to the enhanced meaning, i.e., explicit semantics, that are provided for data) when implementing information sharing infrastructures between discrete content owners. In light of the immense diversity in administration, semantic interoperability is perceived as a key aspect on the road to e-government integration and improved service quality. Multiple interoperability frameworks have put semantic interoperability on the agenda; for example the European Interoperability Framework EIF (European Communities 2004, p.16) defines it as "ensuring that the precise meaning of exchanged information is understandable by any other application that was not initially developed for this purpose" and enabling systems to "combine received information with other information resources and to process it in a meaningful manner." This framework also points out that the semantic interoperability is related to the specific e-government services as they are serving life events or business episodes (European Communities 2004, p. 20).

The key to semantic interoperability is the computer-based production and use of structured data representing the semantics in focus. The basic idea is: if the semantics of an informational resource can be encapsulated in distinct objects (i.e., structured metadata, or annotations) and it is known how those objects are

---

[6]Available at: www.govtalk.gov.uk/schemasstandards/gcl.asp or www.esd.org.uk/standards/ipsv/.
[7]http://www.naa.gov.au/records-management/create-capture-describe/describe/ agift/index.aspx.

constructed – then there is hope for machine interpretation and for paving a common ground for truly seamless services, eventually leading to a Semantic Web for e-government.

The basic pattern of an interoperability infrastructure that we can learn, for example, is from the triangle of web-service provider, service requester, and service registry. In order to enable any service requester to find an appropriate service provider to interact with, it needs a more or less elaborated centralized entity which allows providers to announce their services and the requester to look for a match to their needs. For semantic interoperability, it has been suggested to extend this architecture by a discovery and mediation component (Hauswirth et al. 2008) in order to (a) free requesters from having to know the specific registries and be compatible with their requesting mechanisms, and (b) separate data providing services (registries) from data processing (discovery, mediation). Certainly not all relevant e-government resources on the web have to be considered as services; however, practically all relevant information (e.g., forms, legal requirements, opening hours) is related to providing services, and for this reason the service perspective has emerged as the main conceptualization for e-government projects related to the Semantic Web. Based on this, the informational aspect of the Semantic Web can be exploited by evaluating the annotated service descriptions, and the functional aspect comes into play when, on the basis of the descriptions, the services are actually requested, i.e., specific input is provided and the output is taken for further processing. As indicated above, the process integration (compared to information integration) needs a significantly higher degree of shared abstractions; for this reason the requirements for setting up the semantic interoperability and for enabling "machine-understanding" are much higher as well.

For any discovery component (which itself could be an agent) the most important items to share are the ontologies by which semantic expressions in focus have been generated. Only after obtaining these ontologies an agent may automatically process the structured metadata and generate meaningful conclusions and/or initiate appropriate action. However, the required ontologies are of different types and at different levels. For example, Crichton et al. (2007) have suggested that a set up for semantic interoperability ("semantic framework") should distinguish between components for: "terminology services, providing interpretations for basic terms; metadata registries, holding collections of observations; and model repositories, descriptions of components or data sets, or characterizations of domain information" (Crichton et al. 2007, p. 31). The first one is related to providing a controlled vocabulary and (if possible) defined relationships between the concepts (usually wrapped as ontology); the second one is important for specifying any values that may be used in metadata annotation (e.g., how to denote an address, or opening hours); and the third level refers to more complex abstractions such as forms or life event process models.

Reaping the benefits for Semantic Web users is accomplished through (intelligent) computer-based agents. Basically, a software component as an agent assists human users and may act on their behalf in performing dedicated computer-related tasks (e.g., data mining). To qualify as an intelligent agent, Hendler (2001) points out four important abilities: to communicate with human users (and other machine agents), to act upon an environment as well as to suggest, to do things without supervision (i.e., autonomously), and to make use of its own experience. Hendler (2001) predicted that the area of web services will be one of the most powerful uses of web ontologies. Beyond searching and combining certain information from various sources (information integration), intelligent agents are supposed to search the web for the right services, mediate between the users' task and the service execution, as well as among the various web services (thus achieving process integration). However, combining web services to create higher levels and cross-organizational business processes again requires standards to model the interactions (Peltz 2003).

Meanwhile, experts consider the technical basis for semantic interoperability to be ready for use in real-life applications. The Semantic Web Education and Outreach Interest Group (http://esw.w3.org/topic/SweoIG/) maintains a portal informing about the latest advancements in applications, most of which can be found in the area of social computing (i.e., applications that are carried out by groups of people). In the administrative domain, a number of initiatives and research projects seek to advance the Semantic Web for e-government (Substantial effort of providing infrastructure components for semantic interoperability in e-government has been made within the frame of the R&D projects such as SemanticGov, TerreGov, OntoGov, SmartGov, eGOV, DIP, IPSV;[8]), but so far the applications are still in the experimental or pilot phase. One of these applications in Schleswig-Holstein will serve as the case in focus for the rest of this chapter.

2.2   Upgrading Information Processes in Schleswig-Holstein

The German federal state of Schleswig-Holstein consists of 1,120 municipalities, which belong to eleven different districts. While the larger municipalities each have their own administration, there are more than 900 municipalities with less than 2,000 inhabitants which share a common administration with several municipalities. All administrations offer a set of services to their citizens, like issuing passports, wage tax cards, and different kinds of certificates or registration of enterprises, new places of residence, marriages, deaths, births etc., resulting in a huge amount of municipal services offered all over the state. In addition to these, there are services that are offered by administrations at the district, state, and national level.

In a given life situation, for instance when wanting to build a house, get married, or establish an enterprise, different offices of different administrations have to be

---

[8]See www.semantic-gov.org, www.terregov.eupm.net, www.ontogov. com, www.smartgov-project.org, www.egov-project.org dip.semanticweb.org, www.esd.org.uk/standards/ipsv_internalvo-cabulary, respectively.

contacted by a citizen to get the required documents, forms, permits, etc. At the beginning of such a process, citizens often do not know which offices of which administrations they need to contact, and they need to find the responsible administrations, using, for example, various government websites. The e-government services of the different administrations are usually not integrated and cannot be accessed by citizens through a single platform. Therefore, citizens who want to use the e-government services have to access a variety of websites to get the information on relevant services and, possibly, to also use them. On the other hand, each local administration offers mostly identical information on the same kinds of services.

The state government of Schleswig-Holstein is aiming at integrating the different web resources containing the service information and at making these accessible by a single platform, but still leaving the data and their maintenance in the administrations' legacy systems. The approach suggested in the Access-eGov project builds on the semantic annotation of web resources thus making the meaning of the distributed information explicit. The annotated data can then be used for automatically displaying and searching the services, and also for generating a user scenario in which different services are combined according to a citizen's needs. For the semantic annotation, however, a common conceptual model of the service descriptions is required: the relevant concepts, attributes, and relations that make up a service description and the relevant administrative processes have to be identified and agreed upon.

In two field tests in Schleswig-Holstein, accomplished within this research project, this approach has been followed on the example of the life event "marriage." In this life event, possibly different registry offices have to be contacted one after the other by a citizen to issue the required documents in preparation of the marriage. The services of the registry offices in Schleswig-Holstein were thus to be annotated on the basis of a common conceptual model and to be made accessible to the Access-eGov platform.

The idea of an information process and the basic functional components enabling a semantic e-government application are depicted in Fig. 1. It shows the two groups of users involved in information sharing: The information providers are to the left, and the information consumers are to the right. The information providers create service description and ontologies (used for describing services), thus encoding the information in such a way that the information's context is formalized. This enables Semantic Web applications, like the Access-eGov Core, to process the information, thus making it available to information consumers. The information consumers try to contextualize the information with whatever formalized context may be made available to them through the user interface. Information providers may either use the Annotation Tool provided by Access-eGov (top left corner) or they may use third party CMS, databases or software agents (middle left) that are adopted to provide information to the Access-eGov core in different ways (e.g., a web-service API or by semantically annotated content). Information consumers can use the Access-eGov Personal Assistant (top right) to find services. In the future they may also use other clients or Semantic Web agents developed by third parties

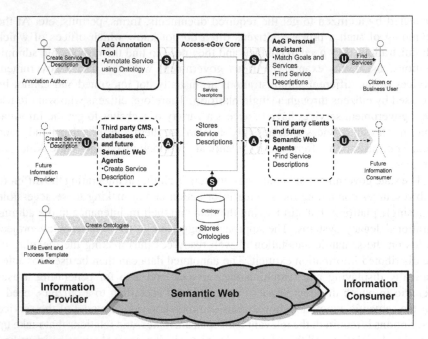

Fig. 1 Information flows from information providers (*left*) through a semantic infrastructure (*middle*) to information consumers (*right*)

(middle right). Figure 1 also indicates interception points for system testing ("S"), user testing ("U"), and agent testing ("A") of which the latter can be used for inspecting if the data and its encoded meaning in focus can be successfully processed ("understood") by another application, i.e., agent (Klischewski and Ukena 2008).

In order to enable semantic interoperability in Schleswig-Holstein, the WSMO conceptual model was reused and adapted for the e-government application as follows (Bednár et al. 2008, p. 68):

- The WSMO-concepts *Goal*, *Ontology*, and *Mediator* were reused as is.
- The WSMO-concept *Service* was extended as follows: While the original concept is only applicable to web services, Access-eGov extends its applicability to electronic services that are not web services, and even to nonelectronic ("traditional" or "offline") services.
- A new concept *Life Event* was introduced. This concept can be used to compose a complex hierarchy of *Goals*. It was introduced as a formal model of users' needs, consisting of multiple goals and services. It is technically used for workflow, control-flow, and data-flow sequences.

Within Access-eGov, a personal assistant component for information consumption and service activation has been developed which provides a user interface for citizens to make use of the new capabilities and which connects to the platform components for finding and brokering information. In addition, promotion campaigns have been launched to attract citizens to use the personal assistant, and several evaluation instruments have been applied to learn from the users' opinions.

All in all the state government considers the project a success, but the question remains how semantic technologies shall be used after the pilot project has been completed. In the following sections we will continue discussing this case in order to identify the most essential pros and cons as well as the example to outline an implementation approach which incorporates the experience of this application pioneer.

3 Administrations as Key Transformers: Challenges and Motivators

Whether the vision of a Semantic Web for e-government ever becomes a reality depends largely on the contribution of the administrations themselves. As information providers, they are the ones who have to establish common conceptual grounds and to transform their web resources on a large scale. It is not an easy task at all and it requires substantial investment. In this section we discuss the required contribution to the transformation in comparison to the capabilities and expectations of administrations; more precisely we summarize the main challenges for administrations as well as the main motivators, and follow up on how the Schleswig-Holstein state government positions itself in this uncertain situation.

3.1 Challenges

1. Information processing is at the core of all e-government operations, but not all information processing can be upgraded and/or automated at the same time. Wang et al. (2007) point out that testing and applying semantic technologies and solutions on a large scale is difficult in PA, being a huge, diverged, and distributed environment that is considered as the "heaviest service industry." The first challenge, therefore, is to prioritize and find an appropriate starting point for semantic processing. Unlike in business, where profit expectations and the selection of a business model usually guide the strategic IT decisions, administrations have to find their own strategic orientation. Unless legislation, politics, or top-management set clear requirements, understanding the wants and needs of e-government users is usually the best way to create strategic guidance. However, identifying the informational needs in practice is a challenge in itself: who are the most relevant users (citizens, business users, or other administrations? which subgroups?) and what exactly are their informational needs?

2. A common ground for abstraction is prerequisite for e-government integration and semantic interoperability. However, the idea that all actors involved adopt exactly one e-government world view, i.e., a certain perspective on what exists and

how it is related, will remain an illusion. With so many actors striving for more interoperability on local, regional, national, and international levels, the source of potential disagreement is unlimited. To reduce the cost and to ensure the highest degree of sustainability, PAs are well advised to use available and accepted standards as much as possible – at best, those which are provided top-down by the most powerful and accepted actor in the region (usually a national government or even an international agency) – and/or implement an accepted mediation strategy (cf. Mocan et al. 2009). But what can be done in case such top-down efforts are not in sight? Should PAs at lower levels of the hierarchy seize the opportunity to suggest and share conceptualizations and resources from their point of view? Or is such an investment too risky, given the unlikely possibility that later on a top-down standard will be enforced which contradicts its own previous efforts?

3. The specific problem in PA is that a wide range of services is offered, requiring a huge effort of annotation, while at the same time existing web resources are poorly structured and/or governed by a multiplicity of different concepts (especially in areas with federate governmental structures). That means annotating and sometimes even restructuring a wide range of service descriptions and web resources is an enormous challenge because even semiautomatic annotation will remain difficult, and manual annotation work will be one of the main cost drivers toward semantic interoperability. In this situation, what is the best approach to achieve sufficient transformation while at the same time keeping work effort, time, and other cost drivers within reasonable limits?

4. Employees in administrations (outside the IT department) are information technology users, not experts. But for many years to come the end-user support for semantic-based information processing will be limited, and as long as this is the case, expertise of semantic technology is indispensable in order to facilitate information provision as well as consumption. But how much technical expertise is actually needed and for which tasks? And who should be a technology expert, and who not?

5. Upgrading the e-government resources and applications also requires an upgrade of the IT infrastructure: additional tools and components are needed as well as new interfaces for interoperation with components from other organizations, or with agents operating on behalf of e-government users. But how much effort is actually needed on the side of the administrations? And how can their IT departments and/or service providers prepare themselves to meet this challenge?

6. On the demand side, preparation for taking up new applications also requires significant effort. Even if we assume that annotations and associated schemata are publicly available – how are these going to be exploited? In contrast to many commercial areas, interacting with PAs rarely involves a profitable business case. Therefore, we can hardly expect entrepreneurs to enter the market and to provide technologies (agents, user interfaces) for bringing out semantic e-government applications on their own. That means PAs investing in semantic technologies also have to take care that the new capabilities are actually being used. But what is the best approach to push the take-up in terms of providing technical components, promotion and/or strategic alignments with other actors moving in the same direction?

7. By nature of the issue, moving toward the Semantic Web is not an individual effort and cannot be supported by stand-alone installations. Therefore, finding partners and building networks is a critical success factor. But from the perspective of the administration, what are the kinds of partners needed and what kind of relationship is most helpful for the envisioned transformation?

3.2   Motivators

From the above analysis, any PA might conclude that it is obviously too early to invest heavily in semantic technologies and related projects. For most PAs this is probably an adequate assessment. However, there are substantial arguments why PAs should care to prepare for or even start such kind of projects now:

- The Semantic Web will reach e-government sooner or later: the demand for e-government integration is increasing, and those who are ready to meet the challenge have the chance to participate in the initial decision-making and can make extensive use of the start-up funding; followers have to cope with what others have established and are likely to be required to pay their own way.
- The use of semantic technologies pays off now: conceptualizing administrative information and processes provides the necessary abstractions as prerequisites for higher integration, thus helping to (re-) organize and streamline the internal affairs, especially in federated regions that currently struggle with distributed systems and uncontrolled growth of websites and resources.
- Creating machine-readable annotation produces long-term assets: in view of the increasing demand for e-government integration, PAs will have to respond to multiple requests for interoperability; having the abstractions ready for an open world signals the PA's readiness and provides the instant basis for any future integration effort.

3.3   Strategic Decision in Schleswig-Holstein

As introduced in the previous section, the state government Schleswig-Holstein has a large-scale integration problem: The e-government services of the different administrations are usually not integrated and cannot be accessed by citizens through a single platform. Therefore, the main reason for participating in the Access-eGov research project and investing own personnel resources is aiming at integrating the different web resources containing the service information and at making these accessible through a single platform but still leaving the data and its maintenance in the administrations' legacy systems. Further, motivators have been upcoming requirements stemming from the central German responsibility finder and the EU service directive: machine-readable service descriptions will be needed for several applications, and it was clear from the beginning that the local administrations cannot meet the upcoming requirements one by one.

The main transformation accomplished within the Access-eGov research project has resulted in two field tests in Schleswig-Holstein. The focus of the test has been on the life event "marriage" in which a citizen has to contact possibly multiple registry offices one after the other to obtain the required documents in preparation of the marriage. Eleven registry offices (responsible for about one-fourth of the state's inhabitants) volunteered to participate in this field test. Their participation was bound to the condition that little time and effort would be required for service annotation and that existing IT systems would not necessarily have to be changed. Therefore, a tool for annotating data, which can easily be used in any environment and by untrained users, and which allows effective service annotation, was required. On the information consumption side, the state government expected a high-quality web-user interface as well as technical interfaces for other IT providers in the region serving a larger number of municipalities in the state.

All in all, the state government's decision for adopting semantic technologies included the expectation of reaching technical solutions for upgrading applications and infrastructure, as well as experience and expertise on how to solve integration challenges on the basis of new semantic technologies.

4   Transitioning to the Semantic Web Step by Step

Today's government websites are automatically created by content-management-systems (CMS) which were designed to deliver HTML-pages for human users to consume with the help of web browsers. The semantic integration of information and services based on Semantic Web technologies requires machine-readable enhancements to web resources and service descriptions which currently reside in CMS or, even worse, in handcrafted HTML-pages.

Thus, transitioning to the Semantic Web cannot be done by a simple one-step procedure. Even though central institutions increasingly provide the tools and standards, the main challenges of actually migrating to a semantic e-government rest with the administrations as the providers of information and services. Administrations who are faced with this paramount annotation effort which is required to enable machine processing are still seeking best practices that may guide them in these activities. The question then is: What are the appropriate approaches which guide administrations effectively and efficiently in transforming their web resources toward the Semantic Web in order to achieve semantic integration of the provided services? By "effectively", we mean successful in meeting the requirements of administrations, citizens, and businesses; and "efficiently" refers to the use of limited resources, scalability, and applicability in real-life administrative environments. In this section, we seek to summarize lessons learnt in Schleswig-Holstein, with the aim of sharing this experience for the benefit of future adopters of semantic technologies in the e-government domain.

4.1 Identifying Informational Needs of Users and Required Information Quality

The informational needs of information consumers (citizens or business users) can be best identified by looking at the information objects that appear in the offline service transactions taking place today. This first step is most important because it will either guide or misguide by applying focus on the specific goals of the PA. If done properly, it will avoid the possibility of getting out of hand and unnecessarily driving the cost. This can be achieved, for example, by identifying the *boundary objects* which are most relevant during the interaction of a PA and its clients and peers (Klischewski and Ukena 2008a).

The relevant boundary objects (good candidates for these are forms, lists, and information leaflets) can be identified by specifying a scenario and use cases in a free-text form, which should then be transformed into a more structured table format containing the identified information needs – goals and corresponding services.

In the Access-eGov project the scenario describes how two citizens want to get married, one with a German citizenship and one with a foreign citizenship, and how they use the system to support them in maneuvering through the administrative process. A list of proposed services together with related information (laws and regulations, required documents, etc.) was thus compiled. Part of this, the final service of receiving the marriage certificate, is depicted in Table 1.

When determining the informational need and the required information quality, it is advisable to plan ahead, especially with regard to evaluation. In particular, the informational needs and quality should not only serve as the starting point for subsequent steps; they should also be used for guiding the design as well as for planning the evaluation of the system from the beginning.

In the Access-eGov project this was done by allowing the user partners to estimate the expected benefits, in particular, the quality and process improvement compared to their current service provisioning practice. During the trials, improvement was measured according to these criteria set by the user partners.

The result of this step should be a list or table that describes the informational needs of citizens (and business users) in such a way that people outside the domain of government (i.e., developers) can understand. This list of informational needs will then be used to design the formal semantic structures and software components

Table 1 Example: Identification of information needs (user's goals) and corresponding administration services

Goal, aim of the citizen	Corresponding service
Get a marriage certificate	*Name:* Issue a marriage certificate
	Description: If the citizens want to, they can obtain a marriage certificate after marriage. Also international marriage certificates can be obtained.
	Responsible: The register office at the marriage location
	Costs: €7 (cost for further copies: €3.50)

for service delivery. In addition, a list of quality criteria and expected improvements should have been produced, including a plan for later evaluation of the degree of achieved improvement.

4.2 Establish and Maintain a Common Conceptual Ground

Another step, typically conducted right after the informational needs and quality have been identified, involves the establishment of a common conceptual ground, which also includes designing new standards or (preferably) identifying existing standards to be reused. In this step, technical standards (like RDF) are left aside and only domain-specific standards (e.g., from the government domain) are considered. Technical standards will play a role after a common conceptual ground has been established.

Using the table of the previous step as an input, a glossary containing all relevant topics and terms related to the services should be created to facilitate the common understanding of all actors, ultimately leading to the development of more structured and formal descriptions. The aim of this step is to identify the general domain concepts, i.e., those concepts that are common not only to the specific scenarios developed in the previous step, but also to other similar scenarios as well.

In the Access-eGov project a second table was created with columns for the terms in German and English language, accompanied with a short description of what the term means and how it relates to other terms. The glossary terms were then grouped and organized into hierarchical categories (see Table 2).

Next, a set of nonhierarchical relations and dependencies were identified between the categories and concepts, using the relationships expressed in the textual descriptions of the categories. This resulted in a conceptual model, of which a fragment is depicted in Fig. 2. The figure shows the identified domain concepts (represented as rounded squares) and their relation (represented as named arrows). The classes of the boundary objects, highlighted in gray, can be directly instantiated and were used to annotate special properties (the so-called nonfunctional properties) of the services.

The result of this step is a conceptual model, i.e., set of concepts, descriptions of these concepts, their relations, and a semiformal representation of this conceptual model. Ideally, this conceptual model represents the common understanding of all actors. The conceptual model will be used by a government officer to understand

Table 2 Category *document* from the Access-eGov controlled vocabulary

Category:	Document
Subcategories	Certificate, Form, Notification, Payment Receipt
Attributes	Title, Description of purpose
Description	Used for concepts that refer to the artifacts as: *certificates* provided by the administration, *forms* to be filled in by citizens, *notifications* issued by an administration in order to inform a service consumer about certain changes in status, *payment receipts* which a citizen receives after having paid a fee

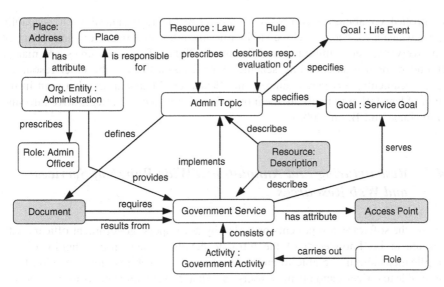

Fig. 2 Fragment of conceptual model, as it was identified for the Access-eGov system

how to annotate services and web resources, as well as by developers to create domain-specific implementations of standards and software components.

In particular, the Access-eGov developers translated the conceptual model into a WSML-representation. To this end, the concepts from the conceptual model were mapped to WSMO-concepts, for example, "Goal: Life Event" was mapped to the WSMO concept Life Event, "Goal: Service Goal" was mapped to the WSMO Goal, and "Government Service" was mapped to (the extended) WSMO Service. When a mapping was not possible (because there was no adequate WSMO concept), the generic WSMO Ontology concept was used to create a new concept.

The benefits of using Semantic Web technology when creating or reusing a domain-specific standard may vary, depending on how the domain-specific standard has been designed by the original authors and how it can be reused. For example, in some cases it might be better to reuse an existing standard which, while not coming from the government domain, is widely accepted and has been designed for the Semantic Web, rather than using a specific government standard which has only a local relevance and is not suited for the Semantic Web. Often, this will be a difficult decision; from our experience administrations should:

- Try to reuse existing standards which were designed (or enhanced) for the Semantic Web whenever possible;
- Choose a widely accepted standard over a standard from the government domain if the widely accepted standard is equally suited for the task at hand.

This does not mean that standards from the government domain should be ruled out from the beginning. On the contrary, well-designed standards from the government domain are a good starting point for building a common conceptual ground (e.g., IPSV/GLC, see above). The available government conceptualizations and controlled vocabularies complement general metadata standards such as Dublin Core which have been developed to identify the relevant aspects for annotation (for an overview, see Tambouris and Tarabanis 2004). These resources are mainly intended for use as encoding schemes for metadata to describe other resources, like documents, services, agencies, and databases. Metadata are also used in the area of legislation to facilitate the integration of, and access to, legislative information (Lupo and Batini 2003).

4.3   Restructuring and Annotating a Wide Range of Services and Web Resources

Using the software components provided by developers, government officers with limited or no knowledge of the intricate details of semantic technologies and applications should be able to annotate services and web resources, making them available to citizens and business users as well as to semantic agents for processing. A basic understanding of the common conceptual model should be enough for the average government officer to successfully annotate services, i.e., to describe services in a formal way, if the right tools are provided. In addition, it may be necessary to restructure the existing resources if the current structure is not adequate for annotation, or if they are not structured at all (e.g., addresses are only provided "buried" within a paragraph of text).

As for annotation and restructuring, it has been pointed out that especially in e-government the variety of concepts and services is a great challenge. Furthermore, each provider of e-government websites has its own particular information management objectives and strategy, leading to individual implementation of informational resources as a result. To some extent mark-up can be supported through shared and standardized ontologies and metadata, but standardization alone does not enable automated annotation, nor avoids the occurrence of semantic mismatches or interoperability clashes.

Through semantic annotation, the content of a web page can be semantically described in a machine-readable way. A number of different annotation tools have been developed for different purposes; some of them also for the special purpose of semantic annotation for the Semantic Web, like the SHOE Knowledge Annotator or the OntoMat Annotizer (cf. Handschuh and Staab 2003). While these tools allow for the annotation of HTML and other kinds of documents, they cannot be used to semantically annotate services, which require a special kind of annotation (e.g., within Access-eGov the semantic annotation is captured in a Service Profile, which is a formal description of a service's inputs, outputs, and other properties). Meanwhile, the labeling of service-related resources has been identified as an important challenge, but the methods and tools for support are still under research (e.g., Lerman et al. 2007).

As part of the Access-eGov project, a web-based application called Annotation Tool has been developed to support administration officers in their task of annotating services. In order to facilitate the annotation effort and support the administration officers, a half-day training workshop was conducted, during which the officers of participating administrations in Schleswig-Holstein began annotating the services that are related to the life event (marriage). The annotation was completed success-fully by all officers themselves within a few weeks following this workshop. Officers who were not able to attend the training were provided with a short handbook on the usage of the annotation. After the officers had completed the annotation, citizens were able to use the Personal Assistant Client to locate services for their particular case.

The results of this step are annotated services and web resources which can be located and automatically combined by software agents in a way that is meaningful to its users. In the case of the Access-eGov, these are WSML-artifacts (documents) which can be directly accessed by software agents through a web-service (e.g., sample of the WSML formalization of life events and web services can be found in Bednár et al. 2008, or Furdik et al. 2008; see also footnote 3 for further reference). Human users will use the Personal Assistant to access the information.

4.4 Processing Information with Semantic Technology

The technical standards and software components that enable the automatic proces-sing of services and service information require an understanding of the semantic technologies available. At the core of automated processing using semantic techno-logies, like the Semantic Web technology stack, lies the definition of standards. A common conceptual model (created in one of the steps described above) should be the starting point to developing a domain-specific standard. The Semantic Web technology stack provides technical standards that can and should be used to implement such domain-specific standards in a machine-readable manner. The use of Semantic Web technology ensures that software components built on this foundation have a level of integration, not only on a technical level but also on a semantic level. By this we mean, that such software components, if properly built, are able to locate, process, and reason upon standards that the developers of these components may not have been aware of.

This step involves two things: (1) using technical standards (like WSMO) to create domain-specific standards from a common conceptual model; (2) using these domain-specific standards to develop new applications or enhance existing applica-tions. The reuse of existing standards should be a main concern during this step.

In the Access-eGov project elements of the WSMO conceptual model (a techni-cal standard for formally representing electronic web services), enhanced and modified for the purposes of the Access-eGov system (see above) to accommodate nonelectronic services also, as well as several existing standards were reused and combined with the categories from the Access-eGov conceptual model. Based on this combined model, ontologies (i.e., formal, machine-readable representations) of life events, service profiles, and domain concepts were developed and implemented using the WSML standard.[9] The resulting ontology was communicated back to the domain experts (in this case the user partners) by rewriting it into the tables of goals and services (Table 2) in order to verify that the formal meaning reflects the informal descriptions in the glossary. This proved to be necessary a couple of times and after several iterations, the meaning of terms and relations was fixed and the formal WSML representation was produced. Other standards (like Dublin Core or vcard) were considered and reused whenever possible.

Within the Access-eGov project, semantic technologies are used to ensure the semantic-based information processing across the developed components as well as in relation to outside components (see Fig. 1). In order to make the asset of annotated services usable for outside operators, the project has followed the suggestion of the Linking Open Data initiative using "linked data" to achieve the goal of publicly available, interlinked data sources. The term "linked data" was coined by Tim Berners-Lee in a note of the same title (Berners-Lee 2006). It can be seen as a recommended good-practice for making data available to Semantic Web applications. The basic idea is to publish data as RDF resources, making these RDF resources available through one or more URLs, thus making the data available for others to read and link to. A community project within the W3C Semantic Web Education and Outreach (SWEO) Interest Group called "Linking Open Data"[10] has taken up the task of creating Linked Data sources using data that is publicly available on the Internet and to promote the creation of Linked Data in general.

The main idea is this: Existing data can be easily republished as Linked Data, as Bizer et al. (2007) have demonstrated by wrapping publicly web services using a straightforward PHP-script. Administrations that publish information or define technical standards should consider reusing information and/or standards that have already been made available using the Linked Data approach. There are two main opportunities for reusing existing Linked Data: (a) linking to "data sets" (i.e., data source), and (b) linking to "data dictionaries" (i.e., standard vocabularies).

Administrations deciding to publish their data and/or their standards using RDF should keep in mind that it is not enough to reuse existing standards by simply mimicking them, as is common practice with XML-based standards. This kind of reuse will not yield the full benefit that RDF can provide. To achieve these benefits the reuse must be made explicit using the means that RDF provides for this purpose. Administrations should also first try to identify what kind of Linked Data has already been published in their domain in order to interlink with those data sources or dictionaries if possible.

The following example describes how the Linked Data approach can be employed: By linking to data sets, an information publisher can make use of existing data sources that provide data about instances of resources. For example, the RDF-Book-Mashup links to the books database of DBLP Berlin to provide meta-data about books without the need to provide this meta-data itself.

---

[9]http://www.wsmo.org/wsml/index.html.

[10]http://esw.w3.org/topic/SweoIG/TaskForces/CommunityProjects/LinkingOpenData.

By linking to data dictionaries a publisher annotates their own data in order to make explicit what the semantics of this data are. For example, if a publisher wants to create a Linked Data of a controlled vocabulary, then she could use (i.e., link to) the SKOS standard[11] which is currently being finalized by the W3C. In both cases, the Linked Data needs to be made available to Semantic Web agents. Usually this can be achieved by making the Linked Data accessible through the administration home-page (using GRDDL[12]).

The key benefit for information consumers (humans and machines) of Linked Data lies in the links between data sets as well as dictionaries. Only by linking to other Linked Data sources, will Semantic Web applications be able to make best use of the published data. The Access-eGov project also investigated how the service information might be made available as Linked Data. A first attempt was to gather all the information available as a single resource as is. While this was easy to implement, the practical benefit was arguably small: to access a single piece of information an information consumer would have to download all the information and then perform a search on that information. A better solution would be to break the information into smaller pieces that can be accessed as resources through multiple URLs and / or to provide a SPARQL[13] end-point that can be easily queried by RDF-enabled information consumers.[14]

4.5   Build and Maintain IT Infrastructure

In all cases the interoperability infrastructure must serve the triangle of service provider, service requester, and service registry. In order to enable any service requester to find an appropriate service provider to interact with, it needs a more or less elaborated centralized entity which allows providers to announce their services and the requester to look for a match to their needs.

If, ideally, all standards that are newly developed during the previous step are fully mapped to the existing domain-specific standards of the Semantic Web, all stakeholders will benefit most because they can also reuse the software components that are able to automatically perform semantic-based processing. A few such software components that are already available are, for example, generic RDF browsers which can be used to explore arbitrary RDF-data, or automatic reasoners,

---

[11]SKOS – Simple Knowledge Organization System – provides a model for expressing the basic structure and content of concept schemes such as thesauri, classification schemes, subject heading lists, taxonomies, folksonomies, and other similar types of controlled vocabulary (see http://www.w3.org/TR/skos-primer).

[12]http://www.w3.org/2001/sw/grddl-wg/.

[13]SPARQL is a query language for RDF and stands for "SPARQL Protocol and Query Language". See http://www.w3.org/TR/rdf-sparql-query/.

[14]Due to limited resources this solution was not implemented during the course of the project.

which exploit the formal meaning of RDF- and OWL-links; however, Semantic Web software agents that can easily be used by the average user are still missing.

Meanwhile, administrations need to provide their own systems and user interfaces for citizens to use, in the case of Access-eGov, the essential components are the Annotation Tool, the Access-eGov Core (including the service registry), and the Personal Assistant Client.

4.6 Creating Take-up

The benefit of Semantic Web applications greatly depends on the amount of data and services that are published using Semantic Web standards. In the future, Semantic Web search engines and agents will be able to locate and process all available information that has been semantically annotated. However, current search engines are limited and do not process all available semantic information. In the absence of widely used Semantic Web search engines, administrations need to take actions to facilitate take-up of the information being made available by them. They should use technical means (like the aforementioned GRDDL), but they might also want to inform relevant actors in the Semantic Web community, like the Linking Open Data project (see above), when they make data with wider relevance available to the Semantic Web.

On the side of service consumers, i.e., mainly citizens and business users, attractive and intuitive user interfaces are needed to foster take-up and acceptance. Access-eGov provides the Personal Assistant Client (see Fig. 3) as a tool

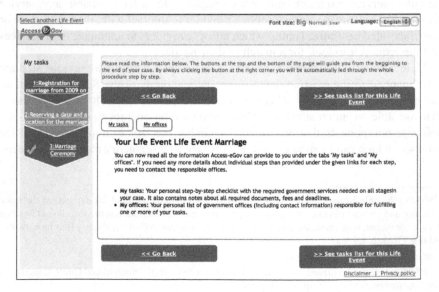

Fig. 3 Personal assistant client, user interface. Browsing the marriage life event

for browsing, discovery, and execution capabilities of services according to the specified life event or goal.

The Personal Assistant can be deployed as part of an Access-eGov installation to allow access to the service information inside the Access-eGov Core component. The Personal Assistant is a web-based application that communicates with the Core component to make information available to citizens and business users. It is not an independent, general purpose Semantic Web agent (because it still relies on the Access-eGov infrastructure for much of the processing), but it can be provided to citizens and business users to take advantage of Access-eGov's semantic technology. In this sense, it can be regarded as a citizen user interface for the Access-eGov platform. The Personal Assistant has been successfully tested in two field tests to verify that:

- Information quality meets the requirements of its consumer
- The information is provided in such units in the semantic mark-up component that it can be displayed in a sufficiently structured manner
- The used information is correct from the service providers' point of view

The Personal Assistant was evaluated by a workshop with public authorities, as well as so-called "think aloud" sessions for usability testing and an online questionnaire, both aimed at citizens. With the online questionnaire, system users were asked to assess the system's information quality aspects, i.e., relevance and comprehensibility of the information, speed, structure, and layout of the website, as well as its navigation and usability in general. The aim of the "think aloud" sessions was to find out whether the tool could support users in the specific life situation to manage the life event, to identify the required steps, the involved offices, and to find out what traditional or electronic services these offer, i.e., to compose the different services in such a manner that it could be understood by citizens. In the workshop for the evaluation, administration workers (service providers and Internet authors) were asked to discuss the Personal Assistant among each other. The results of the discussions were then collected and ordered according to priority from the participants' point of view.

These tests and the workshop resulted in a set of new requirements and change requests regarding usability of the system. With respect to the provided information and its structuring, citizens found that the descriptions were in some cases too long and not sufficiently structured. It seems that the textual descriptions of concepts in the ontology need to be adapted to a greater extent to a hypertext environment, i.e., as short texts with links to additional information instead of one long text. Furthermore, the usage of administrative terminology in the interface proved to lead to misunderstandings in a few cases; the problematic terms were identified and were adapted to common language. Only few changes were required to ensure the correctness of the provided information from the service providers' point of view.

To summarize, the feedback from citizens and administration officers suggests that the main areas that require improvement are usability aspects of the respective user interfaces. The collected data shows no indication that the implemented ontology and the underlying conceptual model have any defects. Thus the current

Personal Assistant component may serve as a starting point for administrations and IT providers to develop new and different Semantic Web applications.

4.7   Finding Partners and Building Networks

Semantic technology is still a mystery to most, both to administrations on all levels and to their IT-service providers. It is far from being commonplace technology. Therefore, it is not an easy task to find partners who are willing to tackle the seemingly overwhelming effort of transitioning to the Semantic Web. Administrations who want to take a step forward into the Semantic Web are even likely to face some resistance. However, administrations willing to take-up this effort do need partners on several levels:

(1) Domain-specific standards yield a much higher benefit if there is consensus across a wide range of stakeholders. This is true for any standard, but because the Semantic Web is built on and around machine-readable standards that were created for the purpose of interoperability, the benefit of a wide adoption of Semantic Web standards will be much higher. Today's web standards (mainly http, HTML, and XML) have been *universally* adopted and this has brought enormous benefits. Semantic Web standards should simply be seen as the next step, with even greater potential. Any PA using these standards is well advised to keep in touch with the working groups on regional, national, or international levels in order to follow up the latest advancements and/or get involved to put forward its own concepts. Schleswig-Holstein, for example, participates in a national working group which recently has issued the list of services for all of Germany ("LeiKa").

(2) Aside from standardization efforts, administrations will need to rely on IT providers to provide them with systems and infrastructure for the Semantic Web. While the Semantic Web does not require any changes to the hardware, existing software systems will need to upgraded or replaced. This requires know–how of semantic technologies and their application which is not very common among IT staff today. However, as increasingly large IT vendors use semantic technologies in their products – not necessarily declaring them as such – this know-how will become more commonplace. In the meantime, administrations should insist and can try to explain the usefulness that these technologies may have for IT providers. Schleswig-Holstein, on the state level, is being served by a large IT-service provider which is also a partner for other German states. For them, the Access-eGov pilot project is of high interest because they will have to serve technology followers in the future.

(3) On the user side there may be more interest in the data that administrations have to offer than one might expect. However, useful and attractive tools for users are still scarce, hindering the take-up as has been described above. Yet, there are pioneer users who are willing to try out new technologies. Users in this sense are not limited to citizens who are looking for services. This can also include IT companies who are providing e-government applications and/or software agents or who are

interested in serving as mediators. Such mediators look for economic ways of exchanging information with multiple stakeholders and therefore are likely to increase the demand for semantic-based information processing. On behalf of the state government, the Access-eGov project has been cooperating with some of these companies being active in Schleswig-Holstein.

(4) As long as the use of semantic technologies is new for the domain, partnership with researchers creates a win–win situation. For administrations this can be an important additional resource if the research institution and the researchers themselves are willing to understand and serve the interest of the administration.

In general, finding partners and maintaining a network should be an agenda by itself: it needs effort in communication, motivation, training, etc. The strategic aims for such a network should include joining forces, establishing long-term working relationships, and exchange of resources – all of which can be very beneficial for all partners.

5   Conclusion: Lessons Learned and Future Work

The Schleswig-Holstein experience shows: transforming information process to the Semantic Web is not an easy task, but it can be done. Although not all steps are yet as efficient and effective as needed for a large-scale application, the overall evaluation reveals that transformation is manageable. This is good news at least for those administrative units which face the challenge of integrating heterogeneous government services provided by geographically and/or hierarchically distributed administration offices. We believe that at least some of these lessons learned can be generalized in the field of e-government as a whole:

- To reduce the cost and to ensure the highest degree of sustainability, PAs are well advised to use available and accepted standards as much as possible; at best those which are provided top-down by the most powerful and accepted actor in the region (usually a national government or even an international agency). If well designed, such standards allow for supplements to be made on lower levels to cover regional or local aspects.
- However, as long as such top-down efforts are not in sight, PAs at lower levels of the hierarchy may seize the opportunity to suggest and share conceptualizations and resources from their point of view: the effort of initial development can easily pay off because the already existing standards on the local level will move bottom-up only to come back top-down later on, i.e., the effort of adaptation can be minimized. Therefore, the investment decision must be made on the basis of an assessment of the e-government community in which it is embedded.
- In any case, PAs are well advised to start small and identify manageable areas for annotation in order to gain experience with manageable effort and costs, preferably within pilot projects.
- The idea of the Semantic Web strengthens the separation of information providers and consumers, but up to now those PAs investing in semantic technologies

also have to take care that the new capabilities are actually being used. This includes the provision of technical components as well as the promotion and strategic alignments with other actors moving in the same direction.

- The importance of the human–computer interface cannot be underestimated as it directly affects the usability of tools and has a significant impact on the user satisfaction and on the efficiency of the entire process. This interface, despite the sophisticated and complex technology behind, needs to be simple and intuitive, and should be in line with the life-event approach. Furthermore, in order to bypass the usability impact, the overall evaluation strategy should be amended by approaches (e.g., an electronic test agent) which do not primarily rely on human user activities and performance.

- Integration of electronic and nonelectronic traditional services (also one important aim of the Access-eGov project) remains a challenge. It seems that on the semantic level the differentiation between traditional and electronic services is necessary, as nonelectronic services need more initial effort for description and explanation in order to enable users to decide and select a proper sequence of services according to their individual preferences.

The field tests and subsequent evaluation also revealed demand for future research, mainly concerning the scalability and efficiency of the transformation approach. The main limitation of these first trials has been the existence of only a few predefined service scenarios (implemented as WSML statements); therefore, it has to be ensured that the overall conceptual model will scale to all kinds of services that administrations have to offer, i.e., that the ontology can be used to represent all government services. This extension implies e.g., the necessity to enrich the functionality of the Annotation Tool which should support creation, customization, and maintenance of all the required service descriptions and complex service scenarios. Furthermore, the modeling of administrative processes needs to be developed in order to enable administrative experts (and not technology experts) to generate templates and business rules for the automatic combination of services based on annotated service descriptions.

Additional research is also necessary to validate that content of legacy systems, which contain (partial) service descriptions that lack semantic annotation, can be integrated as well. Currently, a "content grabber" and a web-service based approach are being investigated as a possible solution to automatically collect relevant service descriptions from annotated web resources and legacy systems.

All in all, the state government of Schleswig-Holstein considers the trial application of the semantic technologies as a successful step toward semantic integration of its e-government services. At the time of writing, dissemination activities are ongoing aiming for continuation of this integration approach, even beyond the state's geographical and electronic borders. While certainly not all PAs are bound to follow this example right away, the experience to share is useful for all stakeholders considering the adoption of semantic technologies now and in the future.

References

P. Bednár, F. Furdik, M. Kleimann, R. Klischewski, M. Skokan, S. Ukena, Semantic integration of eGovernment services in Schleswig-Holstein, Electron. Gov. **2008**, 315–327 (2008)

T. Berners-Lee, Linked Data, www.w3.org/DesignIssues/ LinkedData.html (2006)

T. Berners-Lee, J. Hendler, O. Lassila, The Semantic Web. Sci. Am. **284**(5), 34–43 (2001)

C. Bizer, R. Cyganiak, T. Gauß, The RDF book mashup: from web APIs to a web of data. in *Proceedings of the 3rd Workshop on Scripting for the Semantic Web (SFSW2007)*, Innsbruck, Austria, 6–7 June 2007

C. Crichton, J. Davies, J. Gibbons, S. Harris, A. Shukla, Semantic frameworks for e-government. in *Proceedings of ICEGOV 2007*, Macao, 10–13 December 2007, pp. 30–39

European Communities, *European interoperability framework for pan-European eGovernment services* (IDABC, Luxembourg, 2004) http://europa.eu.int/idabc

J. Farrell, H. Lausen (eds.), Semantic Annotations for WSDL and XML Schema, W3C Candidate Recommendation 26 January 2007, http://www.w3.org/TR/sawsdl/

K. Furdik, J. Hreno, T. Sabol, in *Conceptualisation and Semantic Annotation of eGovernment Services in WSMO*, ed. by V. Snášel. Proceedings of Znalosti (Knowledge) (STU, Bratislava, Slovakia, 2008), pp. 66–77

T. Gill, A.J. Gilliland, M.S. Woodley, Introduction to metadata, Online Edition Version 2.1, http://www.getty.edu/research/conducing_research/standards/intrometadata/. Accessed 25 Jan 2008

S.K. Goudos, V. Peristeras, K. Tarabanis, Mapping citizen profiles to public administration services using ontology implementations of the governance enterprise architecture (GEA) models. in *Proceeding of the Workshop on Semantic Web for eGovernment 2006 at the 3rd European Semantic Web Conference*, Budva, Serbia and Montenegro, 2006, pp. 25–36, http://www.imu.iccs.gr/semgov/final/SemanticWebForEGovernemnt-Proceeding.pdf. Accessed 31 Aug 2008

S. Handschuh, S. Staab, in *Annotation of the Shallow and the Deep Web*, ed. by S. Handschuh, S. Staab. Annotation for the Semantic Web, Frontiers in Artificial Intelligence and Applications, (vol. 96 IOS, Amsterdam, 2003), pp. 25–45

M. Hauswirth, R. Schmidt, M. Altenhofen, C. Drumm, C. Bussler, M. Moran, M. Zaremba, L. Vasiliu, J. Quantz, L. Henocque, A. Haller, B. Sakpota, E. Kilgariff, S. Petkov, D. Aiken, E. Oren, M. Ohlendorf, A. Mocan, *DIP Architecture*. Deliverable 6.2 within the project "Data, Information and Process Integration with Semantic Web Services" (2004), http://dip.semanticweb.org/documents/D6.2-DIP-Architecture.pdf. Accessed 7 Aug 2008

J. Hendler, Agents and the semantic web. IEEE Intell. Syst. **16**(2), 30 (2001)

A. Java, S. Nirenburg, M. McShane, T.W. Finin, J. English, A. Joshi, Using a natural language understanding system to generate semantic web content. Int. J. Semant. Web Inf. Syst. **3**(4), 50–74 (2007)

R. Klischewski, S. Ukena, Test Strategies for Evaluation of Semantic eGovernment Applications, EGOV. Lect. Notes Comput. Sci. **5184**, 291–302 (2008a)

R. Klischewski, S. Ukena, *An activity-based approach towards development and use of E-government service ontologies*. in *HICSS 2008* (2008b), p. 215

H. Kubicek, J. Millard, H. Westholm, Methodology for analysing the relationship between the reorganisation of the back office and better electronic public services. Proceedings of EGOV 2003, Lect. Notes Comput. Sci. **2739**, 199–206 (2003)

H. Lausen, A. Polleres, D. Roman, Web service modeling ontology (WSMO). W3C Member Submission, www.w3.org/Submission/WSMO/ (2005)

K. Lerman, A. Plangprasopchock, C.A. Knoblock, Semantic labeling of online information sources. Int. J. Semantic Web Inform. Syst. **3**(3), 36 (2007)

C. Lupo, C. Batini, A federative approach to laws access by citizens: the 'Normeinrete' system. in *Proceedings of EGOV 2003*, pp. 413–416

D. Martin, M. Burstein, J. Hobbs, O. Lassila, D. McDermott, S. McIlraith, S. Narayanan, M. Paolucci, B. Parsia, T. Payne, E. Sirin, N. Srinivasan, K. Sycara, OWL-S: Semantic markup for web services, W3C Member Submission, http://www.w3.org/Submission/2004/SUBM-OWL-S-20041122/ (2004)

A. Mocan, F. Facca, N. Loutas, V. Peristeras, S.K. Goudos, K. Tarabanis, Solving semantic interoperability conflicts in cross-border E-Government services. Int. J. Semantic Web Inform. Syst. 5(1), 1 (2009)

R. Neches, R. Fikes, T. Finin, T. Gruber, T. Senator, W. Swartout, Enabling technology for knowledge sharing. AI Magazine 12(3), 36–56 (1991)

C. Peltz, Web services orchestration and choreography. Comput. IEEE 36, 46–52 (2003)

V. Peristeras, A. Mocan, T. Vitvar, S. Nazir, S. Goudos, K. Tarabanis, Towards semantic web services for public administration based on the web service modeling ontology (WSMO) and the governance enterprise architecture (GEA). in *Proceedings of the International EGOV'06 Conference*, Electronic Government (Trauner, Sacramento, CA, 2006), pp. 155–162

J.T. Pollock, R. Hodgson, *Adaptive Information: Improving Business through Semantic Interoperability, Grid Computing, and Enterprise Integration* (Wiley, New York, 2004)

E. Tambouris, K.A. Tarabanis, An overview of DC-based e-government metadata standards and initiatives. in Proceedings of EGOV 2004, 40 (2004)

X. Wang, T. Vitvar, V. Peristeras, A. Mocan, S.K. Goudos, K. Tarabanis, WSMO-PA: formal specification of public administration service model on semantic web service ontology. in *Proceedings of HICSS-40* IEEE (2007)

M. Wimmer, E. Tambouris, in *Online One-Stop Government: A Working Framework and Requirements.* ed. by R. Traunmüller. Information Systems: The e-Business Challenge (Kluwer, Boston, 2002) pp. 117–130

Part II

Ontologies and Interoperability

A Semantic Cooperation and Interoperability Platform for the European Chambers of Commerce

Michele Missikoff and Francesco Taglino

1 Introduction

The LD-CAST project aims at developing a semantic cooperation and interoperability platform for the European Chambers of Commerce. Some of the key issues that this platform addresses are:

- The *variety* and *number* of different kinds of resources (i.e., business processes, concrete services) that concur to achieve a business service
- The *diversity* of cultural and procedural models emerging when composing articulated cross-country services
- The limited possibility of reusing similar services in different contexts (for instance, supporting the same service between different countries: an Italian–Romanian cooperation is different from an Italian–Polish one)

The objective of the LD-CAST platform, and in particular of the semantic services provided therein, is to address the above problems with flexible solutions. We aim at introducing high levels of flexibility, both at the time of development of business processes and concrete services (i.e., operational services offered by service providers), with the possibility of dynamically binding c-services to the selected BP, according to user needs. To this end, an approach based on semantic services and a reference ontology has been proposed.

Recently, there has been an acceleration in the use of ontology-based solutions aimed at supporting the cooperation and interoperability among different organizations. Diversities typically lie in the different levels of automation and, when automated, in the characteristics of the information systems having diverging architectures and data format. An ontology-based approach can help in solving the above problems.

M. Missikoff (✉)
National Research Council, Institute of Systems Analysis and Informatics "Antonio Ruberti", Viale Manzoni 30, 00185 Rome, Italy

T. Vitvar et al. (eds.), *Semantic Technologies for E-Government*,
DOI 10.1007/978-3-642-03507-4_6, © Springer-Verlag Berlin Heidelberg 2010

The role of a reference ontology is a central one. In fact, an ontology is "*a formal, explicit specification of a shared conceptualisation*" (Gruber 1993); therefore, it represents:

- The result of a consensus process reached among a group of domain experts (shared conceptualisation), possibly obtained by using focused methods, like a folksonomy, and involving a wider community
- A formal specification, and as such it can be interpreted by a machine

According to that, an ontology is usually adopted:

- At a social level, as a common reference for improving the communication and interoperability among (human or software) members of the same community or of different communities
- At a computational level, for supporting automatic reasoning and *intelligent* querying activities

In the proposed approach we have different components, defined at different levels of abstraction, to achieve a coherent scenario. In particular, we make use of the following notions (see also Fig. 1):

Business Episode. This corresponds to a *user request* (e.g., request a business certificate) that typically falls into a predefined category.

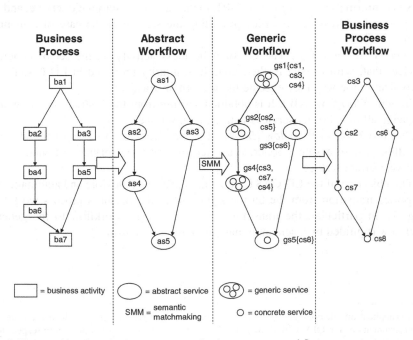

Fig. 1 The transition from business process to business process workflow

Business Process (BP). This is an abstract, generic specification (not yet executable), corresponding to a *Business Episode*. A repository of generic BPs represents the starting point for the flexible composition of the customized workflows.

Abstract Workflow (AW). It is a first level of implementation of a BP. The AW is represented through an executable language, but it is not yet fully executable, since concrete services are not yet referenced here. In general, for each BP there can be more than one abstract workflow (but here we will consider a one-to-one correspondence).

Business Activity (BA). The component of a Business Process.

Abstract Service (AS). The component of an Abstract Workflow. The correspondence between business activities and abstract services is not one to one. For instance, in Fig. 1, the business activities *ba3* and *ba5* are replaced by the only abstract service *as3*.

Semantic Annotation. It is the method adopted to define the semantic specification of an activity. A semantic annotation is built as a vector of concepts selected from the reference ontology. Therefore we refer to it as an ontology-based feature vector[1] (OFV).

Concrete Service (CS). It is an executable service registered by a service provider in the concrete service registry (CSR). A concrete service (CS) can be automatic (e.g., a web service) or manual (e.g., desk services). The stored information is about the name, a natural language description of the service functionality, the service provider, the execution time and price, and where to access the service. This last information is given by an URL in the case of an automatic service, and by the physical address of the office providing the service in the case of a manual service.

Generic Service (GS). The GS of a business activity, is the set of concrete services that, with respect to the semantic similarity proposed in LD-CAST, are equivalent in the way they execute the a given abstract service.

Generic Workflow (GW). It is obtained starting from the abstract workflow and replacing all the abstract services with generic services.

Business Process Workflow (BPW). It is an executable version of the abstract workflow, where a single concrete service of a generic service is bound to the relative abstract service.

The objective of the LD-CAST platform is to allow a flexible and automatically supported transition from the business process to the business process workflow (Fig. 1). In particular, the transition from the abstract workflow to the generic workflow is guided by a semantic matchmaking mechanism.

---

[1]In this application, the components of the OFV are not intended to be ordered. However, ordering the components of the OFV will allow a first level of relevance of the features, with respect to a single OFV to be expressed.

2 The LD-CAST Phased Semantic Approach

The LD-CAST approach is based on 4 main phases: two *setup time* phases and two *run-time* phases, as summarized in the Table 1 and briefly described afterwards.

2.1 Phase 1: Application Resources Set Up

During this first phase the setting up of knowledge resources is performed. The two major activities of this phase are:

(a) *Business processes design (business level)*. BPs are designed by the Chambers of Commerce, with the support of knowledge engineers, by using the ADOe-Gov modeling tool and language (LD-CAST 2006). Corresponding abstract workflows, which are executable code with no attached executable services (concrete services), are also defined. However, for each concrete service to be called, a labeled placeholder is put in the AW as an abstract service.

(b) *Registration of concrete services*. Service providers register concrete services (web services or desk services) in the LD-CAST platform, by filling in pre-defined templates. In particular, information about where each service can be accessed are registered (through the WSDL in the case of a web service and through the physical address in the case of a desk, i.e., manual, service).

2.2 Phase 2: Development of Semantic Contents

During this phase the development of the semantic content repository is performed. The two major activities of this phase are the following (Fig. 2):

(a) *Ontology Creation*. The LD-CAST reference ontology is about the services made available through the involved CoC. It has been built by the Chambers of

Table 1 The four phases of the LD-CAST approach

	Phases	Activities
Setup	(1) Application resources set up	• Business processes modeling
		• Abstract workflow definition
		• Identification and registration of concrete services
	(2) Development of semantic contents	• Ontology creation
		• Semantic annotation of resources
Runtime	(3) Business process work-flow set up	• User's request submission
		• Business process workflow completion
	(4) Business process work-flow (BPW) execution	• Actual BPW execution
		• Monitoring of the actual execution

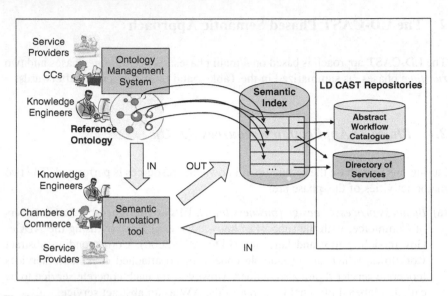

Fig. 2 Development of semantic contents

Commerce, with the support of knowledge engineers, by using the Athos Ontology Management System (ATHENA 2005), based on the OPAL (Object, Process Actor Language) ontology representation method (Missikoff et al. 2007). The ontology is built using a step-wise approach and, in particular, adopting the UPON (Unified Process for ONtology building) methodology (De Nicola et al. 2009).

(b) *Semantic annotation of knowledge resources.* The purpose of the semantic annotation is to associate an ontology-based semantic expression (in our approach an OFV) to an operational resource (i.e., abstract service or concrete service). The objective of this task is to describe all the stored resources in terms of the reference ontology, in order to establish semantic relationships among them.

Summarizing, at the end of the Design Phases we will have the following resources available:

- BP developed by the CoC and abstract workflows
- Registry of the available concrete services to be used to actually execute the AWs
- Ontology of the CoC services
- Semantic indexes consisting in the semantic annotation of concrete services and abstract services (tasks)

Such digital resources will be used in the run-time phases as explained below.

2.3 Phase 3: Business Process Workflow Setup

This phase is triggered by the submission of a request by the end user. The end user
of the LD-CAST platform is someone (e.g., an entrepreneur) who refers to a CoC to
achieve a business service. A user request is matched by a BP. Starting from the
selected BP, the platform identifies the corresponding AW and searches for the
required concrete services for transforming the AW into an executable BPW (see
Fig. 3). This phase is articulated into the following steps.

(a) *User's request submission and business episode selection.* A user submits a
    request asking for a business service corresponding to one of the registered
    business processes.
(b) *Semantic search and discovery for business process workflow completion.* For
    each BP a corresponding abstract workflow has been previously implemented.
    In essence, an abstract workflow represents the control flow, with the sequenc-
    ing of operations but without concrete implementations of the required activ-
    ities (i.e., concrete services), therefore a business process workflow (BPW)
    completion is necessary. We refer to BPW completion as the dynamic binding
    of a business process to concrete services that makes the former executable by a
    workflow engine (see Fig. 4). This BPW completion is supported by a semantic
    similarity matchmaking mechanism that, reasoning on the ontology and using
    the semantic annotation performed on concrete services and abstract services,
    identifies the most suitable concrete services (automatic or manual) able to
    perform the abstract services of an AW. In particular, the application of the
    semantic matchmaking determines the identification of the generic workflow,
    where each abstract service is replaced by a generic service, which is a set of
    concrete service. All the concrete services of a generic service are intended to
    be semantically equivalent and then suitable to be bound to the corresponding
    abstract service. The further selection of a single concrete service from each
    generic service, by using non functional criteria (like for instance execution

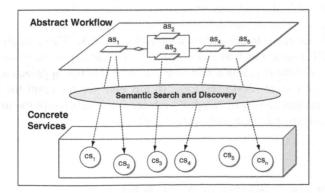

Fig. 3 Binding of concrete services

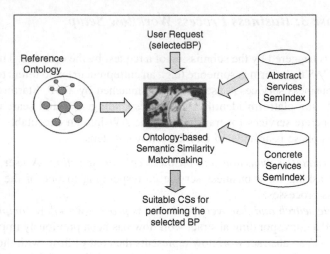

Reference
Ontology

User Request
(selectedBP)

Abstract
Services
SemIndex

Ontology-based
Semantic Similarity
Matchmaking

Concrete
Services
SemIndex

Suitable CSs for
performing the
selected BP

Fig. 4 Semantic search and discovery of concrete services

time and price of the services) will allow the final generation of the BPW that is
fully executable.

(c) *Business process workflow release to the LD-CAST workflow engine.* After the
binding of concrete services to the abstract services, the complete business
process workflow is ready for being executed by the LD-CAST process execution engine.

2.4 Phase 4: Business Process Workflow Execution

This phase concerns the actual execution and monitoring of the business process
workflow. The activities indicated in the AW will be implemented by the concrete
services selected in the previous phase.

An abstract workflow, and the corresponding final BPW, is represented by using
an executable language to this end we adopted BPEL4WS.[2] Then, the BPEL code is
fed to a BPEL engine (such as Active BPEL[3]) for the actual execution, including
the invocation of the concrete services. Please note that this approach accepts also
the binding to manual (desk) services. To this end, we represent the latter with
proxy web services (a sort of "empty" web service) that prompt the users for the
actual execution of the requested manual operations.

---

[2]http://www.ibm.com/developerworks/library/specification/ws-bpel/
[3]http://sourceforge.net/projects/activebpel

2.5   Summarizing the Role of the LD-CAST Ontology

In Fig. 5 a representation of the semantic streamline of the LD-CAST platform is outlined. The figure is mainly to highlight the position and the role of the semantics-based components into the LD-CAST approach. For this purpose, the semantics-based components are bold rounded, to be easily distinguished, while the other components of the LD-CAST platform are not fully represented. The picture focuses on the semantics-based components, their interactions and how they concur to the LD-CAST platform and solution. According to the previous section, the picture is divided into Design Time and Run Time, and the different software components are positioned accordingly.

- *Athos* is the ontology management system which provides support for the ontology construction. Athos is based on the OPAL (Missikoff et al. 2007) ontological framework for the knowledge representation. We wish to recall that the LD-Cast ontology has been developed by applying the ontology engineering method UPON (De Nicola et al. 2009).
- *Semantic Annotation Environment* provides the support for semantically annotate the Business Processes (more precisely, the activities composing them) and the concrete services that are registered and made available to the LD-CAST platform. Such components acquire the ontology from Athos, and the abstract services and concrete services from their respective repositories. Finally, the defined semantic annotation expressions are stored as semantic

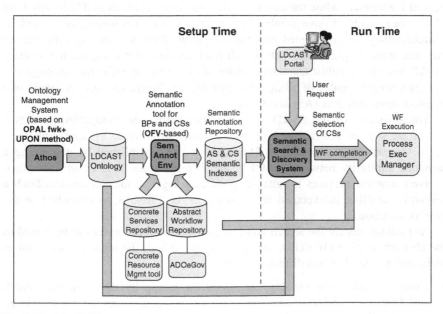

Fig. 5 The LD-CAST semantic streamline

indexes. Semantic annotation expressions in LD-CAST are represented by Ontology-based Feature Vectors (OFV) (Missikoff et al. 2008). An OFV consists of a set of concepts from the ontology that characterize a given resource, which can be a concrete services or an abstract service. From the semantic point of view, the setup phase produces the following two main artifacts: the reference ontology and the semantic annotation of abstract services and concrete services.

- *Semantic Search and Discovery System (SS&DS)* provides a semantics-based support to search and retrieval of concrete services suitable for making the selected business process executable. The selection of the business process (and consequently of the corresponding abstract workflow) triggers the SS&DS. Then the SS&DS searches for the concrete services suitable to be bound to the abstract services composing the abstract workflow. This search is performed through a semantic similarity matchmaking mechanism, which accesses and uses the semantic resources previously built (the reference ontology and the semantic annotations).

As briefly recapped above, the ontology is a key component of the LD-CAST approach and it plays an important role both at the setup and runtime. At setup time, it is used for the semantic annotation of the abstract services composing the abstract workflow and the concrete services. This is a very crucial step since it allows semantic correspondences between the abstract services, which identify what has to be done (i.e., *submitting the request for a fiscal verification*), and the concrete services, which represent actual available implementations be established. BPs, which are the specifications for the abstract workflows, are modeled by the Chambers of Commerce, while the concrete services can be made available by any kind of service provider. Consequently, their descriptions are not homogeneous and, in principle, they are not aligned with the definition of the activities specified in the BP, and more in particular with the abstract services that compose the abstract workflows. The semantic annotation addresses this issue by using the ontology as a semantic bridge capable of filling (large part of) the divergences between these two heterogeneous artifacts (ASs and CSs).

The objective of the SS&D service is to identify the compatibility of two resources, say an abstract service and a concrete service, by analyzing their respective semantic annotations. The analysis is accomplished by computing a semantic similarity between the OFV, and it returns the measure of how much a given concrete services is suitable to execute a given abstract service. Such a semantic coupling is executed at run-time, in the Phase 3, as described in the previous section.

At runtime, during the search and retrieval of concrete services to be bound to the abstract services (Workflow completion), the role of the ontology is crucial as well, and it is used at two different levels:

- *Explicitly*: when the ontology is directly accessed by the Semantic Search and Discovery (SS&D) component for querying its semantic content (e.g., Specialization/Generalization hierarchies, concept weight).

- *Implicitly*: when the ontology-based semantic annotation expressions, built in terms of the reference ontology, are used by the Semantic Search and Discovery subsystem, for coupling abstract services and concrete services.

In LD-CAST, the original method for semantic annotation has been developed, referred to as Ontology-based Feature Vectors. This method will be presented in details in Sect. 3.

3   OFV-Based Annotation in LD-CAST

Semantic annotation is a technique used to describe the meaning of a digital resource by using a reference ontology. This technique is attracting attention for its great potentiality in the Semantic Web (Berners-Lee et al. 2001).

Among typical applications of semantic annotation, we can find:

- *Semantic retrieval*, i.e., the possibility of retrieving digital resources (not only documents) on the basis of their semantic content. This service is at the basis of the following, more specific applications
- *Document management*, for the semantics-based organization and retrieval of digital documents
- *Knowledge management*, for organization and retrieval of enterprise knowledge
- *Web services publishing and discovery*, with semantic matchmaking of requested and offered services
- *Semantic interoperability*, by annotating local resources (information and processes) to support business cooperation among enterprise software applications

In the LD-CAST approach, semantic annotation is at the basis of the semantic search and retrieval of digital resources. In particular, the semantic search is here used to select concrete services suitable for making abstract workflows fully executable.

When we analyzed the possible alternatives in representing a semantic annotation, we considered the following issues:

- *Kind of annotated resources*: i.e., unstructured documents (e.g., textual documents), structured documents (e.g., data schemas), any type of model, web services. In LD-CAST, the annotation process focuses on the annotation of abstract services, and service implementations (human or automatic).
- *Type of user*: human oriented or machine oriented annotation; in LD-CAST, the annotation is mainly for machine oriented consumption, since it is used to support an automatic matchmaking algorithm.
- *Level of formality*: in general, annotations may vary from informal, by using (controlled) natural language, to structured, by using tables and diagrams, to formal, by using formal language-based expressions. In LD-CAST, the annotation is structured as it is represented as Ontology-based Feature Vectors.
- *Terminology restriction*: here there are at least three alternatives: absence (no restriction); mandatory (fully controlled terminology); advised (suggested, but

not mandatory). In the LD-CAST approach, the terminology restriction is mandatory, since the annotation is fully restricted by the terms used in the ontology.

- *Positioning*: embedded to the annotated resource (it needs to modify the original resource); attached (stored in a separated repository). In LD-CAST, an attached approach, through the definition of semantic indexes, has been followed since it is less intrusive with respect to the original resource.

The semantic annotation method used in LD-CAST is based on the usage of OFV. Essentially, an OFV is composed by concepts from the ontology, each concurring to characterize the annotated digital resource. More in general, in such an approach, features vectors are also used to represent requests from the user searching for digital resources. Even if the structure is the same, to avoid confusion, we will refer to it as a *request feature vector* (RFV). A RFV is very similar to the popular way used when searching with Google, where a list of terms is defined. The main difference here is that the RFV cannot use any set of terms, but it is restricted to the labels of the concepts in the ontology.

In LD-CAST, we annotate both concrete services and abstract services, for automatically supporting the workflow completion.

When coupling concrete services to abstract services, three main scenarios have been identified (see Fig. 6). Each scenario is characterized by a different degree of usage of the ontology, which depends on the existing relationships and dependencies among the ontology, the abstract workflows (but also the business processes) and the concrete services:

- *Trivial*: concrete services and abstract services are strictly related; there is a one-to-one matching between CSs and ASs. In this scenario, there is no need of semantic annotation or probably the semantic annotation is trivial: $|ofv_{as}|=1$ and $|ofv_{cs}|=1$, where ofv_{ba} and ofv_{cs} are the OFV for *as* and *cs*, respectively an abstract service and a concrete service.
- *Simple*: there is a one-to-one correspondence between *as* and a concept in the ontology, since the construction of the ontology has been influenced by the BPs definition. Conversely, the CSs have been defined independently. In this case we have $|ofv_{as}|=1$ and $|ofv_{cs}|=n$. Essentially, it means that, in general, there is not only one concept catching the entire semantics of a given concrete service.
- *Full*: ASs and CSs are independently built and both of them are independent with respect to the ontology. In this case we have $|ofv_{as}|=n$ and $|ofv_{cs}|=m$.

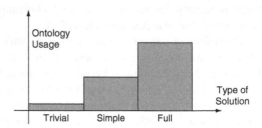

Fig. 6 Ontology usage levels

In the LD-CAST project, we decided to implement the *Simple* case, since it mainly reflects the scenario of the project itself where the construction of the ontology is strongly influenced by the modeled BPs.

Another important feature of the proposed method is represented by the use of a *Weighted Reference Ontology* (WRO), containing the relevant concepts in the given domain. Here, we wish to recall the definition of an ontology, taken from OMG Ontology Definition Metamodel (DSTC 2005):

> An ontology defines the common terms and concepts (meaning) used to describe and represent an area of knowledge. An ontology can range in expressivity from a Taxonomy (knowledge with minimal hierarchy or a parent/child structure), to a Thesaurus (words and synonyms), to a Conceptual Model (with more complex knowledge), to a Logical Theory (with very rich, complex, consistent and meaningful knowledge).

We restrict our view of the ontology to a taxonomy of concepts. This simplified view in our proposal is enriched with a weight, associated with each concept, representing its *featuring power*, which indicates how much such a concept is selective in characterizing the available digital resources. In accordance with the Information Theory (Shannon 1948) a concept weight will be used to determine the (relative) information content of the concept itself. A high weight corresponds to a low selectivity level, meaning that many resources are characterized by the concept. Conversely, a low weight corresponds to a high selectivity, and therefore its use in a request will be more significant.

4   The Weighted Reference Ontology

As anticipated in the previous section, the proposed method is based on a Weighted Reference Ontology, where each concept is enriched with a weight.

The way of associating such weights derives from the structure of the specialization hierarchy and follows a top down approach: the weights are assigned starting from the root of the hierarchy.

In order to have a unique top concept in the specialization hierarchy, *Thing* is added as the root of the hierarchy. *Thing* represents the most general concept in the ontology. Whatever is the specialization hierarchy, *w(Thing)* will always be equal to 1.

As weighting strategy, we adopted a uniform distribution.[4] Therefore, given a concept c_x, having weight equal to $w(c_x)$, the weight of each of the child c of c_x, $w(c)$, is

$$w(c) = w(c_x)/|children(c_x)|$$

---

[4]We are currently analyzing possible other ways of assigning weights to the concepts of the ontology. For instance, considering the relative frequency of each concept with respect to the built OFVs.

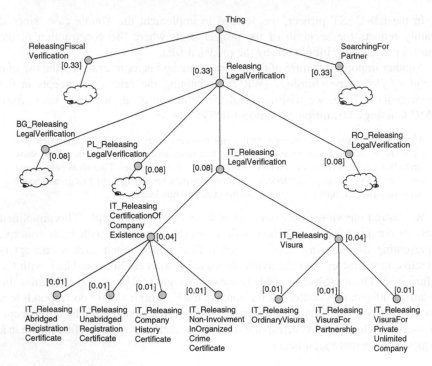

Fig. 7 A fragment of the LD-CAST weighted reference ontology

For instance, consider Fig. 7, assumed that $w(Thing) = 1$, therefore

$$w(ReleasingFiscalVerification) = 1/3,$$

$$w(ReleasingLegalalVerification) = 1/3, and$$

$$w(SearchingForPartners) = 1/3.$$

The rationale behind the presented method for the assignment of the weights is that the weight of a concept expresses how frequently a concept appears in (characterizing) the available digital resources or in other words, the probability of the concept to annotate a resource. For this reason, the leaves in the taxonomy, which represent very specific concepts, are assumed to have the lowest weight (and therefore the highest selectivity factor). For instance, with respect to Fig. 7, there will be a higher probability to annotate a concrete service *cs* with the generic concept *ReleasingLegalVerification*, than to annotate *cs* with *ReleasingOfNon-InvolvmentInOrganizedCrimeCertificate* that is a more specific activity.

In particular, Fig. 7 shows an excerpt of the LD-CAST WRO. This WRO is about three kinds of business services, Legal Verification, Fiscal Verification and

Search for Partners. Furthermore, the WRO describes these three business services for the four countries involved in the project i.e., Bulgaria, Italy, Poland and Romania. The excerpt mainly shows the part of the WRO concerning the Italian Legal Verification.

5 Semantic Search and Discovery in LD-CAST

The role of the Semantic Search and Discovery in LD-CAST is to identify, through a semantic matchmaking mechanism, the concrete services that are suitable for performing the abstract services composing an abstract workflow. This will allow the completion of the abstract workflow into an executable representation via the binding of concrete services.

Since there can be more than one concrete service *cs* suitable for a given abstract service *as*, the semantic search will return, for each *as*, a set of CSs represent a generic service.

Essentially, a Generic Service (GS) is a class of equivalence of concrete services with respect to the semantics of the corresponding *as*.

The fact that for each abstract service there will be a corresponding GS means that, given an abstract workflow *aw*, more than one combination of CSs can be suitable for performing *aw*. The selection of only one out of them is out of the scope of the semantic search. In fact, from a semantic point of view, all the CSs of a GS are considered equivalent.

5.1 The Semantic Matchmaking Mechanism

The Semantic Matchmaking mechanism is based on the identification of a similarity degree between an AS and each CS in order to identify the corresponding GS. All the CSs having a similarity degree equal or higher to a fixed threshold will be in the GS of the considered AS. The semantic matchmaking works on the semantic annotation previously associated to the ASs and the CSs.

The matchmaking mechanism proposed in this approach is based on a semantic similarity technique (Maguitman et al. 2005). A brief comment on the added value of a search mechanism based on semantic techniques and a similarity measure is here reported.

5.1.1 "Semantic Search" Vs. "Keyword-Based Search"

Commonly used search engines are based on string matching techniques. Even if they can be highly sophisticated (i.e., Google) they are only able to compare keywords and finding a match among them. Semantic search techniques, supported by the use of a reference ontology, aim to go beyond keyword-based search. In fact, an ontology defines concepts that are defined not only by labels, but especially by semantic relationships (i.e., specialization/generalization) which can be consequently exploited during the search activities. For instance, considering the fragment of the LD-CAST ontology reported in Fig. 7, we have that the *IT_ReleasingVisura* and the *IT_ReleasingCertificateOfCompanyExistence* concepts are two specializations of the *IT_ReleasingDocumentofCompanyExistence* concept. This means that whenever we are searching for a document about the existence of a given Italian company, we can use a service previously annotated with either a *IT_ReleasingVisura* or a *IT_ReleasingCertificateOfCompanyExistence* since both are specialization of *IT_ReleasingDocumentofCompanyExistence* process.

Please note that, in closed environments, even if very wide, like the LD-CAST community is, such an approach is much more usable than in very open and very heterogeneous environments like Internet is.

5.1.2 "Similarity Matching" Vs. "Exact Matching"

Exclusive exact matching algorithms allow to retrieve only resources that fully match the user request. Nevertheless, partial results can be better than no results and give greater flexibility to the user. In the LD-CAST proposed method, a similarity matchmaking has been introduced which is able to evaluate a similarity measure of available services with respect to the request. The tolerance of the method is defined by a threshold fixed by the user. If for a given resource, the similarity is above a fixed threshold, the resources are retrieved as a satisfying result.

5.2 The Semantic Matchmaking Algorithm

Given a WRO, the notion of similarity here adopted relies on the probabilistic approach defined by Lin (Lin et al. 1998), which is based on the notion of information content and entropy. According to the standard argumentation of information theory, the information content of a concept c_x is defined as:

$$- \ln w(c_x)$$

that is, as the weight of a concept increases the informativeness decreases, therefore the more abstract a concept the lower its information content is. In fact, the weights decrease from the top to the bottom of the specialization hierarchy and whatever is c_x, $0 \leq w(c_x) \leq 1$, we have that $\ln(w(c_x))$, the natural logarithm of $w(c_x)$, has an inverse behavior in the sense that it decreases from the bottom to the top. Essentially, since a leaf is a very specific concept, annotating a resource with a leaf, is considered more relevant than annotating a resource with a more general concept. Finally, $\ln(w(Thing)) = 0$ because *Thing* is the top of the specialization hierarchy and its informative content is null.

Given two concepts c_x and c_y, their concept similarity $consim(c_x,c_y)$, is defined as the maximum information content shared by the concepts divided by the information content of the two concepts (Jaccard 1901). Formally, since we assumed that the taxonomy is a tree, the *least upper bound* (*lub*) of c_x and c_y, $lub(c_x,c_y)$, is always unique and defined and provides the maximum information content shared by the concepts. Therefore, *consim* is the similarity function between concepts, based on the Lin (Lin et al. 1998) similarity. Let be c_x and c_y two concepts[5]

$$consim(c_x,c_y).= 2*ln(w(lub(c_x,c_y)))/(ln(w(c_x))+ln(w(c_y)))$$

Then, whatever are c_x and c_y, $0 \leq consim(c_x,c_y) \leq 1$.

The semantic matchmaking algorithm assumes that the semantic annotations of ASs and CSs have been already performed and in particular, according to the *Simple* scenario:

- Each abstract service *as* is annotated with only one concept ($/ofv_{as}/=1$);
- Each concrete service *cs* can be annotated with more than one concept from the ontology ($/ofv_{cs}/=n$).

The Semantic Matchmaking algorithm assumes that:

- $w(c_x)$ is the weight associated to the concept c_x;
- $ln(w(c_x))$ is the natural logarithm of the weight of c_x;
- $lub(c_x,c_y)$ is the least upper bound between c_x and c_y with respect to the specialization/generalization hierarchy, that is the nearest common ancestor of both c_x and c_y. For instance, with respect to Fig. 1 the least upper bound of *IT_ReleasingAbridgedRegistrationCertificate* and *IT_ReleasingOrdinaryVisura* is *IT_ReleasingLegalVerification;*
- *semsim* is the similarity function that calculates the similarity degree between an AS and a CS. The *semsim* function refers to the semantic annotation of the ASs and the CSs.

Let as_n be an abstract service with $ofv_{asn}=\{c_j\}$
Let cs_m and ofv_{csm} be respectively a concrete service and its OFV, with $/ofv_{csm}/= k$

$$semsim(as_n,cs_m) = semsim(ofv_{asn},ofv_{csm}).$$

Whatever ba_n and cs_m are, $0 \leq semsim(ba_n, cs_m) \leq 1$.
In particular, since with respect to the three scenarios of Sect. 3 we claimed to address the *Simple* one, ofv_{asn} is composed by only one concept c_j, the *semsim* function is calculated by evaluating the average value of the similarity degree between c_j and each concept in the ofv_{csm}

$$semsim(ofv_{asn},ofv_{csm}) = (\sum consim(c_j, ofv_{csm[i]}))/k \text{ with } i = 1...k$$

Now, assuming a business process with two business activities about the verification of the legal and fiscal status of an Italian company (Fig. 8), and the

---

[5]Note that the algebraic sign can be omitted in such rational expression

Fig. 8 An example of business process

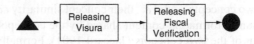

Table 2 Weight of concepts in the ontology

c	w(c)
Thing	1
ReleasingFiscalVerification	0.33
ReleasingLegalVerification	0.33
SearchingForPartner	0.33
BG_ReleasingLegalVerification	0.08
PL_ReleasingLegalVerification	0.08
RO_ReleasingLegalVerification	0.08
IT_ReleasingLegalVerification	0.08
IT_ReleasingCertificateOfCompanyExistence	0.04
IT_ReleasingVisura	0.04
IT_ReleasingAbridgedRegistrationCertificate	0.01
IT_ReleasingUnabridgedRegistrationCertificate	0.01
IT_ReleasingCompanyHistoryCertificate	0.01
IT_ReleasingOrdinaryVisura	0.02
IT_ReleasingVisuraForPartnership	0.02

corresponding AW with two abstract services with the same labels, and the fragment of the ontology in Fig. 7, we annotate the abstract service *ReleasingVisura* with the concept *IT_ReleasingVisura*. According to that, the OFV annotating the abstract service is:

$$ofv_{RLV} = [IT\_ReleasingVisura]$$

On the other hand, we here provide the annotation of 4 concrete services, *cs1*, *cs2*, *cs3* and *cs4*.

$$ofv_{cs1} = [IT\_ReleasingOrdinaryVisura,$$
$$IT\_ReleasingCompanyHistoryCertificate]$$
$$ofv_{cs2} = [IT\_ReleasingLegalVerification,$$
$$BG\_ReleasingLegalVerification]$$
$$ofv_{cs3} = [IT\_ReleasingOrdinaryVisura,$$
$$IT\_ReleasingVisuraForPartnership]$$
$$ofv_{cs4} = [IT\_ReleasingAbridgedRegistrationCertificate]$$

According to Fig. 7 we have the following weight for each concept *c* (Table 2).

Now, the *consim* function between *IT_ReleasingLegalVerification*, which is the only concept in ofv_{RLV}, the OFV annotating *the ReleasingLegalVerification* abstract service, and any concept *c* belonging to at least one OFV annotating a concrete service, is computed (Table 3).

Finally, the *semsim* function between ofv_{RLV} and the OFV relative to the CSs is computed (Table 4).

Furthermore, assuming that the threshold has been fixed at 0.65 (shown by the horizontal dashed line in Table 4), we have that the resulting GS for the abstract

Table 3 Consim values between c_3 and all the other concept c in an ofv

c	Consim ($IT\_ReleasingVisura$, c)
$IT\_ReleasingOrdinaryVisura$	0.90
$IT\_ReleasingCompanyHistoryCertificate$	0.64
$IT\_ReleasingLegalVerification$	0.88
$BG\_ReleasingLegalVerification$	0.39
$IT\_ReleasingVisuraForPartnership$	0.90
$IT\_ReleasingAbridgedRegistrationCertificate$	0.64

Table 4 Ordered *semsim* values between ofv_{RLV} and each ofv_{cs}	ofv_{cs}	semsim(ofv_{RLV}, ofv_{cs})
	ofv_{cs3}	0.90
	ofv_{cs1}	0.77
	ofv_{cs2}	0.68
	ofv_{cs4}	0.64

service *ReleasingVisura* is composed by three concrete services: cs_3, cs_1, and cs_2 that have a *semsim* degree equal to 0.90, 0.77 and 0.68, respectively.

$GS(ReleasingVisura) = \{cs_3, cs_1, cs_2\}$

This means that any concrete service in the GS is a proper concrete service for executing the *ReleasingVisura* abstract service.

Once the GS for the other abstract service, *Releasing Fiscal Verification*, has been identified, the final BPW, which is the actual executable workflow, is obtained by selecting one single CS from each GS and binding it to the corresponding abstract service. This last selection can be seen by the end user considering for instance the execution time and price of the concrete services.

6   Related Works

The main innovations in the use of semantic technologies in LD-Cast are represented by the semantic enrichment of the business process and its components and the semantic search and discovery method used to identify the services that are necessary to realize the business process. Accordingly, this section is organized in two subsections.

6.1   *A Semantic Approach to Web Services and Business Processes*

Semantic description of digital resources and web services, in particular, is one of the key issues of the semantic web activities. Several initiatives are addressing this field. In particular, among the most relevant we recall here WSMO, OWL-S, WSDL-S.

WSMO (Roman et al. 2006) defines an overall framework for Semantic Web Services consisting of four top level elements: Ontologies that provide the semantic terminology definitions used in all other element description as well as for the information interchanged in Web Service Usage, Goals for representing the objective that a client wants to achieve by using Web Services, semantic description of Web Services, and Mediators for resolving possibly occurring mismatches between elements that should interoperate.

OWL-S (Web Ontology Language for Web Services), part of the DAML Program, specifies a set of ontologies based on OWL to describe different aspects of a semantic Web service. There are three core ontologies, i.e., service profile, service model and grounding. Service profile presents "what a service does"; service model describes "how a service works"; service grounding supports "how to access it" via detailed specifications of message formats, protocols and so forth (normally expressed in WSDL). All the three ontologies are linked to the top-level concept Service, which serves as an organization point of reference for declaring Web services.

WSDL-S (Web Service Description Language-Semantics) (Akkiraju et al. 2005), developed by the Meteor-S group at the LSDIS Lab, proposes a mechanism to augment WSDL with semantics, in particular focusing on the services' functional descriptions. Based on the WSDL, WSDL-S has the advantage of attaching semantics building on existing Web services; in the meantime, it does not dictate a specific language for semantic description.

Among the previous initiatives, WSMO seems to be the most complete. In fact, its four top level elements represent the core building blocks for Semantic Web Service enabled systems. Nevertheless, the WSMO philosophy is towards a substitution of the current technologies and not for an integration of them. From this point of view, the Semantic approach defined in LD-CAST is more for a semantic enrichment of existing resources and does not impose any constraint on the technologies to be used for defining business processes, workflows or services.

6.2   Similarity Searching Algorithms

The problem of similarity reasoning has been widely addressed in the literature. The first problem concerns the similarity between pairs of concepts. Some methods to determine semantic similarity in a taxonomy are based on the so-called edge-counting approach (Rada et al. 1989) – that is, the shorter the path between nodes, the more similar the concepts associated with the nodes are. Unfortunately, this approach relies on the assumption that links in the taxonomy represent uniform distances that, in general, is not conform to the reality. For this reason, the approach based on the notion of information content has been proposed in the literature (Resnik 1995), which is independent of the path lengths of the hierarchy. Such an approach has been successively refined in (Lin et al. 1998), where a similarity measure showing a higher correlation with human judgments has been defined.

Other research results concern the similarity between two sets (or vectors) of concepts (Madhavan and Halevy 2003). In the literature the Dice (Frakes and Baeza-Yates 1992; Maarek et al. 1991) and Jaccard (1901) methods are often adopted in order to compare vectors of concepts. However, in both Dice and Jaccard, the concept of similarity is based on the set theoretic intersection and union of the two vectors. Therefore, the adoption of the mentioned approaches requires the exact match of the concepts of the compared vectors. With respect to Dice and Jaccard, our proposal allows a refinement of semantic similarity since the match of OFV components is based on the shared information content.

Finally, several methods for computing semantic similarity have been proposed in the literature (Madhavan and Halevy 2003; Maguitman et al. 2005), and some solutions proposed for the industrial sector, e.g., like the Semantic Tagging proposed by Centiare.

7   Conclusions

In this paper we presented the results obtained in the European project LD-CAST for what concerns the semantic solutions that have been developed. The objective was to achieve a smooth cooperation among European Chambers of Commerce and, furthermore, between the latter and the European SMEs by supporting a flexible construction of executable workflows. Such cooperation should be based on the flexible interoperability of the Information Systems that are used by the different CoC. The main problems encounter are caused by: (1) the above mentioned difference in the IS of the CoC; (2) the difference in the law and regulations that exists from country to country; (3) the fact that the level of automation of the provided business services is very different form one place to another, from a country to another; (4) the need to provide the requested services according to good practices, that may change in time; and finally (5) the possibility of customizing the service provision in accordance with the user profile and user needs.

We addressed the above problems by developing and ontology-based semantic suite capable of: (a) supporting the construction of a weighted reference ontology; (b) supporting the semantic annotation of business processes and concrete services offered to the user; and (c) providing a semantic search and discovery mechanism for the retrieval of concrete services. These three semantic services have been successfully applied in the LD-Cast platform and thoroughly tested in the different pilots. The final results have been very positive and the developed solutions proved that the semantic technologies have reached a good maturity level. Additional tests, and comparison of the *semsim* method with other similarity approaches, have been proposed by Missikoff et al. (2008). We are confident that soon the industrial adoption of semantic technologies will start to spread, and the research results of LD-Cast will produce an interesting result for eGovernment and for the European SMEs.

Acknowledgments We wish to address our warmest thankfulness to all the colleagues and partners of LD-Cast, since without their constructive cooperation these results would not have been achieved. In particular, we owe a special credit to Alessandra Catapano (ElsagDatamat) as the LD-CAST coordinator, to Antonio De Nicola (CNR-IASI) to Alessandro D'Atri and Paolo Spagnoletti (LUISS CeRSI), to Robert Woitsch and Vedran Hergovcic (BOC), to Nicola Christian Rinaldi and Valentina Di Michele (Retecamere).

References

R. Akkiraju, J. Farrell, J. Miller, M. Nagarajan, M. Schmidt, A. Sheth, K. Verma, Web service semantics – WSDL-S (technical note), http://lsdis.cs.uga.edu/library/download/WSDL-S-V1.html, April 2005

ATHENA, D.A3.1, SoA on ontologies and the ontology authoring and management system, with ontology modelling language, ATHENA IP. Deliverable (2005)

T. Berners-Lee, J. Hendler, O. Lassila, The semantic web. Sci. Am. **284**(5), 34–43 (2001)

A. De Nicola, R. Navigli, M. Missikoff, A software engineering approach to ontology building. Inform. Syst. **34**(2), 258–275 (2009)

DSTC, IBM, Sandpiper software; Ontology definition metamodel, Revised submission to OMG, http://www.omg.org/docs/ad/05-01-01.pdf. Accessed 10 Jan 2005

W.B. Frakes, R. Baeza-Yates, *Information Retrieval, Data Structure and Algorithms* (Prentice Hall, Upper Saddle River, NJ, 1992)

T.R. Gruber, A translation approach to portable ontologies. Knowl. Acquis. **5**(2), 199–220 (1993)

P. Jaccard, Bulletin del la Société Vaudoise des Sciences Naturelles **37**, 241–272 (1901)

LD-CAST, D3.1. Common knowledge base specifications. Deliverable (2006)

D. Lin, in *An Information-Theoretic Definition of Similarity*, ed. by J.W. Shavlik. Proceedings of 15th the International Conference on Machine Learning, Madison, Wisconsin, USA (Morgan Kaufmann, San Francisco, 1998), pp. 296–304

Y.S. Maarek, D.M. Berry, G.E. Kaiser, An information retrieval approach for automatically constructing software libraries. IEEE Trans. Softw. Eng. **17**(8), 800–813 (1991)

J. Madhavan, A.Y. Halevy, Composing mappings among data sources. VLDB J. **2003**, 572–583 (2003)

A.G. Maguitman, F. Menczer, H. Roinestad, A. Vespignani, Algorithmic detection of semantic similarity. in *Proceedings of WWW'05 Conference*, May 2005, Chiba, Japan

M. Missikoff, F. Taglino, F. D'Antonio, Formalizing the OPAL eBusiness ontology design patterns with OWL. in *Proceedings of IESA07*, Madeira (Portugal) 26–27 March 2007

M. Missikoff, A. Formica, E. Pourabbas, F. Taglino, Weighted ontology for semantic search. in *Proceedings of ODBASE08* (to appear), Monterrey, Mexico, 11–13 November 2008

OWL-S (Web Ontology Language for Web Service) 1.2 Release, http://www.ai.sri.com/daml/services/owl-s/1.2/

L. Rada, V. Mili, E. Bicknell, M. Bletter, Development and application of a metric on semantic nets. IEEE Trans. Syst. Man Cybern. **19**(1), 17–30 (1989)

P. Resnik, Using information content to evaluate semantic similarity in a taxonomy. Proc. IJCAI **95**(1), 448–453 (1995)

D. Roman, H. Lausen, U. Keller, D2v1.3. Web service modelling ontology (WSMO). Deliverable, http://www.wsmo.org/TR/d2/v1.3/, October 2006

C.E. Shannon, A mathematical theory of communication. BLTJ **27**, 379–423, 623–656 (1948), http://mywikibiz.com/Semantic_tagging

SEEMP: A Networked Marketplace for Employment Services

Irene Celino, Dario Cerizza, Mirko Cesarini, Emanuele Della Valle,
Flavio De Paoli, Jacky Estublier, MariaGrazia Fugini, Asuncion Gómez Pérez,
Mick Kerrigan, Pascal Guarrera, Mario Mezzanzanica, Jaime Ramìrez,
Boris Villazon, and Gang Zhao

1 Introduction

Human capital is more and more the key factor of economic growth and competitiveness in the information age and knowledge economy. But due to a still fragmented employment market compounded by the enlargement of the EU, the human resources are not effectively exchanged and deployed. The business innovation of SEEMP[1] develops a vision of an *Employment Mediation Marketplace (EMM)* for market transparency and effic ient mediation. Its technological innovation provides a federated marketplace of employment agencies through a peer-to-peer network of employment data and mediation services. In other words, the solution under development is a de-fragmentation of the employment market by a web-based collaborative network. The SEEMP-enabled employment marketplace will strengthen the social organization of *public* employment administration, maximize the business turnover of *private* employment agencies, improve citizens' productivity and welfare, and increase the competitiveness and performance of business.

SEEMP has been conceived as an integration project and its adoption has been studied according to the SWOT analysis (Creighton 2003) in terms of migration strategies, cost and performance expectations, and job offer and search modes. Furthermore, as an EU integration project, SEEMP should be compliant with the EIF recommendations (European Interoperability Framework for pan-European e-Government Services, recommendations framed within the EC IDABC – Interchange of Data between Administrations – initiative) (CapGemini and IDA 2004; IDABC-2 2004), which defines a set of guidelines for e-Government services such that public administrations, enterprises and citizens can interact across borders, in a pan-European context.

M. Kerrigan (✉)
STI Innsbruck, University of Innsbruck, Technikerstraße 21a, 6020 Innsbruck, Austria
[1]SEEMP (Single European Employment Market Place): http://www.seemp.org/.

T. Vitvar et al. (eds.), *Semantic Technologies for E-Government*,
DOI 10.1007/978-3-642-03507-4_7, © Springer-Verlag Berlin Heidelberg 2010

The purpose of this chapter is to introduce the SEEMP marketplace of employment mediators, detailing the business objectives and main features of the SEEMP-integrated technology platform. The purpose of SEEMP is to enable the meeting of *Job Offers* from employers and *CVs* of job seekers by developing an e-marketplace, improving the business activity of brokers in an employment market currently characterised by:

Multiplicity of the players on the market and diversity of the distribution networks: Job Seekers and *CVs* are distributed across many online databases, brokers and intermediaries. In order to be sufficiently visible, a candidate or an enterprise has to contact several intermediaries, for example temporary work agencies, employment websites, with a redundancy of information and multiplication of the effort needed to correctly classify, qualify and maintain their data.

Lack of common standard for Job Offer and CV: The lack of standardized descriptions and search criteria shared by the intermediaries prevents them to exchange information easily and effectively.

Insufficient information sharing among the players on the labour market: In spite of various existing information systems for e-employment, data sharing between entities of intermediary networks remains insufficient. The same holds for the cooperation aspects among players in the market, which need cooperative information systems technology.

This paper is organized as follows. In Sect. 2, we state the overall objectives of the SEEMP project and state the market vision of the project. In Sect. 3, we present the methodologies adopted in SEEMP in terms of minimal shared commitment that drives the SEEMP policies, and we describe the adopted best practices which help to clarify the agreement levels established for SEEMP and the SEEMP architecture used to implement the interoperability framework. In Sect. 4, we provide a demonstrative use case of the elements described in the paper; this use case is rather simple but proves difficult to solve at a European scale. Finally, in Sect. 5 we introduce some elements of discussion such as a comparison between SEEMP with EURES and other job boards and employment search engines, and set the stage for evaluating the SEEMP benefits for its intended actors; finally we give the concluding remarks.

2 Employment Market Vision

2.1 Employment Market Need

The request for labour and work is becoming more frequent due to less stability in the employment relationship, dynamic changes in traditional and new sectors, diversification of career development and labour mobility. In reaction to the market need to help in recruitment, the employment mediation industry has experienced fast expansion. It is in fact one of the fastest growing sectors. It is predicted that 1.6 million jobs will be created during the period of 2004–2014, which exhibits a growth rate of 46% as compared with 14% for all industries combined (Jansen et al. 2005; Davis et al. 2006; Le FOREM et al. 2003).

On the European scene, the further pressure for data sharing and exchange across system and organizational boundaries arises from labour mobility (PEP et al. 2006), regional horizontal collaboration in the wake of decentralization in labour market regulations (Le FOREM et al. 2006; SOC et al. 2006), and European and national e-government programs (such as IDABC). An integrated labour market contributes directly to the Euro zone economy (Survey Results Booklet 2002; Survey Results Booklet 2006; OECD 2007). Projects are ongoing with the aim of improving employment market transparency across administrations and regions through inter-connection and integration of employment databases, for example, in the German Federal Employment Office,[2] the Swedish National Labour Market Administration,[3] Public Employment Agency of Wallonia of Belgium,[4] and Regione Lombardia of Italy[5] (Fugini et al. 2003).

On the other hand, due to the poor visibility of labour supply and demand, the problem of unsatisfied need is keenly felt. In addition, the poor visibility of competence shortage makes it difficult for effective measures and policies to be taken to capture labour market trends, and improve human capital in the globally competitive and dynamic economy. The root cause of these problems is the de-fragmentation of the employment market along four dimensions:

- Diversity of the distribution networks through independent databases, publishers, brokers, public, private, off- and on-line.
- Insufficient information sharing among collaborative and competitive actors.
- Geographical, administrative and linguistic boundaries.
- Lack of common standards for data management, such as meta-data about *CVs* or *Job Offers*.

Figure 1 shows a case of five Job Seekers, $S_{1...5}$, with a similar professional profile, looking for a job, and four Employers, $E_{1...4}$, with Job Offers of a similar type.

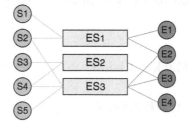

Fig. 1 An illustration of five job seekers in search of a similar job and four employers in search of candidates of similar profile

---

[2]www.arbeitsagentur.de.

[3]www.ams.se.

[4]www.leforem.be.

[5]www.borsalavorolombardia.net.

The Job Seekers and Employers register their requests at three *Employment Services (ESs)* of either public or private nature, $ES_{1\ldots3}$. To ensure a wide visibility of their request, both parties subscribe to different employment service databases. The isolated hosting of data prevents the Job Seekers from seeing all the available *CVs* and the Employers from seeing all the candidates. Moreover, duplication not only results in a waste of resources but it also distorts the global picture of market supply and demand.

2.2 Business Vision: Employment Mediation Marketplace

In line with the above-mentioned labour market needs, the key issue is labour market integration in Europe. The questions that need to be asked for the SEEMP market vision are therefore:

- Who is the customer of the SEEMP technology?
- What customer needs and goals does the SEEMP technology fulfil?
- How should SEEMP technologies facilitate and improve the customer's service?

Initiatives such as centralizing information on *CVs* and Job Offers and adopting uniform standards for data management are not feasible as they fail to adequately recognise the European diversity in regulations and policies, in administrative and business practices, organizational, regional and national differences, and past and future investment in ICT of different operators. They also cause serious operational difficulty in system scalability and data maintenance, in spite of their logical simplicity in system integration. Also many market participants would object that the whole market depends on one federated database. A totally decentralized system paradigm is also not a solution, since the interoperation of business operators requires a regulatory or mediation mechanism to enforce administrative and business policies and rules, to oversee the consensus over data management, and to impose access and security limitations. The concept of a marketplace where traders conduct business in a given framework is a compromise between the need, on the one hand for agreement and complementarities and on the other hand for disagreement and diversity. The framework of such an employment marketplace stresses the interoperability and sharing of data and services, to ensure trading and exchanging of information about CVs and Job Offers.

The *mediator* is a critical link in the employment market. It can de-fragment the market by its increasing number and independent existence as well as contribute to the effectiveness of an integrated employment market. The *Employment Mediator* is one of the two roles of marketers in EMM. In fact, EMM is essentially a mediators' marketplace through a collaborative network. The other role is *Employment Information Provider*, since EMM trades data of vacancy and candidacy.

The Employment Mediator actively engages in matching labour supplies and demands with each other, with motivations in social or political objectives or economic returns. Its value-added service is the introduction to, and advice regarding employment opportunities, channelling high-quality information to clients. Its business process consists of the following steps:

1. Determining labour requirements.
2. Searching for requirement fulfilment (qualified candidates or Job Offers).
3. Validating and assessing the authenticity and legality of information.
4. Comparing profiles and expectations.
5. Proposing a candidate for a job or vice versa.

The Employment Information Provider collects, classifies, stores, distributes and advertises information about *CVs* and *Job Offers* as a channel or media of information. It contributes to the second step in the business process of the Employment Mediator. Some market operators fulfil both roles; others specialize in one.

The EMM is essentially a business enabler for collaboration and interoperation of CVs and Job Offers. An effective EMM enables the exchange of data and sharing of services in four dimensions of interoperability:

* Systemic
* Organizational
* Linguistic
* Domain

The interoperation occurs among its marketers not only across ICT systems, administrative or business entities, but also in different languages with respect to different subject domains. The mechanism of the EMM is a facility for the concept of the *European Employment Mediation Marketplace (EEMM)*. Though it is dedicated primarily to the employment mediators, this information marketplace can be extended to other service providers, such as vocational training providers for operation across domains.

2.3   Actors in EMM

The EMM is a marketplace of service providers (see Fig. 2) rather than consumers such as Job Seekers and Employers. As a B2B market, it primarily targets the *Public Employment Services (PES)* and the *Private Employment Services (PRES)* for mutual complementarities and needs.[6]

The political, social and economic agenda of Public Employment Services is to ensure a citizen-centred set of government services and an efficient employment market. The mission is to effectively help citizens in their employment paths across geographical, linguistic, educational, organizational and systemic barriers to the benefit of society and the economy as a whole. Citizen-centred services mean promoting welfare and productivity by employment and visibility of employment

---

[6]Throughout this chapter we will use the term ESs (Employment Services) when no need arises to distinguish between Public and Private Services.

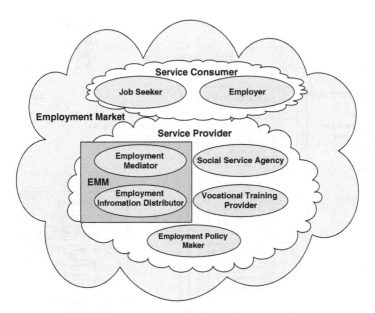

Fig. 2 Key actors in the employment market

needs. On the other hand, Private Employment Services need to constantly expand market access of human resources for economic returns in their staffing business. Whether multinational or regional, they face serious obstacles and costs in a de-fragmented employment market. The synergy between public and private actors towards social and economic goals is the cornerstone of the EMM.

EMM, as an actor in the employment market, is different from the Employment Mediator and the Employment Information Provider. It adopts a B2B business model rather than B2C. It focuses on the facilities that can be provided to enable B2C actors to perform effectively. It is thus based on established employment mediation practices for evolution and enhancement, rather than creating novel business models.

2.4 Goods of EMM

The goods traded in the EMM are, first and foremost, *candidacy* (the publicly accessible part of the *CV* of the Job Seeker) and *vacancy* (the publicly accessible part of Job Offers), as pictorially represented in Fig. 3.

Figure 3 is the starting point for building a reference glossary that is necessary to derive the domain ontology, defining terms belonging to the Domain Objects Description. The main concepts are as follows.

1. *CV*: A CV is a description produced by a Job Seeker for self introduction or for job application. It contains Personal Information (hidden for privacy reasons

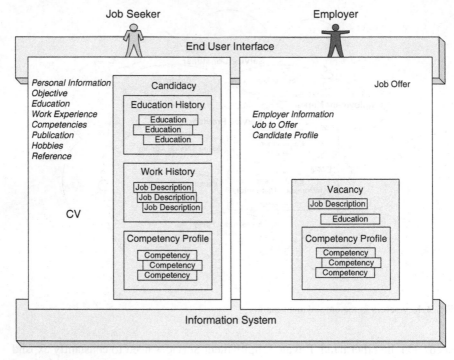

Fig. 3 Overall structure of a CV and a job offer

when circulated in the SEEMP network, until a match is found and the citizen gives his/her consensus to disclose personal data), and various data (see Fig. 3) regarding his skills, education and expectations. In particular, the *CV* is treated in SEEMP anonymously by circulating the so called *Candidacy*, which is a structured set of Personal Information, which includes the following fields:

(a) *Education History:* A set of Education Descriptions constitutes an Education History, describing the courses, classes, etc., attended by the Job Seeker along time. It can be encoded using Education History from the HR-XML recommendation.

(b) *Work History:* A set of Job Descriptions constitutes a Work History, describing the various jobs of the Job Seeker along time. It can be encoded as Work History of HR-XML (HR-XML 2005).

(c) *Competency Profile*: Competency Profile is a set of competencies held by the Job Seeker or expected by the Employer, resulting from education and training. The competency is, according to the HR-XML Consortium, a specific, identifiable, definable, and measurable knowledge, skill, ability, and/or other deployment related characteristic (e.g., attitude, behaviour, physical ability), which a human resource may possess and which is necessary for, or material to, the performance of an activity within a specific business context.

Candidacy information is derived from a *CV*. The node where a Job Seeker is registered is in charge of deriving the Candidacy data from the *CV*. The SEEMP deals with Candidacies and not directly with *CVs*.

2. *Job Offer*: a Job Offer is a description of a job produced by an Employer looking for a candidate to fill a given position. It contains Employer Information (hidden for privacy reasons when circulated in the SEEMP network, until the Employer gives his/her consensus to disclose personal data), and various data (see Fig. 3) regarding the available job. Also the *Job Offer* is treated in SEEMP anonymously; the so called *Vacancy* is circulated. A *Vacancy* is the structured representation of the information derived from a Job Offer. It is composed of the following fields:

   (a) *Job Description*: describes in detail the offered position in terms of location, qualification, tasks, language, salary, benefits and so on.
   (b) *Education*: specifies the educational level required for the position.
   (c) *Competency Profile*: is a set of competencies that are expected by the Employer, resulting from education and training. The competency is, according to the HR-XML Consortium (HR-XML 2005), analogously to what is specified for the *Candidacy*.

The node (Public Employment Service or Job Agency) where an Employer is registered is in charge of deriving the Vacancy data from the Job Description. The SEEMP deals with Vacancies, and not directly with the Job Descriptions.

Access to the above information can be *public* or *private*. It can also be *selective*, in that access can be granted to a specific SEEMP actor to some information subset or to some services, whether according to the permission granted to the subject accessing the information or to the enacted business model.

In order to meet Job Seekers and Employers needs on the marketplace, SEEMP is based on a set of concepts, methods and tools that enable enlarged job matching services, information searches, statistical data production and analysis about the employment market, and other added-value services, such as data quality treatment, or advanced discovery of services in an interoperable environment. The main concepts and tools in SEEMP are as follows (details will be provided in Section 3).

1. *Ontologies*. The peers in the SEEMP marketplace represent their local view of the employment domain in the form of a local ontology. SEEMP peers interoperate with each other via the *SEEMP Reference Ontology* (*RO* from now on). In other words, data and messages encoded in a given ESs local ontology will be transformed to another ESs local ontology via the Interlingua (reference) ontology. A set of scalable, adaptable and maintainable ontologies for the public and private employment services have been designed. From this point of view the ontology related technologies represent a key to addressing problems of terminology and employment vocabulary mismatches.
2. *Interoperability framework*. This is a platform of services into which legacy information systems used by the systems to be federated should be integrated. From this perspective, Semantic Web Services implementing automatic discovery, selection, mediation and invocation are a useful technology.

3. *Policy making tools.* Policies should be defined and enacted paying attention to build effective collaboration and relationships among the involved PESs and at the same time avoid opportunistic behaviours (e.g., a job agency may exploit other agencies CVs while not providing its own).
4. *Statistical services and tools.* New indicators are defined and implemented, to complement existing Employment ones based on regional-local information, namely the ones identified by the Indicators Group of the Employment Committee and used in the Joint Employment Report 2004. The objective is to define a set of cross-governmental indicators derived from statistical and heuristic analysis of the shared knowledge. Data managed by the system may also be used to derive and build statistical information systems (Cesarini et al. 2006), and to provide feedback to improve existing public administration processes and services.
5. *Security services and tools.* Various security issues need to be addressed in a federation (Bellettini et al. 2004), which become even more important when embracing a large number of PESs, as would be expected in a European scenario. Particularly with respect to *privacy*, there are a number of concerns that are related specifically to the domain as in a job market place, the job search and offer relies on the sharing of the data contained within *Candidacy* and *Vacancy* descriptions. This may cause privacy and business issues. In fact, a Job Seeker may like to control the targets to which her/his Candidacy is disseminated (e.g., the *CV* is not disseminated to his or her current Employer), while a private job agency may not wish to share the contact details of a *Vacancy* description due to business reasons. In order to address those and other similar issues, given a *CV*, a *public profile* should be derived from the *Vacancy*, as a subset of terms extracted from the documents provided by the Job Seeker. Analogous considerations hold for the *Job Offer* and the *Vacancy*. In general, contact details must not be present in the public profile; the same applies to all information in SEEMP that would make it possible for the data owner to be identified. Conversely, all the information relevant to match a *CV* with *Job Offers* (e.g., job type, work experiences and so on) has to be presented within SEEMP. Sharing public profiles instead of *CVs* or vacancy descriptions (or *Job Offers* and *Vacancies*) is the solution for privacy and business issues. Should a *CV* public profile match a *Vacancy* public profile, the original *CV* and *Job Offer* descriptions will be shared according to precise business rules and with the acknowledgement of the involved Job Seeker and Employer.

2.5   Benefits and Impacts of EMM

The EMM as a technical platform for collaboration and interoperation is an effective venue for marketing and sourcing candidacy and vacancy for public or private employment mediators. It is both a challenge and an opportunity for existing information marketplaces for the employment information distributor. The EMM is intended to respect the existing business model and practices of the employment industries and seeks to maximize the productivity of machine-assisted human mediation with an ICT platform of interoperability. The technological platform is therefore not intended to be (semi-) automatic self-help systems for the Job Seeker and Employer, but enables multi-party access and an exchange of respective location information about candidacy and vacancy among mediators. The EMM as an e-marketplace provides *four key services* for its customer business-technical needs:

- Shared marketplace services, such as the search and match of candidacy and vacancy, delegated to each participating marketers
- Marketplace data interoperability in semantic terms as well as syntactic formats, such as employment ontology development
- Marketplace policy and compliance enforcement, such as business and administrative rules governing the trading relationship between the marketers
- Cost-effective system integration for marketplace entry.

The main benefits to Public Employment Services can be summarized as below:

- Effective service to citizens in employment and career development
- Fostering transparent, integrated and competitive employment market
- Collaborative network of regional and national agencies on the European scenes
- Market information for policy-making
- Conversely, Private Employment Services will achieve:
- Market access to human resources
- Improved staffing services to the client
- Business performance

The effective collaboration of the public and private employment mediators improves the transparency and de-fragmentation of the employment market. Better candidacy-vacancy matching in turn benefits the job seeker and employer alike. They both can receive high visibility of their requests in the scope of EMM by the registration with one marketer in addition to an improved mediation service. As a result, the job seeker has a wider choice for his/her personal, financial and career development. The employer is able to find the best competencies available in the market for its business operation. It also contributes to the economic performance and facilitates work-related mobility.

The following sections of the paper will provide a detailed description of the technical and development aspects that support such expected benefits.

3   SEEMP Technological Approach

In order to address the challenging problems illustrated in the Sect. 2, SEEMP adopts a mix of methodologies that encompasses both business and technological aspects. In order to analyse the technical vision, SEEMP follows well established methodologies in the area of Software and Knowledge Engineering and Information Systems, with a specific attention to the distributed systems and in particular to the European Interoperability Framework (EIF) (EIF 2004).

The business aspects highlight the need for a system that covers the whole EU and subsumes hundreds of real *heterogeneous systems* existing in EU Countries and Regions. It implies:

- *Language heterogeneity*, e.g., an Italian Java Analyst Programmer may be looking for job offers written in all the different European languages
- *CV and Job Offer structural heterogeneity*, i.e., the use of standards, like HR-XML,[7] is not widespread and a multitude of local formats exist
- *CV and Job Offer content description heterogeneity*, i.e., European level occupation classifications exist, for example ISCO-88;[8] however, they do not reflect legitimate differences and perspectives of political economic, cultural and legal environments; and
- *System heterogeneity in terms of service interface and behaviour*, i.e., no standard exists for e-Employment services thus each ES implements them in their own way

EIF does not prescribe any specific solutions to these problems, but rather recommends a number of principles to be considered for any e-Government service to be established at a pan-European level, namely *accessibility, multilingualism, security, privacy, use of open standards* and *use of open source software* (whenever feasible) and, last but not least, *use of multilateral solutions.* SEEMP is proposed as an implementation of EIF in the domain of e-Employment and it is based on the concepts of services and semantics, as we briefly illustrate below.

SEEMP relies on the concept of "Service." Web services are quickly becoming the standard for Business to Business integration, allowing for loose, decoupled architectures to be designed and built. Following the EIF, each PES and PRES must expose its Business Interfaces as web services. SEEMP uses *Mélusine* (Estublier et al. 2005) as a tool for modelling abstract services and orchestrating the process of delegating the execution to distributed independent service providers. SEEMP, as a marketplace, models a unique consistent set of web services out of those exposed by the PESs and PRESs. Therefore, the services exposed by SEEMP become the actual standard for the distributed independent service providers.

Moreover, *SEEMP relies on the concept of Semantics:* data semantics, captured in ontologies; services semantics captured in semantic description of web services and user Goals; and semantics of heterogeneity captured in mediators. As for services, each local PES and PRES has its own local dictionary of terms and its own classification, which are considered in SEEMP as a local ontology. Such ontology has two purposes: providing an ontology based means for exchanging data (i.e., structure/content of the exchanged messages are classes/instances of such

---

[7]http://www.hr-xml.org/.
[8]http://www.warwick.ac.uk/ier/isco/isco88.html.

ontologies) and describing at a semantic level the capabilities and the interfaces of the exposed web services. All these ontologies differ but share a common knowledge about employment. SEEMP models a unique consistent ontology, called the Reference Ontology *(RO)*, made up of those exposed by the PESs and PRESs. Therefore, the SEEMP *RO* becomes the actual standard for the data exchanged between the PESs and PRESs.

SEEMP adopts the Web Service Modeling Ontology (WSMO) (Fensel et al. 2006) as the conceptual model for described Services and the data they exchange. WSMO is used to semantically describe the data model for data exchanged between SEEMP services, the SEEMP *Web Services* exposed by ESs, the requirements of service requestors as *Goals*, and *Mediators* for resolving heterogeneity issues. WSMO was chosen over other languages, for example OWL due to its basis in both Semantics and Services, which meets the SEEMP needs perfectly. The Web Service Modeling Language (WSML) (de Bruijn et al. 2006a) provides a concrete syntax for encoding these semantic descriptions using the WSMO model. For the purpose of developing and maintaining the ontologies, an extension of METHON-TOLOGY (Gómez-Pérez et al. 2003) is employed as methodology. This methodology specifies a development process and an ontology life cycle that considers the creation of an ontology from scratch, by reusing already existing ontologies, or by taking advantage of data sources that can be converted into ontologies semi-automatically.

A key point in the SEEMP methodology is requiring a *minimal shared commitment* by the PESs and PRESs when joining the marketplace, in order to keep a "win-win" situation for all involved actors. The commitment of each actor, at both the service and the semantic levels, should be minimal to ensure flexibility within the marketplace and to reduce the barriers for new ESs wishing to join. This minimal commitment is made up of two issues: (i) the commitment to expose the standard services expected by the SEEMP marketplace; and (ii) the exposition of information in terms of the SEEMP *RO*. SEEMP Connectors are the means defined in SEEMP to enable the ESs to join the federation, reducing the overhead of meeting this minimum commitment. A number of different architectures for SEEMP Connectors are available, with well defined technological solutions that transform the exposed services and content of ES to those expected by SEEMP. SEEMP Connectors are described in more detail in the next section.

In the following Sections, we detail the concept of minimal shared commitment that drives the SEEMP policies, then describe the best practices adopted in order to clarify the agreement levels established for SEEMP peers, and finally we illustrate the SEEMP architecture.

3.1 Minimal Shared Commitment

In the domain of e-employment, different Employment Services, both public and private, collect CVs and Job Offers in order to match demand with supply. Each ES covers either a region or an occupational sector. As a result, the employment market is severely fragmented and many ESs perceive the need of sharing information in order to provide a better service to their customers. However, they would never exchange CVs or Job Offers, since they contain sensitive information. Instead, these ESs use the "anonymized" versions of CVs and Job Offers, namely the Candidacies and Vacancies. Therefore, if an ES exchanges a Candidacy/Vacancy with another ES, it potentially enlarges the possibilities of finding a match, without giving to the peer a chance to bypass it by directly contacting the Job Seeker/ Employer.

The previous requisite of the employment domain can be generalized to a common industrial need: *parties agree on general principles, but then they only commit to a subset of the possible implications of these principles and keep for themselves all their disagreements.*

Therefore, we draw the conclusion that the common notion of *shared agreement* is not enough to manage the complexity of the industrial scenarios we face. We believe that two important notions have to be made explicit: *commitment* and *disagreement*. It is worth noting that usually when parties provide ontology commitment the intended meaning is that all parties commit to the "entire" ontology. On the contrary, we propose to give a "subjective" meaning to commitment and disagreement which does not presume a common knowledge (Lewis 1969; Aumann 1976) among all the parties: two parties may commit to (or disagree with) different parts of the agreement.

In order to move from the problem statement to the solution conception, we need to find appropriate methods and technologies. We need conceptual elements to capture the notions of agreement, commitment and disagreement, to make them operational and to express the respective relations between them. Ontologies have been used and are good for formalizing and sharing the agreement. The notion of commitment is usually associated to the notion of ontology, and this is certainly true in the context of agent communication. In agent-based systems, all agents usually share a single ontology. The Semantic Web vision, however, foresees an ecosystem of ontologies, because of the very nature of the Web which is "fractal" 0. Ontologies can be co-invented, they can partially overlap and, in developing a new ontology, the importing of existing ones is encouraged (Shadbolt et al. 2006). We believe that the "practical" meaning of ontological commitment in the Semantic Web is slightly different from the original one. In formal terms, committing to an ontology that imports several other ones is the same as committing to one big ontology obtained by the union of all of them; however, in practical terms, committing to the ontology that includes the import annotations is partially an "unconscious" commitment, in that it means trusting the knowledge engineer who decided which ontologies to import.

Therefore, our best practice is to distinguish between the *RO*, which captures the shared agreement, and the *local ontologies*, which captures the commitment and the disagreement of the various parties. We propose to build the *RO* including all the details that are needed to allow for a meaningful communication between each pair of parties, thus including also details that most of the parties would consider either inessential or not sharable. Then, each party can develop its local ontology, partially by importing parts of the reference ontology, and partially by developing its own point of view. Every time a local ontology imports a part of the RO,[9] the party is considered to commit to the imported parts of the RO. Moreover, every time a part of the local ontology is aligned to a part of the RO (e.g., by the means of ontology-to-ontology mediators 0), the party is also said to commit to that part of the RO. A particular attention should be given in capturing also the source of disagreement within the local ontology. Finally, each party should make available to all other actors the part of the local ontology that explains its different point of view without causing conflicts. It should be noted that the responsibility for deciding on the commitment to and disagreement with rests in the hands of the local actor, and specifically with the Ontology and Mapping Engineers responsible for building the local ontology and mapping it to the reference ontology.

3.2   Best Practice in the SEEMP Project

As a consequence of the previous discussion, of the lesson learned and of the best practice, we would like now to share our recipe to express commitment, agreement and disagreement.

To formalize the levels of commitment, agreement and disagreement, we use:

- *Ontologies* as a way to express the general shared agreement among all the parties, which we name *RO*; and the specific points of view of the parties that are only partially sharable with others, which we name *local ontologies*.
- *Ontology-to-Ontology Mediators* as a way to express the *commitment* toward the *RO* by (partially) aligning the local and the reference ontologies; and the formal expression of the *disagreement* of the party, by defining filters that exclude the possibility for facts expressed in the local ontology to be translated in the reference form or vice-versa.

Moreover, with reference to the respect of each party's competitive advantage or private data, we suggest:

- To *make publicly available* to all parties the *RO* and the parts of the local ontologies and the respective mediators which express the local point of view and which are not in contrast with the *RO*
- To *keep private* to each party the disagreement expressed in the rest of the local ontologies and the respective part of the mediators

---

[9]Note that the behaviour of this import feature differs from the behaviour of owl:import annotation, because it allows for a partial importing. However, it can be mapped to owl:import is the reference ontology is correctly modularized.

As already stated, the *RO* is a core component of the SEEMP system: it is the common "language" to describe the details of the employment sector. It is rich enough to support the semantic needs of all the ESs, currently involved or subsequently integrated in the SEEMP marketplace. The *RO*, as well as the Local Ontologies, has been developed by following the METHONTOLOGY approach, as a way to have scalable, adaptable and maintainable ontologies, according to the most common approaches (de Bruijn et al. 2006b).

Given that the *RO* must represent a common agreement among the ESs involved in SEEMP, the specification of the *RO* was based on international standards (like NACE, ISCO-88 (COM), FOET, etc.) and codes (like ISO 3166, ISO 6392, etc.) as much as possible. Basically, the *RO* is composed of thirteen sub-ontologies: *Competence, Compensation, Driving License, Economic Activity, Education, Geography, Job Offer, Job Seeker, Labour Regulatory, Language, Occupation, Skill* and *Time*. The main sub-ontologies are the Job Offer and Job Seeker ontologies, which are intended to represent the structure of a Job Offer and a CV respectively. While these two sub-ontologies were built starting from the HR-XML recommendations, the other sub-ontologies were derived from the available international standards/codes and ES classifications, chosen according to criteria that will be explained in the following section of the paper.

In order to choose the most suitable human resources management standards for modelling CVs and Job Offers, the following aspects have been considered:

- *The degree of coverage in the desired domain*: this aspect has been evaluated taking into account the scope and size of the standard. However, a too wide coverage may move us further away from the European reality; therefore we have tried to find a working tradeoff.
- *The current European needs*: it is important that standards focus on the current European reality, because the user partners involved in SEEMP are European, and the resulting prototype will be validated in European scenarios.
- *The user partner recommendations:* in order to assess the quality of the standards, the opinion of the user partners is crucial since they have a deep knowledge of the employment market.

When choosing the standards, we selected the jobs in the ICT domain as a "proof of concept" and for the prototype being developed in SEEMP. Hence, the chosen standards should cover the ICT domain with an acceptable degree. In the case of the Occupation sub-ontology, for example, we have chosen one standard (ISCO-88 (COM)), but later we have taken into account further concepts coming from other classifications, in order to obtain a richer classification of the ICT domain.

When specifying Job Offers and CVs, it is also necessary to refer to general purpose international codes such as Country codes, currency codes, etc. For this aim, the chosen codes have been the ISO codes, enriched in some cases with classifications provided by the user partners.

Finally, the representation of Job Offers and CVs also require temporal concepts such as interval or instant. So, in order to represent these concepts in the final RO, the DAML[10] time ontology (DAML-S 2002) was chosen among the most relevant time ontologies found in the literature on ontologies, and was transformed into a WSMO Ontology in the WSML syntax.

There are two main approaches for building the ES *local ontologies* within SEEMP:

1. taking the *RO* as seed: in this case, the concepts in the local ontologies are extension, in terms of depth, of the concepts already present in the *RO*; the consequence is that the data exchange between different ESs is easy, while the complexity of the Connectors between the local ontologies and the local schemata is higher;
2. operating a reverse engineering process from ES schema sources: this is the easiest way for ontologizing ESs, since each concept in a local ontology is the semantic expression of a relevant concept in the respective ES; the result of this is that the Connectors between local ontologies and schema sources are not complex, while the mappings between the *RO* and local ontologies can be difficult and cause delay in the data exchange.

The *"SEEMP way"* adopts different options, depending on the piece of the local ontology to be built. On one hand, we select option 1 (building local ontologies from the *RO*) for Job Seeker and Job Offer ontologies and other general purpose ontologies, such as, for example, the Time Ontology. On the other hand, we select option 2 (building local ontologies as a reverse engineering process from ES schema sources) for Occupation, Education, Economic Activity, Language, Compensation, Labour Regulatory, Skill and Driving License ontologies.

Since each ES talks in its own "language" (the local ontology, which represents its view on the employment domain), its respective connector is responsible for *resolving* these *heterogeneity issues*, by translating the local content into the terms of the *RO*. In this way, all the ESs in the marketplace speak the same language, and heterogeneity issues are solved via the reference ontology, the alternative to this would be to create mappings between every possible ES pair (which becomes unmanageable as the number of ESs grows), each ES need only maintain mappings to and from the *RO*.

As a result of the introduction of the *RO*, a set of local ontologies and the various ontology-to-ontology mediators it is possible to support scenarios in which parties agree while disagreeing. For instance each European Country has its own regulation in terms of job legislation and skills/certifications required to apply for a job. This is especially relevant for some professions, such as physician, lawyers, teachers and so on. Those regulations are mandatory for each Country, but, being "local," they cannot fall within the shared agreement (i.e., the *RO*). As a concrete example, let us consider a Swiss ES and an Italian ES. Both express a positive commitment on the concepts related to jobs related to Academic Positions. However, the legislation about the prerequisites to apply for a University Professor position is different between Switzerland and Italy: the two Countries disagree on the necessity of

---

[10]http://www.cs.rochester.edu/~ferguson/daml/.

holding a Ph.D. title. Therefore, the Swiss ES also makes explicit in its local ontology that each candidate for a Professor position should hold a Ph.D. title (whereas in Italy this is not mandatory).

3.3   Technological Employment Marketplace Platform

The technical solution in SEEMP is composed of *a reference level* (see Fig. 4), which reflects the minimal shared commitment illustrated previously, both in terms of services and semantics, and by *the connectors* level toward the various local actors, which ensures that the actors need not change their internal services and data structures.

3.4   Layers and Services Level

The reference level of the SEEMP solution is made up of a logically centralized component (its physical distribution is made possible by the *Mélusine* architecture), named the *EMP* (Employment Marketplace Platform) and a set of services provided to the marketplace, named the *EEMM Services*. The EMP looks and behaves like an ES that "knows" all the CVs and Job Offers across Europe. As such, it provides the usual search and matching operations that all ESs should provide, and therefore can be seen as the ideal ES spanning all of Europe. Users of the SEEMP systems need only to be aware of the EMP.

The upper portion of the EMP is the *EMP Abstract Machine* (EMP-AM), which is depicted in Fig. 5. The EMP-AM machine is implemented as a *Mélusine* application (Estublier et al. 2005), which means it is structured following the *Mélusine* approach in three layers.

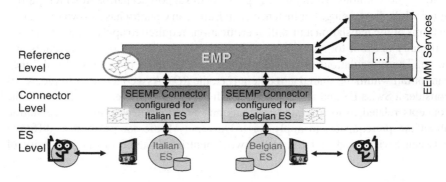

Fig. 4 A bird's-eye view of the SEEMP technical solution

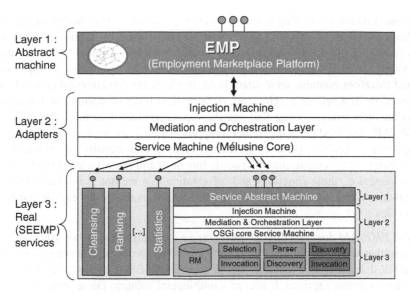

Fig. 5 Detailed view of the SEEMP architecture–reference level

Layer 1: The abstract machine. The higher, EMPAM machine layer is a java abstract program where abstract classes represent the concepts present in the SEEMP Employment Marketplace Platform (EMP). EMP acts as an ES that covers the EU completely, i.e., it acts as if all the CV and vacancies were present in its repositories. However, the EMP is abstract since it does not have any information locally, thus it delegates the functionality of individual components to real ESs. The EMP program defines functions like matching CV and Job Offers that are, indeed, not implemented at all, or only as a stub sketching their function.

Layer 2: The adapters. The role of the second layer is to perform in such a way that empty or dummy methods, found in the abstract layer, really perform what they are supposed to perform. To this aim, this layer itself is structured in three layers:

- *The injection machine*, whose duty is to capture those methods that need to be implemented, and to transfer the call to the following layer.
- *The mediation and orchestration layer*, which is in charge of transforming a single abstract method call into a potentially complex orchestration of real lower level services that together will perform the required function.
- *The Service machine*, whose duty is to transparently find and load the required SEEMP service and to call them. In SEEMP, this service machine is the core Mélusine service machine (an implementation of OSGi).

Layer 3: The SEEMP services. OSGi services that are called accordingly by Mélusine. This solution ensures optimal performance to the EMPAM, while allowing large facilities to future extensions (new SEEMP service) and even dynamic changes (dynamic loading/unloading of services). *Two classes of services* have been identified:

- those dedicated to calling a Web Service exposed by an ES through the Service Abstract Machine (SAM). Most of the issues raised by EMP are related to discovering, selecting, parsing and finally invoking a remote service; more exactly the SEEMP connector of each ES. SAM is itself a Mélusine application and therefore contains an abstract layer in which the fundamental concepts and functions of a service machine are defined. This layer is captured and delegated to an orchestration layer that invokes local services which, in the scope of SEEMP, are WSMX components wrapped as OSGi services.
- additional services, such as cleansing, ranking and statistic functions. These include the implementation of specific functions and repositories of the EMPAM machine, i.e., those functions and information that are not available in the ESs. Functions and information available in ESs are available by calling the SAM service.

The *EMP-AM* does not directly perform any operation, but rather offers abstract services that are made concrete by delegation: when the abstract service is invoked, the EMP delegates its execution to the appropriate ES(s) by invoking the correspondent concrete services. It acts as a multilateral solution (as request by EIF), in which all the services connected to the EMP are made available to all other ESs. *Delegation* is performed in two layers, namely *orchestration* and *EEMM services*. The orchestration layer captures a call to the abstract machine (for example a match request), and call successively the EEMM service that, together, will perform the requested abstract function (for example, select the right ESs to invoke, then invoke these ES, rank and cleanse the results, and finally return the result).

An EMP machine is an ES that subsumes, and makes transparent the access and use of a number of real ESs. An EMP machine is a federation of ESs. Since the connectors provide the same interface as the EMP machine, an EMP machine can be seen as a "real" ES itself. This feature allows EMP machines to cluster a number of existing ESs, for a number of reasons: geographical (a regional or national EMP machine), contractual (a consortium of PRES for example), linguistic, political, or for other reasons. It allows the structuring (possibly hierarchically) of the whole set of ESs, and therefore to satisfy both scalability and evolution constraints. Altogether, the EMP is such that SEEMP meets the EIF requirements: Subsidiary, Transparency, One stop shopping, Scalability, Evolution, Efficiency, Confidentiality.

The *EEMM Services*, provided at the level of European Employment Market Mediators, support the EMP in the execution of operations through the marketplace. EEMM services rely on the fact that each local ES exposes also information regarding the *quality* of the provided services and data, for example in terms of accuracy, timeliness, correctness, or consistency. According to quality of information, users can then shape their requests, either for *Job Offers* or *CVs*, to include also preference parameters that make their search wishes explicit. Moreover, preferences can be weighted to state a level of relevance for each parameter. In such a way, users can enable the EMP to return tailored results. For example, a request may express a wish for a preferred language by assigning it low relevance and a need for a specific location by assigning high relevance.

The reference scenario of SEEMP (see Figs. 4 and 5) requires three basic services

*   Discovery
*   Quality driven query-answering (QDQA), and
*   Ranking

The *discovery* service is offered by the EMP which selects the ES services that are more likely to return relevant Job Offers; for example, an ES could be discarded because the user requested locations are not covered by that particular ES. Once the ESs have been selected, the EMP invokes them using an enhanced version of the Glue Discovery Engine (Della Valle and Cerizza 2005). The match making process is accomplished by mediators that define the matching rules for the involved properties.

The *QDQA* service addresses data quality issues to enhance properties such as completeness and accuracy of the returned data. In fact, it is likely that CV and Job Offers coming from different sources with different quality levels and data schemas carry data that need to be processed to discover missing data that could be added, or inaccurate data that could be corrected by taking advantage of data quality techniques (De Amicis et al. 2006) and of knowledge included in the RO, thesauri and taxonomies. The task is accomplished by adapting and extending techniques designed for structured databases (Batini and Scannapieco 2006).

The *ranking* service is used to merge and classify the results, by providing a homogeneous ranking function of the returned Job Offers. The ranking algorithm is based on the computation of the relevance of Job Offers that states the distance with respect to a given request. The evaluation of the relevance takes into account quality properties as well as actual data. For example, a user may wish to get results coming from public ESs with high completeness first, and sorted by date of issue. In the simple cases, the weights associated with the request parameters provide the information to compute the relevance as a weighted sum. In the case of qualitative parameters, a normalization phase allows for including them into the evaluation process (Comerio et al. 2007).

The components of the Reference level relies on a vocabulary defined in the *RO*. As explained, the *RO* acts as a common "language" or *interlingua* in the form of a set of controlled vocabularies to describe the details of a Job Offer or a *CV*.

3.5   The Connector Level

The Connector level of the SEEMP architecture (see Fig. 4) provides the means to integrate ESs into the SEEMP marketplace with minimal effort and enabling ESs to meet the minimal level of commitment when joining SEEMP. A SEEMP Connector is placed between the EMP and each ES and all communication that occurs between both is made through this connector. However the technological level of a given ES may be very different from other ESs within the marketplace, thus a single architecture for a connecting every ES to the marketplace is untenable. Thus SEEMP

Fig. 6 SEEMP connector for
ES with no infrastructure

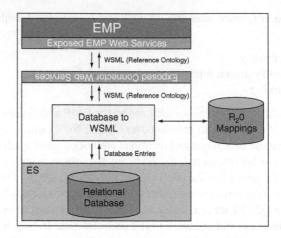

proposes a set of SEEMP Connector architectures that can be employed by a given
ES, at a given level of technological advancement, to reach the minimum level of
commitment required for joining SEEMP. SEEMP identifies four different technological scenarios that may exist and proposes architectures for each. While these
scenarios may not cover all possible technological situations for all ESs, they
provide a guideline for building a SEEMP Connector including the sorts of technologies that may be employed within these architectures. The scenarios are as
follows.

- No Pre-existing Infrastructure (see Fig. 6): There may be scenarios where new
  employment services may appear that have not yet chosen an architecture for
  their system. Also existing ESs may exist that still use paper or electronic
  documents exchanged by hand or by email. In cases where these ESs wish to
  join SEEMP, they may opt to adopt the SEEMP *RO* for storing their data
  internally and the SEEMP services as a mechanism for sharing the content
  externally. In this scenario the ES would adopt a database structure similar to
  the structure of the *RO* and then use the ODEMapster (Barrasa and Gómez-Pérez
  2006) technology for automatically extracting ontological instances from the
  database in terms of the reference ontology. ODEMapster is capable of defining
  mappings in the R_2O language, between the structure of a relational database and
  an ontology, and as the structure of the database and the *RO* are similar, the
  mappings between the structure and the ontology will be trivial. One important
  thing to note is that the functionality for choosing which instances to extract
  from the database depends on the algorithms that will be employed by the ES in
  order to match a given CV with a set of Job Offers (or vice versa) and will vary
  from ES to ES.
- With a Relational Database (see Fig. 7): A more likely scenario exists where the
  ES already contains a relational database that stores the CVs and Job Offers
  which have been registered at the ES, locally. In this scenario, the role of the

Fig. 7 SEEMP connector for ES with relational database

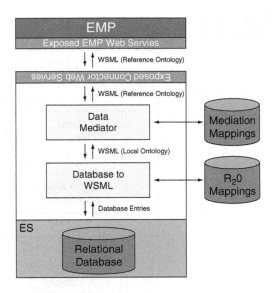

SEEMP Connector is to extract relevant entries from the relational database using ODEMapster and to send them to the EMP in terms of the *RO*. This sort of translation can be very complex, thus the process of performing this translation is broken into two logical steps. Firstly, the ES should design a local ontology that describes their view of the employment domain, when extracting content from the database, using ODEMapster, this information is lifted to the semantic level immediately in terms of this local ontology. Secondly, the ES can create ontology to ontology mappings between their local ontology and the *RO*; thus the instances of the local ontology extracted from the database can be semantically transformed to instances of the RO. The mapping between local and reference ontologies can be performed using the *WSMX Data Mediation* (Mocan et al. 2006) technology, which provides a semi automatic tool for creating the mappings between two ontologies at design time and a fully automated runtime component, which can be embedded within the connector, for applying the created mappings to instances coming from the database. Again it should be noted that the existing algorithms for matching CVs and Job Offers within the ES will be reused for choosing which elements of the relational database must be extracted and returned to the EMP through the connector.

- With an XML Database (see Fig. 8): This scenario is a minor variation of the previous one, where a given ES uses an XML database. XML databases are capable of directly returning XML in responses to queries to the database, rather than returning rows and columns. Usually the output format of such databases can be modified, thus the database can be configured to return instances of the ESs' local ontology directly, removing the need to maintain mappings with ODEMapster between the database and the local ontology structures.

Fig. 8 SEEMP connector for ES with XML database

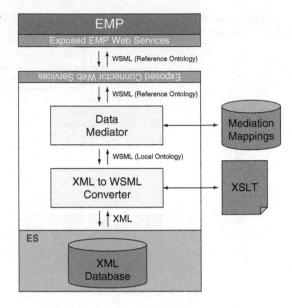

Fig. 9 SEEMP connector for ES with web services

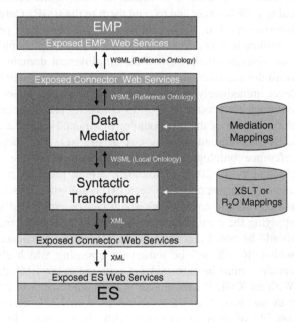

- With web services (see Fig. 9): In advanced scenarios, where the ES already exposes a set of web services that exchange XML content, it is better to layer the SEEMP Connector directly on top of these web services rather than duplicating the function of extracting the XML representation of the ES data from whatever storage mechanism the ES employs. By doing this, the connector is isolated from possible changes to the internal architecture of the ES, thus improving maintenance of the Connector. In this scenario, the use of a local ontology, representing the ESs' view of the employment domain, can also be employed along with ODEMapster, which is also capable of creating mappings between an XML schema and a specified ontology. The SEEMP connector will thus contain some ES specific code for mapping the SEEMP services to the ES services and translating the resultant XML received to instances of the *RO* using a combination of ODEMapster and the WSMX Data Mediation tools.

It should be noted that the last scenario is the most attractive one, since it provides looser coupling between the internals of the ES architecture and the Connector. In all four scenarios it would be possible for the ES to first upgrade its technological level to that of the final scenario, i.e., provide a set of web services that expose XML to the outside world, and then employ the SEEMP connector from this scenario to interact with the EMP.

4   Use Case

As a demonstrative use case of all we have described so far, in the following section, we will consider a simple use case that is rather difficult to solve at a European scale (see Fig. 10):

> Job seekers (or companies) put their CVs (or Job Offers) on a local ES and ask this ES to match them with the Job Offers (or CVs) published by other users in different ESs, using SEEMP.

Although apparently fairly simple, this example demonstrates how, in order to reach its potential EU-wide audience, this e-Employment use case needs to fulfil a wider set of requirements than those of the respective local ES services. A local matching service is designed for national/regional requirements only (i.e., central database, single professional taxonomy, single user language, etc.). SEEMP has to be able to send the request, which an end-user submits to the local ES (the Italian ES on left of Fig. 10), to all the other ESs in the marketplace. In order to avoid asking "all" ESs, SEEMP has to select those ESs that most likely will be able to provide an answer and has to send the request only to them (e.g., the four ESs on the right hand side in the figure). Moreover, the answers should be merged and ranked homogeneously by SEEMP before they are sent back to the user.

By combining the EMP and the connectors, the SEEMP solution enables a *meaningful service-based communication* among ESs. Figure 11 illustrates how such meaningful communication takes place in running the use case:

1. the user inserts a CV into the Italian ES and requests Job Offers,
2. the Italian ES invokes the marketplace matching service with the CV in their local ontology,

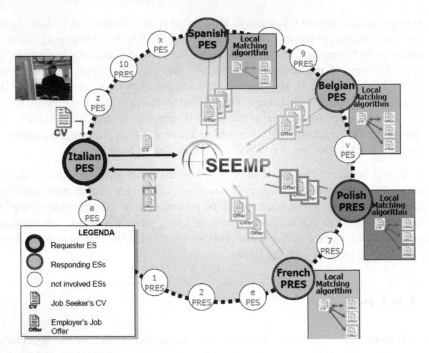

Fig. 10 Distributed matching of CVs against Job Offers: role of candidacies and vacancies data

3. the SEEMP connector translates the CV from the Italian ES ontology to the reference ontology,
4. the discovery SEEMP service analyses the CV and selects the ESs to be contacted,
5. the EMPAM invokes in parallel the local matching service of the selected ESs,
6. the SEEMP connectors of the selected ESs translate the CV from the reference ontology to the local ontology (i.e., the Belgian ES and the French ES ontologies) and invokes the ES's Web service,
7. the Belgian and the French ES compute the matching locally and return a set of Job Offers,
8. each connector translates the Job Offers from their local ontology to the reference ontology,
9. the ranking SEEMP service merges the responses and ranks the Job Offers,
10. the Job Offers are sent back, according to the reference ontology, to the Italian connector, which translates them into the Italian ES's ontology,
11. the connector responds to the Italian ES, and
12. the Italian ES displays the Job Offers to the user.

In Fig. 12 we provide a screen-shot of the page presented by SEEMP to an Italian used who asked for SEEMP-mediated results through his/her own Italian PES.

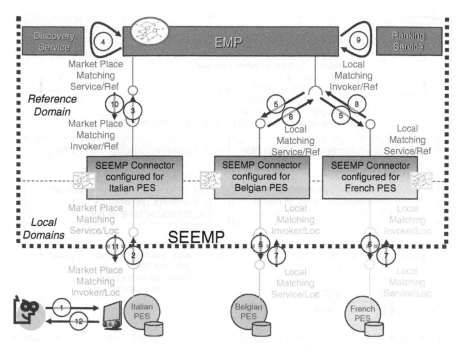

Fig. 11 How the SEEMP technical solution handles the distributed matching of CVs against Job Offers

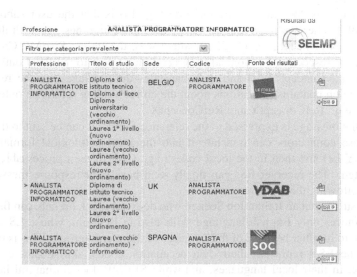

Fig. 12 How the Job Offers, captured by SEEMP from the EU level, are presented to an Italian User

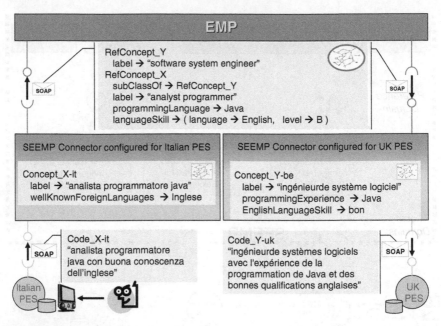

Fig. 13 The way a message payload is translated from one format and code system into another one using the local ontologies and the reference ontology

All information is presented in Italian, although produced by different ESs in different languages.

What happens "behind the scenes" (see Fig. 13) is that the user submits the query, with his/her profile, which is locally translated in a message with the local Italian code system (e.g., Code_X-it); afterwards, the Italian SEEMP Connector generates the respective ontological message which refers to the local ontological concept (e.g., Concept_X-it) and then translates the message into the reference version, which contains indications about the corresponding reference ontological concepts (e.g., RefConceptY and RefConceptX).

Once the message is expressed in the reference format, it can be sent to the other ESs, whose connectors can translate it into the local ontological formats (e.g., Concept_Y-be) and then in the local codes (e.g., Code_Y-be), processable by the local system. The receiver ESs can finally send back their response messages, if any, by following the same process.

The result is that an Italian Job Seeker, who does not speak French, can find a job which requires only English language skills also in Belgium, whose ES was not accessible to him/her because of the language of the user interface. This is possible because the ES's represent their own occupation codes, skill codes, education codes, etc. in their local languages, and while SEEMP does no natural language processing the code from the French ontology is mediated to the code in the Italain system, which is displayed in the Italian language. Moreover, the Italian Job Seeker can access the results of that search with no need of subscribing directly to other ESs and with no need to re-post his/her profile.

5   Discussion and Concluding Remarks

This chapter presents the main theme of the SEEMP project. The SEEMP technology platform is a collaborative network of multiple partners based on the concept of a semantics-based interoperability for service sharing and data exchange. Its business vision is to facilitate employment mediation for PES and PRES to the benefit of job seekers and employers alike. As a result of the virtual de-fragmentation of the employment market, the social position of PES will be strengthened, the business turnover of PRES will be maximized, the citizens' productivity and welfare will increase, the enterprises' competitiveness and performance will improve, and the employment market will be integrated through interoperation. Here we put forward some considerations that motivate some of our organizational and technical choices.

5.1   Alternative Architecture Paradigms

First, we observe that two alternative architecture paradigms are possible to deploy a technology platform for information exchanges and collaboration. One is centralized, using central marketplace resources in an approach of "common standard paradigm." The other is a decentralized collaborative network based on translation gateways for sharing and collaboration. The distinction between the two alternatives can be viewed in terms of three aspects of centralization.

- Process
- Data
- Information model

The centralized process is the use of single resources for information processing, such as a centralized system accessed through a web server with a thin-client browser application. The centralized data are the data accessed at runtime from a single data host. The information model is the data and its semantic model used for indexing, classifying, linking, matching and other intelligent data operations. The centralized information model is the use of single homogeneous models regardless of different data sources, storage, operation and consumer-specific requirements. For example, EMP has an architecture of centralized data and information model.

In view of web-based B2B marketplace, centralizing data on CV and Job Offers gives rise to serious difficulty in keeping information updated from multiple sources and data scalability, though it facilitates real-time information delivery. A centralizing information model by the use of uniform standards for data management and content interoperability is not a feasible solution due to its inability to scale up to diversified realities and needs in spite of their logical simplicity in data integration. They fail to recognize adequately the diversity in regulations and policies in administrative and business practices, organizational, regional and national differences, past and future investment in ICT of different operators and application needs.

If the assumed technical convenience is to be compromised with reality, the architectural model is one of decentralized process, data and information based on distributed systems, federated databases and interoperable information models in the principle of subsidiary. Such a decentralized system paradigm, however, is not a loosely networked virtual community, since the interoperation of business operators in the marketplace requires a regulatory or mediation mechanism to enforce administrative policies and business rules, oversee the consensus over information model and impose access and security. The concept of marketplace where traders conduct business in a given framework is a compromise between the necessity for agreement on the one hand and that to diversify. Such marketplace framework, similar to e-government services, stresses the interoperability of data and sharing the services to ensure trading and exchanging information about vacancies and candidacies.

5.2 Interoperability

The EMM with a decentralized architecture requires interoperability between its decentralized components. It implies four levels of interoperability, which can be described as in Table 1 from the dimension of purpose and informational object.

- Organizational
- Semantic
- Syntactic
- Technical

The decentralized data and information model requires semantic interoperability besides syntactic interoperability. It involves interpretation of information in the data provided or consumed and that by different semantic schemes (information models). This is the key issue for the EMM.

Table 1 Interoperability levels

Purpose	Interoperation	Informational object
Task	Organizational interoperability	Business processes
Collaboration		
Information provision–consumption	Semantic interoperability	Data
Symbolics	Syntactic interoperability	
Sending–receiving	Technical interoperability	Sign

This is not only a technical problem but also a business problem that asks for handling business constraints. When a service is offered by a constellation of actors, a central authority is often difficult to set up and all parties aim at minimizing its role. The central authority should perform only those tasks which cannot be performed effectively by the parties and matters should be handled by the smallest (or, the lowest) competent authority. Each party acts independently and a central system (if any) performs only operations that exceed the capacity of individual parties. This approach assumes that each party is interested in fostering collaboration to create a common value, but it saves room for competing with other parties for market share. Therefore, contemporary solutions to interoperability issues need to protect different positions and ideas. They should take into consideration that looking for a comprehensive agreement sometimes can be useless or counter-productive, because the practice to exclude possible causes of conflict from the agreement can produce agreements that are so limited to be almost empty, thus useless. Last but not least, the explicit formalization of disagreement, if well-known and conflict-safe, is needed in most business domains, in order to prevent invalid business transactions from taking place.

5.3   Best Practice

In this paper, we proposed a best practice that could help in guiding the deployment of interoperability solutions based on Semantic Web which, in our opinion, has a better chance for industrial uptake. It proposes the formalization of the notion of agreement, commitment and disagreement. It recommends the development of a reference ontology, which is the common source of agreement, and several local ontologies, which express commitment and make the disagreement explicit. The adoption of our best practice in the SEEMP project to the employment market gave us several positive feedbacks and we are currently working on applying it in the other projects.

We believe that this approach has to be supported by a full-fledged methodology and a comprehensive tool set. Part of the method that we are formalizing consists in the iterative construction of both reference and local ontologies, based on the analysis of the public positive feedbacks of each partner. Starting from a basic reference ontology, parties provide rough public positive feedbacks. By formally evaluating the part of the agreement that received the commitment of every partner, it is possible to understand the level of *minimal* meaningful communication that can be established among all the parties. At the same time, each partner can understand which part of the agreement it has to commit to, if it wants to achieve a higher level of communication with one or more parties. After this analysis, the un-committed part of the reference ontology can be eliminated and parties are again asked to provide public positive commitment. After each iteration, the sources of conflict in the reference ontology are reduced and a broader positive commitment is reached. In the end, each party is invited to make public the negative commitment that causes no conflict. We need to make this method formal, so as to develop supports tools, especially visualization ones.

5.4 Main Achievements

The following results have been shown:

- *Services and semantics* are the key concepts for abstracting from the hundreds of heterogeneous systems already in place that are evolving separately. They provide a straight forward way to implement the subsidiarity principle of EIF. The use of Semantic Web Services in SEEMP combines semantics and services to enable the automatic discovery and selection of the relevant ES's to invoke for a specific query.
- *The combination of an abstract service machine with a reference ontology* is a technically sound approach to multi-laterality for marketplace implementation. Each actor in the marketplace has to care only about integrating with the marketplace. The marketplace will offer services to support the interaction with the other actors.
- *The introduction of connectors enriched with local ontologies and mediators* is a flexible approach that lowers the barriers to enter a market place. Different variant of the connector has to be developed for different entry levels.
- A *mix of Software Engineering and Semantic approach* is required to achieve flexibility. The two approaches nicely complement each other. By means of "conventional" software engineering design SEEMP build an abstract machine that can run on "conventional" technology and at the same time embeds semantics both in the form of ontology/mediator and in the form of semantic-aware components (i.e., ODEMapster, WSMX data mediation, Glue).

Currently, the SEEMP consortium is running a pilot that shows the integration of EURES and Borsa Lavoro Lombardia. So far, this integration has allowed for testing the functional aspects of SEEMP approach. The next step is integrating Le FOREM PES as a validation case. We expect the RO and the abstract machine to be so well designed that Le FOREM introduction would have almost no impact on them.

Future work includes extending the number of abstract services included in the EMPAM and the respective concepts in the reference and local ontologies. For instance, one essential service of SEEMP should be the possibility to produce on a regular basis (e.g., monthly, weekly, daily) a set of key indicators regarding the labour market in all participant regions (job seekers, job offers, training opportunities, most requested job/skills, etc.), in a common and comparable language, both in terms of methods (definitions, calculation of indicators, etc.) and in terms of technical requirements.

Acknowledgments This work is founded under the IST SEEMP Project. We acknowledge all the partners in the SEEMP Project for common ideas and work.

References

A. Ankolekar, M. Burstein, J.R. Hobbs, O. Lassila, D. Martin, D. McDermott, S.A. McIlraith, S. Narayanan, M. Paolucci, T. Payne, K. Sycara, DAML-S: web service description for the semantic web, in *Proceedings of the First International Semantic Web Conference (ISWC)*, Sardinia, Italy, June 9–12, 2002, vol. 2342 (Springer, Heidelberg, 2002)

R.J. Aumann, Agreeing to disagree. Ann. Stat. **4**(6), 1236–1239 (1976)

J. Barrasa, A. Gómez-Pérez, in *Upgrading Relational Legacy Data to the Semantic Web*, WWW '06. Proceedings of the 15th International Conference on World Wide Web, (ACM, New York, NY), 2006

C. Batini, M. Scannapieco, *Data Quality: Concepts Methodologies and Techniques* (Springer, Heidelberg, 2006)

C. Bellettini, M Fugini (eds.), *Security in Distributed Information Systems: Trends in Methods, Tools, and Social Engineering* (IDEA Book, Virgina, USA, 2004)

CapGemini and IDA, Architecture for delivering pan-European e-Government services, v.1.0, http://ec.europa.eu/idabc/servlets/Doc?id=18944 (2004). Accessed 5 Oct 2009

M. Cesarini, M. Fugini, P. Maggiolini, M. Mezzanzanica, K. Nanini, The Italian e-Government plans. Experiences in the Job Marketplace and in Statistical Information Systems. in *Proceedings of the European Conference on E-Government*, Marburg, Germany, April 27–28, 2006, pp. 57–66

M. Comerio, F. De Paoli, G. Viscusi, An Ontology Management Tool for QoS-based Web Services Design. in *Proceedings of WEBIST (International Conference on Web Information Systems and Technologies) 2007*, Barcelona, Spain, March 3–6, 2007

T.B. Creighton, *The Principal as Technology Leader* (Corwin, Thousand Oaks, CA, 2003)

DAML-S: Web service description for the semantic web, in *Proceedings of ISWC 2002: First International Semantic Web Conference (ISWC)*, vol. 2342, Sardinia, Italy, 9–12 June 2002 (Springer, Heidelberg, 2002)

S.J. Davis, R.J. Faberman, J. Haltiwanger, The flow approach to labor markets: new data sources and micro–macro links. J. Econ. Perspect. **20**(3), 3–26 (2006)

F. De Amicis, D. Barone, C. Batini, An analytical framework to analyze dependencies among data quality dimensions. in *11th International Conference on Information Quality*, Boston, 2006

J. de Bruijn, H. Lausen, A. Polleres, D Fensel, in *The web service modeling language: an overview*. Proceedings of the 3rd European SemanticWeb Conference (ESWC2006), Budva, Montenegro (Springer, Heidelberg, 2006)

J. de Bruijn, M. Ehrig, C. Feier, F. Martìns-Recuerda, F. Scharffe, M. Weiten, in *Ontology Mediation, Merging, and Aligning in Semantic Web Technologies: Trends and Research in Ontology-Based Systems*, ed. by J. Davies, R. Stude, P. Warren (John Wiley, Chichester, UK, 2006b), pp. 95–113

E. Della Valle, D. Cerizza, The mediators centric approach to automatic web service discovery of glue. in *MEDIATE2005*, CEUR Workshop Proceedings, vol. 168, 2005 CEUR-WS.org, pp. 35–50

J. Estublier, G. Vega, Reuse and variability in large software applications. in *ESEC/SIGSOFT FSE*, 2005, pp. 316–325

European Communities, European Interoperability Framework for Pan-European eGovernment Services. Technical report, Office for Official Publications of the European Communities, Europe, 2004

D. Fensel, H. Lausen, A. Polleres, J. de Bruijn, M. Stollberg, D. Roman, J. Domingue, *Enabling Semantic Web Services – The Web Service Modeling Ontology* (Springer, Heidelberg, 2006)

M.G. Fugini, M. Mezzanzanica, in *An Application within the Plan for e-Government*. Annals of Cases on Information Technology (ACIT), IDEA Group, 2003

A. Gómez-Pérez, M. Fernandez-Lopez, O. Corcho, *Ontological Engineering* (Springer, Heidelberg, 2003)

HR-XML's Oct. 3–4 meeting in Nashville, TN, 2005, www.hr-xml.org/. Accessed 5 Oct 2009

IDABC, European interoperability framework for European E-Government services, 2004, http://ec.europa.eu/idabc/en/document/3473. Accessed 5 Oct 2009

B.J. Jansen, K.J. Jansen, A. Spink, Using the web to look for work implications for online job seeking and recruiting. Internet Res. **15**(1), 49–66 (2005)

Le FOREM et al., Employment Brokering Platform – Market Analysis, Deliverable 2.2, EBP, 2003

Le FOREM et al., *User Requirements Definition*, SEEMP Deliverable 1.1, 2006

D. Lewis, *Convention: A Philosophical Study* (Blackburn, Oxford, 1969). ISBN 0-631-23257-5

A. Mocan, E. Cimpian, M. Kerrigan, Formal model for ontology mapping creation, in *5th International Semantic Web Conference (ISWC)*, Attuns, GA, USA, 5–9 November 2006, pp. 459–472

OECD, *OECD Economic Survey of the Euro Area 2007*, January 2007, (OECD, Paris), http://www.oecd.org/document/40/0,3343,en_2649_33733_37849384_1_1_1_1,00.html. Accessed 5 Oct 2009

PEP et al., *Workers Mobility in an Enlarged EU*, SEEMP Deliverable 1.3, 2006

N. Shadbolt, T. Berners-Lee, W. Hall, The semantic web revisited. IEEE Intelligent Systems **21**(3), 96–101 (2006)

SOC et al., *Employment Organisational Aspects and Policies at European, Regional and Local Level*, SEEMP Deliverable 1.2, 2006

Survey Results Booklet, National Online Recruitment Audience Survey (2002), http://www.noras.co.uk/. Accessed 5 Oct 2009

Survey Results Booklet, National Online Recruitment Audience Survey (2006), http://www.noras.co.uk/. Accessed 5 Oct 2009

Semantic Repositories for eGovernment Initiatives: Integrating Knowledge and Services

Matteo Palmonari and Gianluigi Viscusi

1 Introduction

In recent years, public sector investments in eGovernment initiatives have depended on making more reliable existing governmental ICT systems and infrastructures. Furthermore, we assist at a change in the focus of public sector management, from the disaggregation, competition and performance measurements typical of the New Public Management (NPM), to new models of governance, aiming for the reintegration of services under a new perspective in bureaucracy, namely a holistic approach to policy making which exploits the extensive digitalization of administrative operations.

In this scenario, major challenges are related to support effective access to information both at the front-end level, by means of highly modular and customizable content provision, and at the back-end level, by means of information integration initiatives. Repositories of information about data and services that exploit semantic models and technologies can support these goals by bridging the gap between the data-level representations and the human-level knowledge involved in accessing information and in searching for services. Moreover, semantic repository technologies can reach a new level of automation for different tasks involved in interoperability programs, both related to data integration techniques and service-oriented computing approaches. In this chapter, we discuss the above topics by referring to techniques and experiences where repositories based on conceptual models and ontologies are used at different levels in eGovernment initiatives: at the back-end level to produce a comprehensive view of the information managed in the public administrations' (PA) information systems, and at the front-end level to support effective service delivery.

M. Palmonari (✉)
Department of Informatics, Systems and Communication (DISCo), University of Milan, U14 Building, Bicocca viale Sarca 336, 20126 Milan, Italy

T. Vitvar et al. (eds.), *Semantic Technologies for E-Government*,
DOI 10.1007/978-3-642-03507-4_8, © Springer-Verlag Berlin Heidelberg 2010

Although the two kinds of repositories have different targets, namely data source and services, they bring a common perspective to semantic-based approaches in eGovernment initiatives; in particular, they emphasize the role that semantic representations can play as knowledge carrier, beside their exploitation to support automation, e.g. in data integration or Service-Oriented Computing (SOC).

The chapter is organized as follows. The research context is discussed in Sect. 2. In Sect. 3 we focus on repositories of conceptual schemas that represent and organize all the information stored and processed by public administrations into progressive abstraction levels; these repositories of schemas are based on a light-weight approach to ontology modelling, but are rich enough to support semi-automatic Data Reverse Engineering for information sources of other public organizations. In Sect. 4 we focus on semantic repositories of services, describing a repository of Government to Business (G2B) services which connects services to a high-level classification of business processes and implements some techniques to support service selection. Section 5 presents the related work. Finally, in Sect. 6 we discuss the advantages of the integration of the two kinds of repositories, discussing future works and providing some concluding remarks.

2 Background and Motivations: ICT to Support eGovernment Programs

In the above-described scenario, improving the relationship between Government and Businesses (G2B), and between Government and Citizens (G2C), is a major challenge for eGovernment programs. Current trends in Information and Communication Technology (ICT) aim to exploit the development of platforms for supporting G2B and G2C interactions by means of knowledge exchange. Since ICT has been considered the critical enabler to support service-based interactions, a great deal of attention is dedicated nowadays to SOC. Although SOC promises to provide the technological and computational framework on which service centric applications are based in the near future, a large number of services are currently provided with no or partial use of ICT technologies.

This depends on different factors, such as the high costs of the implementation of services and the costs and risks of change management initiatives at the organizational level. Besides other domains of interest, such as healthcare, education, and transport, one paradigmatic case concerns eGovernment, where only few services are available via Web at the transaction level, and most of them are available via Web only at the informative or bilateral interaction levels (Capgemini 2004; Capgemini 2006). In such contexts, the first goal is to support the access to the information about offered services exploiting advanced Web technologies; the second goal consists in enabling citizens and businesses to understand which of the offered services is more valuable from its perspective. Furthermore, these challenges are strictly related to the issues involved in the digitalization of documents and processes at the back-office level of public administration's service infrastructure.

In the past, the lack of cooperation between the administrations led to the establishment of heterogeneous and isolated systems. As a result, two main problems have arisen, i.e. duplicated and inconsistent information and "stovepipe" provision of services. In the old-fashioned style, the interaction between agencies and businesses involves multiple transactions against the agencies' proprietary interfaces. Moreover, in the interaction with businesses, agencies manage both agency-specific information about them, such as e.g. tax reports, balance sheets, and information that is common to all of them, including identifiers, headquarters and branch addresses, and legal form. One major consequence of having multiple disconnected views for the same information is that businesses experience severe service degradation during their interaction with the agencies.

Furthermore, systematically organized file registries, allowing efficient access to official files and documents, are relevant for constituting modern bureaucracies as socio-technical systems (Dunleavy et al. 2006), both when efficiency is the aim of the governments (as in the New Public Management perspective) or to guarantee some pillars of modern bureaucracy based democracies, such as impersonality, equality, and fairness (Cordella 2007). In fact, besides the need for qualified civil servants capable of carrying out knowledge intensive activities and dealing with IT outsourcers (Dunleavy et al. 2006), one of the major requirements for improving eGovernment interactions is to provide an alternative for civil servants to the still predominant paper based archives and to the data quality issues related to the growing number of databases and warehouses spread across different and often not integrated nor shared between the different public administrations.

Civil servants must be able to manage the knowledge about the available data in the public administration archives on the one hand, and the overall service offering available from the different agencies on the other. Furthermore, civil servants must be supported in these information management and data governance activities.

In this scenario, repository technologies have played a relevant role as shared databases of descriptions of engineered artifacts, e.g. software, documents, maps, information systems (Bernstein and Dayal 1994; Moriarty 1991). Considered a common repository, that stores meta-metadata (e.g. data formats and field definitions), metadata (e.g. record and field definitions) and data itself, such a repository is used as a common dictionary that can share information between different agents or organizations.

In the last few years, the traditional repository technologies have been heavily affected by the adoption of semantic models and technologies. Repositories enhanced by light-weight or deep semantics can support different aspects of eGovernment initiatives. In particular, the impact of the adoption of semantic repositories in eGovernment involves both the back-end and the front-end layers. At the back-end layer semantic repositories are relevant to support interoperability among different administrations, improving Government to Government interactions. At the front-end layer, semantic repositories improve the access to existent services, information and delivery of new services through the Web (improving G2B and G2C interactions). A further exploitation of the semantic repository is related to strategic planning, where the improved access to information provides a clear and unified view of the existing resources.

3 Repository of Conceptual Schema of Public Administration Information Systems: Structure and Exploitation

Strong back-end solutions to support the integrated provision of services to citizens or businesses require information integration initiatives based on techniques such as "publish and subscribe," data integration (physical or virtual approaches), service oriented architectures (SOA). Such initiatives involve more or less complex processes, each one dealing with specific issues related to the applied models and techniques. However, any information integration approach and technique used in large and/or federated organizations like PAs face a preliminary problem: that is, to be able to locate the data to be integrated and exchanged and to understand their meaning, which is, their semantic relationships (Halevy et al. 2005; Hauch et al. 2005; Kumar 2008). In other words, a first-class problem that needs to be considered is the governance of the data contained in the many information systems involved in eGovernment information integration initiatives.

3.1 Governance of Data for eGovernment Information Integration Initiatives

One of the challenges that large and/or federated organizations need to address to govern their data consists in the management of (i) the information explicitly represented and stored in the organization's information sources and (ii) the knowledge that is implicitly carried by the domain experts who are responsible for such information sources; such knowledge is often the only key to access data semantics. When information sources are multiple and large in size (e.g. in databases with hundreds of tables) it is not easy to grasp an overall view of the available information, nor to use it in specific applications (Baader et al. 2003). Furthermore, domain-specific knowledge within organizations such as PAs or third parties managing information systems for the PAs often belongs to specific business units or even single data managers; this situation results in difficulties and costs when applications involving different information domains need to be built.

Data dictionaries usually contain the description of all types of data produced, managed, exchanged, and maintained in an organization. However, data descriptions (very often hundreds of schema) are often too specific and are organized into a flat structure (a schema for data source); this makes it difficult for users of the information system to understand the meaning of data and their relationships (Barone et al. 2006). As proposed in (Batini et al. 1993), a set of structuring primitives for a dictionary of entity relationship data schema can be exploited to provide a methodology for dictionary design; this methodology can present the informational content of an information system at different levels of granularity. The above methodology has been applied to a real information integration project in the domain of eGovernment (Batini et al. 2006). The product resulting from the application of this methodology is a repository of conceptual schemas organized according to integration and abstraction primitives, providing a comprehensive multi-level view of the information managed by an organization. In this section we describe the structure of these kinds of repositories and their exploitation e.g. to support reverse engineering tasks.

3.2   The Structure of a Repository

In the following section, we consider a repository as a set of conceptual schemas, each describing all the information managed by an organization area within the information system considered. In particular, the repositories referenced in this paper use the Entity-Relationship (ER) model to represent conceptual schemas. Although the conceptual models – ER schemas – are not represented with semantic Web languages, they can be considered light-weight ontologies concerning the information system in the sense specified in (Guarino 1998).

As for the schema representation, a flat set of schemas does not display the relationships among concepts managed in different areas; the repository has to be organized in a more complex structure, through the use of structuring primitives. The primitives used in our approach, first introduced in Batini et al. (1993), are: *abstraction*, *view*, and *integration*.

Abstractions allow the description of the same reality at different levels, from detailed to abstract ones. We will call *refinement* the inverse primitive, that allows to proceed from abstract representations to more detailed ones. This mechanism is fundamental for a repository, since it helps the user to perceive a complex reality step by step, going from a more abstract level to a local one. Views are fragments of schemas; they allow users to focus their attention only on the part of a complex reality of interest to them. Integration is the mechanism by which a set of local schemas is merged into a unique global schema, after solving all heterogeneities present in the input schemas. By jointly using these structuring primitives, we obtain a repository of schemas. In the following, we name *basic schemas* the conceptual schemas defined at the bottom level of the repository, *abstract schemas* the schemas at the upper levels. In practice, when the repository is populated at the bottom level by hundreds of schemas, as in the case that we will examine in the following, it is unfeasible to manage the three structuring primitives, and the view primitive is sacrificed. Furthermore, integration and abstraction are applied together, resulting in the application of a new composed primitive, the integration/abstraction primitive.

The integration/abstraction is iterated, producing schemas at several levels of abstraction. Figure 1 shows some examples of the schemas represented in the

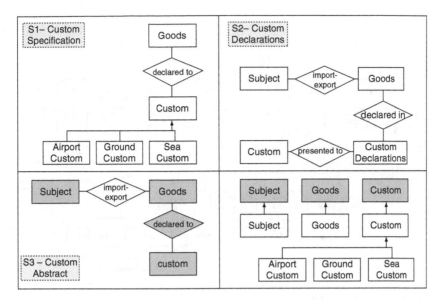

Fig. 1 Some examples of conceptual schemas represented in the repository and generalization hierarchies between entities of schemas at different levels of abstraction.

repository; in particular, *S1* and *S2* represent two schemas related to different databases related to customs; *S3* represents an abstract schema for customs obtained by combining the integration and abstraction primitives on *S1* and *S2*; finally, three generalization hierarchies obtained from the repository are represented.

In Fig. 2 we show the meta-schema of the repository, where meta-attributes are shown within boxes representing entities. The central part of the meta-schema represents the organization of schemas, together with their classification in areas and their relationships with organizational units (managed, owner, and external to PA). The right hand part represents objects defined in the schemas, together with their types. The left hand part represents conflicts defined among objects in schemas that are involved in integration/abstraction primitives.

3.3   *Designing and Maintaining the Repository*

The repository organization described in the previous section has been adopted to provide a structure to a wide amount of conceptual schemas related to the most relevant databases of the Italian central PA. At the bottom level of the central PA repository, approximately 500 conceptual schemas are defined, corresponding to the logical schemas of databases. In order to build the whole repository a methodology based on a three step procedure is adopted (Batini et al. 2006). In step 1, starting from logical relational schemas or requirement collection activities, traditional methodologies for schema design have been used (see e.g. Batini et al. 1992;

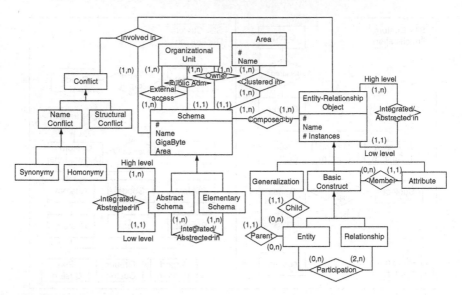

Fig. 2 The meta-schema of the repository

Elmasri and Navathe 1994), that lead to the production of about 500 basic schemas, with approximately 5,000 entities and a similar number of relationships.

In step 2 conceptual schemas representing the different organization areas are grouped in terms of homogeneous classes, corresponding to meaningful administrative areas of interest in central PA, such as social security, finance, cultural heritage, and education. In step 3 each group of basic schemas is first integrated and abstracted, resulting in a unique schema for each area, which populates the second level of the repository, resulting in 32 s level abstract schemas. For instance, the Internal security second-level schema results from the integration/abstraction process, performed over 6 schemas corresponding to 130 concepts.

The integration/abstraction process is iterated, producing higher-level schemas, corresponding to more abstract areas, such as financial resources, human resources, social services, economic services, finally producing a unique integrated schema, which is further abstracted, resulting in a schema at the topmost level of the repository. The schema represents the most significant concepts managed in the information systems of any public administration, i.e. Subject, Individual, Legal person, Property, Place, and Document, and their high-level relationships. The resulting pyramid of schemas provides a natural representation of concepts at different abstraction levels, and, with suitable approximation, finds the common heterogeneous parts among databases pertaining to different agencies. Figure 3 shows a pyramid resulting from the application of the methodology to the 500 base schema of the central Italian PAs; at the base level clusters of base schemas are represented (clusters depend on the area covered by the data sources); each node in all the other levels represents a schema obtained by combining integration and abstraction primitives.

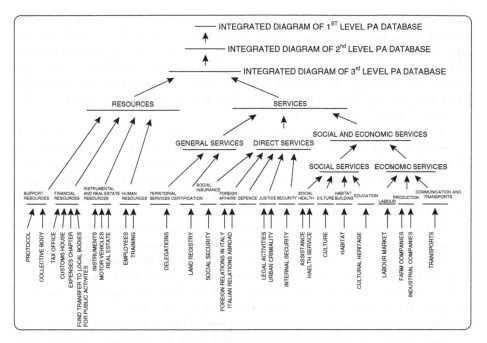

Fig. 3 The pyramid of schemas resulting from the application of the methodology

In order to produce the repository, about 200 person-months were needed in step 1 to produce the 500 basic conceptual schemas, while about 24 person-months in step 3 were needed to produce the 59 abstract schemas of the upper part of the repository (approximately 14 person-days per schema, both for the basic and for the abstract schemas).

3.4 Semi-Automatic Data Reverse Engineering with the Repository

Data reverse engineering (DRE) tackles the question of what information is stored and how this information can be used in a different context (Müller et al. 2000; Perez et al. 2002). An increasing interest for DRE in the reverse engineering community is related to the increasing relevance for businesses and organizations, facing the critical issues of the management of large amounts of data, e.g. related to the diffusion of data warehouses and data mining techniques for strategic decision support systems (Chikofsky 1996; Davis 2001). DRE is a critical task that also addresses (i) business continuity and disaster recovery issues (e.g. in Mergers and Acquisition strategies, allowing to preserve strategic data, e.g. in the public sector the mergers of different agencies), (ii) data integration from various legacy systems in data warehouses, and (iii) mapping of legacy data structures on a common business object model, e.g. in cooperative information systems and Service Oriented Architecture. Data dictionaries structured into repositories of ER schemas provide strategic resources to support DRE by offering knowledge models that can be used to drive conceptualization mechanisms from low-level logical schemas. The methodology presented above can be extended to consider the case in which a repository of schemas covering a domain D is used to support DRE for data sources in D or in domains similar to D.

In particular, in the eGovernment domain, a repository of schemas of central PAs can be exploited for the semi-automatic creation of a repository of schemas of local PAs. In the following section, we discuss the main features of the methodology introduced, with reference to a real experience carried out to semi-automatically build a repository of schemas of the local PAs of the Piedmont region, in Italy (for details see Batini et al. (2006) and Batini et al. (2007)).

In the case of Piedmont region, the set of inputs consists of: the central PA (CPA) repository of schemas made of basic and abstract schemas built during a ten years period from a team of experts see Batini et al. (2006) and Batini et al. (2005); a look up table of CPA most frequent attributes, extracted from the CPA repository of basic schemas; documentation available for the regional databases of the Piedmont region. The logical schemas of the 500 databases are documented in terms of: relational database schemas, tables, description of tables, referential integrity constraints defined among tables, attributes, definitions of attributes, and identifiers. The basic sources of knowledge available for the production of the local PA repository for the Piedmont region, as results from the above discussion, are very rich, but characterized by a significant heterogeneity: the conceptual documentation concerns the central PA, while the logical documentation pertains to local PAs.

A relevant condition of the activity has been budget constraints. Therefore, heuristics and approximate reasoning have been used in order to reduce human intervention as much as possible. Moreover we assumed that, while basic schemas of the central PA repository and the local PA repository may probably differ, due to the different functions between central and local administrations, the similarity should be much higher among the abstract schemas of the central PA repository and basic plus abstract schemas of the local PA repository. In consequence of the above assumption and resource constraints, we decided to exploit the main generalization hierarchies of the CPA repository, whose top elements consists of the concepts defined in the more abstract schema of CPA, namely: Subject, Place, Property, Document.

The methodology is based on different approaches (e.g. schema integration methods, abstraction methods, name conflict analysis methods, etc.) and can be seen as being divided in two main phases. In Phase 1, it aims to reverse engineer a basic local conceptual schema by using the available conceptual/central and logical/local schemas. Phase 1 is composed by the following steps:

- *Step 1.*   Extract entities and attributes from the local schemas on the basis of similarity w.r.t. entities in the central schemas
- *Step 2.*   Add generalizations
- *Step 3.*   Extract relationships

- *Step 4.* Check the schema with referential integrity constraints defined among logical tables
- *Step 5.* Domain expert check of the draft schema and construction of the final schema

Then, in Phase 2, the abstract schemas of the local repository are built. Concerning Phase 2, we initially observe that the schema obtained in Steps 1–3 of the Phase 1 (*draft schema* in the following) inherits high-level abstract knowledge from the central PA repository and basic knowledge from the local PA logical schemas, while the enriched schema obtained in Steps 4-5 encapsulates exclusively basic knowledge from the local PA logical schemas.

Due to the higher level of generality of the entities in the draft schemas (suitable to be adapted to different organizations both in the Italian Central and Local Public administration) and the more specific and local based characteristics of the enriched schema (tied to the knowledge embedded in Piedmont Region public administration), we may conjecture that the draft schema is a candidate for abstract schema for the upper levels of the repository, while the enriched schema, being a more detailed description of a logical schema, populates the basic level.

We now must to associate an abstraction level to the draft schema. By construction, all the entities of draft schemas belong to the central PA generalization hierarchies discussed above. Thus, we may associate an abstraction level to the draft schema that, intuitively, captures the relative position of its entities with regard to the generalization hierarchies. An abstraction level can also be associated with each schema in the central PA repository, defined similarly. Correspondingly, we may associate an average abstraction level to each layer in the central PA repository. The level of the draft schema in the local repository is heuristically set as the closest abstraction level among the layers in the central PA repository. More formally, in order to compute the abstraction level we may use the following algorithm:

1. Split the set of entities of the candidate abstract schema into groups corresponding to the subsets of entities belonging to each of the hierarchies.
2. For each group compute its abstraction level as the sum of the distances from the topmost level in the hierarchy ratio the number of concepts.
3. The abstraction level of the candidate abstract schema is the weighted average of the four abstraction levels.

By iterative application to all draft schemas of the two steps discussed above, we finally obtain the complete local PA repository.

4   A Semantic Repository of Services to Support Service Discovery and Selection in G2B

According to the considerations discussed in Sect. 2, a general perspective on services for eGovernment initiatives is needed. A service is considered as a series of activities of more or less intangible nature, which has a place in an exchange between a supplier and a customer, where the object of the transaction is an intangible good (Grönroos 1990; Lovelock and Gummesson 2004). This general perspective encompasses (1) traditional not web based business services, (2) e-Services, defined as services provided over electronic networks (Roman et al. 2006), and (3) Web services, which are the software systems designed to support interoperable machine-to-machine interactions over a network (Booth et al. 2004). In this context, Semantic Web technologies can also enhance service-based interactions by focusing on the role of knowledge when services are not delivered as Web services or still at an early stage of implementation. In order to enhance service provision, the first goal is to support the access to the information about offered services; the second goal consists in enabling the customer to understand which of the offered services are more valuable from its perspective.

IPAS (Italian Public Administration Services) (Viscusi and Palmonari 2008) is a framework to support the interactions between service providers and customers in the G2B context, addressing the above mentioned goals. The IPAS core consists of a semantic repository of services based on a service ontology that extends OWL-S (Martin et al. 2004) to take into account peculiarities of G2B services (Palmonari et al. 2008). The IPAS approach exploits an explicit representation of the knowledge involved in such interactions to support: (1) providers in the effective delivery of information about services, and (2) customers (businesses) in the value-based selection of the services by exploiting semantic Web technologies. The semantic repository enables semantic navigation, in particular, linking services to business processes they are relevant to, and allowing businesses to browse services starting from business processes they are interested in. Moreover, the repository provides metrics and an algorithm to support businesses in selecting the most valuable services, taking into account the composition of service effects; that is, the case when a service has the same effects of a set of other services. In order to address the reuse of available information, the IPAS ontology has been populated with an existent service registry, described in (Barone et al. 2006), by means of a wrapper. Furthermore, a prototype that implements the navigation functions and the algorithm for value-based service selection has been developed.

Adding semantics to a registry of services, such as the one exploited to obtain instance-level information for IPAS, has a number of advantages (Palmonari et al. 2008). An ontology enhances both the access to knowledge about services and its management, by making the conceptual model according to which the knowledge is organized explicit and understandable. An ontology represented with a semantic Web language such as OWL makes it easier to support the navigation of knowledge, exploiting the ontological linkages between different entities, e.g. between services and business processes. Moreover, the different criteria for the classification of services can be easily integrated to provide users with different browsing paths. Finally, automatic reasoning techniques can be adopted to infer implicit information provided by the repository and to support users both in enriching the repository and in discovering the knowledge contained. Here we discuss the main features of the IPAS repository and of the ontology it is based on (we refer to

Palmonari et al. (2008) and Viscusi and Palmonari (2008) for details and for the formal specification of the ontology axioms).

4.1   The IPAS Ontology

The IPAS ontology has been formalized in SHOIN^D, the Description Logic (DL) behind OWL-DL (Baader et al. 2003). The ontology extends OWL-S to support rich descriptions when Web services are considered. However, the main aim of the IPAS ontology is to address more abstract representation of services in order to achieve a good balance between richness of the descriptions and ease of editing, browsing and maintenance for users of the IPAS framework. The framework is aimed at supporting three types of users:

- Businesses are supposed to navigate the repository through a Web interface, browsing for services, and being supported in the selection of services according to value/quality parameters.
- PA service providers update the knowledge in the repository, by exploiting the ontology when they need to introduce and describe new services. While PA users cannot be assumed to be skilled in ontology management, they should be taught to autonomously update knowledge about services, after a light training.
- Maintainers of the repository provide an ontological framework to possibly enrich the knowledge with concepts and axioms for enhancing the organization of the content and its retrieval. Only ontology maintainers are supposed to have strong skills in Semantic Web technologies.

The link between the IPAS ontology and OWL-S is established by linking IPAS services to the OWL-S concept of ServiceProfile. However, as for the IPAS concept of service, some issues concerning the institutional context of service production and delivery need to be considered. Public Administration (PA) is organized in many countries at two levels, corresponding to *central PAs*, e.g. ministries, departments, etc., and *local PAs*, e.g. municipalities, districts, regions. Consequently, an important ontological problem related to service granularity arises. As shown in Fig. 5, services can be represented at two levels: *abstract services*, established by law with an owner (e.g. the "update business address" service at the Chamber of Commerce), and *concrete services*, provided by a specific provider, e.g. the previous service provided by a Chamber of Commerce itself or by a private provider.

Due to the above distinction, the ontology includes two fundamental disjoint classes – AbstractService and ConcreteService – and the two DL roles have ConcreteService and AbstractService (one is the inverse of the other one); a concrete service has one and only one abstract service associated to it. Abstract and concrete services are therefore represented as individuals, along with further organized in a set of relevant classes according to the classification given in Barone et al. (2006) and Palmonari et al. (2008).

Figure 4 shows the top-level concepts of the ontology and some of their subclasses (arcs represent `is-a` relations). Figure 5 represents the information about abstract and concrete services. A set of top-level concepts in the ontology which directly refers to service descriptions (in the figure, on a darker background) is `Service`, `AbstractPreconditions` (representing the conditions at which a service can be accessed), `AbstractEffects` (representing the effects of a

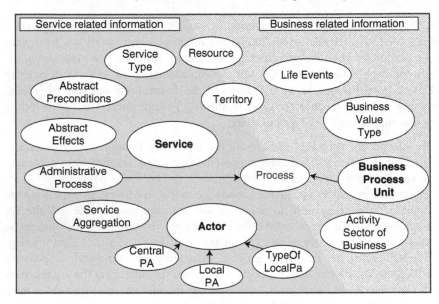

Fig. 4 Top-level concepts of the ontology

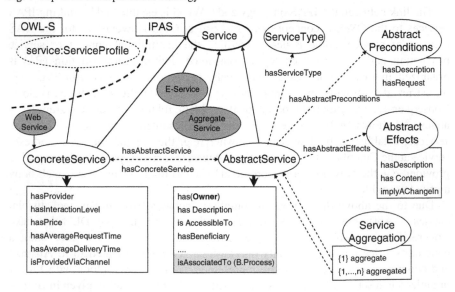

Fig. 5 The IPAS service ontology

service), ServiceType (representing the type of a service based on the business processes it is associated with), Actor (representing the different kinds of stakeholders involved in G2B interactions such as businesses, central and local PAs) and ServiceAggregation. ServiceAggregation is an important concept that reifies a relation pattern holding among an abstract service and a set of other abstract services when the effects of the first one (the aggregate service) equal the effects of the set of services (the aggregated services). Consider the following example: a service A provides the update of a business address to the Social Security registry; a service B provides the update of a business address to the Social Insurance registry; a service C provides the update of a business address to both the Social Security and the Social Insurance registries; service C is said to aggregate services A and B. Service aggregations need to be taken into consideration in order to support service selection because e.g. the price of a service of type C needs to be compared to a sum of prices of services A and B and not to the price of one service.

The top-level concept Process in Fig. 4 concerns both administrative processes and business processes, respectively grouped under the disjoint classes AdministrativeProcess, on the service side, and BusinessProcessUnit. The top-level concepts related to business related information (in the figure, on a clearer background) are BusinessValueType (referring to the Porter's business values *primary* and *support*), ActivitySectorOfBusiness (representing a standard classification of activity sectors), and LifeEvent (representing life events associated to services). Two further top-level concepts on the borders of the two areas are Territory – representing the areas ruled by local PAs where businesses are located and where services are provided – and Resource – representing resources involved in service provision, such as financial resources, channels and non physical objects such as capabilities.

Business related knowledge is represented through a set of concepts in the ontology, where the most relevant aspect of the information related to the business perspective is the association between services and business processes. Businesses perceive processes, made of atomic activities. They do not perceive services needed, and the impact of services on processes. Business process representation is based in our ontology on the value chain model (Peristeras et al. 2007b), which is considered a tool for diagnosing and enhancing the competitive advantage of a business, by disaggregation of its most relevant activities. The ontology provides a hierarchical model of business processes (see Fig. 6) based on Porter's value chain. Moreover, according to Porter's distinction between primary activities and support activities, one BusinessValueType (that is, *primary* or *support*) is associated to process units through the role hasPorterType; based on these associations, business processes are classified as instances of the (defined) concept PrimaryProcess or SupportProcess.

4.2   The IPAS Application Framework for Service Selection

In order to support the access to and the update of the repository, in Palmonari et al. (2008) we make use of NavEditOW (Bonomi et al. 2007), a tool for the

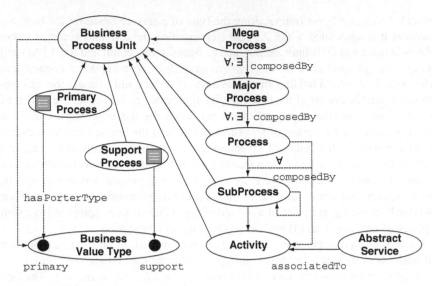

Fig. 6 The IPAS Business Process Ontology

development of semantic applications, where non-skilled users are supported in updating via Web a knowledge base through ABox editing. In order to populate the IPAS ontology at the instance level, an IPAS wrapper was developed and applied to a G2B service registry containing 450 services from the Italian eGovernment initiatives (Viscusi and Palmonari 2008). Support for service selection is based on the identification of a number of properties relevant to evaluate the services.

In particular, the value $v(s)$ of a service s is determined by the function: $v(s) = r(s)/t(s, \mathbf{w})$, where $r(s)$ is a *relevance* parameter, $t(s,w)$ is a *total cost,* and w is a set of weights associated to a set of individual cost considered. In IPAS the relevance is evaluated for clusters of triples $<s,a,p>$, where a is an abstract service, a is an activity sector of business, and p is a business process. Requesters specify weights for each of the individual costs composing the total cost: price (C^P), cost of the service request time (C^{RT}), cost of the service delivery time (C^{DT}) and of a relevance value. On the basis of these parameters the *Compare* algorithm calculates the value of concrete services, taking into account the semantics of service aggregations; that is, it compares concrete services according to equivalence classes based on service aggregations.

A detailed description of the algorithm is given in Palmonari et al. (2008). Here we present a summary of the algorithm and an example of the application of the *Compare* algorithm to give an idea of the service evaluation process. The main problems that the algorithm needs to solve are: initial selection is performed choosing a set of abstract services of interest (by browsing the ontology); costs are related to concrete services, where the relevance is given for abstract services; information about the equivalences between the abstract services with respect to their effects is fragmented in different RDF molecules representing the service aggregations. The algorithm therefore proceeds in six steps.

(i)   A set S of abstract *services is selected.*
(ii) Starting from the service aggregations *Local (abstract) service Composition Trees* (LCT) for services in S are built: the set of services that each aggregate service is recursively compound of (up to effects equivalence) is collected and represented as a tree.
(iii) *Global (abstract) service Composition Trees* (GCT) are built by compounding the LCTs and identifying a number of equivalence classes among the involved services; the set of services occurring in the GCTs is a set S', such that $S \subseteq S'$.
(iv) *Concrete Composition Trees* (CCT) are built by applying all the possible substitutions of the concrete services associated with the abstract services in S' to each of the services in S'; the result is a tree whose nodes consists of sets of possible concrete service composition lists.
(v)   The *value of each concrete composition list* in the CCTs is calculated (sum of the costs and average relevance); the concrete composition lists falling within a same equivalence class are ordered.
(vi) FA *table* summarizes the results for the requester.

As for an example of value-driven selection, consider the following scenario: a business has moved its headquarters and is obliged by law to communicate the change of address to several central/local PAs. The PAs involved are Social Security (SS), Chamber of Commerce (CC) and Social Insurance (SI). A number of abstract services of the repository respond to this need: services uA_SS, uA_CC, and uA_SI respectively update the business address in the SS registry, in the CC registry and in the SI registry (uA is used here as the short form for updateAddress); service uA_SS-CC updates the business address in both the SS and CC registries; service uA_SS-CC-SI updates the business address in all the three registries. These abstract services are members of the superclass UpdateBusinessAddress and have a set of concrete services associated each: uA#1 (with Price = €9) for uA_SS, uA#2 (€81) for uA_CC, uA#5 (€40) and uA#6 (€36) for uA_SI, uA#3 (€105) and uA#4 (€115) for uA_SS-CC, and uA#7 (€155) for uA_SS-CC-SI. Three instances of ServiceAggregation have been introduced in the repository: the first one has uA_SS-CC as aggregate service, and uA_SS and uA_CC as aggregated; the second one has uA_SS-CC-SI as aggregate, and uA_SS, uA_CC and uA_SI as aggregated; the third one has uA_SS-CC-SI as aggregate, and uA_SS-CC and uA_SI as aggregated. In order to choose the most valuable concrete service, we use the evaluation method described (Palmonari et al. 2008). According to the approach described by Palmonari et al. (2008) and Viscusi and Palmonari (2008), users play a major role weighting their preferences for the quality parameters.

Figure 7 provides an example of the evaluation of total cost (c^s) and service value (v^s) that assumes $w_1 = 60\%$ (C^P), $w_2 = 20\%$ (C^{RT}) and $w_2 = 20\%$ (C^{DT}). As far as the service compositions equivalent to the equivalence class of uA_SS-CC-SI are concerned, the algorithm Compare suggests the combination of the

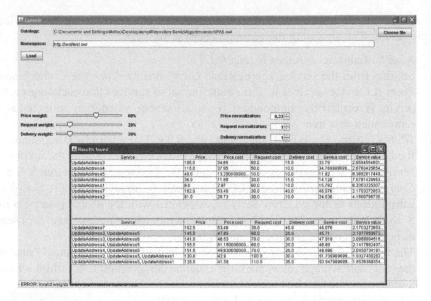

Fig. 7 IPAS evaluation component (a)

aggregate service uA#3 and the atomic service uA#6 as the best choice; that is, the choice that minimizes the total cost according to user preferences (emphasized in grey in the picture). Notwithstanding, the good values for the service request time, service uA#7, providing a joint update of all the registries, is not evaluated as the best choice because the delivery time is long and prices are highly weighted. If saving on the service request time is weighted much more than saving on the delivery time, e.g. weights are $w_1 = 60\%$, $w_2 = 30\%$ and $w_3 = 10\%$, then service uA#7 becomes by far the best choice (with a value equal to 2.20, where the second best is 2.02). Conversely (see Fig. 8), if saving money is the main concern, e.g. weights are $w_1 = 90\%$, $w_2 = 5\%$ and $w_3 = 5\%$, the more valuable solution results in getting all the services separately, and in particular preferring uA#6 to uA#5.

5   Related Work

Integration is a key issue in all information systems where several levels of cooperation have to be established between different organizations or players. As an example, Shoval et al. (2004) discuss the need for agencies to integrate their IT infrastructures, in order to improve their competitiveness by integrating their systems with suppliers, or other trading partners. In Perez et al. (2002) a solution and methodology for reverse engineering of legacy databases using formal method-based techniques is presented. In Castano et al. (1997) criteria and techniques to support the establishment of a semantic dictionary for database interoperability are

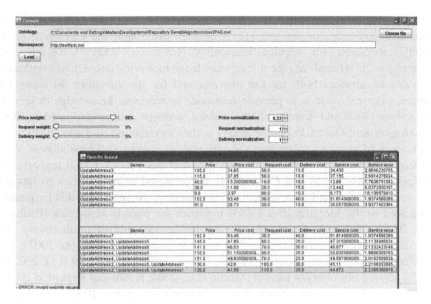

Fig. 8 IPAS evaluation component (b)

proposed. Similarity-based criteria are used to evaluate concept closeness and, consequently, to generate concept hierarchies. The techniques allow the analysis of conceptual schemas of databases in a federation and the definition and maintenance of concept hierarchies. Furthermore, methodologies for conceptual schema integration have been developed in the past (see Batini et al. (1986) for a comprehensive comparison). A survey of the approaches to schema matching, a critical issue in schema integration, appears in Porter (1985). In Mirbel (1995) a descriptive model based on words and concepts and a set of primitives for integration of object oriented schemas that generate abstract concepts as a result of the integration process is proposed. A repository of relational schemas is described by Motro et al. (2004) within a global-local as view data integration system. In Sheth et al. (2006) the conceptual schema package is introduced as an abstraction mechanism in the ER model. Several effective techniques are proposed to group entities and relationships in packaging such as dominance grouping, accumulation and abstraction absorbing.

In Halevy et al. (2003) and Madhavan et al. (2005) a corpus-based approach is introduced, where a corpus is a collection of any kind of information related to structured data, e.g. schemas and mappings between some schema pairs. Schemas in the corpus are loosely related and belong to a single domain, but need not be mapped to each other. Moreover, repositories of conceptual schemas are proposed in several application areas, e.g. in Palopoli et al. (2003) a data repository is used as the core structure of a mediator-like module supporting the user-friendly integrated access to available data resources. The core of the system is to extract and exploit the inter-schema knowledge (in the form of inter-schema properties) relative to the involved database schemas.

In the following we provide a brief overview of research works related to semantic repositories of services (for a detailed discussion see Palmonari et al. (2008)). Research on service marketing (Grönroos 2006; Lovelock and Gummesson 2004) analyzes the role of knowledge in service interaction to enhance the value of services both for the provider and for the customer. In computer science, a critical issue is to provide semantics to represent knowledge in service interactions (Rust and Kannan 2002). Indeed, a major area investigated in SOC (Papazoglou and Georgakopoulos 2003) is the organization and specification of repositories of services to support the retrieval, discovery and provision of Web services. In the area of Service Oriented Architectures (SOA), UDDI registries of services (Themistocleus and Chen 2004) are proposed as repositories to support discovery, selection and composition of Web services. Nevertheless it is frequently recognized in the literature that UDDI registries are poor in semantics (Paolucci et al. 2002a). The role of semantics for service design, publishing, discovery and selection has been largely recognized by the SOC community (Cardoso 2007), and is addressed using several solutions for service description (Paolucci et al. 2002b), and for service discovery/selection (Martin et al. 2004; Rahm and Bernstein 2001). Focusing on business processes, their representation in the IPAS ontology is inspired by Johannesson (2007) and Osterwalder (2005), where a business model is defined as a conceptual tool containing a set of objects, concepts and its relationships with the objective to express the business logic of a specific business. In our case, business modeling is based on Porter's value chain, in order to encompass strategic issues also. The ontological choices of IPAS, discussed in details by Palmonari et al. (2008) are mainly oriented to achieve a good balance between the richness of the descriptions to support service search and simplicity to reduce the effort in describing the services; moreover, the distinction between abstract and concrete service is related to the requirements coming from the specific domain (see Sect. 4).

As a state of the art in the eGovernment area, several frameworks provide a comprehensive approach to service description and delivery by exploitation of semantic Web technologies (UDDI.org 2004). Among these frameworks, GEA (Perez et al. 2002; Peristeras et al. 2007a; UDDI.org 2004) provides strong support to service description and discovery. However, the GEA approach focuses less on the problem of supporting the selection of services according to quality parameters; this issue has been addressed by IPAS in the G2B context through the compare algorithm.

6 Integration of the Two Repositories: Conclusions and Future Perspectives

In this chapter we discussed two approaches based on repositories to support back-end and front-end activities in eGovernment programs. The back-end approach is more oriented to supporting data governance for public administrations, while the front-end approach focuses on the improvement of service-based interactions. Both the approaches are based on the elicitation of semantics although with different tools and techniques.

The integration of the two kinds of repositories has several advantages. One of the major bottlenecks in providing semantic representations of services is related to the cost of building ontologies to annotate the service descriptions. Although some ontologies are available on the Web, in this context there is usually the need to exploit ontologies developed in the mother tongue of the country involved in the eGovernment project; as a matter of fact it is very difficult to find ontologies expressed in languages other than in English on the Web. Moreover, it is worth noting that most of the services offered by governments provide information about and execute operations on the information sources of the organization. The concepts used in the service descriptions are likely to deeply overlap with the concept describing the information content represented in the repository of conceptual schemas at different levels of abstraction.

Generally, the integration of a repository of conceptual schemas of the kind discussed in Sect. 2, with a repository of service of the kind discussed in Sect. 3, allows to bridge the gap between back-end and front-end activities. Finally, the different abstraction layers in which the repository of conceptual schemas are structured may provide people with a navigation layer to discover services related to the concept of the ontology in a way which is analogous to the process-based discovery of services currently implemented in the G2B service repository.

Our current research focuses on this integration. Some significant problems are related to the gap between the conceptual modelling language ER on which the current repositories of schema are based and the semantic Web language (OWL) with which the services are described in the repositories of services. Future work will address some issues that need to be considered in order to carry out the desired integration. First, RDF and OWL can represent only binary relationships as properties, while the ER model also represents n-ary relationships. Furthermore, the representation of the repository cannot be directly reduced to pure ER, since relationships between schemas are considered and meta-data about the repository structure need to be represented. Finally, the language should be as simple as possible in order to reduce the costs of designing and maintaining the repository; for "simplicity" of the language we mean that the language should be (i) easy to understand for people in the organization having a little knowledge of knowledge representation formalisms, and (ii) easy to be manipulated w.r.t. to editing of the repository and retrieval of knowledge.

According to these considerations, translations of ER into Description Logics (and therefore OWL-DL) like the one proposed by Calvanese et al. (1998) risk producing representations of schemas that are too difficult to be understood and manipulated (e.g. the introduction of "ER roles" produces many language elements with little intuitive significance and correspondence in the original models).

The search for a good balance not only between expressiveness and computational complexity but also between expressiveness and simplicity of semantic Web languages is a challenging topic for the success of semantic Web technologies to support real-world communities of users (Hepp 2007); this problem that is being acknowledged by the semantic Web community is particularly relevant for semantic Web-based solutions to the problem of data and service governance in eGovernment initiatives.

Acknowledgments The work presented in this paper has been partially supported by the FIRB project NeP4B – Networked Peers for Business(RBNE05XYPW). Special thanks go to Professor Carlo Batini for the previous work this chapter is partially based on.

References

F. Baader, D. Calvanese, D.L. McGuinness, D. Nardi, P.F. Patel-Schneider (eds.), *The Description Logic Handbook: Theory, Implementation, and Applications* (Cambridge University Press, Cambridge, 2003)

D. Barone, G. Viscusi, C. Batini, P. Naggar, in *A Repository of Services for the Government to Businesses Relationship*. ed. by O. Etzion, T. Kuflik, A. Motro, Proceedings of Next Generation Information Technologies and Systems (Springer, Berlin, 2006)

C. Batini, M. Lenzerini, S.B. Navathe, A comparative analysis of methodologies for database schema integration. ACM Comput. Surv. **18**(4), 323–364 (1986)

C. Batini, S. Ceri, S.B. Navathe, *Conceptual Database Design: An Entity-Relationship Approach* (Benjamin/Cummings, Redwood, CA, 1992)

C. Batini, G.D. Battista, G. Santucci, Structuring Primitives for a Dictionary of Entity Relationship Data Schemas. IEEE Trans. Softw. Eng. **19**(4), 344–365 (1993)

C. Batini, R. Grosso, G. Longobardi, Design of repositories of conceptual schemas in the small and in the large. in *Proceedings of the eGovernment Workshop '05 (eGOV05)*, Brunel University, Middlesex, UK, 13 September 2005

C. Batini, D. Barone, M.F. Garasi, G. Viscusi, Design and use of ER repositories: methodologies and experiences in eGovernment initiatives. in *Proceeding of Conceptual Modeling – ER 2006, 25th International Conference on Conceptual Modeling*, Tucson, AZ, USA, November 6–9, 2006, vol. 4215 (Springer, Heidelberg, 2006), pp. 399–412

C. Batini, G. Viscusi, D. Barone, A repository based approach to data riverse engineering. in *Proceedings of the First International Working Session on Reverse Engineering Techniques for Application Portfolio Management, (RE4APM 2007), co-located with the 23rd IEEE International Conference on Software Maintenance (ICSM 2007)*, Paris, 5 October 2007

P.A. Bernstein, U. Dayal, An overview of repository technology. in *VLDB '94: Proceedings of the 20th International Conference on Very Large Data Bases*, Santiago de Chile, 12–15 September 1994, pp. 705–713

A. Bonomi, A. Mosca, M. Palmonari, G. Vizzari, NavEditOW – a system for navigating, editing and querying ontologies through the web. Lect. Notes Comput. Sci. **4694**, 686–694 (2007)

D. Booth, H. Haa, F. McCabe, E. Newcomer, M. Champion, C. Ferris, D. Orchard, Web services architecture – w3c working group – note 11, February 2004, http://www.w3.org/TR/ws-arch/#whatistis

D. Calvanese, M. Lenzerini, D. Nardi, Description Logics for Conceptual Data Modeling, ed. by J. Chomicki, G. Saake, in *Logics for Databases and Information Systems* (Kluwer Academic, Norwell, 1998), pp. 229–264

Capgemini, *Online Availability of Public Services: How is Europe Progressing?* Web Based Survey on Electronic Public Services Report of the Fifth Measurement (European Commission Directorate General for Information Society and Media, Europe, 2004)

Capgemini, *Online Availability of Public Services: How is Europe Progressing?* Web Based Survey on Electronic Public Services Report of the 6th Measurement. i2010 Information

Space Innovation & Investment in R&D inclusion (European Commission Directorate General for Information Society and Media, Europe, 2006)

J. Cardoso (ed.), *Semantic Web Services: Theory, Tools and Applications* (IGI Global, New York, 2007)

S. Castano, V. De Antonellis, Semantic dictionary for database interoperability. in *Proceedings of the 13th International Conference on Data Engineering*, University of Birmingham, Birmingham, UK, 1997

E.J. Chikofsky, in *The Necessity of Data Reverse Engineering*. Foreword for Peter Aiken's Data Reverse Engineering (McGraw Hill, London, 1996)

A. Cordella, E-government: towards the e-bureaucratic form? J. Inf. Technol. **22**, 265–274 (2007)

K.H. Davis, in *Lessons Learned in Data Reverse Engineering*. WCRE (IEEE Computer Society, Washington, DC, USA, 2001), pp. 323–327

P. Dunleavy, H. Margetts, B. Simon, J. Tinkler, *Digital Era Governance – IT Corporations, the State, and E-Government* (Oxford University Press, London, 2006)

R. Elmasri, S. Navathe, *Fundamentals of Database Systems*, 5th edn. (Addison-Wesley, England, 1994)

C. Grönroos, *Service Management and Marketing – Managing the Moments of Truth in Service Competition* (Lexington Books, Lexington, USA, 1990)

C. Grönroos, Adopting a service logic for marketing. Market. Theor. **6**(3), 317–333 (2006)

N. Guarino, in *Formal Ontologies and Information Systems*, ed. by N. Guarino. Proceedings of FOIS'98 (IOS Press, Amsterdam, 1998)

A.Y. Halevy, J. Madhavan, Corpus-based knowledge representation. in *Proceedings of the International Joint Conference on Artificial Intelligence (IJCAI 03)*, vol. 18 (USA, 2003), pp. 1567–1572

A.Y. Halevy, N. Ashish, D. Bitton, M. Carey, D. Draper, J. Pollock, et al., Enterprise information integration: successes, challenges and controversies. in *SIGMOD '05: Proceedings of the 2005 ACM SIGMOD International Conference on Management of Data (2005)*. pp. 778–787

R. Hauch, A. Miller, R. Cardwell, Information intelligence: metadata for information discovery, access, and integration. in *SIGMOD '05: Proceedings of the 2005 ACM SIGMOD International Conference on Management of Data (2005)*, pp. 793–798

M. Hepp, Possible ontologies: how reality constrains the development of relevant ontologies. IEEE Internet Comput. Mag. **11**(1), 90–96 (2007)

P. Johannesson, The role of business models in enterprise modelling. in *Proceedings of the Conceptual Modelling in Information Systems Engineering* (Springer, Berlin, 2007)

S. Kumar, *Data Governance: An Approach to Effective Data Management* (Satyam Computer Services, India, 2008)

C. Lovelock, E. Gummesson, Whither services marketing?: in search of a new paradigm and fresh perspectives. J. Serv. Res. **7**(1), 20–41 (2004)

J. Madhavan, P.A. Bernstein, A. Doan, A.Y. Halevy, Corpus-based schema matching. in *International Conference on Data Engineering (2005)*, pp. 57–68

D.L. Martin, M. Paolucci, S.A. McIlraith, M.H. Burstein, D.V. McDermott, D.L. McGuinness, B. Parsia, T.R. Payne, M. Sabou, M. Solanki, N. Srinivasan, K.P. Sycara, Bringing semantics to web services: the OWL-S approach. SWSWPC **3387**, 26–42 (2004)

I. Mirbel, Semantic integration of conceptual schemas. in *Proceedings of the First International Workshop on Applications of Natural Language to Databases (NLDB'95)*, Versailles, France, 28–29 June 1995, pp. 57–70

T. Moriarty, Framing your system. Database Program. Des. **4**, 38–43 (1991)

A. Motro, P. Anokhin, Fusionplex: resolution of data inconsistencies in the integration of heterogeneous information systems. Inf. Fusion **7**(2), 176–196 (2004)

H.A. Müller, J.H.Jahnke, D.B. Smith, M.-A.D. Storey, S.R. Tilley, K. Wong, Reverse engineering: a roadmap. in *ICSE – Future of SE Track*, Limerick, Ireland, 4–11 June 2000, pp. 47–60

A. Osterwalder, Clarifying business models: origins, present, and future of the concept. Commun. AIS **16**(1), 751–755 (2005)

M. Palmonari, G. Viscusi, C. Batini, A semantic repository approach to improve the government to business relationship. Data Knowl. Eng. **65**(3), 485–511 (2008)

L. Palopoli, G. Terracina, D. Ursino, DIKE: a system supporting the semi automic construction of cooperative information systems from heterogeneous databases. Software Pract. Ex. **33**(9), 847–884 (2003)

M. Paolucci, T. Kawamura, T.R. Payne, K. Sycara, Importing the semantic web in UDDI, in *Proceedings of the Workshop on Web Services, E-business and Semantic Web* (Springer, Heidelberg, 2002a)

M. Paolucci, T. Kawamura, T. Payne, K. Sycara, Semantic matching of web services capabilities, in *Proceedings of the First International Semantic Web Conference (ISWC)* (Springer, 2002b), pp. 333–347

M.P. Papazoglou, D. Georgakopoulos, Service-oriented computing. Commun. ACM **46**(10), 25–28 (2003)

J. Perez, I. Ramos, J. Cubel, F. Dominguez, A. Boronat, J. Carì, Data reverse engineering of legacy databases to object oriented conceptual schemas. Electron. Notes Theor. Comput. Sci. **74**(4), 1–13 (2002)

V. Peristeras, N. Loutas, S. Goudos, K. Tarabanis, Semantic interoperability conflicts in pan-European public services. in ed. by H. Österle, J. Schelp, and R. Winter, *Proceedings of the 15th European Conference on Information Systems (ECIS2007), June 7–9 2007* (University of St. Gallen, St. Gallen 2007), pp. 2173–2184

V. Peristeras, K. Tarabanis, N. Loutas, Cross-border public services: analysis and modeling, in *Proceedings of the Fortieth Annual Hawaii International Conference on System Services* (IEEE Computer Society, Waikoloa, Big Island, HI 2007), p. 10

M.E. Porter, *Competitive Advantage* (The Free Press, New York, 1985)

E. Rahm, P.A. Bernstein, A survey of approaches to automatic schema matching. VLDB J. **10**(4), 334–350 (2001)

D. Roman, J. de Bruijn, A. Mocan, H. Lausen, J. Domingue, C. Bussler, D. Fensel, WWW: WSMO, WSML, and WSMX in a nutshell. ASWC **4185**, 516–522 (2006)

R.T. Rust, P.K. Kannan, *E-Service: New Directions in Theory and Practice* (ME Sharpe, Armonk, NY, 2002)

A. Sheth, K. Verma, K. Gomadam, Sematics to energize the full services spectrum. Commun. ACM **49**(7), 55–61 (2006)

P. Shoval, R. Danoch, M. Balaban, Hierarchical entity-relationship diagrams: the model, method of creation and experimental evaluation. Requir. Eng. J. **9**(4), 217–228 (2004)

M. Themistocleus, H. Chen, Investigating the integration of SMEs' information systems: an exploratory case study. Int. J. Inform. Tech. Manag. **3**(2/3/4), 208–234 (2004)

UDDI.org, Introduction to UDDI: Important Features and Functional Concepts (2004)

P. Vassilios, L. Nikolaos, T. Konstantinos, Organizational engineering in public administration: the state of the art on eGovernment domain modeling, in *Proceedings of the 2008 ACM Symposium on Applied Computing*, ACM, Fortaleza, Ceara, Brazil, 2008

G. Viscusi and M. Palmonari, IPAS: an ontology based approach to government to business service selection. in *Proceedings Database and Expert Systems Application, 2008, DEXA '08. 19th International Conference on Database and Expert Systems Application (2008)*, pp. 749–753

Toward an E-Government Semantic Platform

Marco Luca Sbodio, Claude Moulin, Norbert Benamou,
and Jean-Paul Barthès

1 Introduction

This chapter describes the major aspects of an e-government platform in which semantics underpins more traditional technologies in order to enable new capabilities and to overcome technical and cultural challenges. The design and development of such an e-government Semantic Platform has been conducted with the financial support of the European Commission through the Terregov research project: "Impact of e-government on Territorial Government Services" (Terregov 2008).

The goal of this platform is to let local government and government agencies offer online access to their services in an interoperable way, and to allow them to participate in orchestrated processes involving services provided by multiple agencies.

Implementing a business process through an electronic procedure is indeed a core goal in any networked organization. However, the field of e-government brings specific constraints to the operations allowed in procedures, especially concerning the flow of private citizens' data: because of legal reasons in most countries, such data are allowed to circulate only from agency to agency directly. In order to promote transparency and responsibility in e-government while respecting the specific constraints on data flows, Terregov supports the creation of centrally controlled orchestrated processes; while the cross agencies data flows are centrally managed, data flow directly across agencies.

In order to allow a comprehensive use of such processes, it also provides means of supporting and helping civil servants in their daily use of the system.

While the implementation of electronic processes across organizations is a well-studied domain, technical solutions based on traditional workflows and business process automation become unpractical due to the increasing number of actors and

M.L. Sbodio (✉)
Italy Innovation Center, Hewlett-Packard, Corso Trapani 16, 10139, Torino, Italy

T. Vitvar et al. (eds.), *Semantic Technologies for E-Government*,
DOI 10.1007/978-3-642-03507-4_9, © Springer-Verlag Berlin Heidelberg 2010

services. For instance French Districts are responsible for Social Care; they allocate between 50% and 80% of their budget and staff to this end. Each District manages close to 25 different types of social allowances (not taking into account post-allowance services). For this purpose the District collaborates with several hundreds of local agencies that use their own information systems from tens of software providers for each social care domain (family/childhood, inclusion, housing, elderly and impairments, etc.). In such a complex environment, implementing an application to support the simplest social allowance takes almost two years of studies and development, thus leading to slow and expensive deployment of e-government in districts. This example shows the necessity to go beyond pure technical interoperability for effectively supporting government policies characterized by multiple services, actors or IT suppliers.

More generally, there are several situations in which semantics needs to be added to information systems, in order to ensure a shared understanding among system actors by referencing a common vocabulary/language. Among them, we find:

- Change management: changes in actors or services or processes are frequent, thus requiring dynamic selection of services
- Resilience: changes in information systems or architectural components should not disrupt the processes
- Complexity: end users need help to find the suitable services and processes among a high number of heterogeneous services

The Terregov platform offers a set of software components and technologies that enable an e-government semantic platform. Such a platform is based on formal ontologies. It provides advanced capabilities such as enhanced collaboration tools for civil servants, use of semantic web services for simplifying the definition and enactment of e-government processes, and automatic identification of social-care and healthcare services based on a citizen's profile.

The Terregov software is usable both as a whole system and as a set of subsystems and components that can be used for embedding advanced functionalities in other e-government platforms. The software is distributed under Open Source licenses and is available online on the Terregov open source site.[1]

The chapter is organized as follows: the first three sections introduce the needs of semantics in the e-government domain, the engineering process used in the project for developing the ontology and the resulting structure of the ontology. The next section presents the semantic indexing and searching tools that integrate the ontology. Then two sections explain the role of semantic web services and their uses in e-government platforms. The four following sections describe a real scenario that has been implemented using the technology described before. We conclude with an evaluation section.

---

[1]http://terregov-oss.eupm.net.

2 Semantics for E-Government

A shared and formal knowledge representation is a key resource to enable the use of semantic technologies. Recommendations about using standards led us to choose ontologies for the definition of shared vocabularies with formal semantics. According to Gruber (Gruber 1993) "an ontology is an explicit specification of a conceptualization." An ontology contains a description of the concepts of the application domain and of the relationships that hold among them.

Our intent in creating an ontology for e-government was not only to create a conceptualization of the domain, but also to build a formal vocabulary providing operational semantics for software applications and for interoperability. In this context, the Arianna approach (Barone and Di Pietro 2005a, 2005b) is interesting since it provides one of the best examples of operational ontologies used in e-government applications. However, the Arianna domain does not cover entirely the Terregov domain. Other ontologies developed in European projects like Onto-Gov[2] or Dip[3] are also worth noticing. Unfortunately, they were developed in parallel with the Terregov project and it was not possible to reuse them. The OntoGov ontology defines a high-level generic semantics for the e-government service lifecycle (i.e., covering all the phases from definition and design through to implementation and reconfiguration of e-government services). Its objectives are different from ours. Our objectives in defining an ontology for the e-government domain are summarized in the following points:

- Defining a formal conceptualization of a basic set of e-government concepts and their respective relationships; such a basic set constitutes a *core ontology*[4] for the e-government domain
- Ensuring the extensibility of the core ontology in order to cover specific subdomains, and in particular those analyzed in the Terregov project
- Providing operational support for the software components of an e-government semantic platform

Some research approaches (Missikoff and Schiappelli 2005) propose a unified method for modeling an ontology in the business domain.Nevertheless, we decided to keep the subdomains and operational extensions separated[5] from our core ontology in order to ensure better scalability and modularity. In this section we present the engineering process and the structure of our core ontology. Such an ontology serves as a common foundation to develop various capabilities for an e-government semantic platform. Firstly, the core ontology provides a common knowledge representation used throughout the various components of our e-government semantic

---

[2]http://www.ontogov.com/.

[3]http://dip.semanticweb.org/.

[4]The term "core ontology" should be understood by reference to the expression "core business." It denotes a regional ontology developed for the domain of social services.

[5]Essentially meaning in different name spaces.

platform. Secondly, it allows the enhancement of information retrieval tools with advanced capabilities, which copes with the ever-growing need of civil servants for a better access to information in order to face the continuously evolving and complex scenarios of their daily working tasks. Finally, the core ontology is the basic extensible vocabulary of concepts used in the semantic description of web services, thus enabling an increased level of automation in service-based e-government processes.

3 Engineering Process of the Core Ontology

We decided to build a new ontology following well known methodologies like those presented in (Fernándes-López et al. 1997; Uschold and Gruninger 1996). A summary of the main methodologies for building ontologies can also be found in (Fernándes-López et al. 1997; Fernández-López 1999). We slightly adapted some recommended methods in order to fulfill all the ontology objectives. In particular, we integrated a step on corpus analysis (Aussenac-Gilles et al. 2000) and we took into account end-user comments to iteratively refine the ontology. In designing our core ontology we also considered the evolutions of the Government Enterprise Architecture as described in (Peristeras and Tarabanis 2004).

The four-step method we adopted (Fig. 1) involves several actors and information sources, namely: (1) collecting and analyzing a corpus of text; (2) submitting the result to experts; (3) enhancing the ontology; and (4) introducing end-user observations.

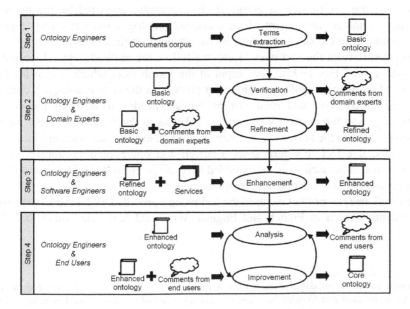

Fig. 1 Engineering process of the core ontology

The first step consists in collecting a corpus of administrative, legal and government-related documents, and in extracting the most important terms and expressions from this corpus using natural language processing tools. Thanks to morphologic and syntactic analysis, such tools can extract a set of terms from the analyzed documents, and classify them. Ontology engineers organize the concepts and relationships represented by the terms into a formalized ontology. The output of this step is a *basic ontology*, which is essentially a taxonomy expressing the semantics of the most relevant concepts from the corpus of documents.

During the second step, several domain experts, with the help of the ontology engineers, verify the content of the basic ontology, and iteratively refine it. The refinement substep is done by the ontology engineers on the basis of comments from the domain experts. The output of the second step is what we call a *refined ontology* that effectively maps the concepts and relationships of our domain. Although it is adequate for providing a shared formal vocabulary of the domain, or to be used in enhanced collaborative tools and in information retrieval systems, it does not effectively support the definition of formal semantics for services.

The third step consists in the enhancement of the refined ontology, in order to add those concepts and relationships that are necessary to map relevant inputs, outputs and parameters types of semantic web services. This step is performed by a mixed team of software engineers and ontology engineers. Software engineers bring the necessary knowledge about web services and corresponding data domains, ontology engineers incorporate such knowledge into the ontology. The outcome of the third step is an *enhanced ontology*, the concepts and relationships of which map not only the knowledge of the domain experts, but also the general data structure needed to model the relevant web services.

During the fourth step, a group of civil servants supported by the ontology engineers analyze the content of the enhanced ontology, and iteratively improve it. The improvement substep is done by the ontology engineers on the basis of a set of comments from the end users. Here, we follow the methodology advocated by (Grüninger and Fox 1995). The output of the fourth step, which is also the final output of the whole ontology engineering process, is the *core ontology*. It contains the general concepts and relationships that are needed to describe the domain knowledge and the domain web services. Thanks to the iterative process we just described, and to the active involvement of domain experts, software engineers and end users, it effectively represents a shared and operational vocabulary of the domain. It can be used as is, or extended to map specialized subdomains that may require specific subconcepts and relationships.

In the Terregov project we used the technology provided by Nomino[6] to analyze documents written in French and English. We could have used other tools like

---

[6]Nomino was freely available at the beginning of the project. However, its site was disconnected and we understand that Nomino has been integrated to a set of services at the following address: http ://www.nominotechnologies.com.

Lexter for French (Bourigault 1996) or Sandra.[7] The reasons for using Nomino were the following: (1) Nomino was freely available; (2) from its Canadian origin, Nomino could process English and French; and (3) Sandra was not available at the beginning of the project.

4   Structure of the Core Ontology

The core ontology is organized in a text file structured into manually defined chapters and sections[8] in order to gather together concepts concerning the same entities in the documentation. Obviously, this internal organization has some limits but is a good approach for someone wanting to explore the ontology. The main chapters concern: geographical areas, territories and administrative zones, authorities, social services, documents, facilities and buildings, organizations, people, time and information technology.

It is not simple to give a complete overview of an ontology, either graphically or textually. Graphical tools give only partial representations, and lack the ability to show the complex structure of an ontology or a satisfying rendering of the concepts and relations. In order to support the iterative engineering process of the core ontology, and to simplify its presentation and discussion among experts, we designed a module for exporting our ontology into a visualization tool.[9] Such a visualization tool provided both a hypertextual and a graphical navigation of the ontology. Figure 2 shows a fragment of the Terregov core ontology displayed by this tool.

The left panel contains the hypertextual representation of the ontology, where each concept is presented with its corresponding description and links to possibly related concepts in the ontological hierarchy. The right panel gives a graphical representation of the concept selected on the left side, and provides a clustered view of connected concepts. The two panels are synchronized: when the user selects a concept in the right panel, its documentation appears in the left panel.

For representing the ontology and for obtaining an operational version, i.e., directly manageable by platform tools, we used the technology recommended by the W3C and in particular the OWL format (Bechhofer et al. 2004). However, the available ontology editors like Protégé or SWOOP had some problems with coping with multilingual ontologies easily and gave a very local view of the edited ontology. Thus, we developed a specific format called Simple Ontology Language

---

[7]Sandra is a linguistic tool that has been developed during the Terregov project. It is available on the Terregov site.

[8]See later for the ontology formalism.

[9]We used Touchgraph Wiki Browser that was freely available at the time from http://www. touchgraph.com/.

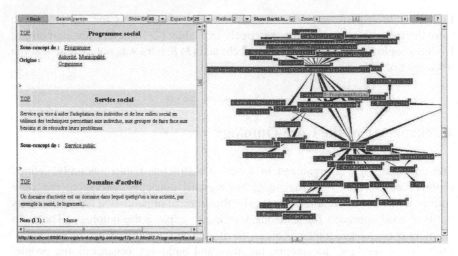

Fig. 2 Hypertextual and graphical views of the core ontology

(SOL[10]) that can be handled by a simple text editor and some related tools for parsing and exporting an SOL ontology into the OWL standard. SOL uses a frame formalism, but translates into OWL definitions. Thus, its semantics is that of OWL. However, we introduced a number of additional features like: (1) an easy way to express multilingual labels and synonyms; (2) the possibility of expressing rules (A-Box); (3) the possibility of annotations for later creating indices; and (4) the organization in chapters and sections. The SOL-to-OWL compiler further checks the consistency of the ontology, adds inverse relations automatically (inverse object properties), produces either JENA[11] or SPARQL (Prud'hommeaux and Seaborne 2008) rules, produces various output files, e.g., for display. SOL was developed for allowing the ontology specialist to create and maintain a large ontology using a simple text editor, and catching most of the syntactic and consistency mistakes.[12] The detailed presentation of the SOL language is outside the scope of this chapter; more information can be found in (Moulin et al. 2008; Terregov 2008).

When modeling the ontology, we observed that some concepts could be specialized according to different semantic axes. For example, the central concept "People," which is important in e-government applications, can be considered from different points of view like handicap (physically/visually impaired people, etc.), occupation (civil servant, mayor, jobless, etc.), marital status (married, single, etc.), etc. The different points of view yield different specializations of the concept of "People," each of which spans a hierarchy of subconcepts. We decided to take a different modeling approach. Instead of having several distinct subconcepts

---

[10]The SOL tool suite and the ontology are available on the Terregov open source site: http://terregov-oss.eupm.net/my_spip/index.php.

[11]http://jena.sourceforge.net/.

[12]The approach is somewhat similar to the Latex approach.

hierarchies, we maintain a single hierarchy of fundamental concepts (such as "People"), and we mark concepts belonging to the same semantic axis. The OWL formalism enables such a representation through the "oneOf " construct.

This way of modeling simplifies the building of concepts, avoiding specifying disjoint and complementary concepts for representing a semantic axis. In this way, reasoning on a knowledge base for categorizing people is greatly simplified (Moulin et al. 2008). Indeed, it is possible to write simple rules and use rule engines for dynamically extracting a semantic axis (for example, people with a certain handicap or married people).

In the Terregov project we analyzed scenarios from different European countries, and built several applications. Our core ontology serves as a common ground for all scenarios and applications, and can be extended and customized to answer specific needs. The core ontology contains only the subset of generic reusable concepts for the e-government domain. Such concepts are multilingual, i.e., they are identical in each involved country. Each concept in the core ontology has a description with translations into various languages (English, French, Italian, and Polish). The use of multilingual concepts corresponds to the "enrichment of an ontology with multilingual information" (Espinoza et al. 2008).

Culture-specific concepts fall into the extensions of the core ontology: they are concepts that depend on a specific administrative domain and have no equivalent in other countries. Each culture-specific concept has a description in the native language of the corresponding administrative domain, and an equivalent description in English to simplify general understanding.

A simple example involves administrative partitions that differ in European countries. The concept of "département" in France has no equivalent in the United Kingdom; the concept of "préfecture" is different in France and in Italy, etc. Such concepts receive an English tag (e.g., "French department," "Italian prefecture"), and an associated description.

5   Indexing and Searching Tools

Once the semantics of procedures and services is made explicit in order to support semantic interoperability, a large part of the administrative burden is supported by automated procedures. The role of civil servants involved in such e-government processes is therefore radically modified. They increasingly act as a front-end to citizens providing advices, identifying the most adequate services, activating the procedures for specific citizen cases. To this purpose, civil servants involved in delivering a service to citizens must become familiar with the whole offer of government services and procedures in which they are involved. This requires both an extension of the semantics for human usage and the availability of knowledge services shared among the community of civil servants. Hence, we present how knowledge management tools enhanced with semantic indexing of resources can support a community of practice. This involves two different tools.

The first tool is based on the semantic indexing of documents: official documents, but also any kind of private document that a civil servant thinks should be indexed, e.g., e-mails or notes. Indexing is done automatically.

Unlike standard keyword indexing technologies that are designed to generate inverted indexes containing every word occurring in a document, semantic indexing techniques associate documents only with items from a predefined vocabulary – the so-called controlled vocabulary. Actually, the term "semantic" is justified only if such a controlled vocabulary is an ontology. In such a case, a concept label is merely a textual representation of a semantic unit (concept) formally defined in the underlying ontology, and thus a technical means to associate a document with that semantic unit. Accordingly, semantic indexing allows identifying a document by its meaning rather than merely by its vocabulary.

Semantic indexing is useful when searching for documents. The relations defined in the ontology allow connections among concepts, which can be exploited to refine and/or to enlarge the search. For example, starting from the documents associated with the concept "Allowance," it is possible to look for related documents, such as those associated with concepts having some ontological relations with "Allowance," or those having the same "Author," or published by the same "Organization," etc.

Starting with concept labels extracted from an ontology, semantic indexing must then attempt to match such labels with the text in a document. Techniques derived from natural language processing (NLP) overcome the wide range of difficulties related to the matching. In particular, NLP deals with morphological and syntactical issues: singular and plural forms, verbs, nouns, etc. For example, if a concept label contains a singular noun, then a document containing a verb derived from that noun is indexed under the same concept. The core ontology provides the semantics required for a controlled vocabulary. However, this is not sufficient with respect to the difficulties encountered in the matching process. Accordingly, an additional, auxiliary ontology was developed and integrated into the semantic indexing tool. The auxiliary ontology encapsulates the lexical, semantic and grammatical knowledge necessary to correctly detect items from that controlled vocabulary in the documents. See the work from Moulin et al. (2006) for more details about semantic indexing.

A second transparent tool is associated with the user interface and allows querying the document base or the registry of services. Civil servants can send questions to the system. The auxiliary ontology developed in Terregov specifically for semantic indexing provides also an effective means for querying, using natural language. As mentioned previously, semantic indexing transforms the Terregov ontology into an inverted index. The approach we followed is to treat a query just as any other natural language input, i.e., as a very short document. The same methodological approach applied to the semantic indexing of documents is thus also applied to the queries. Consequently, the same concept labels that were successfully detected in the indexed documents will be successfully detected in the queries. This approach ensures a complete consistency between the query processing results, and the indexing of the documents that are targeted by this query. According to the nature of queries, a civil servant can receive information from the ontology itself (e.g., the definition of a concept), or references to documents or services associated with specific concepts.

Furthermore, the introduction of cross-organizational procedures and knowledge services also enables the emergence of collaborative practices (among peers) where bureaucracy was often the rule. The Terregov e-government platform supports such practices with the provision of customizable workflow templates for collaborative practices based on committees. However, transforming practices and procedures is a challenge that goes far beyond technology; it requires strong political willingness and commitment.

6 Semantic Web Services for E-Government

With a diversity of in-house IT systems (information sources, databases, legacy applications, etc.) and the increasing availability of third party applications and service providers, the web services technology is becoming a major building block for application interoperability and integration. Not only enterprises, but also e-government IT environments are adopting the paradigm of service-oriented architecture (SOA), which facilitates the creation of business processes from distributed interoperable components built as web services. However, the availability of technically interoperable web services is not sufficient to ensure the correctness and validity of the assembled processes. Moreover, business processes should not assume the use of concrete and specific web services; otherwise, the processes themselves become highly coupled to the services, and lose their modularity, flexibility and adaptive character.

Semantic descriptions of services are a key factor to ensure that the proper web services are used when building processes in a service-oriented architecture, and that the resulting processes are flexible and adaptive. In the remainder of this section we give an overview of semantic web service technologies, and we describe an application framework for semantic web services giving examples of its usefulness in the e-government domain.

Semantic Web Services aim at overcoming the lack of expressiveness of the current syntactical definitions, providing formal and unambiguous descriptions of the indented purpose of web services operation, and enabling a higher degree of automation in tasks such as discovery, composition and monitoring. Although the WSDL[13] description of a web service is a precise definition of its functional interface, it does not declaratively and unambiguously denote the semantics of the operations offered by the web service.

The semantic web services vision (McIlraith et al. 2001) is pursued by several formalisms and frameworks, such as WSMO (De Bruijn et al. 2005a, 2005b),

---

[13]http://www.w3.org/2002/ws/desc/.

OWL-S (Burstein et al. 2004), and the recent W3C recommendation SAWSDL (Kopecký et al. 2007). An in depth description of semantic web services formalisms is out of scope in this chapter; the interested reader may find a comparison between OWL-S and WSMO in (Lara et al. 2004); possible interactions between SAWSDL and OWL-S are described in (Paolucci et al. 2007). An overview of recent trends and developments in the area of Semantic Web Services is available in (Martin et al. 2007a, 2007b).

Our work is largely based on OWL-S. We selected OWL-S because of its openness, simplicity, and modularity, and because it is based on standard W3C Semantic Web technologies (OWL-S is in fact a set of OWL ontologies). However, the application framework for semantic web services, the architecture of which is described in the following section, also supports SAWSDL. The specific implementations of the framework components take care of handling the peculiarities of OWL-S or SAWSDL.

7   An Application Framework for Semantic Web Services

Semantic Web Services are a valuable technology that enables a variety of powerful applications. Here, we present the architecture of a framework for semantic web services that offers a set of reusable software components. The framework facilitates the creation of applications that take advantage of semantic web services capabilities. The design principles that underpin the architecture of the application framework are the following:

- Modularity: the architecture consists of separate components that interact among one another
- Separation of concern: each architectural component has specific capabilities that do not overlap with those of other components
- Independence from semantic web services formalisms: the architecture does not make any assumption on the formalisms used to describe the semantics of web services; both OWL-S and SAWSDL are supported
- Generality: the architecture is general enough to be reused in several application domains other than e-government
- Stratification: the architecture extends the existing service-oriented architecture paradigm, ensuring co-existence of traditional and semantic web services, and minimizing deployment impacts

The following figure shows the components of the framework, and its layering on top of existing SOA components (Fig. 3).

The *Semantic Registry* holds the semantic descriptions of web services, and provides high level search functionalities for the Discovery Agent and the Composition Engine. The Semantic Registry may work in parallel with a standard UDDI Registry: the former keeps only semantic information of the web services, and the latter stores their traditional descriptions. In a scenario where a UDDI Registry is

Fig. 3 Architecture of the
application framework for
semantic web services

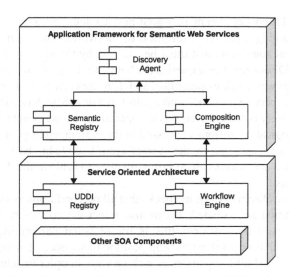

coupled with the Semantic Registry, the former acts as a master, and an additional software layer bridges the two registries and keeps them synchronized. In our solution the bridging module is named *Semantic Binder*: it is an end-user application allowing the user to manage syntactical (WSDL) and semantic descriptions of services. The Semantic Binder acts as a single publishing service for both UDDI and Semantic Registry: whenever a WSDL is published into (removed from) the UDDI, its associated semantic descriptions are also published into (removed from) the Semantic Registry.

The Semantic Registry is organized in *Entries*. Each Entry represents the semantic information of a web service operation; the Entry has a unique identifier within the Semantic Registry, and a type (allowing distinction among different types of semantic descriptions, such as OWL-S or SAWSDL). Specialized Entry implementations provide access to detailed information from the corresponding semantic description.

The Semantic Registry keeps also internal data structures that model the *preconditions* and *effects* of web services operations (the former are logical expressions that must be evaluated to be true in order to properly invoke the web service operation and the latter are logical expressions that hold after the invocation of the web service operation. Such data structures are used to answer search queries. A search query essentially consists of a set of logical conditions, which must hold after the invocation of an appropriate web service operation. The Semantic Registry checks the satisfiability of the logical conditions expressed in a search query against its internal data structures, and returns search results consisting of the Entries corresponding to web services operations whose effects ensure the satisfiability of the search conditions.

The Semantic Registry is usually queried by the *Discovery Agent*, which is a software module specialized in the automatic discovery of semantic web services.

The Discovery Agent is a goal-based intelligent agent. It has a knowledge base containing a partial description of the world. The agent goal contains the set of logical conditions that must be satisfied by the effects of a web service operation. The Discovery Agent queries the Semantic Registry to identify the set of potentially useful web service operations, and then, for each of them, checks the satisfiability of the respective preconditions against its knowledge base. The result of the automatic discovery is a set of web service operations whose effects ensure the satisfiability of the logical conditions expressed in the current agent goal, and the preconditions of which are satisfied by the current agent knowledge base. Any of the returned web service operations can be safely invoked to achieve the desired effect, and to fulfill the goal.

The Discovery Agent checks that all preconditions associated with a web service operation are satisfied. It can also select the operations whose preconditions are only partially satisfied: this is useful when performing searches with relaxed constraints or for dynamic composition of services. It is the task of the *Composition Engine* to build sequences of web services in order to achieve a complex goal. The dynamic composition handles the cases when a web service operation has both a desired output, and an effect that satisfies a specific goal, but only a subset of its required inputs is available and/or its preconditions are only partially satisfied. In such cases, the Composition Engine can search for web service operations whose output is semantically compatible with the missing required inputs (Paolucci et al. 2002) and whose effects can contribute to the satisfiability of the necessary pre-conditions (Sbodio and Moulin 2007). The composition process is recursively iterated with a backtracking algorithm, the result of which is a sequence of web services that can be invoked in order to achieve the desired effect and get the expected output.

Another possible approach to the dynamic creation of workflow is the so called *template approach* (Martin et al 2007a). In this case, the workflow that describes a process has (some) *abstract steps*. An abstract step does not specify the exact service to be invoked, but it only gives a description of the service type and/or the desired output and effects. When such a workflow is invoked, the Composition Engine must go through it, and find out appropriate services that can be invoked at each abstract step. This is a semiautomatic approach to dynamic workflow creation: the abstract workflow is created by humans, but its instantiations are automatically generated, and may vary in time according to service availability. The template approach ensures a very high level of flexibility and adaptive character.

The Composition Engine can also interact with a traditional Workflow Engine in an SOA environment. The sequence of web services created by the Composition Engine can be translated into a BPEL[14] workflow that is deployed into a BPEL compatible workflow engine for subsequent execution. Specific implementations of the software bridging the Composition Engine with the Workflow Engine can handle formalisms different from BPEL.

---

[14]http://docs.oasis-open.org/wsbpel/2.0/wsbpel-v2.0.pdf.

Both the Discovery Agent and the Composition Engine are designed to offer low-level interfaces that can be used by higher-level software components that are part of a domain-specific application, and that directly interact with end users.

8 E-Government Applications

The e-government domain, like modern enterprise environments, is adopting the service-oriented architecture paradigm. SOA helps in coping with the scalability and manageability requirements of modern IT infrastructure, and with the ever growing need for interoperability among heterogeneous and distributed systems. The application framework for semantic web services enables a number of interesting applications for the e-government domain.

Firstly, the framework offers support for the creation of flexible and adaptable e-government processes. The increasing availability of web services wrapping existing legacy systems offers a unique opportunity to create e-government processes that cross the boundaries of several local or regional organizations and departments. The framework components allows creating even more flexible processes, where one or more steps are not tightly bound to a specific web service implementation but rather specify the required output and effects. The Composition Engine can enact such processes finding at every execution the most appropriate service for each step. This fully dynamic approach may have obvious impacts on performance, but intermediate solutions are possible: for example, the Composition Engine may be used only on first-time invocation, and then the composed workflow is reused until some services happen to be unavailable or until new better services become available.

The template approach to service composition can be extremely useful in the e-government domain, where a process may be linked to (or represent) some law or governmental procedure. The template process can be designed by a central authority, and then distributed to local authorities with possible customizations. It is quite common that local authorities have their own implementations of services, and in this scenario the Composition Engine and Discovery Agent offer a unique opportunity to (semi)automatically deploy the centrally designed template process, by finding the appropriate web services in the local Semantic Registry. This ensures a high degree of flexibly, and allows a controlled distribution of template processes that support or map governmental procedures or laws.

Using the framework for semantic web services can also enable some novel applications, that provide better support to specialists working in the e-government domain, and increase the overall efficiency of some processes. A very common use case in the e-government domain is the identification of appropriate assistance services for some categories of citizens (typically elderly or physically/mentally impaired people). The assistance services range from social services, to economical or healthcare services, and they may differ from one local or regional authority to another. Usually a citizen may benefit from one specific assistance service only if some eligibility criteria are met: for example an economical support for elderly people may be available only for citizens who are older than a specific age, and whose annual income is below a certain threshold. The eligibility criteria for a given assistance service may vary from a local authority to another, and may also change over time due to updates in related laws. Such aspects, together with the broad variety of local assistance services, create a very complex, dynamic and heterogeneous scenario, which makes the identification of appropriate services for a citizen a challenging and time/resource consuming task. Such a task is usually performed by domain experts who know the details of available assistance services and examine the various citizen cases, evaluating the peculiarities of each of them in order to select the most appropriate services.

We exploited semantics to build novel applications that support domain experts in this scenario. The eligibility criteria of assistance services are analogous to the preconditions of web services operations: a citizen is eligible for an assistance service only if she/he meets the corresponding eligibility criteria. Similarly, a software client may safely invoke a web service operation only if its preconditions are satisfied. Exploiting this similarity, it is possible to perform an automatic discovery of appropriate assistance services for citizens. It is obviously necessary to give at least a partial semantic description of each assistance service, which specifies the corresponding eligibility criteria as preconditions of a fictitious web service operation. OWL-S can be effectively used to build such a partial description (Moulin and Sbodio 2007), giving the minimal amount of semantics to declaratively specify the eligibility criteria as preconditions. We use SPARQL, the W3C standard query language for RDF, to express preconditions and effects of services (Sbodio and Moulin 2007). The Semantic Registry can store the semantic descriptions of the assistance services, and the Discovery Agent can automatically identify the services that a citizen is eligible for. In this kind of application, the Discovery Agent takes the so called citizen profile as knowledge base. The citizen profile is a formal semantic representation of the relevant information about a citizen. The Discovery Agent checks if such a profile can satisfy the preconditions (that is the eligibility criteria) of some services.

The following figure (Fig. 4) illustrates a fragment of the OWL-S description of an example: the "Economic assistance service" (for reasons of space we do not give the whole description, but only the fragment specifying the SPARQL query that defines the services eligibility criteria and effects). The service description contains an instance of *SPARQL-Condition* (a class defined in the OWL-S *Expression* ontology), whose property *expressionData* gives the SPARQL query defining the eligibility criteria and effect. The WHERE clause (lines 15–30) defines the eligibility criteria, which gives two alternatives for being eligible for this service: (1) either the citizen has a job and an annual income of less than 5,000 (lines 16–22), or (2) the personal-wealth-indicator of the citizen contains the string "low" and the citizen is possibly job-less (lines 24–29). If the eligibility criteria are met, then the SPARQL query creates an RDF graph (lines 12–14) specifying that the citizen is entitled to an instance of the service *EconomicAssistance*. Note that the SPARQL query makes use of several concepts and relations coming from the Terregov

```
 1  @prefix expr: <http://www.daml.org/services/owl-s/1.2/generic/Expression.owl#> .
 2  @prefix xsd: <http://www.w3.org/2001/XMLSchema#> .
 3  @prefix : <http://www.regione.veneto.it/terregov/services/EconomicAssistance.ttl#> .
 4
 5  :Condition_1 a expr:SPARQL-Condition .
 6  :Condition_1 expr:expressionData "
 7    PREFIX foaf: <http://xmlns.com/foaf/0.1/>
 8    PREFIX xsd: <http://www.w3.org/2001/XMLSchema#>
 9    PREFIX rdf: <http://www.w3.org/1999/02/22-rdf-syntax-ns#>
10    PREFIX tgv: <http://www.terregov.eupn.net/ontology/2006/10/terregov.owl/terregov#>
11
12    CONSTRUCT {
13      ?citizen tgv:hasSocialBenefit [ a tgv:EconomicAssistance ] .
14    }
15    WHERE {
16      {
17        ?citizen a tgv:Z-Person ;
18          tgv:hasJob ?job ;
19          tgv:hasGainedIncome ?gainedIncome .
20        ?gainedIncome tgv:hasAmount ?amount .
21        FILTER ( ?amount <= 5000 )
22      }
23      UNION
24      {
25        ?citizen a tgv:Z-Person ;
26          tgv:hasPersonalWealthIndicator ?wealth .
27        OPTIONAL { ?citizen tgv:hasJob ?job . }
28        FILTER ( ! bound(?job) && regex(?wealth, "low", "i") )
29      }
30    }
31  "^^xsd:string .
```

Fig. 4 Eligibility criteria and effect of an Economic Assistance Service encoded as a SPARQL query in an OWL-S description

```
 1  @prefix foaf: <http://xmlns.com/foaf/0.1/> .
 2  @prefix xsd: <http://www.w3.org/2001/XMLSchema#> .
 3  @prefix tgv: <http://www.terregov.eupn.net/ontology/2006/10/terregov.owl/terregov#> .
 4  @prefix : <http://localhost:7532/kbs/alfa_beta.ttl#> .
 5
 6  :AlfaBeta a tgv:Z-Person;
 7    foaf:family_name "Alfa"^^xsd:string ;
 8    foaf:givenname "Beta"^^xsd:string ;
 9    tgv:hasJob _:myJob ;
10    tgv:hasGainedIncome _:myGainedIncome ;
11    tgv:hasPersonalWealthIndicator "low"^^xsd:string .
12
13  _:myJob a tgv:Z-Work;
14    tgv:isJobOf :Citizen_AlfaBeta .
15
16  _:myGainedIncome a tgv:Z-GainedIncome ;
17    tgv:hasAmount "4000"^^xsd:decimal ;
18    tgv:hasYear "2009"^^xsd:gYear ;
19    tgv:isGainedIncomeOf :AlfaBeta .
```

Fig. 5 Fragment of a citizen profile matching the eligibility criteria of the Economic Assistance Service

ontology ("tgv" prefix), which are essential to express the eligibility criteria and effects of the service.

The following figure (Fig. 5) shows a fragment of a semantic representation of a citizen profile having characteristics that match the eligibility criteria of the Economic Assistance Service.

Note that it is necessary to construct a partial representation of the citizen profile in a language having formal semantics (at least RDF): such a translation is not an understatement, and requires a careful mapping between the data collected in the citizen profile and ontological concepts. We have implemented a custom translation that consistently extracts the subset of information that is necessary to evaluate the eligibility criteria of existing services. Note that this subset may become insufficient when new eligibility criteria are defined. However, since our Discovery Agent can also perform partial matches of preconditions, it can find services even when the semantic translation of the citizen profile is incomplete.

The described approach enables the creation of applications that support the domain experts by automatically identifying appropriate assistance services that a specific citizen is eligible for, and can considerably speed up the corresponding e-government processes.

9   A Real-World Scenario

This section presents a real-world use case that has been analyzed and implemented as the Italian pilot application in the Terregov project.

The scenario of the use case is situated in a large local authority (Regione Veneto) based in northern Italy. Its territory spans an area of about 18,000 km^2 with a population of about five million inhabitants. This local authority is very active in the social care sector, and has an on-going initiative sponsoring the implementation of an "integrated on-line social care system." Such a system aims at increasing the use of information technology to achieve greater efficiency in the provision of services to citizens, and to offer better support to domain expert working in this sector.

The local authority representatives and the domain experts identified the service selection process as a bottleneck that highly delays the provisioning of social services to citizens. Although the area benefits from a very strong, active and dynamic community of volunteers and specialists in social services, the services selection process is affected by several problems:

- Huge heterogeneity of services: the provision of social care services is entrusted to many different actors (about 500 municipalities, 21 local social care units, and several nonprofit organizations and private companies)
- Amount or requests: the number of citizens requests for social care services is constantly increasing
- Poor IT support: there is a huge heterogeneity of existing infrastructures and application services that need to coexist and interoperate in order to deliver an integrated end-to-end solution

We have worked with the local authority representatives and domain experts to understand the scenario, to identify its weakness, and to design a solution. We have created mock-ups of the proposed solution, presented them to the final end users, and incorporated their feedbacks in successive refinements. We followed an iterative development process, with a strong involvement of the end users, who tested the application in three trial phases. In the following sections we describe the initial use case for the service selection process, and the semantics-based application that we have developed.

10   Use Case Description

The selection of social care services is done through a complex collaborative process that involves several human actors. Figure 6 illustrates the process, showing the main actors.

The process starts when a citizen gets in touch with a civil servant to ask for some kind of social service. Note that elderly or physically/mentally impaired people may be unable to perform this task (and the following ones) autonomously, and so some other person will act on their behalf. Nevertheless, for the sake of simplicity, we refer to the requesting citizen throughout the use case description.

The civil servant is a clerk working at a help-desk or a front-end office of the local public authority. Note that the citizen may or may not know in advance which services are available, and so the request may be specific (the citizen would like to benefit from a specific service) or generic (the citizen would like to know if there is any service for which she/he is eligible). Similarly, the civil servant does not necessarily know all the services provided by the various social care entities of the local authority. Finally, note that neither the citizen nor the civil servant may know in advance potential prerequisites for being granted a social service. It is in fact quite common that a citizen may benefit from a service only if she/he meets some eligibility criteria.

The citizen's request triggers various data collection steps. The first one is performed by the civil servant, who gathers some general information such as

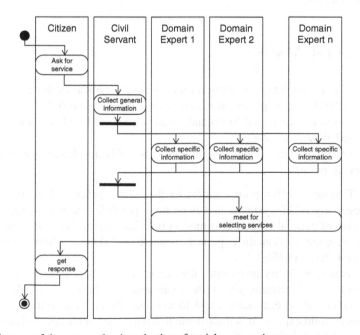

Fig. 6 Diagram of the process for the selection of social-care services

home address, contact information, family status, etc. The civil servant, in order to complete this task, may need to access several information systems, and/or ask information directly to the citizen. Sometimes the citizen is required to go to some specific office, get the required information, and bring it back to the civil servant (this process causes delays and inefficiency). The outcome of this first data collection step is a *General Citizen Profile*.

At this point the process forks into several independent data collection activities, each of which is performed by a corresponding domain expert. Each domain expert will perform some kind of medical examination or assessment of the citizen who has asked for social care. Each domain expert works independently, and at the end of her/his task fills in a *Domain Status Form*, which gives specific information on the citizen status with respect to that particular medical or social domain.

After the domain experts have completed their tasks, all the information (General Citizen Profile and all the Domain Status Forms) are gathered together into a *Complete Citizen Profile*. Note that this information is available on paper. The Complete Citizen Profile is the input for the last step of the process, which consists of a meeting among all the domain experts. During the meeting, the domain experts assess the complete status of the citizen who made the request for social care services, and evaluate if she/he is eligible for any social service. The services selection is based on the knowledge of the domain experts, who evaluate the information collected in the Complete Citizen Profile and check if the eligibility criteria for the various services are satisfied. The output of such a meeting is a response to the citizen; the response lists the selected social service that the user is entitled to receive.

11 Use Case Analysis

The use case for the service selection process is very typical in the e-government domain: in the Terregov project we found that another scenario that was independently assessed and analyzed in Poland, could also be reduced to such a use case (Siemek and Wozniak 2008).

The assessment of the scenario highlighted several issues that are summarized in the following points.

- The IT systems offer poor support to the whole process. Due to the huge heterogeneity of IT systems, and poor interoperability among them, even the gathering of general citizen information is a challenging task; besides, most of the work done by domain experts is paper based (Domain Status Forms and General Citizen Profile).
- There is no possibility to monitor the status of the whole process, and to give feedback to the citizens about the evaluation of their request. Due to the involvement of several actors, and to the distribution of activities among the various domain experts, it is impossible to have a constantly updated and precise status of all the different citizens' requests.

- The final selection of services requires a meeting among the various domain experts. Although domain experts tend to evaluate several citizen requests during a single meeting, this step is obviously a bottleneck within the process itself.
- The evaluation of the citizen profile against the eligibility criteria of the various services, being a human activity, is not necessarily conducted in a systematic way. It may be inaccurate (not all eligibility criteria of a given service are evaluated), or incomplete (not all possible services are taken into account). The service selection activity is largely based on the experience of the domain experts: they usually try to compare some relevant information of the current citizen profile with previous cases that they examined, and if such information matches, then they decide that the citizen is eligible for an already established set of services. This approach basically reduces a citizen case to some established *Standard Case*, where the set of services for which the citizen is eligible is already known. The domain experts perform a detailed evaluation only when the citizen case does not fall into any known Standard Case.

The use of semantics offers several improvement opportunities for the use case of social-care service selection. The need for interoperability among isolated and heterogeneous systems is a typical scenario for semantic web services. The need of collaboration among domain experts may be fulfilled by a mixture of traditional collaborative technologies and semantic technologies. Eliminating the need for actual meetings among the domain experts to evaluate the Standard Cases greatly increases the overall efficiency of the whole process. Interviewing domain experts who participated in the Italian pilot of the project, we discovered two interesting facts: about 60% of the citizen cases are reduced to a Standard Case, and such a reduction is often based on the evaluation of eligibility criteria that involve a specific subset of the information contained in the Complete Citizen Profile. This suggested that the use of semantics to automate the selection of social care services was a promising approach: the encoding of relatively simple eligibility criteria as preconditions of semantic description of services, and the use of the Discovery Agent helped in avoiding a meeting among domain experts in many cases, thus speeding up the whole process.

12 Application Description

We extended the Terregov core ontology in order to model the characteristics of the various social care services, and some relevant part of the General Citizen Profile (we only modeled those parts containing relevant information to evaluate the eligibility criteria of Standard Cases for the selection of social care services).

The IT department of the local authority had already initiated a progressive migration to service-oriented architecture, and this approach has enabled the adoption of our application framework for semantic web services. Isolated legacy systems were wrapped into web services, thus enabling the creation of a complete workflow that supports the gathering of information among the various distributed data sources. This workflow crosses the boundaries of several organizations ranging from the municipalities to the local health care agencies. We assessed that the dynamic composition of services was not necessary in this use case, because the workflow is fairly static. Therefore, we adopted the template workflow approach, where some steps (those collecting information from heterogeneous back-end systems) do not bind to specific web services implementation, but gives the semantic definition of the required output and effects.

We designed and built a web-based application that supports the civil servant in initiating the whole process and in collecting the information of the General Citizen Profile. Such a data collection step is performed though the invocation of various web services that fetch data from various legacy systems. The application also supports the domain experts providing web-based versions of the Domain Status Forms. Each domain expert is notified by e-mail whenever a new citizen case requiring his attention is opened. The civil servant can monitor the overall progress of the process, because the application has a status console that shows which Domain Status Form has already been filled in. When all the domain experts have completed their work, the Complete Citizen Profile is automatically assembled by the application. The application produces also the *Relevant Citizen Profile*, which is a semantic description of the subset of information that is relevant to evaluate the eligibility criteria of Standard Cases for the selection of social care services. At this point the application exploits the Discovery Agent of our framework to automatically identify the services for which the citizen is eligible. The result of the automatic discovery is an *Assistance Plan* that is sent by e-mail to the domain experts, who can verify it with their experience and eventually approve it by a single click. If all domain experts approve the proposed Assistance Plan, then the process completes without the need for a meeting of domain experts. If some domain expert does not approve the proposed Assistance Plan, or if no Assistance Plan is automatically identified by the application, then it is necessary to have a meeting. However, during our trials, we assessed that the meeting step was skipped for all Standard Cases.

The following figure (Fig. 7) shows the process for the selection of social care services with the support of our application.

The new process for the selection of social care services is entirely supported by a web-based application. Note that the activity *"collect general information"* is performed transparently through the invocation of web services. Similarly the activities *"collect specific information"* and *"approve/reject services"* are performed on-line through web forms, which communicate with back-end systems through web services. Finally, note that the Discovery Agent is an actor of the new process, and it effectively identifies services in all Standard Cases, thus reducing the need for a meeting among domain experts in about 60% of the cases.

The use of semantic technologies has brought added value to the application supporting the overall process, and has considerably increased the efficiency of the process itself, thus giving a better perception of the e-government effectiveness both to the civil servants and domain experts, and to the citizens.

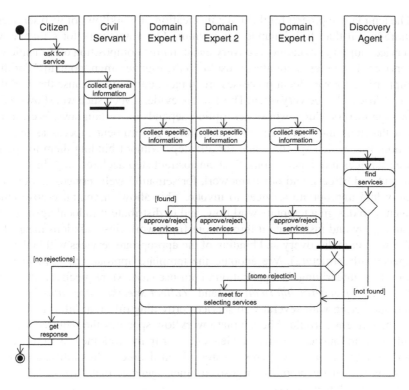

Fig. 7 Diagram of the new process for the selection of social-care services

13 Evaluation

Here, we present some lessons learned while implementing the application supporting the use case described in the previous sections, and the major results of the end users' evaluation.

- Semantic description of services is based on a set of ontologies, whose engineering process is long, difficult and involves several experts from different domains. We have developed an e-government ontology, which provided us the concepts and relations necessary to unambiguously describe key information and services. Such an ontology must be properly maintained: not only the ontology must evolve to coherently reflect changes in the e-government domain, but it may also require customizations for specific local scenarios. Although we designed the Terregov ontology in a modular and extensible way, its maintenance is not an easy task, and it requires a strong cooperation between domain experts and ontology engineers. The same considerations apply to the semantic description of social-assistance services, which must be properly updated to reflect changes in the existing services, and to incorporate new services.

- The template approach for the dynamic creation of workflows of web services is more useful than full dynamic composition. Our framework for semantic web services supports dynamic discovery and dynamic composition of semantic web services. The latter is not always useful in the e-government domain. Workflow supporting e-government processes are in fact quite static because the workflow steps do not change very often. This is more evident when such workflows reflect or support procedures whose description depends on certain laws. We can find out that it is more convenient to describe e-government process as template workflows, which specify some (or all) steps without binding them to specific web services implementations. Such an abstract step declares only the expected output and effects, and our framework for semantic web services can dynamically find appropriate services to invoke. This allows a central e-government agency to design a template workflow, and to distribute it to local agencies that can deploy and instantiate it through our framework (instantiations means here the automatic discovery and binding of the appropriate services within the local agency infrastructure). We adopted the template approach to implement the workflow underlying the application of our use case. More precisely, the activities *"collect general information,"* and *"collect specific information"* requires the interaction with several web services providing different information items of the citizens' profile. The template workflow specifies the required semantic information for each activity, and leaves to our framework the task of finding the appropriate web services. This ensures a high degree of flexibility, and allows deployment of our application also in other agencies that have different web services implementations.
- The use of semantics effectively automates the selection of social care services, and improves the overall efficiency of the associated process. Our work showed that it is possible to give semantic descriptions of the social care services and of their associated eligibility criteria. This enables the use of our framework to automate the selection of services matching the characteristics of a citizen's profile. An obvious prerequisite is the translation of the citizen profile in a language with formal semantics. However, the eligibility criteria are based only on a small set of information items coming from the citizen profile (less than 20% of the whole citizen profile), and so their translation does not bring a huge overhead. Moreover, since the Discovery Agent of our framework can discover services whose preconditions are only partially satisfied, it is possible to find services even when the semantic translation of the citizen profile is incomplete. Our experiments showed that the Discovery Agent was able to automatically build assistance plan in 65% of the test cases, and that such plans were accepted without changes by the domain experts in 95% of the test cases. This effectively reduces the need of meetings among domain experts in about 60% of the cases.
- Civil servants, domain experts and citizens were positively impressed with the use of our application. We performed several interviews with the three categories of end users, collecting their feedback. We received several suggestions to

improve the usability of the application, but the overall impression was positive. Moreover, end users' feedbacks confirmed that our application succeeds in improving the overall efficiency of the selection process for social care services. In fact end users reported that reducing the need for meetings among domain experts, considerably improves the response time of the whole process.

14 Conclusions

This chapter described some major aspects of an e-government platform where semantics underpins more traditional technologies to enable new capabilities, and to overcome technical and cultural challenges.

First, we recognized that shared knowledge representation is a key resource to enable the use of semantic technologies, and therefore we presented the engineering and the structure of a core ontology for the e-government domain to be used as a common foundation for developing various capabilities of a semantic platform. Second, we recalled that civil servants are increasingly required to face new situations, and that better access to information and services is a key to improved public service. Hence, we presented how knowledge management tools enhanced with semantic indexing of resources can support a community of practice.

Third, we acknowledged the growing need for interoperability among heterogeneous systems: e-government environments are moving to the paradigm of service-oriented architecture, which facilitates the creation of business processes packaged as services. We described how semantic web services can improve the level of automation in the creation of such processes. We also extended the approach to a broader definition of service encompassing social-care and health-care services provided by Public Agencies. We showed how formal semantic descriptions of these services can be defined and enable novel applications.

Finally, we presented a real-world use case, where semantic technologies have brought added value to an application that reengineers a typical e-government process in the domain of social services and health care.

Acknowledgments The work presented in this chapter has been developed within the project Terregov (Terregov 2008), an integrated project cofunded by the European Commission under the IST (Information Society Technologies) Program, e-government unit, under the reference IST-2002-507749.

References

N. Aussenac-Gilles, B. Biébow, S. Szulman, Revisiting ontology design: a methodology based on corpus analysis, in *12th International Conference in Knowledge Engineering and Knowledge Management (EKAW)*, Juan-Les-Pins, France, 2000

A. Barone, P. Di Pietro, in *Ontologies to Support the Definition of the Knowledge Society*, ed. by P. Bouquet, G. Tummarello. Semantic Web Applications and Perspectives, vol. 166. CEUR Workshop Proceedings, Trento, Italy, 2005a

A. Barone, P. Di Pietro, in Semantic of egovernment processes: a formal approach to service definition, *International Workshop on Semantic and Orchestration of eGovernment Processes, Web Intelligence and Intelligent Agent Technology conferences* (Compiegne, France, 2005b), pp. 5–17

S. Bechhofer, F. van Harmelen, J. Hendler, I. Horrocks, D.L. Mcguinness, P.F. Patel-Schneider, L.A. Stein, M. Dean, G. Schreiber (eds.), *OWL Web Ontology Language Reference W3C*, 2004

D. Bourigault, Lexter: a natural language processing tool for terminology extraction. in *Proceedings of Euralex'96*, Department of Swedish, Göteborg University, 1996, pp. 771–779

M. Burstein, J. Hobbs, O. Lassila, D. Mcdermott, S. Mcilraith, S. Narayanan, M. Paolucci, B. Parsia, T. Payne, E. Sirin, N. Srinivasan, K. Sycara, D. Martin (eds.), *OWL-S: Semantic Markup for Web Services*, W3C Member Submission, 2004

J. De Bruijn, D. Fensel, U. Keller, R. Lara, Using the web service modeling ontology to enable semantic e-business. Commun. ACM **48**, 43–47 (2005b)

J. De Bruijn, C. Bussler, J. Domingue, D. Fensel, M. Hepp, U. Keller, M. Kifer, J. Kopecky, B. Knig-Ries, R. Lara, H. Lausen, E. Oren, A. Polleres, D. Roman, J. Scicluna, M. Stollberg, *Web service modeling ontology (WSMO)*, W3C Member Submission (2005b)

M. Espinoza, A. Gómez-Pérez, E. Mena, in *Enriching an Ontology with Multilingual Information*. The Semantic Web: Research and Applications (Springer, Heidelberg, 2008), pp. 333–347

M. Fernández-López, in *Overview of Methodologies for Building Ontologies*. ed. by V.R. Benjamins, B. Chandrasekaran, A. Gómez-Pérez, N. Guarino, M. Uschold, Proceedings of the IJCAI-99 workshop on Ontologies and Problem-Solving Methods (KRR5), Stockholm, Sweden, 1999

M. Fernándes-López, A. Gómez-Péres, N. Juriso, METHONTOLOGY: From ontological art towards ontological engineering. in *Proceedings of AAAI-97, Spring Symposium on Ontological Engineering* (Stanford University, California, 1997)

T.R. Gruber, Toward principles for the design of ontologies used for knowledge sharing. Int. J. Hum. Comput. Stud. **43**(5–6), 907–928 (1993)

M. Grüninger, M.S. Fox, Methodology for the design and evaluation of ontologies. in *IJCAI'95, Workshop on Basic Ontological Issues in Knowledge Sharing*, Canada, 1995

J. Kopecký, T. Vitvar, C. Bournez, J. Farrell, SAWSDL: semantic annotations for WSDL and XML schema. IEEE Internet Comput. **11**, 60–67 (2007)

R. Lara, D. Roman, A. Polleres, D. Fensel, L. Zhang (eds.), *A Conceptual Comparison of WSMO and OWL-S*. ECOWS, vol. 3250 (Springer, Heidelberg, 2004), pp. 254–269

D. Martin, J. Domingue, M.L. Brodie, F. Leymann, Semantic web services, Part I. IEEE Intell. Syst. **22**, 12–17 (2007a)

D. Martin, J. Domingue, A.P. Sheth, S. Battle, K.P. Sycara, D. Fensel, Semantic web services, Part II. IEEE Intell. Syst. **22**, 8–15 (2007b)

S.A. McIlraith, T.C. Son, H. Zeng, Semantic web services. IEEE Intell. Syst. **16**, 46–53 (2001)

M. Missikoff, F. Schiappelli, A method for ontology modeling in the business domain. in *EMOI-INTEROP*, Porto, Portugal, 2005

C. Moulin, M.L. Sbodio, Exploiting semantics to automate selection of services for citizens, in *Proceedings of the eGovernment Interoperability Campus 2007*, Paris

C. Moulin, F. Bettahar, J.-P. Barthès, M.L. Sbodio, N. Korda, Adding support to user interaction in e-government environment, Adv. Web Intell. Data Mining **23**, 151–160 (2006)

C. Moulin, J.-P. Barthès, F. Bettahar, M.L. Sbodio, Representation of semantics in an e-government platform. in 6th Eastern European eGovernment Days, Prague, Czech Republic, 2008

M. Paolucci, T. Kawamura, T.R. Payne, K.P. Sycara, I. Horrocks, J.A. Hendler (eds.), Semantic matching of web services, in *Capabilities International Semantic Web Conference (ISWC)*, vol. 2342 (Springer, Heidelberg, 2002), pp. 333–347

M. Paolucci, M. Wagner, D. Martin, B.J. Krämer, K. Lin, P. Narasimhan (eds.), Grounding OWL-S in SAWSDL. in *ICSOC*, vol. 4749 (Springer, Heidelberg, 2007), pp. 416–421

V. Peristeras, K. Tarabanis, Advancing the government enterprise architecture -GEA: the service execution object model. in *Database and Expert Systems Applications*, DEXA, Zaragoza, Spain, 2004

E. Prud'hommeaux, A. Seaborne, SPARQL Query Language forRDF. W3C Recommendation, 2008

M.L. Sbodio, C. Moulin, SPARQL as an expression language for OWL-S. in *Proceeding of the Workshop "OWL-S Experiences and Future Developments", 4th European Semantic Web Conference 2007 (ESWC 2007)*, Innsbruck, Austria

A. Siemek, D. Wozniak, Semantic integration of social services on the basis of TERREGOV solution. in *Proceedings of the 6th Eastern European eGovernment Days*, Prague, Czech Republic, 2008

Terregov, TERREGOV: "Impact of e-Government on Territorial Government Services" – FP6/IST 507749, http://www.terregov.eupm.net/ (2008)

M. Uschold, M. Gruninger, Ontologies principles, methods and applications. Knowl. Eng. Rev. **11**(2), 96–137 (1996)

Part III

Portals and User Interaction

Semantic-Based Knowledge Management in E-Government: Modeling Attention for Proactive Information Delivery

Konstantinos Samiotis and Nenad Stojanovic

1 Introduction

E-government has become almost synonymous with a consumer-led revolution of government services inspired and made possible by the Internet. With technology being the least of the worries for government organizations nowadays, attention is shifting towards managing complexity as one of the basic antecedents of operational and decision-making inefficiency. Complexity has been traditionally preoccupying public administrations and owes its origins to several sources. Among them we encounter primarily the cross-functional nature and the degree of legal structuring of administrative work. Both of them have strong reliance to the underlying process and information infrastructure of public organizations. Managing public administration work thus implies managing its processes and information. Knowledge management (KM) and business process reengineering (BPR) have been deployed already by private organizations with success for the same purposes and certainly comprise improvement practices that are worthwhile investigating. Our contribution through this paper is on the utilization of KM for the e-government.

The public sector is by far one of the most knowledge-based and intensive organizations, thus making it ideal for KM interventions. Already several issues related to the management of knowledge have been identified in public administrations: (1) information is not up to date, (2) required information is not available, (3) too much information is collected, (4) very little information is used in actual decision-making, and (5) there has been information explosion (Misra 2007). Information and knowledge are thus needed for a variety of purposes

K. Samiotis (✉)
Research & Innovation, PLANET S.A, 64, L.Riencourt Street, Apollon Tower, 115 23, Athens Greece
e-mail: ksamiotis@planet.gr

T. Vitvar et al. (eds.), *Semantic Technologies for E-Government*,
DOI 10.1007/978-3-642-03507-4_10, © Springer-Verlag Berlin Heidelberg 2010

contributing to decision making or problem solving. Making right decisions requires access to relevant information, when it is needed, by the people who need it. However, decision-making tasks suffer from two seemingly competing requirements. On the one hand, there is a need to have access to all sources of information, including sources of tacit knowledge. On the other hand, information overload of the knowledge workers can be as bad as having no access to relevant information at all. To avoid such deadlocks, we capitalize on a KM approach that is based on a model of information delivery, which utilizes human attention capacity as a means to tackle "proactively" any information requests of the knowledge worker.

This knowledge perspective recognizes workers as a source of knowledge in their respective roles (Devadoss Paul et al. 2002). Any intervention in this respect should make allowances for the support of the human factor and in particular its on-the-job requirements and significations. Our claim goes beyond existing empowerments for the structuring, searching and discovery of knowledge, concentrating on the importance of making information more readily and meaningfully available to its seekers, and therefore any reaction to it more (pro)active. The realization of this approach necessitates the understanding of the functioning of human attention in order to capture and model the requirements for proactive information delivery.

Our ideas for proactive information delivery are realized in the SAKE project[1] and subsequently in the SAKE system. The main aim of the SAKE (Semantic-enabled Agile Knowledge-based e-Government) system is to support public administrators in performing knowledge-intensive tasks. Required support can be provided in the following ways: integration of all relevant information sources, integration of information processing and integration of information flow with the current process and user context. The spearhead of the SAKE system is the utilization of semantics (i.e., ontologies) in traditional (i.e., content management and collaboration) but also novel KM functions (i.e., attention and change management). Moreover, SAKE draws its claims from three real business cases (three PAs), where the technical solution will also be validated.

In this paper we demonstrate the origins but also the products of our KM approach, which is based on the idea of proactive information delivery. We first address the specificities of the business environment that inspired us. Then we present the basic conceptual strands of our approach and conclude the paper with the details of its technical implementation.

[1]SAKE (Semantic-enabled Agile Knowledge-based E-Government) Project (IST-027128) is a European Commission project in the 6th Framework Program. The work presented in this chapter is funded by the SAKE project. For more information visit the project's website: www.sake-project.org.

2 Conceptual and Empirical Background

2.1 The Knowledge Landscape in Public Administrations

Public administrations represent the backbone of any political system. Involved at all stages of the policy-making process, public administration also plays the role of the interface between citizens and the political system, thus acting as an efficient catalyst for the process of transferring political measures to society. Nowadays, contemporary societal developments impose the modernization of PAs in order to achieve higher levels of efficiency in the delivery of public service. In this realm, KM introduces new options, capabilities, and practices that can impact and assist public administration to great advantage (Wiig 2000). For public administrations, the management of their knowledge landscape comprises a new responsibility.

As knowledge landscape, we define the structure of knowledge sources that are relevant for a problem domain. It can be represented as a classification of available knowledge sources, according to their content/structure, that enables, e.g., better search for a relevant knowledge type. The real challenge, however, lies in managing knowledge based on its usage and actuality, what we call as "changeability." Knowledge changes often are reflected on metadata, like creation date, last modification, how often a document has been changed, etc. However, metadata alone are not sufficient to capture the dynamic nature of knowledge or even of information during its "actuality/living" mode. In this mode, knowledge transforms thus affecting its purpose and scope of application. In several cases, changes in the knowledge landscape of the organizations remain unnoticed and thus unexploited. Managing people's attention will enable more relevant and important information and knowledge to reach its seekers. Our approach to KM is built on this premise.

Conception of knowledge acquires different meaning during its treatment in this knowledge landscape. This perspective of knowledge differs significantly from the one ascribed by traditional and static information management views (Panagiotis 2005). Knowledge is no longer manifested by static and reactive information structures such as usage stamps (time, person, purpose, etc.) and cataloging rules (clustering, etc.) but could be continuously redefined based on its role in the organizational landscape. In its new structure, knowledge codification is enhanced with information elements acquired during its "living" trajectory rather than any human ex post attributions. In knowledge-based environments like the ones in PAs, where information is endless and chaotic and human mediation is overwhelming, KM needs to facilitate efficient access to information by enabling information seekers' attention with appropriate IT-based mechanisms. Our proposition is greatly motivated by this principle.

2.2 Public Administrations in Need for KM

Our proposition does not stem only from conceptual inquiries but is also grounded
in the requirements of actual PA workplaces. Our work draws on three cases of PA
organizations located in three different countries, Hungary, Poland, and Slovakia.
Due to their recent endorsement by the European Union (EU), these countries are
still struggling to meet the quality criteria of EU in several aspects of public
services. This task becomes harder considering the PAs' heterogeneity within the
boundaries of a single country, let alone at a pan-European level. This heterogeneity is increased due to the complexity of activities of the PAs, the continuous change
as well as their scope (regional, national, international). Amidst these conditions,
we were called to support three PAs on three different areas:

1. LATA (Mestska cast Kosice – Sidlisko Tahanovce): pilot user has chosen the
   involvement of the public into the process of making local legal regulations by
   annotation of the city ward general binding regulation.
2. MEC (Ministry of Education and Culture): pilot process is the higher education
   portfolio alignment with the world of labor needs.
3. UMC (Urząd Miasta Czestochowy): pilot process is the management of education institutions' material resources.

All three cases concern processes in the PA environment addressed to citizens,
businesses, or PA-internal groups. Several features demonstrate the knowledge-
and information- intensiveness of these processes:

- They depend on a number of applicable laws, regulations, court decisions, etc.
- They typically process a huge amount of information and documents from
  different sources
- They require continuous monitoring of the content of the employed knowledge
  resources as they frequently become subject of change
- The application and interpretation of law and regulation is often not trivial,
  ambiguous, such that it requires experience in the field but also constantly
  updated knowledge
- Content items logically belong together (e.g., a regulation interprets a law in a
  more or less binding manner, while example cases illustrate the borders of
  applicability) and are only valid in a certain, complex application context
  (which region, which timing of events, which kind of citizen or decision, etc.)

2.3 Motivations for Technical Development

The formation of our KM propositions was based on a multiangle approach taking
into consideration SAKE's project proposal predefined ideas and requirements
from the three pilot public administration organizations. Special care was also
given to issues related to technological complexity and organizational adoption

so as to increase its possibilities for uptake. User requirements were collected through several workshops, where potential stakeholders and the project's technology team were participating. Our on-site inquiry led to the inception of a technical and management intervention constituted by empowerments on the content and collaboration functions of the PAs. Particularly, the following content- and collaboration-oriented scenarios have been elicited:

- Content-oriented scenarios
    - Resolving a difficult case
    - Storing an interesting case
    - Receiving proactive help
    - Coping with changes in law

- Collaboration-oriented scenarios
    - Finding an expert
    - Defining an expert
    - Storing an interesting communication
    - Building/Analysing Communities of Practice

Our requirements analysis also included detailed mapping of the knowledge landscape of the three pilot PAs as constituted by processes, knowledge assets and knowledge agents.[2] Specifically our inquiry focused on eliciting detailed description of the targeted processes in terms of knowledge inputs/outputs, communication modes and knowledge agents, the detailed description of knowledge assets (as the main input for the ontology population), and the detailed description of knowledge agents.

Our analysis of the public administrators' knowledge environment unveiled the need to control information in its context of use. Consequently, we adopt the notion of changeability to address the breadth of possible situations that an information resource can be found in during its life-span. Given information lives within a social context, it would be a mistake from our behalf to leave the human factor unaddressed (Brown and Duguid 2000). People comprise the basic sense-giving instrument for information. We perceive sense as a blend of value and meaning that is enacted by humans during the utilization of information in work. The maximization of these two aspects will inevitably lead to better decision making and problem solving. Apparently, access to information is not the problem; accessing information that is relevant, meaningful and valuable for our work is. However, given humans' bounded capacity to process information, proactive delivery of knowledge and information becomes an imminent priority. Our treatment for this matter comes through managing the attention of knowledge

---

[2]Mapping of the knowledge landscape was based on the CommonKADS methodology (Knowledge Engineering and Management, The CommonKADS Methodology", G. Screiber et al.)

workers. In our approach, there are three main requirements for modeling attention (to be further discussed later):

1. Modeling information sources that should be accessed, in order to enable focusing on relevant ones
2. Modeling context in which information should be received, in order to define the business context in which information will be consumed
3. Modeling preferences of users, in order to express individual "context" in which information will be used

Based on the requirements of three public administration organizations and also on our technical aspirations for the future KM solution, we endeavored to implement a technical solution that provides:

1. An integrated knowledge space (instead of a set of isolated and heterogeneous knowledge resources) that will unify different perspectives and interpretations of knowledge resources and will enable their treatment on a far more fine grained level: now any bit of information or any knowledge object could be given identity (so called virtual content) and assigned attributes (metadata) allowing for more sophisticated applications and services in e-government
2. A collaborative working environment (instead of a single-person decision-making process) that will bring every public servant to the same level of effectiveness and productivity and will ensure more efficient knowledge sharing by guaranteeing at the same time reliability and consistency of the decision-making process
3. A change management system (instead of ad hoc management of changes) that will ensure harmonization of requests for changes, resolution of changes in a systematic way and their consistent and unified propagation to the collaborative and knowledge space, in order to ensure the high quality of the decision-making process
4. A platform for proactive delivery of knowledge (instead of an one-way knowledge access) that enables creation of an adaptable knowledge sharing environment through learning from the collaboration between public servants and their interaction with the knowledge repository and supporting in that way the full empowerment of public servants

3 Proactive Information Delivery: A Role for Ontologies

Information and communication technologies (ICTs) have been used in several purposeful manners in order to support and facilitate KM activities (Alavi and Leidner 2001). The basic usages of ICTs refer to supporting creation, storage/retrieval, transfer, and application of knowledge in organizations. Typical examples of ICTs used for the aforementioned purposes comprise communication and collaboration tools, brainstorming tools, knowledge mapping and mining tools, workflow and content and document management systems, Intranets, and many more which were named KM tools following the concept's hype in the last decade (Ngai and Chan 2005). Lately, a new technological concept, called ontologies, lends its capacity on encapsulating shared and common understandings as a means to support knowledge sharing and reuse. Ontologies are increasingly seen as a key technology for enabling semantics-driven knowledge processing (Maedche et al. 2003). Our technical proposition also draws on ontologies' capabilities to model possible transformations of information inside an artefact, i.e., interaction among components, changing of content and metadata, etc.

Ontologies have been primarily and largely used for enabling the sharing of common understanding of the structure of information among people and software agents as well as enabling reuse of domain knowledge and making domain assumptions explicit to name just few of the reasons for their necessity (Noy and McGuinness 2001). The problem that we are trying to tackle in this paper lies in the effective delivery of information to its seekers, the resolution of which requires grasping and modeling the transformations of the information while being used. Given its existence in a shared context (e.g., PAs) the ontological treatment of information as resource (enclosing both content and action) deems appropriate and necessary. Ontologies are sufficient in capturing both the concepts and the relations about information resources as well as the changes affecting them. Modeling information in that way allows mapping and switching between different contexts i.e., context of resource creation, (individual) context of resource application (business) context of living.

The deployment of ontologies as a means to model the e-government domain for the purposes of our solution has its own value.

4   Modeling Attention: A New Challenge for Knowledge Management

The main challenge for modeling a KM system in e-government nowadays is modeling (efficiently) the attention of public administrators. Indeed, (human) attention capacity is the only resource which cannot be increased by improvements in the technology, as illustrated in Fig. 1.

On the other side, the amount of (relevant) information around public administrators is increasing dramatically, leading to the well known information overload problem. Therefore, managing access to relevant knowledge includes managing attention of knowledge workers.

Figure 2 presents our framework for Attention Management. It is developed along three axes, which corresponds to the aforementioned requirements:

1. Information represents all relevant chunks of knowledge that can be found in the available information repositories and sources. In the business environment of an organization, sources of information can be both internal and external to the organization. Moreover, information can be represented either formally (e.g.,

Fig.1 The importance of
managing attention efficiently

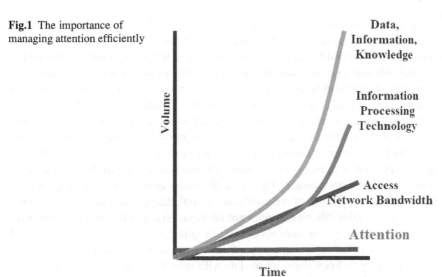

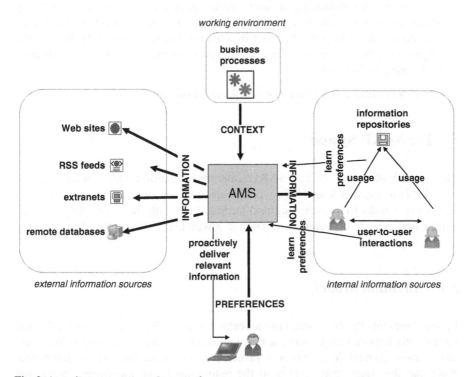

Fig. 2 Attention management framework

using information structuring languages such as XML) or informally. Finally, information may be stored in structured repositories such as databases that can be queried using formal languages or in unstructured repositories such as discussion forums. We use a set of ontologies for representing information (and sources).
2. Context defines the relevance of information for a knowledge worker. Detection of context is related to the detection of the user's attentional state which involves collecting information about users' current focus of attention, their current goals, and some relevant aspects of users' current environment. The mechanisms for detection of user attention that have been most often employed are based on the observation of sensory cues of users' current activity and of the environment; however others, non-sensory based, mechanisms also need to be employed to form a complete picture of the user's attentional state (Roda and Thomas 2006).
3. Preferences enable filtering of relevant information according to its importance/relevance to the given user's context. In other words, the changeability of resources is proactively broadcasted to the users who can be interested in them, in order to keep them up to date with new information. Users may have different preferences about both the means they want to be notified and also about the relevance about certain types of information in certain contexts. User preferences can be defined with formal rules or more informally by means e.g., of adding keywords to user profiles. Moreover, even when employing mechanisms capable of formalizing the users' preferences, a certain level of uncertainty about users' preferences will always remain. For this reason, dealing with uncertainty is an important aspect of attention management systems. Equally important is the way preferences can be derived: by explicitly specifying them or be learning techniques.

In the next section we give more details about our approach.

5   The SAKE System

The overall objective of the SAKE enterprise attention management system (EAMS) is to support knowledge workers always keep their attention focused on their current tasks by preselecting and feeding them with the most relevant information resources to complete their tasks in a way that will not disturb them more than they prefer.

5.1   Attention Model

Figure 3 presents the conceptual model behind SAKE. The model assumes that the interactions between users and internal information sources are logged including the business context (e.g., business process) in which the interactions happened. Note that the figure corresponds to the requirements we mentioned. Some log entries can be defined as Events that cause Alerts, which are related to a user, a

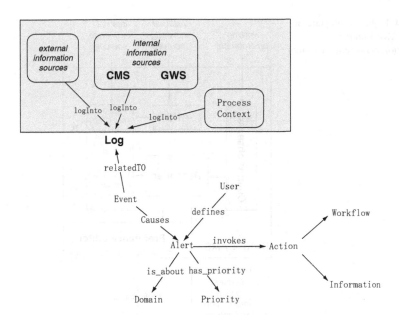

Fig. 3 Conceptual attention model

problem domain and associated to a priority level. Every Alert invokes Actions, that can be purely informative (i.e., an information push) or executable (i.e., to execute a business process).

In the core of the SAKE approach are ECA (Event–Condition–Action) rules; their general form is:

> ON *event* AND *additional knowledge*, IF *condition*
>
> THEN DO *something*.

Relevant events and actions are usually triggered by interactions taking place in organizational systems, such as the SAKE content management system (CMS) and the groupware system (GWS) or by external change detectors. The later are implemented with the change notification system (CNS), a component that can be configured to monitor web pages, RSS feeds and files stored in file servers for any change or specific changes specified by regular expressions (e.g., new web content containing the keyword "sanitary" but not "pets").

6 The SAKE Enterprise Attention Management System

Figure 4 depicts the logic architecture of the SAKE EAMS system that suits to the general EAMS framework given in Fig. 2.

Relevant events and actions are usually triggered by interactions taking place in organizational systems, such as the SAKE CMS and the GWS or by external change

Fig. 4 Logic architecture of
the SAKE Enterprise
attention management system

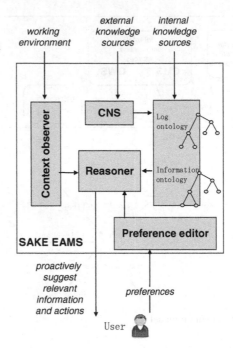

detectors. The later are implemented with the CNS, a component that can be configured to monitor web pages, RSS feeds and files stored in file servers.

The SAKE CMS enables storage and provision of content by:

(1) Supporting the annotation of content with metadata as well as relations between different content items
(2) Semiautomatic population of metadata using text mining methods and
(3) Realizing semantics-based search that retrieves content based on both full-text and metadata

The SAKE GWS supports information sharing and creation by:

(1) Supporting the annotation of the interactions between users
(2) Enabling identification of communities of practice from mining their interactions and their specific vocabularies by social tagging and
(3) Searching for experts based on their profiles as these are created explicitly and implicitly during their interaction with the system

In the rest of this section we present the most important ontologies for EAMS:

• The log ontology models change events, following a generic and modular design approach, while
• The Information ontology contains the domain concepts and relations about which we want to express preferences, such as documents and forum messages

In the following, we describe the log and information ontologies as well as the main components of the SAKE EAMS in detail.

6.1 Information Ontology

The Information ontology (Fig. 5) contains the concepts and relations about information resources for which we want to express preferences, such as documents and forum messages. On the top level we have separated the domain concepts from value types. The FiletypeValue class defines the different file types a file in the SAKE system can have.

In the InformationSource subtree we differentiate between information sources which are of an abstract nature (such as persons), external information sources such as Web pages and RSS feeds, and information sources which physically exists in the SAKE system, such as documents, forums or e-mails. We further divided the physical information sources into CMS-specific and GWS-specific entities.

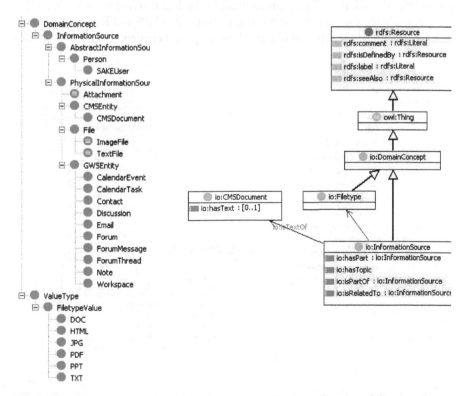

Fig. 5 Information ontology: class hierarchy represented in a tree-like view (*left*), class diagram (*right*)

This FiletypeValue class represents the file type (indicated by the file extension) of a document, for example PPT, PDF, DOC, etc. Note that one subclass of filetype can describe multiple file extensions, such as JPG can be a .jpg or .jpeg file.

6.2 Log Ontology

There are many sources of changes that can affect an information resource, like adding, removing, deleting a new document or starting a new discussion. The Log ontology is used for representing these changes in a suitable format. There are four subclasses of Event: AddEvent, RemoveEvent, ChangeEvent and AccessEvent.

AddEvent is responsible for the creation of new events, e.g., a new document has been added to the SAKE CMS. It contains two subclasses: AddToCMSEvent, meaning the addition of a resource to the CMS and AddToParentEvent, meaning the addition of an existing child to a parent element, e.g., posting a new message to a discussion thread (Fig. 6).

RemoveEvent is dedicated to the deletion of the existing elements from the system, like the deletion of a document from CMS. It consists of RemoveFromCM-SEvent, meaning the removal of a resource from the CMS and RemoveFromParentEvent, meaning the removal of a child from a parent element, but the child is still existent.

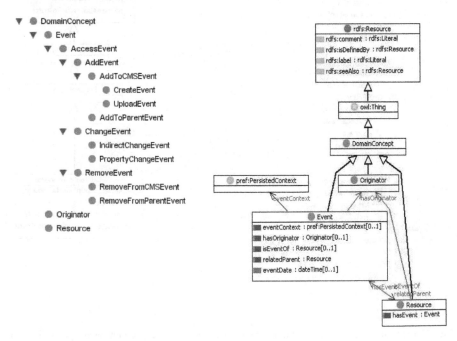

Fig. 6 Log ontology, class hierarchy (*left*), class diagram (*right*)

ChangeEvent is responsible for the modification of an existing individual, e.g., the change in the name of the author of a document. It consists of: Property-ChangeEvent, meaning that some properties of an individual have changed and IndirectChangeEvent, meaning a change caused by some other event.

AccessEvent is dedicated to the access of an existing individual. It represents a very broad class of events like reading a document, for which is very complicated to define the semantics clearly. For example, if anyone has opened the document and closed it after five minutes, read the document or just opened it, considered it as not interesting, but has forgotten to close it immediately.

We differentiate subclasses AddEvent and RemoveEvent by addition/removal of resources to/from the CMS and by addition/removal of a resource to/from a parent/child relationship using the isPartOf property. AddToCMSEvent is further differentiated by either creating a resource within the SAKE system or uploading an existing resource. For ChangeEvents, we distinguish between changes of the resource's properties (e.g., metadata) and changes which are caused by some other event.

Properties of an event are the resources the event relates to, the user who originated the event, a timestamp when the event occurred, an optional description of the event and a copy of the current runtime context. In the case of ChangeEvents, we add the names of the changed properties of the resource, and optionally link to another event which caused this ChangeEvent.

The following considerations are assumed:

- An information resource is associated with multiple events, and the first event is always an AddToCMSEvent (addition to the CMS). Then multiple events of different kinds can follow. After a RemoveFromCMSEvent (removal of the resource) no other events follow.
- In order to see which aspect of the resource has changed, we associate the names of the changed properties with the event.
- If the event has been caused by another event (e.g., the modification of a thread has been caused by the addition of a new message, see below), then an IndirectChangeEvent is generated which links to the original event via the causedBy property.

Special attention has to be paid if we define events for "compound" resources, i.e., resources which have child resources. Consider a forum in the SAKE GWS for instance: There we have forums, which consist of multiple threads which consist of multiple messages. Now, imagine that someone adds a new message to a thread. It is clear that by adding a new message to a thread we can consider the thread as changed, thus creating an AddToParentEvent for the message and an IndirectChangeEvent for the thread.

In order to resolve this issue, we define the following as the default behavior:

- Compound resources state their parent/child relationship by the property isPartOf or a subproperty thereof.
- For compound resources, a ChangeEvent will be generated if (1) the properties of the resource itself change (i.e., title of a forum thread changes) ==>

PropertyChangeEvent; or if a child object has been added or removed (e.g., adding a new message to an existing thread) ==> IndirectChangeEvent.

- The modification of a child object does not result in a modification (i.e., IndirectChangeEvent) of the parent.
- The developers programmatically create only the most basic event, e.g., a PropertyChangeEvent or a AddToParentEvent. SWRL rules decide whether this event triggers an IndirectChangeEvent or not as described in the following paragraph. IndirectChangeEvents are never created by the developers.

We do not hard-code the propagation of events from child to parent; instead we define them in SWRL rules, such as:

$$addToParentEvent(?E) \land resource(?RES) \land hasEvent(?RES, ?E) \land$$
$$relatedParent(?RES, ?RES2) \land swrlx : createIndividual(?E2) \Rightarrow$$
$$indirectChangeEvent(?E2) \land hasEvent(?RES2, ?E2)$$

Default rules state that the addition/removal of a child object triggers a ChangeEvent for the parent object. However, in order to be more flexible, we could also state that the modification of a specific child object also causes the modification of its parent. Note that in this way, we may use events to specify more complex events (e.g., *indirectChangeEvent*). Those complex events are created using SWRL[3] (Semantic Web Rule Language) rules and a number of built-in predicates supported by KAON2.[4] Although realized in a declarative way, complex event processing (CEP) in SAKE is still limited, and it is subject of our future work. Particularly, we will continue developing declarative CEP. The advantage of such an approach is that the definition of a complex event may easily be altered by changing only a logical rule. Further on, inconsistencies in CEP are handled by means of logic.

6.3 Change Notification System

The CNS is a server-based change detection and notification system that monitors changes in the environment which is external to SAKE. It can be configured to monitor web pages, RSS feeds and contents of file servers.

Users and the administrator can create new notification queries for finding and displaying interesting changes. When creating a query, users can define if they want to monitor a web page for any change or specific changes in links, words or a selected section specified by a regular expression. Moreover, users can select a topic of interest from a list. If new web page content is added that is related to the

---

[3]http:// www.w3.org/Submission/SWRL/
[4]http://kaon2.semanticweb.org/

topic or an RSS feed update contains information related to the topic, then the user is notified.

CNS relies on the services of Nutch (http://lucene.apache.org/nutch/), an open source crawler, which is used for fetching and parsing HTML documents, RSS feeds as well as resources in other supported formats. Moreover, Nutch periodically indexes the selected external resources, compares consecutive indexes and evaluates notification queries. When a difference between two indexes is found and this difference matches the specified query criteria, the old cache copy of the index is updated by the new copy. Note that this index is only used for the purpose of detecting changes. Query criteria supported include identification of changes in particular keywords, regular expressions, hyperlinks, or any changes in the monitored resources. For queries of keyword change, the system positively evaluates queries in cases where the keyword has appeared, disappeared, changed number of appearances or changed position within the text. Moreover, the system supports combining many keywords by using NEAR, AND, OR operators. Detecting changes in text specified by regular expressions is also supported. For detecting changes in hyperlinks, the hypertext tag href is used to identify the all hyperlinks in a page. For detecting any changes to a resource, the new document checksum is computed and compared to the old checksum. This approach works with both static and dynamic Web pages. In cases of RSS feeds, a simple timestamp comparison is performed.

6.4 Context Observer

The business context is derived using the Context Observer, a component that links to enterprise systems (such as workflows) and extracts the current business process, activity, and task the user is working on. The business context describes the situation which a user is currently present in, and is utilized for derivation of information resources based on context-sensitive preferences.

SAKE proactively delivers information resources (e.g., different documents and files) to a user. The resource delivery is realized in a process of matching the business context on one side, and user's preference rules on the other side). Relationship between the business context and user defined preferences is handled via the *validIn* relation in the preference ontology, Fig. 7 (e.g., particular preference rule is *validIn* a certain context). The preference ontology is typically imported by another ontology which maps its own concepts to this ontology. More specifically, by subclassing *PreferredResource* the importing ontology defines for which type of resources (i.e., individuals) the user can define preferences. Similarly, subclasses of *ContextObject* should be defined in order to indicate which type of individuals the *Context* consists of (i.e., the business process, activity, task, and the user).

Furthermore, we differentiate between a *RuntimeContext* and a *PersistedContext*. The RuntimeContext reflects the user's current context and changes dynamically with the user's interactions within the system. This context may be used to

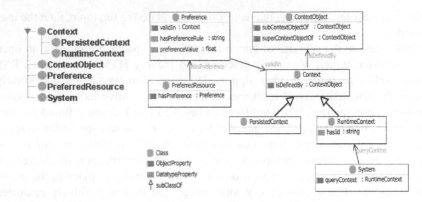

Fig. 7 Preference ontology, class hierarchy (*left*), class diagram (*right*)

track user's behavior in the system. However, if a user's interaction is logged in the system as a persistent activity (e.g., the creation of a new document) the user's current context will be persisted (using the *PersistedContext*).

The RuntimeContext and PersistedContex are utilized by the Context Observer to extract the current business context, and hence, enable resource delivery based on that business context.

6.5 Preference Editor

A preference is an *n*-ary relation between a user, multiple resources, and a preference value. Figure 8 shows how such a preference relation is formally modeled using the preference ontology.

Each preference (i.e., *n*-ary relation) is expressed as a logical rule, represented in SWRL. Figure 9 illustrates a preference rule: if userA is in the processZ, then userA has preference of value 1.0 for documents created in 2006. Among the preferred values, preferences include the business context of the user, in order to support context-awareness of the whole system (e.g., userA and processZ are related to each other by the same runtime context: ctx.

Utilizing logical rules, for expressing context-sensitive user preferences, SAKE features a very flexible preference model. One rule is used to assign different preference values to different information resources based on relevant criteria of a particular user. Therefore, every information resource may be assigned with different preference values by different preference rules (i.e., by different users and/or business contexts). Another flexibility of the SAKE preference model comes from an implicit representation of preferences. Since preference values are not precomputed and persisted in the system, just adding one preference rule may significantly influence the whole preference model. Also adding a common

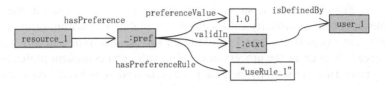

Fig. 8 Preference as *n*-ary relation between a resource, value, user and rule

```
Document(?res)^yearCreated(?res,"2006") ^
RuntimeContext(?ctx) ^ queryContext(sakesystem,?ctx) ^
isDefinedBy (?ctx, userA) ^ isDefined By (?ctx, processZ) ^
swrlx : CreateIndividual (?x)
   ⟹ Preference (?x) ^ hasPreferenceRule (?x, "rule_2") ^
      preferenceValue(?x, "1.0") ^ hasPreference (?res, ?x)
```

Fig. 9 A sample preference rule expressed in SWRL

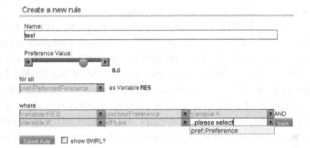

Fig. 10 Preference editor: step-wise, interactive rule development

preference to the SAKE preference model (i.e., a preference valid for all users) may be as easy as adding only one preference rule. Moreover updating existing resources, or adding new ones, does not mess up all previously created preference values. In this way, a user is given a great freedom to create particular preferences for particular processes, activities, tasks, and even to aggregate multiple preference values[5] for one resource into a final score.

The Preference Editor supports the creation of preference rules by providing a GUI for step-wise, interactive rule development, as presented in Fig. 10. The user starts with selecting what kind of resources (i.e., file, forum, workspace, email etc. that is a subclass of pref:PreferredResource) she/he wants to define a preference for. This information is specified in the information ontology (Fig. 4), and is represented as a variable ?RES. The preference rule is then further extended, narrowing down the preference criteria in several subsequent steps (possible introducing new

---

[5]Preference aggregation is computed in cases where there exist more than one preference rule for an information resource.

variables). For each of these steps, SAKE reasoner is used to find out the list of possible properties or property values that are available. Further on, values entered by a user are syntactically checked out (e.g., for the data type). In this way, the Preference Editor eases the process of creating valid and consistent preferences.

Preference rules, created by the editor, are serialized to its SWRL representation and stored in the preference ontology. Finally, preference rules may also be removed (or updated) using the Preference Editor.

6.6   Reasoner

Rule-based, formal, reasoning plays a central role for managing user's attention in SAKE. The knowledge base of the system comprise of nine SAKE specific ontologies. The purpose of these ontologies is to formally describe information resources, preferences, and events in SAKE, supporting a user in knowledge-intensive and highly dynamic business environments.

As we already explained in the previous section, a preference is expressed as a logical rule, represented in SWRL. The rule matches an information resource with the desired criteria (i.e., particular business context etc.) and assigns a preference value to them. Preference rules are stored in the SAKE knowledge base, and they are evaluated by the reasoner when certain events occur within the system. Events are triggered whenever a user changes her/his run-time context. A user may utilize these events to create ECA rules. ECA rules offer extensible and flexible approach to realizing active KM Systems. Such systems are enabled to actively respond on events or state changes.

Currently we allow the user to use preference rules as the action part of an ECA rule, and do not explicitly define the condition part.[6] Since a few preference rules may be defined for one particular event, SAKE may be seen as a reactive system capable of executing basic form of complex actions (i.e., actions that comprise of simple or atomic actions). Enhancing SAKE with more complex operators, for combining atomic action into complex actions, is a subject of our future work.

It is a task of the reasoner to react on events and evaluate appropriate ECA rules. The evaluation procedure is as follows: on an event, the system issues a SPARQL query which starts the reasoner engine. The reasoner takes into account a relevant preference rule (with the respect to the SPARQL query) and evaluates the rule. In case, there are more than one preference rule, defined for a particular information resource, the reasoner applies an aggregation function combining the single preference values into an aggregated score.

---

[6]The condition, if required, may be formally expressed in the action part (i.e., in the preference rule).

Once the rules are positively evaluated, a notification is generated and provided to the user both as a web bulletin and an RSS feed. The RSS feed points to a web page containing the results of the evaluated rules. By adopting RSS as a notification mechanism instead of sending emails, we allow the user to select whether she/he wants to be notified immediately about relevant information, periodically or when she/he wants to be notified. Most RSS readers allow the user to specify when and how they want to be notified about updates in the feeds they receive.

We use KAON2 as an underlying inference engine for managing, querying and reasoning about the ontologies in SAKE. KAON2 supports the SHIQ(D) subset of OWL-DL, and DL-safe subset of SWRL rules. Also a good portion of (but not entire) SPARQL specification is supported, and a number of built-in predicates have been implemented in this reasoner.

7 Technical Implementation

The SAKE prototype is based on J2EE and Java Portlets following a three-tiered architecture (Fig. 11). The presentation tier contains Portlets, JavaServer Pages (JSPs) and an auxiliary Servlet. Portlets call business methods on the Enterprise Java Beans (EJBs), preprocess the results and pass them to the JSP pages. The JSPs contain Hypertext Markup Language (HTML) fragments as well as placeholders for dynamic content (such as the results passed from the Portlets). The auxiliary Servlet is used for initializing the connection to the KAON2 ontology management system (http://kaon2.semanticweb.org/, part of the integration tier).

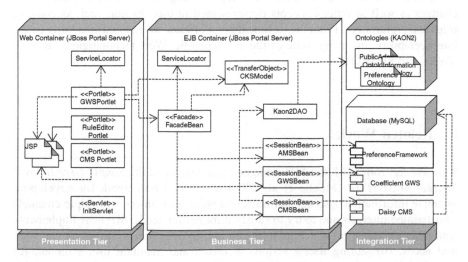

Fig. 11 SAKE technical implementation

The business tier consists mostly of EJBs, which provide the business logic and communicate with the components of the integration tier that comprise a third-party CMS component (Daisy) and GWS component (Coefficient) as well the Preference Framework. The interface to these components is represented using EJBs which all use the Kaon2DAO in order to access the ontologies: the CMSBean and GWSBean enhance the CMS and GWS with semantic meta-data, the AMSBean manages the preference rules. KAON2 stores the semantic meta-data for these entities with ontologies and provides the facilities for querying them using SPARQL. The KAON2 reasoner is used for evaluating the user's preference rules. The integration tier contains also a MySQL relational database, which stores CMS- and GWS-related content, such as forums, discussions, documents etc.

Since the development of the SAKE system has not been completed yet (mainly integration of components is still pending), a comprehensive user-driven evaluation of the system as a whole is planned but not performed yet. On the contrary, we have performed an early evaluation of the main SAKE components, independently. Evaluation has been performed in three case studies: two local administrations and one ministry. We validated the usability of these components and their relevance to the knowledge-intensive work of public servants. We collected useful comments for further improvement regarding the functionality and interface of the SAKE components. Early evaluation of the Preference Framework in particular has revealed noticeable improvement in relevance of system-generated notifications when user preferences are taken into account. In the future we plan to perform formal experiments to measure the degree of improvement of notifications. Moreover, as soon as the SAKE system is integrated, we plan to test the system's ability not only to send relevant notifications to users but also to execute relevant actions such as the initiation of a workflow process.

From a conceptual point of view, we have ensured that all components are based on a common ontological model for representing information resources and changes as well as other concepts not presented in this chapter, such as context, roles and preferences. From the technical point of view we ensured standards-based interoperability by using state-of-the-art Semantic Web technologies, such as SWRL and SPARQL.

8   Related Work

Researchers from IBM and MIT designed and developed the *Simple User Interest Tracker* or *SUITOR* (Maglio et al. 2001) which is a framework for developing attentive information systems that track computer users through multiple channels to determine interests and to try to satisfy information needs. SUITOR implements four main modules: (a) watching user's actions to infer user's current mental state and needs, (b) storing user's actions to create and maintain user's model, (c) searching information from the digital world and scanning user's local hard disk and (d) ranking and suggesting relevant information sources through peripheral display. Having enough input information from these modules, SUITOR can infer users' current interests and propose relevant information sources from the local and remote databases that have been previously gathered and stored.

The *Attentional User Interface project* (Horvitz et al. 2003) developed methods for inferring attention from multiple streams of information, and for leveraging these inferences in decision-making under uncertainty. These methods have been used in illustrative applications of the use of attentional models. Applications focus on the design of new interfaces that take into account visual attention, gestures and ambient sounds as clues about a user's attention. These clues can be detected through cameras, accelerometers and microphones or other perceptual sensors and, along with the user's calendar, current software interaction and data about the history of user's interests, they provide valuable information about the status of a user's attention. The same project built Bayesian models aiming at dealing with uncertainty and reasoning about current or future user's attention taking as input all of the above clues. Moreover, it introduced the economic model of attention and information. The model computes the expected cost of disruption user's current activities and infers whether and how to alert the user and display incoming messages.

A significant stream of related work deals with the design of attentive user interfaces (e.g., see Vertegaal (2003); Vertegaal et al. (2006)). Shell et al. (2003) identify five key properties of attentive user interfaces: sensing attention, reasoning about attention, communication of attention, gradual negotiations of turns, and augmentation of focus. Wood et al. (2006) make the distinction between visual and auditory attention and discuss five themes that concern the nature and measurement of visual attention.

In order to analyze the issues related to the design of attention aware systems, Roda and Thomas (Roda and Thomas 2006) have identified three aspects of attention management: (1) detection of current user's attentional state – the system needs to establish what the user's goals and current tasks are, where the user's attention is focussed, and what is happening in the environment; (2) detection and evaluation of possible alternative attentional state – the system establishes whether alternative foci are available, how important they may be for the user, and the cost-effectiveness of possible focus switches; and (3) strategies for presentation of alternative states to the user (or maintenance of current focus) – the system defines the strategies best suited to present the user with alternative foci.

In comparison to attention aware systems, our system does not include sensor-based mechanisms for detecting the user's environment. We argue that for enterprise attention management, non-sensory based mechanisms provide a wealth of attentional cues such as users' scheduled activities (e.g., using online calendars), users' working context (e.g., by querying workflow or enterprise systems) and user's communication and collaboration patterns (e.g., using groupware and other communication tools). However, our system is tailored to support enterprise attention management by taking into account the business context and working preferences.

9 Conclusion

In this chapter we presented a novel approach for managing attention in an enterprise context by realising the idea of having a reactive system that manages not only alerting a user that something has been changed, but also supporting the user to react properly on that change. In a nutshell, the corresponding system is an ontology-based platform that logs changes in internal and external information sources, observes user context and evaluates user attentional preferences represented in the form of ECA rules.

Since the presented system is currently under deployment in a real-world environment, results from the formal evaluation are still missing. However, initial assessments have shown that the users find the system useful and usable. The system's validation, planned to take place in three public administration organizations, will hopefully generate insights for the applicability of our model and system in this context and its contribution in performance improvements as instantiated in decision quality.

Future work will focus on further refinement of ECA rules for preference description and automatic learning of preferences from usage data using and machine learning techniques. Considering the existence of hierarchical relations that exist in the Log Ontology which models interactions (events) that happen in the SAKE system, we can further utilize Generalized Association Rules in order to mine and discover interesting patterns in the system's usage. Generalized Association Rules improve upon standard association rules taking into account a taxonomy.

References

M. Alavi, D.E. Leidner, Knowledge management and knowledge management systems: conceptual foundations and research issues (Review). MIS Q. **25**(1), 107 (2001)

J.S. Brown, P. Duguid, *The Social Life of Information* (Harvard Business School Press, Boston, 2000)

E. Horvitz, C.M. Kadie, T. Paek, D. Hovel, Models of attention in computing and communication: from principles to applications. Commun. ACM **46**(3), 52 (2003)

A. Maedche, B. Motik, L. Stojanovic, R. Studer, R. Studer, R. Volz, Ontologies for enterprise knowledge management. IEEE Intell. Syst. **8**(2), 26–33 (2003)

P.P. Maglio, C.S. Campbell, R. Barrett, T. Selker, An architecture for developing attentive information systems, in *Knowledge-Based Systems*, vol. 14 (Elsevier, Amsterdam, 2001), pp. 103–110

D.C. Misra, Ten guiding principles for knowledge management in e-government in developing countries. in *First International Conference on Knowledge Management for Productivity and Competitiveness*, New Delhi, 2007

E.W.T. Ngai, E.W.C. Chan, Evaluation of knowledge management tools using AHP. Expert Syst. Appl. **29**, 889 (2005)

N.F. Noy, D.L. McGuinness, *Ontology Development 101: A Guide to Creating Your First Ontology.* Stanford Knowledge Systems Laboratory Technical Report KSL-01-05 and Stanford Medical Informatics Technical Report SMI-2001-0880 (Stanford University, Stanford, 2001)

B. Panagiotis, From information to knowledge management: a critical approach on differences and common ground under the integration rhetoric. in *Proceedings 14th Pan-Hellenic Conference of Academic Libraries*, Athens, Greece, 2005, pp. 63–71

D. Paul Raj, L. Pan Shan, C. Huang Jimmy, Structurational analysis of e-government initiatives: a case study of SCO. Decis. Support Syst. **34**, 253–269 (2002)

C. Roda, J. Thomas, Attention aware systems: theory, application, and research agenda. Comput. Hum. Behav. **22**, 557 (2006)

J.S. Shell, T. Selker, R. Vertegaal, Interacting with groups of computers. Commun. ACM **46**(43), 40 (2003)

R. Vertegaal, Attentive user interfaces, introduction to special issue. Commun. ACM **46**(3), 30 (2003)

R. Vertegaal, J.S. Shell, D. Chen, A. Mamuji, Designing for augmented attention: towards a framework for attentive user interfaces. Comput. Hum. Behav. **22**, 771 (2006)

K.M. Wiig, Application of Knowledge Management in Public Administration. Paper Prepared for Public Administrators of the City of Taipei, Taiwan, ROC (2000)

S. Wood, R. Cox, P. Cheng, Attention design: eight issues to consider. Comput. Hum. Behav. **22**, 588 (2006)

Personalization in E-Government: An Approach that Combines Semantics and Web 2.0

Kay-Uwe Schmidt, Ljiljana Stojanovic, Nenad Stojanovic, and Susan Thomas

1 Introduction

In Europe, large parts of the population use the Internet in their daily life: at work, during their leisure time, or for accessing information, purchasing goods or communication. They now expect public administrations to provide the same level of service that they are accustomed to when using online banking, flight booking or electronic shops. Increasingly, they also expect the types of personalization and user adaptation offered by such commercial services.[1]

The current norm for e-government portals, which is to confront different citizens with a one-size-fits-all Web interface, is not the optimum way to deliver public sector services because every person is an individual with different knowledge, abilities, skills and preferences. The conventional brick-and-mortar office has a more human face because the clerk can respond to different people in different manners. That is why people tend to use the conventional office rather than the e-government services. To transfer some of the humanity to e-government portals, it is necessary to build adaptive portals for public services. Such user-adaptive portals will increase the usability, and, thus, the acceptance of e-government, enabling administrations to achieve the, as yet, elusive efficiency gains and user satisfaction, which are the primary goals of e-government projects.

In this chapter we present an approach for front-office adaptation that enables public administrations to offer more usable services, and to even exceed current user expectations, by providing support (like proactive recommendations) which cannot be realized in the brick-and-mortar environment. This approach results in

K.-U. Schmidt (✉)
SAP AG, Vincenz-Prießnitz-Straße 1, 76131, Karlsruhe, Germany

[1]See, for example, E-Government Handbook, www.cdt.org/egov/handbook/.

T. Vitvar et al. (eds.), *Semantic Technologies for E-Government*,
DOI 10.1007/978-3-642-03507-4_11, © Springer-Verlag Berlin Heidelberg 2010

a user-adaptive portal. "User-adaptive" means that the interactive system acquires a model of the individual user, and utilizes that model and the background knowledge to adapt itself to the user. Such adaptation usually involves some form of learning, inference or decision making.

User-adaptivity is achieved by using a new approach that combines the power of Ajax, the underlying technology of Web 2.0, with Semantic Web technologies to create a client-side (which means faster and more powerful) semantic framework for capturing the meaning of user behavior, recognizing the user's situation, and applying rules to adapt the portal to this situation.

As indicated by the definition of user-adaptivity, acquisition of a model of the user is the indispensable prerequisite to adaptation. The second step is then to use this model to perform the adaptation. We assume that the system has no previous information about a user, so that in each user session the user model may have to be acquired from scratch. Effectively, this means that the user model is based on the user actions during a session. Therefore, it is essential to be able to track and interpret these actions as accurately as possible.

With Ajax the range of user actions that can be tracked is extended beyond just mouse clicks. For example, scrolling, mouse-over and keystroke events can be tracked, enabling the detailed recording of user actions on the client side.

The advanced user tracking possibilities are also accompanied by sophisticated adaptation techniques formerly only seen in desktop applications, like tool tips and fading help windows. However, this rich model of user actions and new adaptation options can only be leveraged if they are described in a machine-understandable way that enables their automated processing. Hence, ontologies, as formal and explicit models of a domain of interest, are used to model actions and potential adaptations. Additionally, ontologies enable the sharing of lessons learned (e.g., adaptation rules) between public administrations offering similar services (e.g., two municipalities in one state are similar), since they are partners and work together to realize the vision of the electronic government.

Additionally, ontologies are used in the formulation of rules, which derive adaptations from the user model and user behavior. Adaptation rules can be created based either on patterns found in the collective behavior of users (e.g., as found in web logs) or on a priori rules suggested by an application expert.

In this chapter, we present the whole approach of achieving user-adaptive eGovernment portals by combining Web 2.0 and semantic technologies, including its evaluation in a field trial. The work is based on research done within the FP 6 ICT project FIT – Fostering self-adaptive e-government service improvement using semantic technologies.

The chapter is organized as follows.

In the second section, we motivate the research problem and gather requirements for its resolution. In the third section, we give the logic architecture of such a solution, while in the fourth section we describe the role of ontologies in it. Section 5 contains the most important implementation details, whereas Sect. 6 elaborates on the evaluation of the approach. In Sect. 7, we present the related work and Sect. 8 contains concluding remarks.

2   Motivating Example

In this section, we present a real-world scenario that serves as the illustration of the problems users are experiencing in the "traditional" eGovernment portals. At the same time we use this scenario for gathering requirements for our approach.

E-government portals face many usability challenges. One of the most demanding is the perceived decreased quality in service provisioning. This challenge seems to be contradictory to one of very important goals of e-government portals: to enable the provision of an easy and convenient access to public services for everybody. But citizens are accustomed to a clerks sitting in a mortar-and-brick environment that can be talked to either directly face to face or via telephone. In (Mardle 2007) it is argued that citizens most often are not only looking for information but also for immediate help from public authorities.

A typical problem of online public services is: Finding the right form.[2] In Austria as well as in Germany, the building process is constrained by building law. The law regulates the administrative process for building up or pulling down any kind of building. The trigger of this process is the request of a building permit. There exist several processes with distinct online forms for different kind of constructions. The Austrian legislator defines three types of building permissions: Construction permit (Baubewilligung), construction notification (Bauanzeige) and construction projects for which notification of the authorities is unnecessary (nicht anzeigepflichtiges Bauvorhaben).

Wrongly committed forms lead to increased costs for the public administration and to increased work and dissatisfaction for the citizens:

- Increased costs for the public administration – Every received form has to be checked for validity by the public administration. In the case of not matching the construction project of the citizen, it must be resubmitted. This causes not only a delay in the approval process, but, also generates costs as the clerk has to contact the citizen and to process the resubmitted form. The same holds for submitted construction permit forms or construction notification forms where the construction project does not need any permission or notification at all.
- Dissatisfaction for the citizens – Without explicit user guidance it is hard to find the right form for an inexperienced client not familiar with the building law. This already causes confusion while searching for the right form. The client feels unsure about the correctness of the form he/she has chosen. But, in the case of a wrongly submitted form he/she is even more dissatisfied after receiving the request to resubmit his/her building project because he/she used the wrong online form.

The building permission service is actually a complex process, subject to regulations that require the submission of different forms at different times, depending

---

[2]SAP Public Sector reported that public administrations are often overwhelmed by wrongly chosen forms or by forms not necessary at all.

on the type of building project. For an inexperienced user the challenge starts here. With lack of background knowledge of the building regulations the user is confused and does not know which form to choose for her building project. Such users, who are unfamiliar with the portal and the specific service, need guidance to prevent them from getting stuck in the portal shallows. On the other hand, for an architect who works daily with the virtual building application within an e-government portal, any guidance would only hinder her smooth sailing. Therefore, there is, among other things, a need to cater for different skill levels like novice, average and expert.

Moreover, adaptation, for example adaptation to skill level, is needed for each service, since an expert in one service may be a novice in another. For example, the architect, expert at building applications, may be a novice when it comes to submitting an application for child support. In fact, many services will only rarely be used by any one user, so the majority of users will probably remain novices in their use.

Given this scenario we derive five basic requirements for adaptive e-government portals. Firstly, a portal must provide guidance and information that matches the users, e.g., the different skill levels and interests of its citizens. Secondly, as citizens typically use e-government services rarely they should not be bothered with providing and maintaining any user profiles. The third important requirement is to observe the crucial usability principles such as responsiveness, predictability and comprehensibility, controllability and unobtrusiveness. Initial emphasis, in regard to usability, is placed on providing accurate, but unobtrusive, guidance, when and where it is needed by the user. The fourth general requirement is that the portal should be subject to continual improvement. Explicit user feedback can be enormously helpful here, but the feedback requested should be relevant to the services that the user executed. A fifth, and final, important requirement is related to the nature of e-government services, and the fact that there are multiple units of e-government at different levels, e.g., local, regional and national. Given the similarity of many of the services offered by these different units, there is an enormous potential for efficiency gains through sharing best practices. Therefore, the fifth general requirement is the ability to share successful adaptation strategies and rules.

We analyzed the online portal of the Austrian city of Vöcklabruck[3] in order to find usability gaps of current web-based e-government applications. The web portal is reachable via the official web address http://www.voecklabruck.at and is hosted and developed by the administration itself. The online portal serves as Internet resource for getting any kind of information related to the town, for downloading forms related to public services like the application for a building permit or birth certificate, and, finally, also for the complete online handling of public services like for instance the submission of the meter reading.

---

[3]Vöcklabruck is a regional center town with 13,000 inhabitants at the northern edge of the Salzkammergut region of Austria.

In the rest of this chapter we present an approach that meets these identified requirements.

3 Logical System Architecture: The Adaptation Loop

The logical architecture of an adaptive eGovernment system is depicted in Fig. 1. It is a two-stage approach consisting of three cycles forming the adaptation loop. The design-time stage and the run-time stage logically divide the components of our architecture into off-line and online components respectively. That is, the stages refer to the invocation time of the components comprising our architecture. The three cycles, the modeling cycle on the left, the adaptation cycle on the right and the larger transfer cycle in the middle illustrate the self-adaptive character of our architecture (one of the requirements from previous section).

The modeling cycle stands for the design time components in charge of constructing the adaptation rules. At design time, an indispensable prerequisite for our RIA (rich internet application) adaptation approach, the portal must be annotated by using a portal annotation tool (Stojanovic et al. 2007b) (cf. Portal Annotation in Fig. 1). After annotating the structure and content of the RIA, user access log data, collected in the past, can be mined for useful Web usage patterns, which will differ for each group of users (first requirement form previous section). This is done by the semantic Web usage mining component (cf. Semantic Web Usage Mining) (Dai and Mobasher 2002; Rahmani et al. 2008). Once useful patterns are found, they can be formulated as adaptation rules by using a rule design tool (cf. Rule Design). The adaptation rules are stored in an ontology format. After designing the adaptation

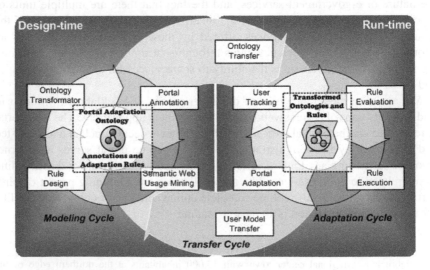

Fig. 1 Logical system architecture: the adaptation loop

rules on a conceptual level, based on the annotated RIA, they are translated at design-time by the rule transformer (cf. Ontology Transformator) into a client-readable format like JavaScript.

The rightmost cycle in Fig. 1, the adaptation cycle, is executed, like the transfer cycle in the middle of the figure, at run-time. The aim of the adaptation cycle is to adapt the RIA based on the predefined adaptation rules and the current user model. The adaptation rules are obtained from the modeling cycle via the transfer adaptation rules component of the transfer cycle (cf. Ontology transfer). The user model is built up by the user tracking component, which records the user's interactions with the RIA, without disturbing the user in her/his work (second requirement). Based on the user model, which is constructed on the fly (cf. User tracking), the adaptation rules are evaluated (cf. Rule Evaluation) and, if the condition part holds, are fired (cf. Rule Execution). It is the task of the rule evaluation component and the rule execution component to carry out rule processing. If a rule fires, the corresponding actions are executed and the RIA adapts itself directly on the client-side without server requests (third requirements) (cf. Portal Adaptation).

At the end of the session, the tracked user model is sent back to the server (cf. User model transfer). On the server-side all user models are collected and fed back into the modeling cycle in order to mine new behavioral patterns. Thus, the adaptation loops starts again.

Note that the usage of the rich domain model (ontologies) enables the exploitation of the knowledge that has been gained in one eGovernment portal in a form that could be used in another portal (fifth requirement).

4 Ontology-Based Adaptation of Public Services

In this section, we show how semantic technologies and in particular ontologies can be utilized for automatic adaptation of an e-government portal to the individual requirements of the users, according to the architecture presented in the previous section. We firstly motivate the reasons for using ontologies and thereafter we introduce the semantic model of adaptive portals. Even though the paper is motivated by using e-government examples, the proposed approach is general enough to be applied in any other domain.

4.1 Advantages of Using Ontologies for Adaptation

There are several reasons to build our approach upon the intensive use of semantic technologies. Firstly, ontologies enable semantic interpretation of user behavior in a portal, which enables meaningful, effective and context-aware adaptation (Stojanovic et al. 2007a).

The building permission example from Sect. 2 is elaborated next to show how Ajax and semantics together enable such context-aware adaptation. Assume that the user, who wants to apply for building permission, goes to the appropriate e-government Web site. And, on this site, the user finds a list of hyperlinks to the forms related to building permits. But, she does not know which one is appropriate for her building project. Being based on Ajax, the Web site implements mouse-over help for these hyperlinks. The user knows this, and places the mouse on a hyperlink for a time to make the help appear. Then the user does this for a second hyperlink, but still does not choose a form. Assuming that the hyperlinks have been associated with concepts in the ontology, the system can now make a semantic interpretation of the user's behavior. In this case, the conclusion would be that the user has a strong interest in the concepts associated with the two mouse-over hyperlinks, and that the user needs help choosing a form. In response to this context, the system can offer the user help. Not only that, this help can be tailored to the user by taking account of the concepts in which the user showed interest, concluded from her current navigation path and behavior. As explained later, adaptation such as this is based on using semantic annotation of a page and its structural elements (e.g., hyperlinks).

The second reason to use ontologies is that ontologies used in rules can make adaptation logic more explicit. This declarative representation, expressed as rules using concepts and relations from the ontology, helps the domain experts inspect, understand and even modify the rationales behind adaptive functionality. For example, the hierarchical organization of e-government services allows the expert to model adaptation rules on a more abstract level, i.e., covering more than one concrete service (e.g., building permission service, independently of the type of building such as house, office, etc). This significantly reduces y the number of rules and makes maintenance of the system much easier.

Finally, ontologies facilitate sharing knowledge between portals, especially for those offering similar services (e.g., two municipalities in one state are similar). For example, the best practices gathered in issuing building permits in one portal (e.g., inexperienced users need an additional explanation regarding the hyperlink "required documents") can be easily transferred to other portals that implement the same regulations for issuing building permits. This sharing is greatly facilitated by the fact that all of the terms used (e.g., additional explanation, hyperlinks, "required documents" etc.) are well defined. It is clear that the benefits for the users as well as for e-government are enormous, since the public administration can improve its performance at much less expense.

We note here that transferring best practices is especially important for e-government where all governmental institutions are motivated to share their knowledge, since they are partners and work together to realize the vision of the electronic government. In all other domains, the owners of portals do not have interest to exchange experiences and best-practices with similar portal (e.g., Amazon and e-Bay), since they are competitors. Therefore, e-government seems to be an ideal environment for new research regarding collaboration between adaptive web portals. It is also a good testbed for the evaluation of results.

4.2 Ontology-Based Model of Adaptive Portals

Since the data relevant for adaptation is rather sparse, or a great deal of interpretation must be done to turn it into actually useful information, we have developed the ontology-based model of adaptive portals. This model (the so-called Portal Adaptation Ontology) is used to decide if an adaptation should take place and how to do that. A part of the ontology is shown in Fig. 2. The full version can be found in (Schmidt et al. 2007). The ontology represents all aspects relevant for adaptation such as Web site structure (Web Portal Ontology), Web site content (Content Ontology), user profiles (User Ontology), and Web site usage data as well as knowledge about the adaptation process itself (Adaptation Ontology). Ajax-enabled Web pages as well as the UI elements contained by those pages will be annotated with individuals and concepts from the Portal Adaptation Ontology.

Web Portal Ontology: The way that the Web site is physically laid out as well as the structure of each page can be useful toward understanding usage behavior and interpreting system suggestions. Additionally, the semantic information about the reasons why the structure exists in the way that it does may also be useful. Thus, the Web Portal Ontology contains entities representing the types of pages (such as Head Page, Navigation Page, FAQ, Combined Page etc.) and the structural elements of a page (e.g., Hyperlink, Figure, Table, Content, etc.). We note here that the

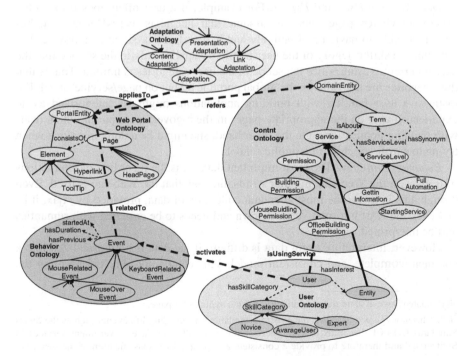

Fig. 2 A part of the Portal Adaptation Ontology showing several entities of the included ontologies as well as dependencies between them

information about page structure can be used to derive or to verify the type of a page (Crockford 2006). For example, a Navigation Page is a page with small content/link ratio; a short time is spent on the page and it is not a maximal forward reference.

Content (Domain) Ontology: The content[4] of Web pages themselves is essential to determine particular topical interests and understanding the relationships between pages. The Content Ontology consists of concepts and relations modeling the meaning of services/information offered by an e-government portal. This includes already existing categorization[5] of e-government services (such as residential affairs, residential permissions, identification, certifications, naturalization citizenship, moving, education, etc.) as well as typical e-government terminology (e.g., building permission, building application, etc.).

User Ontology: The user is modeled through the concept User and its properties such as *hasInterest, hasSkillCategory*, etc. As already mentioned, the values of these properties are determined on the basis of user actions during the session. For example, to determine the interest of the user and the content/meaning of the pages the user visited is taken into account. Indeed, semantic annotation of pages using the entities from the Content Ontology is used to derive this information. Returning to the example from Sect. 2, the system would conclude that the user has a strong interest in the concepts associated with the two moused-over hyperlinks, since these concepts define the meaning of hyperlinks.

The hierarchy of user skill categories includes, at the first level, concepts such as *Novice, Average User* and *Expert*. For example, if a user often goes back to the previously visited page, then we assume that he/she is overwhelmed and has become unable to navigate effectively and is therefore classified as a novice. We note that the skill category of the user implicitly applies only to the service that the user is currently using, since the scope of the user categories is limited. That is that the categories are not valid on the global portal level but on page/service[6] level. For instance a user familiar with building applications might be categorized as an experienced user on the appropriate pages in the e-government portal which deals with building applications. On the other hand, she might be a domain novice when trying to enroll her child in a public school.

Behavior Ontology: The most important data set is the recording of interactions of users with the Web site, in other words, the way that the Web site is used. Even though, this is by far the most abundant collection of data, provided by Ajax, it is, however, the least informative on its own and needs to be enriched with semantics and be interpreted.

However, interpreting event data is difficult if the data is not normalized into a common, complete, and consistent model. This entails not only reformatting the

---

[4]By "content" we assume the meaning and not the syntax of a page.

[5]It has been developed based on the existing standards for modeling life events such as the Swiss Standard eCH-001 that aims to give an overview over all relevant e-Government services in Switzerland and therefore to provide a consistent and standardized classification of the services.

[6]A page must be annotated with the service it belongs to in order to enable the system to link the user with a service.

data for better processing and for achieving readability, but also breaking it down into its most granular pieces. For example, the system has to be able to recognize all mouse-related events such as mouse-down, mouse-move, mouse-out, mouse-over, mouse-up, etc. Moreover, interpretation involves filtering out unwanted information to reduce analytical errors or misrepresentations. For example, the system should be able to condense the received events into a single event directly indicating a problem. Returning to the example from the beginning of this section, the adaptation should be generated only if two mouse-over events occur sequentially within a session. Finally, interpretation involves acquiring more information from outside the scope of the original event data, for example, from a page the event occurred on (e.g., replacing the meaningless information such as name and target of a hyperlink with the meaning of this hyperlink).

To cover all these requirements we have developed the Behavior Ontology that structures information about the user's interactions and relationships and/or dependencies between interactions. The main purpose of the ontology is to store all the interactions of the user which might help to identify her experience, actual context and goals.

The most important concept of this ontology is the concept Event that describes what happened, why it happened, when it happened, and what the cause was. The structure of the hierarchy of events reflects the underlying technology used for capturing events, i.e., Ajax. For example, events are decomposed at the first level into the event categories: keyboard, button, mouse, focus and general events. Each of these categories is further specialized. For example, keyboard-related events that occur when a user hits a key include key-down, key-up and key-press. The category of general events cover load, unload, submit, error handling, etc.

Adaptation Ontology: This ontology was derived from the taxonomy of adaptive hypermedia systems (Bechhofeer et al. 2004). We distinguish between content, presentation and link adaptation. Each of these types can be further categorized. For example, adaptation of navigation which realizes adaptation by changing the links of the system (i.e., *Link Adaptation*) can be realized by several techniques such as *Direct Guidance, Link Sorting, Link Hiding, Link Annotation, Link Generation* or *Map Adaptation*. Each technique might also be realized in several ways. For example, *Link Hiding* concerns links that are not considered relevant for a user (at the current time), and can be realized by hiding, disabling or removing links.

As shown in Fig. 2, all the previously mentioned ontologies are combined in the Web Portal Adaptation ontology that models adaptive functionality formally and explicitly. Moreover, it is enriched with rules to enable automation of the adaptation process. In this way, we provide a logical characterization of self-adaptive e-government systems. The rules can be designed either manually or by applying usage mining techniques. Here we give an example we learnt from the annotated web log file: "*All users that filled in the marriage certificate form and the wedding day form also filled in the birth certificate form.*" The corresponding adaptation rule is shown below:

portal:Form((?a)) ∧ portal:isVisited(?a, true) ∧

domain:WeddingDay(?b) ∧ portal:isAnnotated(?a, ?b) ∧

portal:Form((?c)) ∧ portal:isVisited(?c, true) ∧

domain:MarriageCertificate(?d) ∧ portal:isAnnotated(?c, ?d) ∧

domain:BirthCertificate(?e) → portal:showLink(?e)

This example shows how an ontology and rule engineer could formulate the rule described above in SWRL. Translated into English the rule states that whenever a form annotated with *Wedding Day* and a form annotated with *Marriage Certificate* were visited show all links to forms annotated with *Birth Certificate* as link recommendations. *Wedding Day, Marriage Certificate* and *Birth Certificate* are concepts taken from the Content (Domain) ontology. Schmidt et al. detail in (Schmidt et al. 2008) how to derive adaptation rules form business rules.

5 Architecture of Adaptive Portals for E-Government

The logical system architecture of our framework enabling the design and execution of intelligent e-government services is decomposed into a design- and run-time architecture. The design-time architecture embraces all components in charge of definition, configuration and maintenance of intelligent e-government services. The run-time architecture in turn comprises all components covering the real-time algorithmic detection of events and the execution of adaptation rules.

5.1 Design-Time Architecture

The design-time architecture consists of the components constituting the modeling cycle as depicted in Fig. 1. These tools and components are executed off-line during the annotation, mining, design and transformation phases.

Suitable ontologies are crucial for our RIA adaptation approach. We developed an approach amalgamating ontology learning, ontology refinement and annotating RIAs into one coherent tool. Based on this approach we developed the ontologies as described before. As a proof of concept we annotated our internal demo portal and the e-government portal of the city of Vöcklabruck with our ontologies under supervision of e-government experts. All ontologies are described using the Ontology Web Language (OWL).

The adaptation rules are designed based on the results of applying semantic Web usage mining to Vöcklabruck's access-log files (Berendt et al. 2004). The discovered patterns needed to be analyzed by an e-government expert. The domain expert judged, whether the patterns are useful or not. Patterns, which have been judged useful, were then encoded into a rule language as adaptation rules by an ontology engineer with the help of customary ontology and rule editors. We are using the Semantic Web Rule Language (SWRL) because it nicely fits to our OWL ontologies.

Having the ontologies, annotations and adaptation rules in place, the last step in the modeling cycle is still the transformation of all of these parts into a client-readable format that can be executed by a browser's JavaScript engine. As an Internet browser on a client machine has only limited processing power and main memory capacity, both ontologies and rules must be translated beforehand in an easy-to-parse format that can be effortlessly executed on the client-side. Due to the lack of a client-side reasoner we materialize all ontologies at the server-side. By using an OWL reasoner we check the consistency of the ontology at design-time, classify the instances and infer the class hierarchy. We decided to represent ontologies, annotations and rules in the compact and directly executable data interchange format JSON (JavaScript Object Notation).

5.2 Run-Time Architecture: A Client-Side Intelligent Adaptation Engine

The core responsibility of the run-time architecture is to ensure the user-centric adaptation of the RIA. The run-time architecture is constituted by the adaptation and transfer cycle as depicted in Fig. 1. After transforming the ontologies, annotations and adaptation rules into a client-readable format at design-time, they can be transmitted as JavaScript code in answer to a client request at any point in time. When a user requests the RIA, not only content and layout data are send to the client, but also the JSON representation of the ontologies, annotations and rules. On the client-side the user model is built up and the portal is adapted by tracking user interactions and executing adaptation rules. Figure 3 shows the interplay of the constituent run-time components.

In a Web browser HTML pages are internally represented as a DOM (Document Object Model). Whenever a user interacts with the Web page, the DOM fires appropriate events which can be caught by the event handler component. In order to catch events, the event handler has to register first to specific event types. In our

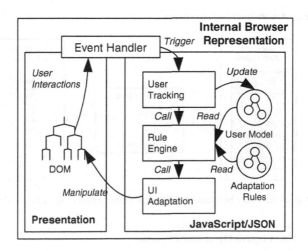

Fig. 3 Logical client-side run-time architecture

current implementation this is done manually. The Web programmer has to explicitly specify which kinds of events shall be tracked. Each recognized event results in a call of the user tracking component and, in a second step, the invocation of the rule engine. The user tracking component resolves the relationships between the JavaScript events, the user interface elements and their annotations. Furthermore, it records the events to the user model. In this way, the user model materializes the browsing history of the current user on the level of JavaScript events. The user tracking component is depicted in Fig. 4.

Based on the Web usage data stored in the user model the rule engine evaluates the adaptation rules. We implemented a stateless rule evaluation based on the sequential algorithm (Berstel et al. 2007). The rationale behind this approach is that each of the independent rules fires once its conditions hold. There is no agenda to resolve any eventual conflicts caused by the executing rules. Furthermore, this approach implies that the rules do not affect each other. Despite the disadvantages of this approach we chose the sequential algorithm because of its simple loop-like implementation. Once a rule has fired, the rule body, in most of the cases translated SWRL built-ins, is executed by the UI adaptation component and the user interface is manipulated. The cooperation of the user model component, the Rule Engine (AHS[7] Engine) and the UI Adaptation model component is clarified in Fig. 5.

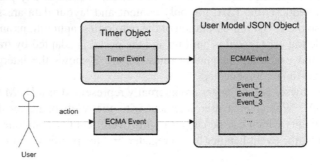

Fig. 4 User tracking component

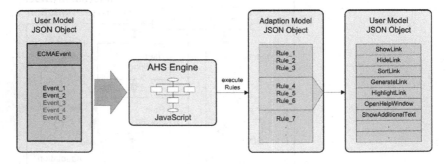

Fig. 5 Interplay between the different components of the client-side intelligent adaptation engine

---

[7]AHS: Adaptive Hypermedia System.

At the end of the session, the user model is sent back to the server using the asynchronous communication facility of AJAX. The accumulated user models form the basis for a further modeling cycle. Further details to the client-side run-time architecture can be found in (Schmidt et al. 2008).

6 Evaluation

We conducted a comparative usability evaluation as part of the User Centered Design Methodology (Norman and Draper 1986) in order to verify the validness of our approach. We chose the city portal of Vöcklabruck for this evaluation study.

7 Hypotheses

The next five hypotheses formulate our confidence about the advantage of adaptive over nonadaptive web sites. The goal of the evaluation test is to gain significant test data that allow drawing conclusions whether or not these hypotheses hold.

7.1 Main Hypothesis

H1. The usability of an adaptive city portal is greater then the usability of a nonadaptive portal.

Based on the motivating example we argue for the introduction of a client-side and context-sensitive adaptation of user interfaces for web-based public services. In H1 the main hypothesis is formulated that an adaptive e-government portal is superior to a nonadaptive portal. In order to test this hypothesis we conducted a comparative usability test based on the following subhypothesis. The subhypotheses concretize the main hypothesis by breaking it up into several measurable and more concrete hypotheses.

7.2 Subhypotheses

H2. Citizens more likely choose the correct form according to their current working context in an adaptive environment than in an environment not adapting to the current user context.
H3. Citizens spend less time searching for the correct form in an adaptive than a nonadaptive portal.
H4. Citizens call search or help pages less often in an adaptive portal than in a nonadaptive portal.

H5. The perceived usability of an adaptive e-government portal is higher than the perceived usability of a nonadaptive e-government portal.

H2 states that an adaptive portal supports the citizen better in finding the right form than a nonadaptive portal. This also includes decision support for the question whether or not it is necessary to submit a form at all. Furthermore, we hypothesize in H3 that an adaptive portal not only supports citizens in finding the right form but also shortens their search time. Another indicator for H1 is hypothesized in H4. We assume that citizens do not so often call search or help pages in an adaptive portal as the user guidance is much stronger than in nonadaptive portals. H5 aims at the perceived usability of adaptive and nonadaptive portals. We hypothesize that the perceived usability in the case of adaptive portals is much higher than the perceived usability in the nonadaptive case.

8 Planning

We decided for the usability testing methods of *logging actual use* plus *questionnaires*. We did not go for on-site execution of usability tests. So we were able to reach more test persons at less cost.

We planned the evaluation of our hypotheses by comparing two versions of the same city portal: a static version without and an adaptive version with the adaptive technology. In order to accomplish this, we needed a highly dynamic architecture that allows running two distinct versions of the same portal. The sources of the original portal should stay untouched while the adaptive technology should be added on the fly. This is somewhat crucial for lower evaluation costs.

The evaluation portal has to choose randomly the version of the portal to be tested. Whenever a test user enters the evaluation portal the web browser "throws a coin" and either loads the adaptive or the nonadaptive version of the city portal of Vöcklabruck. On average this ensures that both versions are tested equally.

Nielson (1989, 1990, 1993, 1994; Nielsen and Hoa 2006) and Krug (2005) argue that about five people discover 85% of the usability problems. As e-government portals aims to support all citizens and not only construction law experts, the selection of the test users is not constrained by any target group constraints. Actually, Nielson and Krug argue that target groups do not really matter except for portals only designed for special target groups. As we wanted to conduct a comparative evaluation five test users for each version of the portal would not be enough. In order to draw statistical conclusions, we needed more test users. Our goal was to have at least 15 test users for each version. Taking this into account, we decided to recruit the test users from colleagues and friends.

To reach a high ratio of responses it is crucial for a usability test not to take too long. As we didn't give any incentives to the test user we were dependent on their good will. As the good will of test persons shrinks the longer the test lasts, we planned a test that does not take longer than 10 minutes. Additionally, we planned a time frame of two weeks for the whole test. This duration gives some freedom to the test users to choose the time point for doing the evaluation which fits best into their schedule.

With our usability test we want to evaluate three out of four usability goals: performance, accuracy, and emotional response. Performance is measured in time or number of steps required to complete predefined tasks. Accuracy measures the number of mistakes test users make while completing predefined tasks. The feelings of the test users about the tasks completed are recorded in a questionnaire as emotional response. Recall, the fourth usability goal, is not addressed by our test setup. Recall is the measure of how much a test person remembers after a while.

We considered the validity of our usability test framework by asking a domain expert for the validity of our test cases. We presented our test task to a construction domain expert of the city of Vöcklabruck and she confirmed that our test cases are valid, sound and address real world problems. She also confirmed the selection of test users.

9 Design

Figure 6 shows the evaluation wizard as a finite state machine. State transitions are preformed by the user either by clicking the navigation buttons *Next* or *Back*, or by clicking the *Task finished* button during the processing of a task. Usually, the Back button resets the evaluation wizard to the previous state.

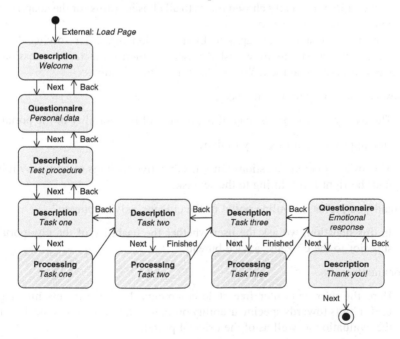

Fig. 6 Finite state machine of the evaluation wizard

After requesting the evaluation portal from a browser the wizard is loaded. A welcome page is shown to the test user. After pressing the *Next* button a questionnaire is loaded asking for the test user's personal data. Every piece of information is voluntary. We asked for: age, gender, mother tongue, intensity of using the Internet, and expertise in construction law. The age is interrogated in intervals in the range of 0–25, 26–35, 36–45, 45–open-ended. The options for the gender attribute are female and male, for the mother tongue attribute the options are German and others, for the intensity of using the Internet: seldom, often, intensive; and for the expert in construction law: yes or no.

The subsequent web page explains the evaluation procedure. The next six states are conceptually the same. They all are paired with a state describing the task, and a subsequent processing state in which the user tries to accomplish the task described before. Here the quantitative measures are recorded.

As already explained in the motivating example, one problem of e-government portals is: finding the right form. Therefore, we designed three tasks asking the user to find the right form for a given problem from the building law domain. After the user processes the task, we record the time the user needed for finishing it. Additionally, we track the user behavior, which means we record the user's click stream, and we store the chosen form. All these measures serve as quantitative benchmarks. The time spent for solving a task can be compared between the adaptive and nonadaptive version of the city portal. The recorded click stream provides deep insights into the browsing behavior of the current user. The frequency of calling internal help or search pages can be evaluated. Finally, we can compare the ratio of correctly chosen forms to all chosen forms for the adaptive and nonadaptive version of the portal.

The emotional response is captured by a questionnaire after solving the first three tasks. In the questionnaire we ask the users for their subjective impressions of the city portal of Vöcklabruck. We ask the following questions:

- How satisfied are you with the portal?
    - The user is asked for his overall impression of the usability of the portal.

- Are the appropriate forms easy to find?
    - This more concrete questions aims at subjective feelings of how easy it is to find the right form, fitting to the set task.

- Would you prefer the online portal or the citizens' advice bureau?
    - In this question, we ask the user whether the usability of the city portal is superior to the citizens' advice bureau.

- Comments
    - Here the user can enter free style comments. User comments might give useful hints towards specific usability problems, not foreseen in the design of the evaluation as well as of the original portal.

Finally, a farewell screen is displayed in the *Thank you!* state.

10 Architecture and Implementation

The architecture of the evaluation portal is depicted in Fig. 7. The design follows the major design directive of not making the city portal of Vöcklabruck twofold, on the one hand, for the static and unchanged version of the portal, and, on the other hand, for the adaptive version. Therefore, the evaluation test server relies for both versions on the same original and unchanged city portal of Vöcklabruck. The original web portal is depicted on the right in Fig. 7. The test portal, also depicted on the right, delivers the intelligent Rich Internet Application consisting of User Tracking and UI Adaptation. The test portal also provides the evaluation wizard and construction wizard.

Both, the User Tracking and the UI Adaptation components are initialized with the rules and annotations retrieved from the test web server. While initializing the adaptation components, the start page of the city portal of Vöcklabruck is loaded from the portal web server. After successfully initializing the adaptation components and after successfully loading the start page, the adaptation components decide what kind of portal will be tested by the current test user: the adaptive or the nonadaptive version. This decision is made randomly every time the evaluation portal is accessed. This ensures that on average the adaptive portal is evaluated as often as the static portal by the test users.

In the case of the adaptive version, the original start page is altered. A link to the construction wizard is added dynamically. The static version of the portal is not altered at all, and, thus, will not have a construction wizard supporting the test user to fulfill the test tasks.

For both versions in common events are registered according to the tracking rules. Additionally, listeners are implemented for dynamically adapting the original forms, menus, help and search pages. Then the evaluation wizard is started.

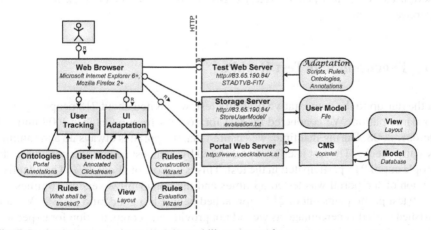

Fig. 7 Design and implementation of the usability test portal

The user model recorded during processing the three task and the questionnaire data are stored at the storage server in a file in JSON format.

10.1   The Adaptive Portal

In order to make the static e-government portal adaptive the construction wizard is dynamically injected. The construction wizard is a component for guiding the user, based on a question/answering mechanism, to the right construction form. A construction wizard is a finite state machine where a state represents the choices the user has made and the transitions are the choices themselves. The states and transitions are defined in the construction wizard rules. The rules comprise the three building law test cases. During run time the rules are evaluated and depending on his/her previous answers the user is guided to the right form. What the right form is depends on the given task.

10.2   Test of the Evaluation Portal

Before going public we tested the usability test portal intensively. These tests ensured the compatibility of our software with all major browsers.

Additionally, we tested the usability test itself by a randomly chosen test person. During this test it turned out that there was too much continuous text that could not be easily understood. We changed that in the final version of the evaluation wizard. Also, a completely new path to the construction forms was discovered. Furthermore, that test impressively exhibited the "Where is the cow?" problem (Gould 1988). First, the nonadaptive version of the portal was tested. Afterwards, the test person tested the adaptive version. Surprisingly, the construction wizard was not used, because the test person went exactly the path, she already took for the nonadaptive version.

11   Execution and Test Results

In the run-up to the comparative usability test, we invited about 215 people by mail for participation. We conducted the test for 16 days from 6 October 2008 until 21 October 2008. During that time, we ensured that the portal is always up and running by daily checks. The test itself was performed by each test person autonomously. 49 people out of 215 participated in the test. This is a quota of about 23%. The adaptive version of the portal was tested 33 times and the nonadaptive version 16 times.

49 test participants out of 215 approached people is a good ratio of 23%. We are satisfied with this percentage as we did not provide any compensation for expenses. The test participation was only based on the good will of the approached people.

The ratio of static test runs to adaptive test runs is 1:2. That is a little bit surprising, because intensive prerelease laboratory tests showed that in the long run the average ratio is 1:1. One possible explanation for the observed imbalance is that some test users gave up working on the tasks in the static version of the portal. One reason could be the lack of the construction wizard and with that the lack of user guidance. It is conceivable that they had serious problems finding the right form and therefore canceled the whole test procedure.

11.1 Demographics

Most of the test users (54.2%) were between 26 and 35 years. As we mainly approached scientific and administrative staff, this percentage is only natural, as most of them already finished their professional training or study. The same explanation holds for the 20.8% of the people who are between 36 and 45 years. The 20.8% of people under 26 are owed to recruiting also students for our comparative usability test. Only 4.2% were older than 46 years.

One third of our test participants were women. That corresponds to the ratio of women to men we addressed by our invitation emails.

87.5% of the test persons were native speakers; only 12.5% did not have German as mother tongue. This meets our expectations as we mainly approached German speaking persons.

Our test users were very familiar with the Internet. Among them 78.7% stated that they intensively use the Internet, 21.3% declared using the Internet often. None of them uses the Internet only rarely. That is not surprising as our usability test is web-based. Furthermore, we asked for participation via email and administrative and scientific staff work daily with the Internet.

Unfortunately, no expert in building law participated in our test. As the portal is designed for common people, this is negligible, although it would have been nice to have their browsing behavior as a comparison value.

11.2 Quantitative Test Results

In H2 we hypothesize that the ratio of rightly chosen to wrongly chosen forms is higher for the adaptive version of the portal than for the static version. The test users working with the static version of the portal were never able to choose the right form, not a single time. In contrast, working with the adaptive version leads in 78.8% of the cases to the selection of the right form. 0% of right forms for the static and about 80% of right forms for the adaptive portal speak a clear language. The adaptive portal leads to a significant higher percentage of chosen right forms. With regard to this measure the adaptive portal is more effective and more efficient than the static one, H2 is proven.

The Hypothesis H3 could be partially proven. Test results reveal that the fastest test user, although not finding the right form, used the static version of the portal. He/she was three times faster than the fastest user of the adaptive portal. This could mean that experienced users familiar with building permissions might be faster using a static portal. On the other hand, it pointed out that on average the maximum time for finding a form is faster using the adaptive portal.

The frequency of using search or help pages is an indicator for the usability of a portal. We hypothesized in H4 that users of the adaptive portal call search and help pages less frequently than users of the static version. The collected click stream data revealed that a call to the search page is four times more likely in the static portal. With five times more, visiting the help page is even more likely in the static portal. With the click stream data we proved the fourth hypothesis.

11.3   Qualitative Test Results

We hypothesized in H5 that the perceived usability of an adaptive e-government portal is higher than the perceived usability of a non-adaptive e-government portal. To prove this hypothesis we presented a questionnaire to each test user, asking three questions.

In the first question, we asked the test users for their overall impression of the usability of the portal. The answers to this question are broken down in Fig. 8. 73% of the test users who evaluated the adaptive portal were enthusiastic or very satisfied with the portal in contrast to 7% of the test users who evaluated the static portal. This is a strong vote for the use of adaptive portals in e-government.

Another strong vote for adaptive portals is given by the answers to question two. Here we asked for the subjective feeling of how easy it is to find the right form, fitting the set task. 84.9% of the test persons investigating the adaptive portal found it very easy or easy to get to the right form. Compared with that, only 21.4% users

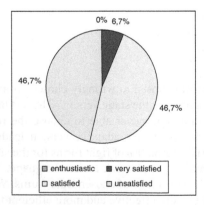
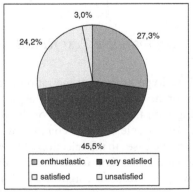

Fig. 8 User satisfaction (**a**) static portal and (**b**) adaptive portal

testing the static portal stated that it is very easy or at least easy to find the right form.

Additionally, we have got yet another evidence of the dominance of adaptive to static portals given by the answer to the third question. In the third question we asked the test users whether the usability of the city portal is superior to the citizens' advice bureau. The answers draw a clear picture. About 80% of the test users investigating the adaptive portal answered with yes whereas only about 30% of the users testing the static portal answered with yes.

12 Discussion

The evaluation of the comparative usability test, between an adaptive and a static version of the city portal of Vöcklabruck, gave evidence to our main hypothesis H1, that the usability of an adaptive city portal is higher than the usability of a static portal. The qualitative as well as the quantitative test results impressively demonstrated the advantage of the adaptive over the static portal.

The quantitative test results showed that only the adaptive portal enables inexperienced users to choose the right form out of many. Additionally, on average, users working with the adaptive portal navigate faster to forms and they also visit less frequently help and search pages.

The qualitative test results illustrated the subjectively perceived advantage of adaptive portals over static portals. The perceived usability of the adaptive portal in comparison to the static portal was more than twelve times higher, the ease of finding the right form was more than four times and more than twice as many prefer the online portal over the citizens' advice bureau.

After performing the evaluation our conclusion for public administrations is: The FIT framework greatly enhances the usability of e-government portals, increases the effectiveness and efficiency both of the citizens and the public service, and lowers costs by decreasing the wrongly submitted forms.

13 Related Work

In (Honghua and Bamshad 2002) the integration of semantics in Web usage mining techniques is shown applied to a movie website. On the basis of movie ontology and the user behavior, user profiles were constructed, which are used for online recommendations. In the center of our approach are e-government websites consisting of forms, services and information.

Comparing our work with standard models for adaptive hypermedia systems like e.g., AHAM (Romero et al. 2005), we observe that they use several models like conceptual, navigational, adaptational, teacher and learner models. Compared to our approach, these models correspond to ontologies presented in Sect. 4, but miss their formal representation. Moreover, we express adaptation functionalities as encapsulated and reusable OWL-DL rules, while the adaptation model in AHA uses a rule based language encoded into XML.

The Personal Reader (Dolog et al. 2004) provides a framework for designing, implementing and maintaining Web content readers, which provide personalized enrichment of Web content for each individual user. The adaptive local context of a learning resource is generated by applying methods from adaptive educational hypermedia in a semantic Web setting. Similarly (Frasincar and Houben 2002) focuses on content adaptation, or, more precisely, on personalizing the presentation of hypermedia content to the user. However, both approaches do not focus on the on-line discovery of the profile of the current user that is one of the main features of our approach. Another difference would be the self-adaptivity.

In (Ankolekar et al. 2006) the authors suggest the use of ontologies and rules in order to find related content on the Web, based on the content currently displayed to the user. We enhance this work by not only adapting the content based on concept similarity but rather based on accumulated Web usage data. Furthermore, we show a way how to link semantics and content. Still the main difference remains the introduction of the autonomous client, as we are dealing with Rich Internet Applications and not with common dynamic Web applications executed on a Web server.

14 Conclusion and Future Work

The major benefit of our approach for designing Adaptive Portal is that it facilitates continuous, ongoing improvements in portal usability, helping public bodies to realize their goals of more efficient and flexible service delivery, tailored to individual users.

The main advantages of the approach are based upon its intensive use of semantic technologies. First, semantics can guide the design of the portal. Then usage analysis can be combined with the semantics to discover opportunities for improvement and personalization of that design, leading to increasingly better design. Ontologies enable semantic interpretation of user behavior in a portal, which enables meaningful, effective and context-aware adaptation.

The presented approach has been evaluated comparatively to a static front office, in our Austrian pilot. The results presented in the Evaluation section are indicative of the value added of our approach. More specifically, the evaluation of the comparative usability test, between the adaptive and the static version of the city portal of Vöcklabruck, gave evidence to our hypothesis that the usability of an adaptive city portal is higher than the usability of a static portal. The qualitative as well as the quantitative test results impressively demonstrated the advantage of the adaptive over the static portal.

The future work has two main lines: the inclusion of other sources of information about users and the development of SaaS (Software as a Service) solutions. Examples of other information sources are: search logs, user-supplied and historical data. The last two will become available as citizen cards become more widely used. Easily managing and mining this vast amount of information to convert it into adaptation rules is a complex task, beyond the capabilities of most public sector organizations, as experience in FIT showed. One promising solution, therefore, is to develop SaaS solutions that collect and mine the data, converting it into reports and rules that can be understood and used by web site maintainers. The FIT Final Report (Legal and Thomas. D35: Identification of typical problems in e-government portals. Public FIT deliverable, Online resource. Created January 2009) outlines such a SaaS solution for the public sector.

References

A. Ankolekar, D.T. Tran, P. Cimiano, Rules for an ontology-based approach to adaptation, in *First International Workshop on Semantic Media Adaptation and Personalization*, Athen, Greece, December 2006

S. Bechhofeer, F. van Harmelen, J. Hendler, I. Horrocks, D. McGuinness, P. Patel-Schneider, L. A. Stein, Owl – web ontology language reference. Recommendation, W3C, 2004

B. Berendt, A. Hotho, D. Mladenic, M. van Someren, M. Spiliopoulou, G. Stumme, A Roadmap for Web Mining: From Web to Semantic Web. In *Web Mining: From Web to Semantic Web*, vol. 3209, (Springer, Heidelberg, 2004), pp. 1–22

B. Berstel, P. Bonnard, F. Bry, M. Eckert, P.-L. Patranjan, Reactive rules on the web. Lect. Notes Comput. Sci. **4636**, 183–239 (2007)

D. Crockford, *Rfc4627: Javascript object notation*, Technical Report (IETF, San Francisco, 2006)

H. Dai, B.Mobasher, Using ontologies to discover domain-level web usage profiles, in *2nd Semantic Web Mining Workshop at ECML/PKDD-2002*, 2002

P. Dolog, N. Henze, W. Nejdl, M. Sintek, The *personal reader: personalizing and enriching learning resources using semantic web technologies*, in International Conference on Adaptive Hypermedia and Adaptive Web-Based Systems (AH 2004), August 2004

F. Frasincar, G.-J. Houben, Hypermedia presentation adaptation on the semantic web. Lect. Notes Comput. Sci. **2347**, 133–142 (2002)

J. Gould, in *How to Design Usable Systems*, ed. by M. Hel, Handbook of Human-Computer Interaction (North-Holland, Amsterdam, 1988), pp. 757–790

D. Honghua, M. Bamshad (eds.), Using Ontologies to Discover Domain-Level Web Usage Profiles, 2002

S. Krug, *Don't Make Me Think: A Common Sense Approach to the Web*, 2nd edn. (New Riders, Thousand Oaks, CA, USA, 2005)

M. Legal, S. Thomas, *D35: Identification of Typical Problems in e-Government Portals*. Public FIT deliverable, Online resource. Created January 2009

E. Mardle, e-Government – a citizen's perspective. Multilingual **18**(4), 41 (2007)

J. Nielsen, Usability engineering at a discount, in *Proceedings of the Third International Conference on Human-Computer Interaction on Designing and Using Human-Computer Interfaces and Knowledge Based Systems*, 2nd edn. (Elsevier, New York, 1989), pp. 394–401

J. Nielsen, Big paybacks from 'discount' usability engineering. IEEE Softw. **7**(3), 107–108 (1990)

J. Nielsen, *Usability Engineering* (Morgan Kaufmann, San Francisco, CA, USA, 1993)

J. Nielsen, in *Guerrilla hci: Using Discount Usability Engineering to Penetrate the Intimidation Barrier*. Cost-Justifying Usability (Academic, Boston, 1994), pp. 245–272

J. Nielsen, L. Hoa, *Prioritizing Web Usability* (New Riders, Berkeley, California, 2006)

D.A. Norman, S.W. Draper, *User Centered System Design; New Perspectives on Human-Computer Interaction* (L. Erlbaum, Hillsdale, NJ, USA, 1986)

T. Rahmani, S.M. Thomas, K.U. Schmidt, L. Stojanovitc, in Using semantic web usage mining to improve e-Government websites, ed. by F. Enrico, H.-J. Scholl, M.A. Wimmer. In *Schriftenreihe Informatik, EGOV*, vol. 27 (Trauner Druck, Linz, 2008)

C. Romero, S. Ventura, C. Herváas Martinez, P. De Bra, *Extending aha!* in *Proceedings of the Fifth International Conference on Human System Learning* (ICHSL, Europia, 2005)

K.-U. Schmidt, J. Dörflinger, T. Rahmani, M. Sahbi, L. Stojanovic, S.M. Thomas, An user interface adaptation architecture for rich internet applications. Lect. Notes Comput. Sci. **5021**, 736–750 (2008)

K.-U. Schmidt, L. Stojanovic, N. Stojanovic, S. Thomas, On enriching ajax with semantics: the web personalization use case. Lect. Notes Comput. Sci. **4519**, 686–700 (2007)

K.-U. Schmidt, R. Stühmer, L. Stojanovic, From business rules to application rules in rich internet applications. *Scalable Computing: Practice and Experience, Scientific International Journal for Parallel and Distributed Computing, Special Issue: The web on the Move*, **9**(4), 329–340 (2008)

L. Stojanovic, K.-U. Schmidt, N. Stojanovic, S.M. Thomas, in *Adaptive Portals Based on Combining Semantics and Ajax in Expanding the Knowledge Economy: Issues, Applications, Case Studies*, ed. by C. Miriam, C. Paul. Proceedings of E-Challenges 2007 (IOS, Amsterdam, 2007a), pp. 230–237

L. Stojanovic, N. Stojanovic, J. Ma, An approach for combining ontology learning and semantic tagging in the ontology development process: egovernment use case. Lect. Notes Comput. Sci. **4831**, 249–260 (2007b)

A Semantically Enabled Portal for Facilitating the Public Service Provision

Nikolaos Loutas, Lemonia Giantsiou, Vassilios Peristeras, and Konstantinos Tarabanis

1 Introduction

During the past years, governments have made significant efforts to improve both their internal processes and the services that they provide to citizens and businesses. These led to several successful e-Government applications (e.g., see www. epractice.eu). One of the most popular tools that was used by governments in order to modernize their services and make them accessible is e-Government portals, e.g., (Drigas et al. 2005), (Fang 2002). The main goals of such portals are:

- To make available complete, easy to understand, and structured information about public services and public administration's modus operandi, which will assist citizens during the service provision process.
- To facilitate the electronic execution of public services.

Nevertheless, most of such efforts did not succeed. Gartner argues that most e-Government strategies have not achieved their objectives and have failed to trigger sustainable government transformation to greater efficiency and citizen-centricity (DiMaio 2007).

This work tries to enhance the efficiency of public service provision. The process of finding the public services to address a Public Administration (PA) Client's need is a tedious and cumbersome task. One of the main reasons for this is, what we call in our work, the service versioning problem. This problem deals with the fact that public services comprise generic service types and usually a large number of service versions. The service versions usually differ from one another due to differences in:

1. The profile of the eligible PA Client
2. The service inputs

N. Loutas (✉)
Center for Research and Technology Hellas, CERTH, 1st km Charilaou-Thermis Rd, Thessaloniki, 57001, Greece

T. Vitvar et al. (eds.), *Semantic Technologies for E-Government*,
DOI 10.1007/978-3-642-03507-4_12, © Springer-Verlag Berlin Heidelberg 2010

3. The service outputs
4. The service workflow

It has to be mentioned that only the service versions can be executed. The service versioning problem exists in almost all public services. It is interesting that even for public services that are considered simple, such as Issuance of Driving License, different versions of the same service type exist e.g., Issuance of Driving License for people over 60, Issuance of Driving License for disabled people, Issuance of Driving License for driving small or large vehicles, etc.

The service versioning problem is not tackled by the existing e-Government portals. Thus, the PA Client usually has a need, but s/he generally does not know, firstly, which PA services are currently available for addressing his/her specific need (Peristeras and Tarabanis 2002, 2008) and secondly, which specific versions of these PA services fit his/her profile. But, even when these obstacles are overcome and the PA Client manages to identify the appropriate PA service version, another issue crops up.

The complexity of service provision is scaled by the fact that the descriptions of public services are fragmented and determined by different laws and regulatory acts. In order to provide to the PA Client a complete and coherent description of a public service this diverse, and often conflicting or difficult to understand, the information has to be put together and homogenized. Until today, this has been only partially done, and hence the PA Clients usually have many questions during the provision of a service; for example, for which service version (if any) s/he is eligible, where the public service is provided and by whom, what are the necessary inputs and/or the expected output, what is the average waiting time, cost etc. To address this, we introduce in this chapter an infrastructure (henceforth referred to as SemanticGov Portal or Portal) (Loutas et al. 2007a; Mocan et al. 2007) with the following objectives:

- To help PA Clients find the specific public service version among the various versions that a public service has, which will both address their needs and fit their profiles through a user-friendly, self-explanatory interface that offers them the necessary guidance throughout the public service provision process.
- To inform the PA Client about his/her eligibility for a specific public service.
- To provide complete and well-structured information for the identified public service version.
- To allow the PA Client to invoke the public services that are available online.

From the technology perspective, the SemanticGov Portal capitalizes on the use of semantic technologies and in particular on the Web Service Modeling Framework (WSMF) (Fensel and Bussler 2002), i.e., WSMO (see Sect. 2.2) and WSML (see Sect. 2.4) and on the Governance Enterprise Architecture PA Service Model (see Sect. 2.1). The SemanticGov Portal, as such, is a part of the SemanticGov project (Loutas et al. 2008a), in which within the overall platform architecture, it has the role of the national EU Member State Portal.

The public services made available through the Portal follow a formal description which we call as WSMO-PA specification and is presented in Sect. 2.3. The SemanticGov Portal is heavily based on the use of ontologies. Different types of ontologies that are used by the Portal are discussed in Sect. 3. The SemanticGov Portal offers functionalities both to the PA Clients for finding and executing public services and to the domain experts for managing the Portal's content as discussed in Sect. 4. The internal Portal architecture is modular and extendable and is presented in Sect. 5. An overview of the chapter with conclusions and future research directions are discussed in Sect. 6.

2 Background Technologies

This section describes the core models and technologies upon which the development of the SemanticGov Portal was based. These are the PA Service Model of the Governance Enterprise Architecture (GEA), the Web Service Modeling Ontology (WSMO), and the Web Service Modeling Language (WSML).

2.1 Government Enterprise Architecture Public Administration Service Model

GEA (Peristeras and Tarabanis 2002, 2008) is a modelling effort which aims at introducing a consistent set of object and process models that describe public administration in a generic fashion. A key aspect of GEA is that it attempts to be technology-neutral, thus being applicable to different technological environments. GEA proposes object and process models for the overall governance system, covering two major areas: public policy formulation and service provision. This section focuses on one of the GEA models, henceforth referred to as the Public Administration (PA) Service Model (Peristeras and Tarabanis 2004). A brief description of the model (Fig. 1) follows.

There are two categories of Governance Entities participating in service provision: the Political Entities and the Public Administration Entities. The PA Entities can acquire one of the following roles during the PA service execution phase:

- Service Provider that provides the PA Service to the Societal Entities
- Evidence Provider that provides necessary Evidence to the Service Provider in order to execute the PA Service
- Consequence Receiver that should be informed about a PA Service execution
- Service Collaborator that takes part in the provision of the PA Service

The Political Entities define the PA Services, which are governed by pre-conditions usually specified by the law. The pre-conditions set the general framework in which the PA Service should be performed and the underlying business rules that

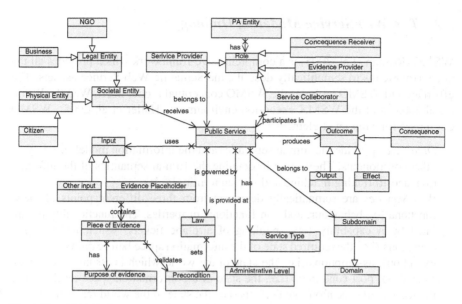

Fig. 1 The GEA PA Service model

should be fulfilled for its successful execution. The pre-conditions can be formally expressed as a set of clauses (or rules) and are validated by a piece of evidence serving a purpose. As the evidence is pure information, it is stored in the Evidence Placeholders (e.g., documents).

The Outcome refers to the different types of results a PA Service may have. GEA defines three types of outcomes. The first one is the Output, which is the documented version of the Service Provider regarding the service requested by a Societal Entity. This is currently embedded and reaches the client in the form of an administrative document. Then, the Effect is the change in the state of the real world (e.g., transfer of money to an account) that is caused by the execution of a service. In the PA domain, the service Effect is the actual permission, certificate, restriction or punishment the citizen is finally entitled to. In cases where the PA refuses the provision of a service, there is no Effect. Finally, the Consequence is the information regarding the executed PA Service that needs to be forwarded to the interested parties, e.g., other PA agencies.

Finally, the PA Services are categorized in several Domains. Each Domain is divided into several SubDomains (Council 1999).

GEA, and the PA Service Model in particular, has been used, validated and further extended in EU-PUBLI.COM IST FP5 Project and in the SemanticGov (Loutas et al. 2008b) and OneStopGov (Tambouris et al. 2006) IST FP6 Projects. Moreover, GEA has been combined with the WSMO Framework for expressing PA-specific semantics in Semantic Web Services. The result of this exercise is the WSMO-PA specification which is described in the next section. Finally, the GEA PA Service Model is currently used by the Cypriot Government in order to document more than 100 public services.

2.2   The Web Service Modeling Ontology

WSMO (Roman et al. 2005) is a comprehensive framework which provides all the necessary means to semantically describe the Semantic Web Service aspects. The effort around WSMO includes the WSMO conceptual model itself, WSML (Bruijn et. al 2005) and the WSMX execution environment (Haller et al. 2005). WSMO comprises four top level elements:

- *Ontologies* provide the formal semantics and the information models used by all other components. They serve in defining the formal semantics of the information, and in linking machine and human terminologies.
- *Web Services* are semantically described from three different points of view: functionality, behaviour, and non-functional properties. The functionality is captured by a capability (e.g., booking of airplane tickets) which include: preconditions (i.e., the required state of the information space before the Web Service execution), assumptions (i.e., the state of the world which is assumed before the execution), post-conditions (i.e., the state of the information space reached after the successful execution), and effects (i.e., the state of the world reached after the successful execution). The behaviour of a Web Service is described by its interface from two perspectives: communication (i.e., choreography) and collaboration (i.e., orchestration). The non-functional properties specify non-functional information about the service such as reliability, robustness, scalability, security, etc.
- *Goals* specify objectives that a client might have when consulting a Web Service (e.g., find a public service that gives a monthly allowance to unemployed people). In WSMO, a goal is characterized in a dual way with respect to the Web Services: goal descriptions include the requested capability and the requested interface.
- *Mediators* provide interoperability facilities between the WSMO's top level elements in order to enable the effective goal-driven Web service interaction. They describe elements that aim to overcome structural, semantic or conceptual mismatches that appear between the different components. There are four types of mediators: *ooMediators* resolve terminological (data level) mismatches between two ontologies; *wwMediators* connect two different Web services, resolving any data, process and protocol heterogeneity; *ggMediators* connect different goals, enabling goals refinement and by this the reuse of goal definitions; and finally *wgMediators* connect goals and Web services, resolving any data, process, and protocol heterogeneity.

2.3   A Formal Description of PA Services: The WSMO-PA Specification

The SemanticGov project aims at achieving interoperability amongst different agencies both within a country as well as amongst countries, easing the discovery

Table 1 The WSMO-PA
specification

GEA	WSMO
Societal entity, service provider, evidence placeholders, evidence etc.	Ontology
PA Service	Web Service
Pre-conditions	Pre-conditions
	Assumptions
Outputs	Post-conditions
Effects	Effects
Consequences	Orchestration
	Choreography
Needs	Goal
	Mediator

of public services by the PA Clients, and facilitating the execution of complex services often involving multiple PA agencies in inter-organizational workflows.

To achieve these objectives, Semantic Web technologies were employed, such as WSMO (Roman et al. 2005). Although these technologies provide important technical tools, they have a shortcoming. Their expressivity in terms of public administration-specific semantics is rather limited.

Within the project, a public administration domain ontology was developed (Goudos et al. 2007), which is based on the GEA Public Administration Service Model (Peristeras and Tarabanis 2004). The ontology provides additional public administration domain knowledge that is required for developing SWS for public administration.

Thus, the challenge was to create WSMO Web Services that would be able to "understand" public administration semantics. Remaining compatible with WSMO allows us to use the already available execution environment, namely the WSMX (Haller et al. 2005) to provide Public Services as SWS to citizens and businesses within Europe.

The outcome of this effort has been the drafting of the WSMO-PA specification, as a mapping of the concepts of the PA Service Model to WSMO elements (Wang et al. 2007) (see Table 1). The mapping shows which elements of the PA Service Model are already covered by the elements of the WSMO Web Service. A direct mapping is created between the PA Service Model element and the corresponding WSMO Web Service one, e.g., the PA Service's pre-conditions map to the WSMO Web Services pre-conditions and assumptions. All the PA Service elements that do not have a direct mapping to some WSMO Web Service element, e.g., the Service Provider, are expressed in a WSMO Ontology which is linked to the WSMO Web Service.

2.4   The Web Service Modeling Language

WSML (Bruijn et al. 2005) offers a set of language variants for describing WSMO elements that enable modelers to balance between expressiveness and tractability according to different knowledge representation paradigms.

The conceptual syntax of WSML has a frame-like style (Kifer et al. 1995). The information about classes, attributes, relations and their parameters, instances and their attribute values are specified in one large syntactic construct, instead of being divided into a number of atomic chunks.

A way of using the logical expression syntax in WSML is by the means of axioms (lines 39–45). The GreekCitizenRule axiom states that if a person has as birthplace (hasBirthplace with a given value y), the birthplace is a city situated in a country (hasCountry with value z) and this country is Greece, then the person has the Greek citizenship.

WSML has direct support for different types of concrete data, namely strings, integers, and decimals, which correspond to the XML Schema[1] primitive data types and they can then be used to construct complex data types.

WSML combines different formalisms, most notably Description Logics and Logic Programming. Three main areas can benefit from the use of formal methods in service descriptions: Ontology description, Declarative functional description of Goals and Web services, and Description of dynamics. WSML defines a syntax and semantics for ontology descriptions. The underlying logic formalisms are used to give a formal meaning to the ontology descriptions in WSML, resulting in different variants of the language: WSML-Core, -DL, -Flight, -Rule, and -Full.

WSML-Core is based on the intersection between the Description Logic and the Horn Logic and it has the least expressive power of all the WSML variants. WSML-DL captures the Description Logic. WSML-Flight is an extension of WSML-Core, which provides a powerful rule language; it is based on a logic programming variant of F-Logic (Kifer et al. 1995) and is semantically equivalent to Datalog with inequality and (locally) stratified negation. WSML-Rule extends WSML-Flight with further features of Logic Programming while WSML-Full aims to unify WSML-DL and WSML-Rule under a First-Order umbrella.

3   Organizing Public Service Information as Ontologies

After analyzing the domain of the public service provision, we concluded that public services have a tree structure, which expressed the way the different service versions of a service type are organized or in other words the way a public service type is decomposed into different service versions. Thus, in the root node the concept of a generic service type is found while in the rest of the nodes (both internal and leaf nodes) different versions of this generic service type exist depending on specific characteristics of the service (e.g., profile of aPA Client, difference in workflow, types of output etc.).

We utilized the means provided by WSMO in order to formalize this structure. These logical abstractions, namely the generic public service types and service

---

[1]http://www.w3.org/TR/xmlschema11-2/.

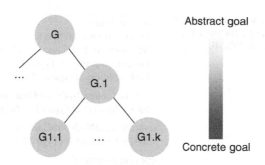

Fig. 2 Sample goal tree ontology

versions, have been formalized and expressed by means of WSMO Goals. As a result, mappings from public service types and versions to WSMO Goals of different granularity were made. In particular, we distinguish mainly between the abstract and concrete Goals. The more concrete a goal is, the more details it contains about the profile of the PA Client who wishes to use the public service that is modelled by the tree structure.

The tree structure that is created helps to organize the various types of Goals (abstract and more concrete ones – see Fig. 2) efficiently and enables the system to provide the PA Client with better guidance through the PA Client-Portal interaction, which will be explained later on in this chapter. We have encoded these tree structures into formal ontologies, which we call as *Goal Tree Ontologies*. Hence, a Goal Tree Ontology is an ontology that aims at modelling and expressing in a formal way the different service versions of a public service type by means of WSMO Goals.

In order to facilitate and formalize the process of developing the Goal Tree Ontologies, the *meta-ontology for Goal Tree Ontologies* was defined. The meta-ontology provides the building blocks for creating the Goal Tree Ontologies for public services.

All the aforementioned ontologies have been developed using WSML and the WSMO Studio (Dimitrov et al. 2007). These ontologies are described in detail in the next section.

3.1 The Meta-Ontology for Goal Tree Ontologies

This meta-ontology acts as a template and defines the concepts, which are used for developing the Goal Tree Ontologies. These concepts are (see also Table 2):

- *The Node*. This concept represents the nodes of the Goal Tree Ontology. All nodes are actually Goals with different levels of granularity, starting from abstract Goals and going to more concrete ones. We define the following attributes for the Node concept:
- The *hasDescription* attribute provides a brief description of the node, as to what the node represents in the Goal Tree Ontology.

Table 2 The concepts of the meta-ontology for Goal Tree Ontologies in WSML

concept Node
  hasDescription ofType (1 1) _string
  hasParentNode ofType (1 *) Node
  hasQuestion impliesType (1 *) Question
  hasCondition ofType (1 1) _string

concept InternalNode subConceptOf Node
  hasChildNode ofType (1 *) Node

concept LeafNode subConceptOf Node
  hasPostcondition ofType (1 1) _string

concept Question
  hasData ofType (1 *) _string
  hasAnswer ofType (1 *) _string

- The *hasParentNode* attribute shows the ancestor node of the current node. The parent node indicates a WSMO Goal at a higher level of abstraction, which when further refined gives the current node.
- The *hasQuestion* attribute expresses the question to be asked to the PA Client. There can be more than one *hasQuestion* attribute at a node.
- The *hasCondition* attribute is used to validate the answer of the question asked. In fact each *hasCondition* is connected with an axiom, in which the pre-conditions of the current Goal are expressed.

All the nodes of the Goal Tree Ontologies, either internal or leaf nodes, are subconcepts of the *Node* concept and inherit all its attributes.

- *The InternalNode*. This concept represents the internal nodes of the Goal Tree Ontology, i.e. nodes that have descendants. Apart from the attributes that they inherit from *Node*, *InternalNodes* have also the *hasChildNode* attribute which indicates the descendants of the current node. There can be more than one *ChildNode*. The *ChildNodes* constitute specializations of their *ParentNode*, mainly by containing more information about the PA Client's profile (Table 3). An example of an *InternalNode* is presented in Fig. 3.
- *The LeafNode*. This concept represents the leaf nodes of the Goal Tree Ontology, namely nodes that have no descendants, and thus, the list of concrete Goals that exist in this ontology. Apart from the attributes that they inherit from *Node*, *LeafNodes* have also the *hasPostcondition* attribute which expresses what the output of the public service version will be and thus corresponds to the post-condition of the concrete WSMO Goal.
- *The Question*. The *Question* concept represents the questions that the Portal poses to the PA Client. We define the following attributes for the *Question* concept:
- The *hasData* attribute models the question itself, e.g., "what is your marital status?"
- The *hasAnswer* attribute models the possible answers.

Each question instance is related to a *hasQuestion* attribute of a *Node*.

Table 3 A fragment from the "GreekCitizen" ontology in WSML	1	concept City
	2	name ofType (1 1) _string
	3	hascountry ofType Country
	4	
	5	concept Country
	6	name ofType (1 1) _string
	7	isoCode ofType (1 1) CitizenshipCode
	8	
	9	instance Greece memberOf Country
	10	name hasValue "Greece"
	11	isoCode hasValue GR
	12	
	13	concept Person
	14	hasFirstName ofType (1 1) _string
	15	hasSecondName ofType (0 *) _string
	16	hasSurname ofType (1 1) _string
	17	hasGender ofType (1 1) Gender
	18	hasCitizenship ofType Citizenship
	19	hasMaritalStatus ofType (1 1)
	20	maritalStatus
	21	hasBirthday ofType (1 1) _dateTime
	22	hasBirthplace impliesType (1 1) City
	23	
	24	instance Maria memberOf Person
	25	hasFirstName hasValue "Maria"
	26	hasSurname hasValue "Papadopoulou"
	27	hasGender hasValue F
	28	...
	29	
	30	concept Address
	31	streetName ofType (1 1) _string
	32	streetNumber ofType (1 1) _int
	33	city ofType (1 1) City
	34	country ofType (1 1) Country
	35	zipCode ofType (0 1) _string
	36	
	37	concept HomeAddress subConceptOf Address
	38	
	39	axiom GreekCitizenRule
	40	definedBy
	41	?x[hasBirthplace hasValue ?y]
	42	memberOf City and
	43	?y[hasCountry hasValue Greece] implies
	44	?x[hasCitizenship hasValue
	45	GreekCitizenship]

3.2   The Goal Tree Ontology

As described in the previous sections, a Goal Tree Ontology models and organizes the different service versions of a generic public service type. A Goal Tree

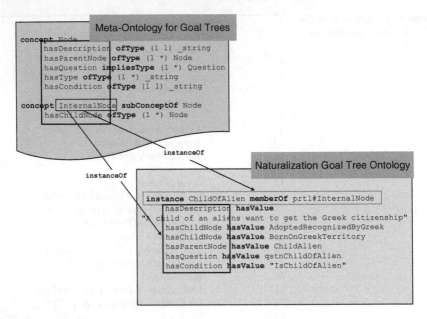

Fig. 3 InternalNode in the goal tree ontology

Ontology has to be created for every public service that will be made available through the Portal.

The Goal Tree Ontologies play a key role in the SemanticGov Portal. They provide the base upon which the Portal builds its core functionalities and makes them available to the PA Clients. Moreover, the user interface (html forms) of the Portal is dynamically created based on information encoded in the Goal Tree Ontologies.

The Portal guides the PA Client from the root of the Goal Tree Ontology down to the specific leaf (concrete Goal), that matches the PA Client's profile and addresses his/her need using a pre-defined set of questions. At the same time the eligibility of the PA Client for the specific public service is also checked.

In the SemanticGov project two such ontologies were developed, namely:

- The Naturalization Goal Tree Ontology, which models the Greek Naturalization public service. In the case of the Greek Naturalization, the Goals differentiate based on attributes like the applicant's citizenship, age, place of birth etc. There, if the applicant has the citizenship of another EU member state or if s/he has a Greek parent, the service requires different inputs and has different execution paths. A part of the Greek Naturalization Goal Tree Ontology which models the root node and a question asked to the citizen is presented in Table 4.
- The Change of Residence Goal Tree Ontology, which models the Italian Change of Residence public service. In the Change of Residence, there are differences in the service provision based mainly on the different nationality of the applicant.

Table 4 Part of the Greek
Naturalization Goal Tree
Ontology

instance NaturalizationService memberOf InternalNode
hasDescription hasValue "Root node"
hasChildNode hasValue Alien
hasChildNode hasValue FellowGreek
hasQuestion hasValue {qstnCitizenship, qstnFellowGreek,
qstnYearsOfResidence,qstnCriminalRecord}
instance qstnCitizenship memberOf Question
hasData hasValue "What is your citizenship?"

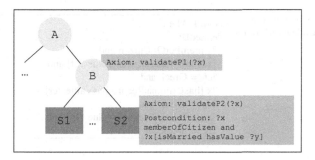

Fig. 4 A sample goal tree ontology

For example, different service versions are suitable for applicants with an Italian citizenship and for applicants with different citizenships.

The Goal Tree Ontologies are based on the concepts defined by the meta-ontology for Goal Tree Ontologies, as described in the previous section. This means that all the elements of a Goal Tree Ontology are instances of the *InternalNode*, the *LeafNode* or the *Question* concepts of the meta-ontology. Figure 3 depicts the relationship between the meta-ontology and a Goal Tree Ontology. Figure 4 shows a very simple Goal Tree Ontology where all the *InternalNodes* are represented as circles and all the *LeafNodes* as rectangles.

An interesting feature of the Goal Tree Ontologies is that they contain a set of keywords that can be used by the PA Clients in order to search for one. The keywords aim at expressing what kind of public service is modelled by the Goal Tree Ontology, what is its purpose, in which case would one use it, etc. The keywords of the Greek Naturalization Goal Tree Ontology are shown in Table 5.

The questions asked each time are designed so as to collect information which will then be used for validating the pre-conditions that differentiate the various Goals in the ontology. In their turn, the pre-conditions of the Goals have been designed according to the service pre-conditions that were identified during the service analysis that has to precede the encoding of the Goal Tree Ontology. From another perspective, or to put it better in other words, the pre-conditions express the attributes of the PA Client's profile that have to be validated so as to decide the PA Client's eligibility for a specific service version and allow him/her to invoke it. The pre-conditions of each of these Goals are expressed in a respective axiom. A sample axiom from the

Table 5 Keywords for the Greek Naturalization Goal Tree Ontology

ontology GreekNaturalization
  non-FunctionalProperties
  keywords hasValue "Naturalization, citizenship, acquire citizenship, Greek citizenship, acquire
Greek citizenship, become Greek, region, naturalization, acclimatization, acculturation,
accustoming, adapting, conditioning, habituation, nationalization, rooting, citizen, region"
  endNonFunctionalProperties

Table 6 Sample axiom from the Greek Naturalization Goal Tree Ontology

axiom IsAlien
  definedBy
    ?x memberOf Citizen and
    ?x [hasCitizenship hasValue ?ct] and
    ?ct != Greek and
    ?x [hasCriminalRecord hasValue ?cr] and
    ?cr = "clear" and
    ?x [isFellowGreek hasValue ?fg] and
    ?fg = _boolean("false")

Greek Naturalization Goal Tree Ontology which checks if the PA Client who applied for the public service is an alien (i.e., a person that does not have Greek ancestors) or a fellow Greek (i.e., a person that has Greek ancestors) is presented in Table 6.

4 Actors and Functionalities

This section presents two simple use cases: the actors and the main functionalities of the Portal. Two main types of actors have been identified:

- The PA Client, as defined in the SemanticGov domain ontology (Goudos et al. 2007), refers to citizens and businesses that use the Portal in order to express their needs (which the Portal formalizes as Goals) and to find the public services that fulfil these needs.
- The domain expert supports a central public agency, such as a ministry. The domain expert adds (and updates) the content of the Portal. The domain expert can be either a public servant or a private software company.

The Portal provides a set of functionalities which can be grouped in two parts:

- The PA Clients can:
- Find the exact public service version that fits to their personal characteristics/ needs among the various service versions of a specific public service type
- Check whether they are eligible for receiving a public service
- Access a complete set of information with respect to the public service which contains, among others, information on the service inputs and outputs, the service provider, the channels of provision, the electronic point of execution etc.

- Invoke a public service
- The domain experts can add/update/delete the Portal's content by managing the Goal Tree Ontologies.

This role-based grouping of functionalities, which are described in the rest of this section, results in two separate subsystems in the Portal's architecture: (a) the PA Client's subsystem and (b) the domain expert's subsystem. These are separately discussed in Sect. 5.

4.1 Find Public Service

In a nutshell, the Portal helps the PA Clients to find the exact public service version(s) that can be consumed in order to address their needs among the various service versions of a generic public service type. In addition to that, the Portal helps the PA Client to personalize the public service according to his/her profile and checks his/her eligibility for the service. At the end of this process the PA Client receives detailed information about the specific public service version that fits his profile or is informed that s/he is not eligible for the specific public service, depending on whether s/he fulfils or not the respective pre-conditions. This is the core functionality of the Portal and its internal workflow is described below:

1. The PA Client visits the Portal and describes the public service that s/he needs using a set of keywords.
2. The Portal uses the keywords and finds the Goal Tree Ontologies that correspond to the public services that possibly address the PA Client's need.
3. The PA Client selects one of the Goal Tree Ontologies and the online dialogue with the Portal is initiated.
4. At this point an iterative process starts. The Portal starts traversing the Goal Tree Ontology and asks the questions that have been encoded in its nodes. The PA Client answers the questions. The Portal validates the answers and decides on the next step. If the next step can not be decided, it means that the PA Client does not satisfy one of the conditions that have to be validated before invoking the public service. Thus s/he is informed that s/he is not eligible for the specific public service. If a *LeafNode* is reached then a concrete WSMO Goal has been identified and the dialogue is terminated.
5. Once the dialogue is terminated successfully, the Portal sends the information to Discovery Engine. The Discovery Engine performs a search in the public service repositories and returns the matching public service along with all the related information about it. If no public service is found, it means that no public service is found that could address the PA Client's need. Thus, s/he is informed accordingly.
6. The Portal pareses the semantic description of the identified service (WSMO-PA service) and a summary report is prepared and presented to the PA Client.

4.2   Invoke Public Service

In some cases, a PA Client (citizen or business) goes beyond finding information about a public service and uses the Portal in order to invoke the electronic execution of the public service that s/he has found. The service execution process is described below:

1. The PA Client invokes the service that s/he found in the previous use case.
2. The Portal asks for a set of information. In fact, the Portal parses the semantic description of the service to be invoked and creates the service interface, which is then used by the PA Clients in order to provide the information required by the public service.
3. The PA Client provides the information and submits the form.
4. The public service is executed successfully and the PA Client is informed about its outcome. If this fails, it means that the execution of the public service was not successful either due to the invalid information or due to the unavailability of the server. In any case, the PA Client is informed accordingly.

This functionality is loosely coupled with the rest of the SemanticGov Portal as it is very much dependent on the underlying service execution environment. In the prototype that has been implemented and described in this chapter, WSMX (Haller et al. 2005) has been used.

4.3   Manage Goal Tree Ontologies

The domain expert adds and/or edits the content of the Portal using the administrative tools that are discussed later. In order to do so, the domain expert opens the administrative tool and starts creating/updating a Goal Tree Ontology. Once s/he is finished, the domain expert saves the Goal Tree Ontology and publishes it to the Portal.

5   SemanticGov Portal Architecture

The SemanticGov Portal is loosely coupled with the rest of the SemanticGov platform (Vitvar et al. 2006, 2007). It is a part of the front-office layer, which provides access to the system for the SemanticGov stakeholders. Access to citizens and businesses is provided through Member State portals, while public servants access the system through management tools, e.g., ontology management tools, monitoring tools etc.

As said earlier, the Portal is divided into two subsystems: the *PA Client subsystem* and the *Domain Expert (administrative) subsystem*.

The *PA Client subsystem* implements the functionalities that the Portal provides to the PA Clients. As depicted in Fig. 5 the PA Client subsystem of the Portal consists of the following components:

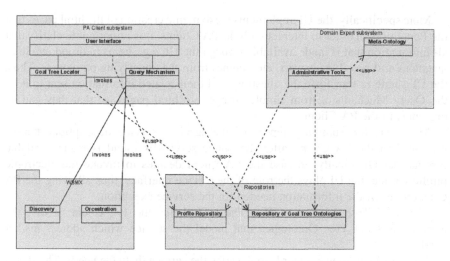

Fig. 5 Semanticgov portal's components

- The User Interface
- The Goal Tree Locator (GTL)
- The Query Mechanism

The Domain Expert subsystem supports the administrators of the Portal and allows them to manage the Portal's content. The Domain Expert subsystem consists of the following components:

- The Administrative Interface and Tools
- The Meta-Ontology for the Goal Tree Ontologies

The two subsystems are supported by an underlying repository infrastructure which comprises the following:

- The Repository of Goal Tree Ontologies
- The Profile Repository

Moreover, the Portal communicates with the SemanticGov platform and in particular with the discovery and orchestration of components.

The subsystems of the SemanticGov Portal are presented in the next section.

5.1 The PA Client subsystem

The User Interface (UI). The UI provides the means that the PA Clients can use in order to interact with the Portal. The main functionality of the UI is to present to the PA Clients the questions asked by the Query Mechanism and collect their answers. The answers are then forwarded to the Query Mechanism.

More specifically, the UI implements the dynamic creation of the html pages that the Portal uses in order to interact with the PA Clients. It is important to clarify that all information that is made available through the UI, e.g., items in dropdown lists, questions and possible answers, etc., comes from the underlying ontologies. Thus, the UI is able to transform the questions and their related information sent to it by the Query Mechanism, from simple strings into html pages, so that they can be presented to the PA Client.

Moreover, the summary report of the service (service description) that is presented to the PA Client, after the public service is found is made available through the UI. Finally, in case the PA Client decides to invoke the electronic public service, the UI plays the role of the service interface, thus allowing the PA Client to insert the information needed for the service execution.

The Goal Tree Locator (GTL). The GTL helps the PA Client to find the appropriate Goal Tree Ontologies that model the service which address his/her need.

The PA Client uses keywords to describe the service that s/he needs. The Portal receives these keywords and sends them to the GTL. Then, using these keywords the GTL queries the Repository of Goal Tree Ontologies and finds the matching Goal Tree Ontology (-ies). More specifically, the queries are formed with the aid of SPARQL.[2] Finally, the matching Goal Tree Ontologies are returned to the PA Client in order for him/her to select the appropriate one. A snapshot of the process is illustrated in Fig. 6.

The Query Mechanism (QM). The QM is the core component of the Portal as it carries out the traversal of the Goal Tree Ontology. The QM takes as input:

- The PA Client's profile information (either from the PA Client Profile Repository, if the PA Client has registered a profile in the Portal, or directly from the information that the PA Client fills in the Portal). The two options that the Portal provides with respect to the PA Clients' profiles are presented later. This information is stored in an ontology instance, which models the profiles of the PA Clients. From now on we will refer to this instance as the Service-based PA Client Profile.
- The Goal Tree Ontology that the PA Client has selected.

The QM traverses the Goal Tree Ontology and for each loop, it has to decide the next step. It is important to highlight the fact that each time the next step option is unique. This means there is no case where the PA Client could follow two different paths in the same Goal Tree Ontology (at a technical level this means that at any time the axiom of only one of the *ChildNodes* of the current *InternalNode* can return true).

If the current node is an *InternalNode* (which means that it has *ChildNodes*), the QM has to verify the *ChildNodes'* pre-conditions, which are in fact expressed as axioms written in WSML. Therefore, the QM first checks if the necessary

---

[2]See http://www.w3.org/TR/rdf-sparql-query/ for more details.

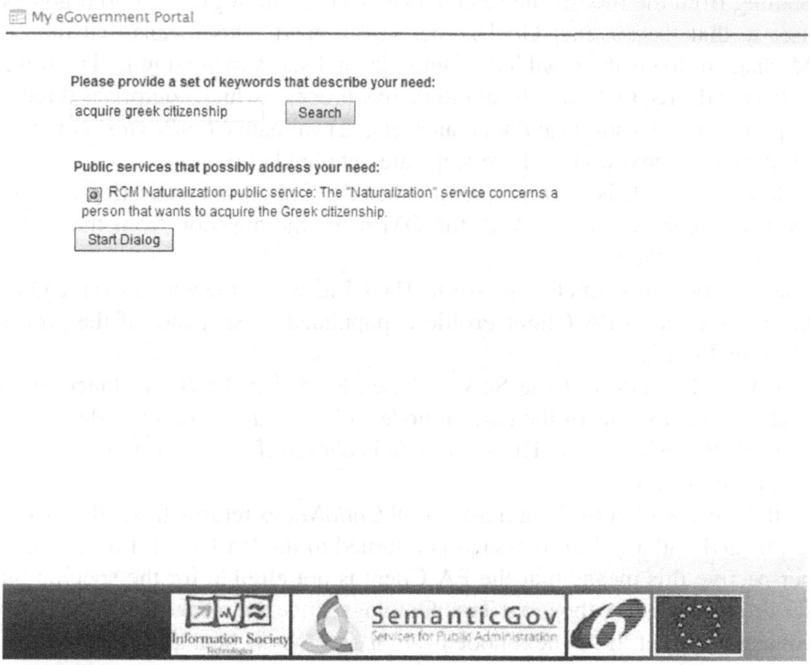

My eGovernment Portal

Please provide a set of keywords that describe your need:

acquire greek citizenship   Search

Public services that possibly address your need:

RCM Naturalization public service: The "Naturalization" service concerns a
person that wants to acquire the Greek citizenship.

Start Dialog

SemanticGov
Services for Public Administration
Information Society
Technologies

Fig. 6 Searching for a public service

information can be found in the PA Client Profile Repository or else it takes the
appropriate question from the Goal Tree Ontology and forwards it to the UI so that
the question can be posed to the PA Client.

In case the current node is a *LeafNode* (i.e., it has no *ChildNodes*), the end of
the structured dialogue has been reached. By now the Portal has collected all the
necessary information for identifying the specific Goal and consequently, the
WSMO-PA service that matches the PA Client's profile. At this point the QM
contacts the WSMX and forwards to the Discovery Engine the post-conditions of
the concrete Goal and the completed Service-based PA Client Profile. The QM does
not need to forward the pre-conditions, since these have already been checked
during the PA Client's interaction with the Portal and they have been included in
the instance of the Service-based PA Client Profile.

As described above, the execution of the QM is terminated successfully when it
reaches a *LeafNode* (a concrete Goal). In case the PA Client is not eligible for one of
the specific Goals of this Goal Tree Ontology, the QM terminates its execution and
returns a failure message. The failure message explains to the PA Client the reason
why s/he is not eligible for the service, e.g., "You are not eligible for this service
because you are under 18-years-old."

The workflow of the algorithm that is implemented by the QM is described in
detail hereafter.

1. Starting from the root of the selected Goal Tree Ontology, the Portal guides the user so that the abstract Goal is stepwise refined. This means that the Query Mechanism loads the Goal Tree Ontology and starts traversing it. The traversal of the Goal Tree Ontology is an interactive process, which comprises three main steps: (1) Ask questions and read answers, (2) validate *ChildNodes'* axioms, and (3) decide on next node. These steps are detailed below.
2. If the current node is an *InternalNode* then the QM reads its question and in case the PA Client has to be asked, the QM reads the question from the node and forwards it to the UI.
3. The PA Client answers the question. The UI forwards the answer to the QM and the Service-based PA Client Profile is populated. A snapshot of the process is illustrated in Fig. 7.
4. Based on the values of the Service-based PA Client Profile instance, the QM evaluates the axioms of the current node's *ChildNodes* in order to decide which one will be visited next. The next node is chosen if its axiom is validated, i.e., returns the true value.

   If the evaluation of the axioms of all *ChildNodes* returns false, the process is terminated and a failure message is returned to the PA Client. From a business perspective this means that the PA Client is not eligible for the specific public service modelled by the Goal Tree Ontology since the respective pre-conditions could not be met. If the next node is an *InternalNode* the algorithm goes back to Step 3.
5. If the next node is a *LeafNode* the algorithm is considered to have reached a complete, successful termination (a concrete Goal has been formed).

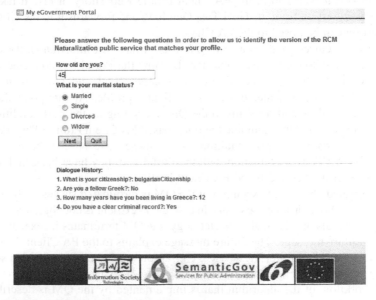

Fig. 7 The PA Client–Portal online dialogue

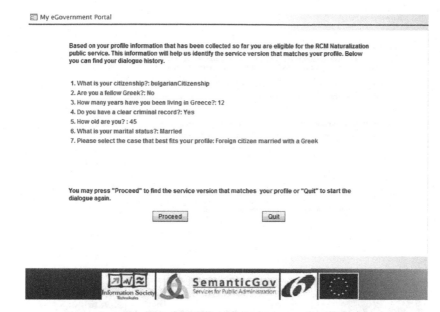

Fig. 8 A summary report of the PA Client's answers

The Portal provides a textual description of the Service-based PA Client Profile, and the PA Client confirms that all the information is accurate. But what is most important at this point, is that by now the Portal has collected all the information required for deciding on the PA Client's eligibility for the specific public service. This means that at this point the PA Client knows that s/he can use the specific public service and by clicking *Proceed*, s/he will also find out which version of the public service fits his/her profile. A snapshot of the process is illustrated in Fig. 8.

6. After clicking *Proceed*, the QM contacts the WSMX and forwards to the Discovery Engine the post-conditions of the identified concrete Goal and the completed Service-based PA Client Profile.

   The Discovery Engine performs a search in the public service repositories and returns back the URI of the matching WSMO-PA service. Using this URI the Portal accesses and parses the semantic description of the service, thus producing the report which is shown in Fig. 9.

   If no public service is found, it means that no public service is found that could address the PA Client's need. Thus, s/he is informed accordingly.

7. If the PA Client wishes to invoke the electronic execution of the public service, s/he has to click on the link. At this point the PA Client is informed that a direct communication between him/her and the service provider will be established and that the validity of the information that s/he provided will be checked. This is shown in Fig. 10.

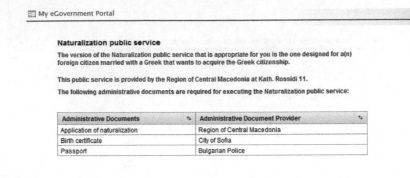

Naturalization public service

The version of the Naturalization public service that is appropriate for you is the one designed for a(n) foreign citizen married with a Greek that wants to acquire the Greek citizenship.

This public service is provided by the Region of Central Macedonia at Kath. Rossidi 11.

The following administrative documents are required for executing the Naturalization public service:

Administrative Documents	Administrative Document Provider
Application of naturalization	Region of Central Macedonia
Birth certificate	City of Sofia
Passport	Bulgarian Police

If you wish to use this public service electronically please click here

Fig. 9 The summary report of the identified service

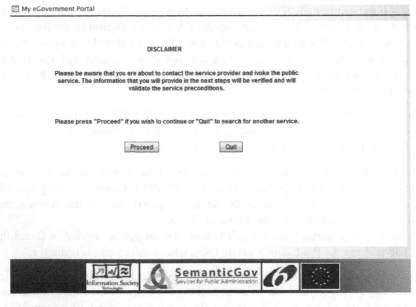

My eGovernment Portal

DISCLAIMER

Please be aware that you are about to contact the service provider and ivoke the public service. The information that you will provide in the next steps will be verified and will validate the service preconditions.

Please press "Proceed" if you wish to continue or "Quit" to search for another service.

Proceed   Quit

Fig. 10 The Portal's disclaimer

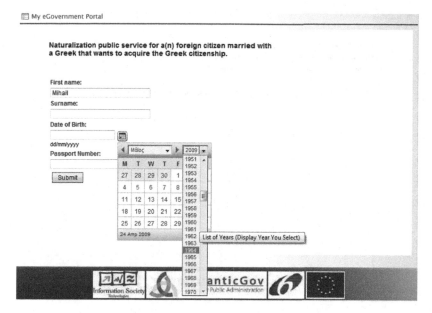

Fig. 11 The public service interface

8. After clicking *Proceed*, the Portal loads the service interface and asks from the PA Client to provide the information that is required by the service provider for executing the service. A snapshot of the process is illustrated in Fig. 11.

9. On clicking the *Submit* button, the Portal contacts the Orchestration Engine, via its WSMX entry point, and forwards the information that the PA Client has provided. The Orchestration Engine carries out the execution of the electronic public service. If the information provided by the PA Client is accurate, then the electronic public service is executed successfully and the PA Client is informed accordingly as shown in Fig. 12. Otherwise, the PA Client is informed that the execution of the electronic public service failed due to inconsistent information. This is the final step of the algorithm.

5.2   The Administrative Subsystem

The *Administrative Subsystem* targets at facilitating the management tasks of the Portal. Thus, the domain experts can use the Portal's administrative subsystem in order to register Goal Tree Ontologies in the Portal, monitor the Portal's usage statistics, edit or delete existing Goal Tree Ontologies etc. With the term *Domain Expert*, we refer to the employee of a central public administration unit who is responsible for adding and updating the content of the Portal using the administrative subsystem. The domain experts should have good knowledge both of the domain and of the SemanticGov technologies and tools.

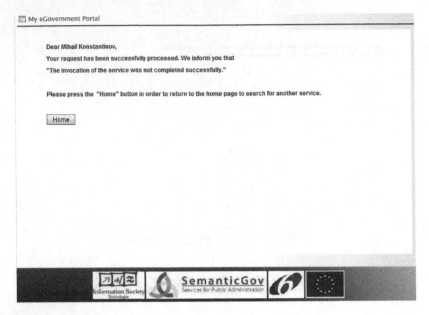

Fig. 12 The result of the execution of the electronic public service

The administrative subsystem comprises of the *Administrative Interface and Tools* and is implemented as a plug-in for WSMO Studio. The domain experts use the *Administrative Interface* (AI) in order to interact with the Portal. Actually the AI is implemented via the Portal's administrative tools.

Currently the only administrative tool that has been developed is the Goal Tree Editor. The screenshot in Fig. 13 outlines the editor with its major components. The Goal Tree Editor allows the user to:

- Register a new Goal Tree Ontology in the Portal
- Edit or delete an existing Goal Tree Ontology

The outcome of the tool is a representation of a userdefined Goal Tree Ontology. The Goal Tree Editor allows updating of the set of services offered through the Portal at a relatively low cost and in an easy and well structured way. Once a new Goal Tree Ontology is developed and stored in the underlying repository, it can be accessed by the PA Clients.

During the creation of a new Goal Tree Ontology, the domain expert provides also the specification (e.g., text, expect answer datatype etc.) of every question of this Goal Tree Ontology. For example, the domain expert should indicate that the "What is your date of birth?" question will be followed by a date control which will be used by citizens in order to give their date of birth in a standardized way and not in free text (see also the properties panel in Fig. 13). This kind of information is stored in an XML file that accompanies each Goal Tree Ontology.

Since all the information needed for the UI is provided at the design-time and is stored in the above-mentioned XML file, the automatic generation of the html

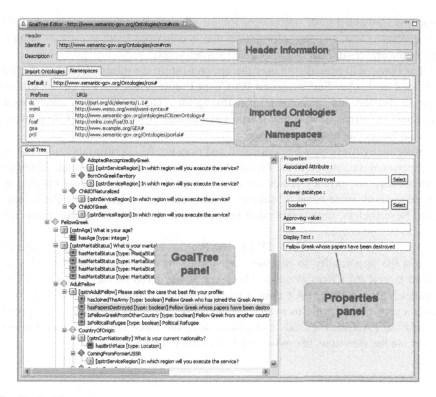

Fig. 13 GoalTree editor overview

forms by the Portal's UI at runtime is enabled. This saves significant time and programming effort and makes the Portal more agile and easily adaptable and extendable.

5.3 The Common Repositories

Repository of Goal Tree Ontologies. This is a semantic repository for WSML ontologies, where all the Goal Tree Ontologies are stored. We have used ORDI[3] for the semantic repository implementation.

Profiles Repository. This is a repository where the Stored PA Client Profiles of all the PA Clients and the profiles of the domain experts are kept.

The Service-based PA Client profiles are populated with the PA Client's answers to the Portal's questions during their interaction. The Service-based PA Client

---

[3]http://www.ontotext.com/ordi/.

Profile is forwarded to the Discovery Engine after the PA Client has identified his/her concrete Goal, and the information that is contained there is used in order to verify the pre-conditions of the WSMO-PA Services.

The Portal will provide the user the option to store the information that s/he has provided for his/her Service-based PA Client Profile. Thus, the PA Client will not have to give the same piece of information again. . This functionality addresses an important requirement in public administration that says that the PA Client should give his/her personal data only once.

Since many users may be concerned and may not feel comfortable with having their personal data stored in the Portal, this functionality is only optional. Although, data security and privacy issues are out of scope of the SemanticGov project, we intend to apply some basic techniques in the prototypes to protect the PA Clients' data. Nevertheless, more elaborated methods and technologies of data protection have to be considered.

Apart from the Service-based PA Client Profiles, the Portal will also give the PA Clients the opportunity to register their profile in the Portal. These profiles are called *Stored PA Client Profiles*. The level of the detail of the Stored PA Client Profiles is also up to the PA Clients to decide. The PA Clients could choose to store from a very basic profile to a very detailed one. The level of detail of the profile affects the PA Client–Portal interaction, since the more detailed the profile, the fewer are the questions that will be asked to the PA Client.

6 Conclusions

In this chapter, we presented in detail a semantically-enabled e-Government portal, which aims at:

- Finding the public service version that best matches the PA Client's profile among the usually large number of versions that a public service type has
- Checking the PA Client's eligibility for consuming the specific public service
- Providing all the information the PA Client needs to know for going through the process of executing the service; and
- Invoking the electronic public services

A running prototype of the Portal is available at: http://www.semantic-gov.org/SemanticGovPortal/.

The "Intel inside" the Portal is basically the different ontologies that the Portal uses, namely the Goal Tree Ontologies that are developed following a meta-Ontology as a template. The meta-Ontology ensures re-usability and extensibility as it is not difficult for a domain expert to use it in order to model public services as the Goal Tree Ontologies.

The Portal's architecture is modular and as such easily extendable. It is decoupled from the service execution environment that may be available in different technologies and communicates with it using the Web Services.

There are two main reasons that have led us to use the WSMO framework for developing a prototype of the Portal.

- One important reason is the fact that the WSMO framework supports both a client (using WSMO Goal) and a service (using WSMO Web Service) view, which are both useful when modelling the PA domain and public services in particular.
- The Web Service Modeling Language (WSML) provides a formal syntax and semantics for WSMO. We have used WSML-Flight, which has a rich set of modelling primitives for modelling the different aspects of attributes, such as value constraints and integrity constraints. Furthermore, WSML-Flight incorporates a fully fledged rule language, while still allowing efficient decidable reasoning.
- Additionally, the reasoners for the ontologies encoded in WSML are available in order to build an efficient semantic application. In the SemanticGov Portal the IRIS reasoner[4] has been used.

Nevertheless, in order to validate the applicability of our approach in using different technologies, another implementation of the Portal is also available (Loutas et al. 2007b) which follows the OWL-S framework (Martin et al. 2004) instead of WSMO.

Summarizing, the experience that was gained while implementing the Portal says that using Semantic Web technologies for developing an e-Government portal allows:

- To make use of the power provided by the ontologies and reasoning. Thus, the online structured dialog does not have to comprise pre-defined paths, but each time the next step is defined on the fly depending on the answers of the PA Client.
- To update the Portal's content in a plug-n-play way. Once a new Goal Tree Ontology is added to the Portal's ontology repository, a new public service is automatically made available through the Portal.
- To reuse the ontologies already available online as building blocks for the Goal Tree Ontologies, for example ontologies that model the citizens or public services, etc.
- To connect with different SWS execution environments, such as WSMX, where the Portal provides an interface that will gather the necessary semantics from the PA Clients, which will then be used for the discovery and execution of SWS.
- To enable the Portal to be used with some customization in the different domains beyond e-Government. This means that once the Goal Tree Ontologies that model services from other domains, e.g., e-Banking, e-Business, are developed, the Portal can process them without requiring any changes in its core components, i.e., Query Mechanism.

---

[4]http://iris-reasoner.org/.

Our test results so far have shown that our approach is scalable and can possibly be extended in other fields, apart from e-Government. As part of our future work, we plan to enhance the Portal both in matters of user interface and functionality. Moreover, we plan to extend the functionalities of the GTL by supporting synonyms for the keywords entered by the PA Client. We plan to do this by using functionalities offered by Wordnet, and we expect this to improve significantly the GTL's search capability and, consequently, the Portal's efficiency. Moreover, we plan to implement and extend further the ability to create and store PA Client profiles in the Portal.

Another interesting item on our future research agenda is to compare the pros and cons of using different sets of technologies, namely WSMO or OWL-S, for implementing the Portal and how the functionalities of the Portal benefit from each one.

Finally, it has to be mentioned that the Portal has been evaluated by its end-users and the feedback that was collected regarding the usability of the Portal was very positive. The PA Clients answered that the SemanticGov Portal's functionalities are easy to be used and quite intuitive. For example, the keyword search provided by the Portal is thought to be quite fast, but it should be tested in a wider context, e.g., with more services registered in the Portal. The search functionality, from the user's point of view, is similar to that of a common search engine based on keywords. Thus, the users are pretty familiar with it. Finally, the question and answer dialog is browsed quickly. The users commented that it might be easier to group and show the related questions together. Moreover, they are happy with the question and answer dialog, because they feel like being at the center of the service provision process and they look forward to use a public service customized to their needs and profiles.

References

D.J. Bruijn et al., The Web Service Modeling Language WSML, Technical Report, WSML Working Draft, http://www.wsmo.org/TR/d16/d16.1/v0.2/ (2005)

CIO Council, Federal Architecture Enterprise Framework v.1.1 (1999)

A. DiMaio, *Web 2.0 in Government: A Blessing and a Curse*. Presentation (Gartner, Stanford, USA, 2007)

M. Dimitrov, A. Simov, V. Momtchev, M. Konstantinov, *WSMO Studio* – A semantic web services modelling environment for WSMO (System Description), in *4th European Semantic Web Conference*, Innsbruck, Austria, 3–7 June 2007

A.S. Drigas, L.G. Koukianakis, Y.V. Papagerasimou, An e-Government web portal. WSEAS Trans. Environ. Dev. **1**, 150 (2005)

Z. Fang, e-Government in digital era: concept, practice, and development. Int. J. Comput. Internet Manage. **10**, 1 (2002)

D. Fensel, C. Bussler, The web service modeling framework (WSMF). Electron. Commerce Res. Appl. **1**, 113 (2002)

S. Goudos, N. Loutas, V. Peristeras, K. Tarabanis, Public administration domain ontology for a semantic web services e-Government framework, in *International Conference on Services Computing*, Salt Lake City, Utah, USA, 2007, pp. 270–277

A. Haller et al., WSMX – A semantic service-oriented architecture, in *4th International Conference on Web Services*, Galway, Ireland, 2005

M. Kifer, G. Lausen, J. Wu, Logical foundations of object-oriented and frame-based languages. J. ACM **42**, 741 (1995)

N. Loutas, V. Peristeras, S. Goudos, K. Tarabanis, Facilitating the semantic discovery of e-Government services: The semanticGov portal, in *3rd VORTE at the 11th EDOC*, Annapolis, MD, USA, 2007a

N. Loutas, L. Giantsiou, E. Tambouris, V. Peristeras, K. Tarabanis, How to discover eGovernment services efficiently: An ontology-enabled portal, in *Proceedings of the IADIS e-Commerce 2007 conference*, Algarve, Portugal, 2007b

N. Loutas, V. Peristeras, K. Tarabanis, Providing public services to citizens at the national and pan-European level using semantic web technologies: The semanticGov project, in *6th Eastern European eGov Days*, Austrian Computer Society, Prague, Czech Republic, 2008a

N. Loutas, L. Giantsiou, A. Simov, V. Peristeras, K. Tarabanis, A tool for annotating services with domain specific semantics, in 2nd IEEE International Conference on Semantic Computing, IEEE, Santa Clara, California, USA, 2008b

D. Martin et al., OWL-S: Semantic Markup for Web Services, W3C Member Submission, http://www.w3.org/Submission/OWL-S/ (2004)

A. Mocan et al., D5.2, Design and Development of SemanticGov Software Components v.2. SemanticGov Project Deliverable (2007)

V. Peristeras, K. Tarabanis, Towards an enterprise architecture for public administration: a top down approach. Eur. J. Inform. Syst. **9**, 252 (2002)

V. Peristeras, K. Tarabanis, Advancing the government enterprise architecture – GEA: the service execution object model. Lect. Notes Comput. Sci. **3183**, 476 (2004)

V. Peristeras, K. Tarabanis, in *The Governance Architecture Framework and Models*, ed. by Pallab Saha. Advances in Government Enterprise Architecture (IGI, Hershey, USA, 2008)

D. Roman, H. Lausen, U. Keller, Web Service Modeling Ontology (WSMO), Technical Report, WSMO Final Draft, http://www.wsmo.org/TR/d2/v1.2/ (2005)

E. Tambouris, M. Vintar, K. Tarabanis, A Life-Event Oriented Framework and Platform for One-Stop Government: The OneStopGov project, in *4th Eastern European eGov Days*, Austrian Computer Society, Prague, Czech Republic, 2006

T. Vitvar, M. Kerrigan, V.A. Overeem, V. Peristeras, K. Tarabanis, Infrastructure for the Semantic Pan-European E-government Services. *2006 AAAI Spring Symposium on The Semantic Web meets e-Government* (2006)

T. Vitvar et al. D3.2: SemanticGov Architecture v.2, SemanticGov Project Deliverable (2007)

X. Wang, S. Goudos, V. Peristeras, T. Vitvar, A. Mocan, K. Tarabanis, WSMO-PA: Formal Specification of Public Administration Service Model on Semantic Web Service Ontology, in *40th Hawaii International Conference on System Sciences* (IEEE Computer Society, Hawaii, USA, 2007)

Index